A. C. LITTLETON'S FINAL THOUGHTS ON ACCOUNTING: A COLLECTION OF UNPUBLISHED ESSAYS

STUDIES IN THE DEVELOPMENT OF ACCOUNTING THOUGHT

Series Editor: Gary J. Previts

Recent Volumes:

Volume 10:	The Contributions of John Lansing Carey to the Profession of Accountancy
Volume 11:	Abraham J. (Abe) Briloff: A Biography
Volume 12:	Early Warning and Quick Response: Accounting in the Twenty-First Century
Volume 13:	Gerhard G. Mueller: Father of International Accounting Education
Volume 14A:	A Global History of Accounting, Financial Reporting and Public Policy: Europe
Volume 14B:	A Global History of Accounting, Financial Reporting and Public Policy: Americas
Volume 14C:	A Global History of Accounting, Financial Reporting and Public Policy: Asia and Oceania
Volume 14D:	A Global History of Accounting, Financial Reporting and Public Policy: Middle East and Africa
Volume 15:	Understanding Accounting Academic Research: Before and after Sarbanes-Oxley
Volume 16:	The Big Four and the Development of the Accounting Profession in China
Volume 17:	Management Accounting at the Hudson's Bay Company: From Quill Pen to Digitization
Volume 18:	History of Management Accounting in Japan: Institutional & Cultural Significance of Accounting
Volume 19:	Count Down: The Past, Present and Uncertain Future of the Big Four Accounting Firms

STUDIES IN THE DEVELOPMENT OF ACCOUNTING THOUGHT VOLUME 20

A. C. LITTLETON'S FINAL THOUGHTS ON ACCOUNTING: A COLLECTION OF UNPUBLISHED ESSAYS

EDITED BY

MARTIN E. PERSSON
Western University, Canada

Emerald

United Kingdom – North America – Japan
India – Malaysia – China

Emerald Group Publishing Limited
Howard House, Wagon Lane, Bingley BD16 1WA, UK

First edition 2016

Reprints and permissions service
Contact: permissions@emeraldinsight.com

British Library Cataloguing in Publication Data
A catalogue record for this book is available from the British Library

ISBN: 978-1-78635-390-0
ISSN: 1479-3504 (Series)

A. C. Littleton 1887–1974

Source: This picture has been reproduced courtesy of *The Accounting Review* and the American Accounting Association. The picture was originally published in Bedford and Ziegler (1975).

Dedicated to

Hiram Thompson Scovill
Accountant, Teacher, Author, Administrator,
Friend, Colleague, Mentor

"History is experience, and all experience is historical."

— Ludwig Von Mises
(The Ultimate Foundations of
Economic Science, 1962)

CONTENTS

PART III

PART IV

PART V

PART VI

PART VII

PART VIII

PART IX

PART X

PART XI

PART XII

PART XIII
LATE REFLECTIONS

APPENDICES

LIST OF TABLES

APPENDICES

ACKNOWLEDGMENTS

It is an honor and joy to be the Editor of A. C. Littleton's final accounting manuscript. The journey of editing this manuscript into a book began in 2014, and the final product would not have been possible without the assistance of several individuals and organizations. Foremost, I would like to thank Gary J. Previts for believing in this project as the Series Editor of Emerald's *Studies in the Development of Accounting Thought*. I cannot think of a more fitting home for this manuscript. I would also like to thank Stephen A. Zeff for early directions on the project and Bill Black for his assistance in proofing the final draft. Finally, I would like to thank Littleton's grandchildren as well as the American Accounting Association, the American Institute of Certified Public Accountants, the Illinois CPA Society, and the Vernon K. Zimmerman Center for International Education and Research in Accounting at the University of Illinois at Urbana–Champaign for kindly granting me the necessary copyright permission of the material contained in this book. I am also grateful for the funding provided by the Ivey Business School and the University of Western Ontario.

FOREWORD

This edited book represents Ananias Charles Littleton's (1886–1974) final monograph on accounting theory. I first became familiar with Littleton and his ideas as a doctoral student in the United Kingdom, while writing my dissertation on the Australian academic Raymond J. Chambers and his contribution to accounting theory (Persson, 2013). In a letter to Chambers from Sir Alexander Fitzgerald, who held the first full-time professorship in accounting in Australia and was one of the few accounting scholars who had visited the United States in the early 1900s, Littleton is described as "... regarded in [the] U.S.A. as being the most scholarly man in the profession."[1] After Littleton's passing, his colleagues shared similar sentiments writing "... the world of accounting lost one of the founders of its intellectual base" (Bedford & Ziegler, 1975, p. 435).

Yet, when Littleton passed away in the 1970s, great changes were underway in academic research in the United States. Interest in the individual and his or her contribution to the accounting discipline was giving way to capital market research, led by (among others) the Universities of Rochester and Chicago. Correspondingly, the goal of accounting research shifted, from scholarly discussions concerned primarily with the improvement of accounting practice to the examination of accounting numbers from financial statements and share-price data, using new methods from financial economics and statistics (see, e.g., Whitley, 1986).[2] Coupled with the pressures of increased publishing requirements for faculty in universities, the result of this transition has been such that contemporary accounting scholars have reported little attention to their intellectual forefathers such as Littleton. This shift is an unfortunate turn of events and unlike developments in disciplines such as economics, where the thoughts of great economists such as Adam Smith, Irving Fisher, and John Maynard Keynes, continue to receive considerable attention (Ashraf, Camerer, & Loewenstein, 2005; Dimand & Geanakoplos, 2005; Skidelsky, 2010).

With the shift in accounting research as a backdrop, this edited book was composed with the intention of renewing interest in Littleton's contribution to the accounting discipline. It is also fitting that it is being published in the same year as the centennial celebration of the American Accounting Association, an institution that Littleton and his colleagues founded as the American Association of University Instructors in Accounting shortly after the turn of the 20th century.

Littleton was born in Bloomington, Illinois, in December 1886, where he remained until he moved to attend university in Urbana–Champaign. Littleton describes his early upbringing and time at Bloomington High School, from which he graduated in 1905, as quite ordinary. He had found bookkeeping, English literature, and written composition interesting but mathematics and the natural sciences unappealing. While still in high school, Littleton also worked part-time in the local railroad shops, and, after graduating, took up full-time employment as a telegrapher on the Chicago & Alton Railroad, which operated railroad lines with stops in the states of Illinois and Missouri. At the time, the railroad company operated large terminals in Chicago, Kansas City, Peoria, and St. Louis, but Littleton found himself working the night shifts in smaller stops and switching towers located between these larger destinations (see the last chapter, "Reminiscing," for more about Littleton's early life).

After two years of working as a telegrapher, Littleton had saved enough funds to enroll in an undergraduate program in railway administration, at the University of Illinois at Urbana–Champaign. Littleton consequently moved 50 miles from Bloomington to Urbana–Champaign and took up residence in a university rooming house. In his new residence, Littleton learned from two roommates about the new public accountancy laws in Illinois and the opportunities that were presented to those willing to enter public practice. Inspired by these roommates, who had come from Chicago to study accountancy at the university, Littleton switched his major and graduated in 1912 with a Bachelor of Arts in Accountancy.

After graduation, Littleton moved to Chicago and took up employment in public accounting with the British firm Deloitte, Plender, Griffiths & Co. (today Deloitte), which had set up offices in the United States in 1893 (Parker, 1980). His stay in public practice, however, proved short-lived. After serving as an audit assistant to a senior accountant, who was a part-time instructor and fellow alumnus, Littleton was persuaded to return to the University of Illinois at Urbana–Champaign in 1915 to teach elementary accounting courses and pursue a graduate degree in business administration. Littleton recalls finding both the graduate coursework and teaching experience gratifying, and he was appointed to an assistant professorship with the university soon after graduating with a Master of Arts in 1918.

While working as an assistant professor, Littleton qualified as a Certified Public Accountant in the state of Illinois; developed the first graduate course in accountancy at the university (combining accounting theory and history); and, together with his colleague Hiram Thompson Scovill, founded Beta Alpha Psi, an honors organization for accounting students. These activities led to a promotion to associate professor in 1925, and, as graduate enrollment in accounting grew, Littleton used the material he had developed for his course as the basis for pursuing a doctoral degree by dissertation. The university awarded Littleton a PhD in Economics in 1931 and the resulting dissertation, *Accounting Evolution to 1900*, was published in book form in 1933. This book is today considered one of Littleton's greatest works and a seminal contribution to the accounting literature.

Littleton was promoted to full professor shortly after the completion of his doctoral studies, and he remained with the university until his retirement in 1952. During his time as full professor, Littleton and Scovill established the first doctoral program in accounting in the United States. Littleton's first doctoral student, John W. McMahan, graduated in 1939 and went on to work as an accountant for the Atomic Energy Commission.[3] Another graduate from 1942, Robert K. Mautz, was inducted into the Accounting Hall of Fame in 1978 and received the American Institute of Certified Public Accountants' Gold Medal in 1979. In total, Littleton supervised 24 doctoral and 76 graduate dissertations and, as a result, a significant portion of accounting academics during this period was graduates from the University of Illinois at Urbana–Champaign (for more about Littleton's former students, see Appendices A and B).

In addition to his work in the supervision of graduate research, Littleton served in various external academic capacities such as the Vice-President (1936), Director of Research (1940–1942), and President (1943) of the American Accounting Association as well as the Editor of *The Accounting Review* (1943–1947). Littleton also served on various committees of the American Institute of Certified Public Accountants. After retirement from his full-time appointment at Illinois in 1952, Littleton taught part-time at the universities of Arizona, Colorado Boulder, Denver, and Michigan; was elected into the Accounting Hall of Fame in 1956; and received an honorary doctoral degree from his alma mater in 1967 (for further biographical detail, see Bedford & Ziegler, 1975; Gaffikin & Aitken, 2014; Zimmerman, 1967).

Littleton began publishing accounting research as a graduate student and continued through his retirement (for a complete list of publications, see Appendix C). In total, Littleton published over 100 articles in journals such as the *Harvard Business Review*, *Journal of Accountancy*, and

The Accounting Review. An avid reader since high school, Littleton also published 25 book reviews and, for a period, wrote a column titled "The Accounting Exchange" in *The Accounting Review*, in which he offered his thoughts on events in the discipline of accounting. It is for his eight books, however, that Littleton is most well know. In his second sole-authored book, *Accounting Evolution to 1900* (1933), Littleton traced the evolution of bookkeeping into modern accountancy.[4] In his third sole-authored book, *Structure of Accounting Theory* (1953b), he continued this line of inquiry into the present and examined contemporary accounting practices in order to inductively derive an underlying theory that can explain those practices. And, in his fourth sole-authored book, *Essays on Accountancy* (1961a), Littleton brought together extracts from his published work and arranged them in accordance with four categories: accounting education, history, theory, and the profession.

Prominent co-authors joined Littleton for his remaining four books. In his first such book, *An Introduction to Corporate Accounting Standards* (1940), William A. Paton, a professor of accounting at the University of Michigan, and Littleton deductively elaborated what has become known as the quintessential theoretical defense of historical cost accounting. In the second one, *Accounting Theory: Continuity and Change* (1962), Littleton and Vernon K. Zimmerman, a former graduate student, returned to examine the antecedents of modern accountancy using the inductive method. Their aim was to provide a theoretical structure of accountancy broader than that derived through the examination of the evolution of practices and logical deduction.

The remaining two books were edited volumes. The first volume, *Studies in the History of Accounting* (1956), was co-edited with Basil S. Yamey, then a Reader at the London School of Economics. The second volume, *Significant Accounting Essays* (1965), was co-edited with Maurice Moonitz, then a professor of accounting at the University of California, Berkeley. Both volumes were on the topic of accounting history and drew contributions from authors such as Louis Goldberg in Australia; Harold Edey in the United Kingdom; and Eric L. Kohler, Henry R. Hatfield, and Robert H. Montgomery in the United States.

The sum of Littleton's writings have contributed to the establishment of the inductive approach to accounting theory construction, the veracity of historical cost measurements, and the viewpoint that accounting principles and standards should guide practice. According to Bedford and Ziegler (1975), the introduction of the inductive approach to theory construction in accounting was novel at the time and a harbinger of the research methods later developed at the Universities of Chicago and Rochester in the 1970s. Littleton's ideas, however, also spurred much critique and fierce debate among accounting theorists in the 1950s. Whereas there were some support from the traditional leaders of the discipline such as George O. May and Robert N. Anthony, most of Littleton's contemporaries favored a deductive approach to theory construction and shunned measurements based on dated entry prices (historical cost).[5] Chambers (1966) and Robert R. Sterling (1970b) supported measurements based on current exit prices. David Solomons (1961) and William T. Baxter (1971) preferred current entry prices (either replacement cost or deprival value). John B. Canning (1929) and George J. Staubus (1954), on the other hand, welcomed measurements based on discounted future cash flows (i.e., as proxies of current prices).

Whereas the bulk of Littleton's ideas were published in the 1930s and through the 1950s, his later critics published most of their work in the 1960s and onward. The exception to this was Littleton's last book, authored together with Zimmerman, which was published in 1965. This volume, however, contained little more than categorized excerpts from earlier publications. The result of this situation was that most of the criticism directed toward Littleton's ideas went unanswered. This lack of response seems to have even caught some of his fiercest critics' off-guard. For example, in a letter to Ernest Weinwurm in the 1950s, Chambers writes that he had expected "... something quite devastating of Littleton. But it turned out to be rather disappointing."[6]

Although Littleton did not publish much in terms of substantive responses to his critics (for what is available, see Littleton, 1956a, 1956b, 1965), it appears that he was working on the present edited book for this specific purpose. From information contained in the draft of the manuscript, Littleton had at least written some of the chapters by 1966, and his plan had been to dedicate the publication to his former colleague Scovill.[7] If this information is correct, it seems like Littleton would have begun working on the present manuscript sometime after the publication of his edited book together with Moonitz. Contained with the manuscript in the archives, there is also correspondence between Zimmerman, acting on Littleton's behalf, and an editor from a publisher dated September 1972. The content of this correspondence indicate that the manuscript was at least in full draft form at this time, but that no agreement had yet been reached with this publisher. It is likely that Littleton, who passed away just two years later, simply ran out of time.

I discovered the carbon copy of the manuscript in May 2014, and, to my best knowledge, this is the only version of the manuscript that remains. I was moving from Charleston, South Carolina, to London, Ontario, and I had arranged to visit the archives at the University of Illinois at Urbana–Champaign on the way up to Canada. From the list of content published on the university website, I had expected that three days would be enough to take inventory of the personal papers of Arthur R. Wyatt, Edward J. Filbey, and Littleton. My initial intention had been to start with the former two collections, as these were located in the Main Library at the center of campus, but I was unable to find parking because I was arriving a week before finals. As fortune would have it, I therefore began with the Littleton papers instead, stored in the Horticulture Field Lab Building, which is located slightly off the university center.

Littleton's papers were donated to the university archives in two batches, the first one in 1996 and the second one a year later. The archive does not have a donation record, but it is likely that the donor was one of Littleton's children (he had a daughter and a son). There is a total of 2.3 cubic feet of material contained in three boxes. The archivist that received this material created a list of contents that was published on the university website. This list contains the usual items of articles, books, and correspondence. Because this person is not a trained accounting historian, however, he or she would not have been able to separate drafts of Littleton's published material from that which has not been published, without further research. As such, the present manuscript was simply labeled as "late reflections."

Viewing the label "late reflections", I had opened the third box with the expectation of finding the usual collection of annotated articles, disjointed notes, and news-clippings. Instead, I discovered a carbon copy of a 600-page manuscript neatly tucked into an archival folder. Once I realized that I had discovered an unpublished manuscript, I spent the remainder of my time at the archives taking photos of its content.

Once I arrived in Canada, I began to make inquiries regarding the copyright status of the material. For the few items that had previously been published, copyright was obtained from the American Accounting Association, the American Institute of Certified Public Accountants, the Illinois CPA Society, and the Vernon K. Zimmerman Center for International Education and Research in Accounting at the University of Illinois at Urbana–Champaign. For the unpublished materials, which make up most of the manuscript, my first reference was the university archivist William J. Maher. Maher was most responsive and helpful but did not have more information than the names of Littleton's two children, Barbara and Scott, both of which had already passed away.

Using this new information, I eventually managed to locate one of his grandchildren who ran a personal blog. In another fortunate turn of events, this person happened to be a retired higher education professional and was therefore sympathetic towards what I was attempting to accomplish. With her help, we managed to round up the remaining grandchildren; a necessity given that the copyright would have been split evenly between them upon the passing of both Barbara and Scott. These grandchildren gracefully gave me their copyright permission and blessing to reproduce Littleton's manuscript for publication.

Once the copyright permission had been obtained, I approached Gary Previts about the project at the annual meeting of the American Accounting Association in Atlanta, Georgia, in 2014. Previts believed that the project had considerable merit for potential publication as part of Emerald's Studies in the Development of Accounting Thought, and, upon my return from Georgia, I began the process of transcribing the original manuscript.

Once transcribed, I made a series of editorial changes to the original draft. Formatting and referencing were changed throughout, as each entry in the original volume was written as an individual manuscript with its own peculiar layout and citation style. Several references were also either missing or incomplete and therefore had to be retrieved. Littleton's comments, some of which were typed into the manuscript and others scribbled in its margins, were all moved to the endnotes. My editorial comments appear in the footnotes.

In the process of retyping the material for the volume, Littleton made editorial changes to some of his previously published articles. All of these modifications were kept, but a reference to the original article was inserted as a footnote at the beginning of each of these items. The part "Late Reflections," which Littleton wrote last, was moved from the front to the back of the manuscript to maintain a chronological order. My editorial assistant, Bill Black, and I modified the writing only when we felt that such changes would make the manuscript more accessible to the reader. In this process, one chapter, "Assume or Debate," was deemed unsatisfactory and removed. With these exceptions, Littleton's writing is otherwise presented in the format that he had intended.

The manuscript contains 52 chapters, including the introduction, which are divided into 13 parts. Each part appears to be structured according to a theme, but only two parts were given actual titles. These are the first and last parts, titled "Even with Changes, Patterns Remain" and "Late Reflections," respectively. The former contains excerpts from Littleton's writings prior to the present manuscript, and the aim is to bring readers up-to-date on his thoughts. Had the manuscript been published as envisioned in the 1970s, it is likely that this would have been a useful exercise. To the contemporary reader, however, these excerpts provide little more than a starting point for consulting the original publications. On the other hand, the latter part contains some of the best and most succinct expression of Littleton's final thoughts on accounting. These can be read without any knowledge of Littleton's earlier publications.

Out of the 51 chapters, five have appeared as articles published in the *Journal of Accountancy*, *The Accounting Review*, and *The International Journal of Accounting Education and Research* (later *The International Journal of Accounting*). Another six chapters have been previously published in *The Illinois Certified Public Accountant*, which is the predecessor of the Illinois CPA Society's *INSIGHT Magazine*. As mentioned earlier, the sum of these chapters represents Littleton's response to his critics in the 1960s and his last "... excursion into accounting theory" (p. 25)" It marks Littleton's concluding attempt to inductively examine aspects of accounting practices with the goal of deriving "... elements of implicit logic capable of convincingly demonstrating the existence of natural interrelations between accounting actions and ideas" (p. 25).

Readers familiar with Littleton's work will recognize reoccurring themes from earlier publications throughout the manuscript. Littleton continues to argue for the view that the purpose of accounting is the recording of transaction experience (i.e., dated entry prices) emanating from management decisions. This leads him to exclude the use of measurements of current entry and exit prices as well as the valuation of future expected prices in the traditional financial statements, although he is open to supplementary information provided in separate statements. This also leads him to disapprove of the use of a price index to calculate changes in general price-levels (a popular idea at the time, see, e.g., Sweeney, 1936), as economic forces such as these are outside of management's control and, if recorded, would distort the transaction history of the enterprise.

Along with familiar themes on the measurement function and purpose of accounting, Littleton offers new lines of inquiry as well. The most interesting of these is Littleton's increased incorporation of the philosophical tradition of pragmatism into his thoughts on accounting theory. He appears particularly keen on the writings of the American philosopher John Dewey (1859–1952). Faced with arguments from his contemporaries that accounting should reflect current economic conditions and be grounded in "sound" scientific principles (Mattessich, 1964; Sterling, 1970a, 1979), Dewey's line of thought must have appealed to Littleton. Consistent with the tradition of pragmatism, Littleton saw the primary function of accounting as being that of an instrument to aid decision-making, as opposed to trying to represent an accurate depiction of current economic conditions (most of which were taking place independently of management action). As such, just as pragmatism considers most philosophical ideas in terms of their usefulness to facilitate human action, Littleton saw accounting in terms of its usefulness in informing management of their past transaction decisions and results.

Littleton ends the last chapter, written before his 85th birthday, with the hope that some of his activities and thoughts "… may have proved useful to others" (p. 593). At the eve of his 130th birthday, I believe that Littleton would have found comfort in the fact that his activities and thoughts certainly have, despite changing trends in accounting research. The American Accounting Association, which he and his colleagues started as an unassuming teaching association, has grown to become an organization of international significance that is now celebrating its centennial. His parting thoughts, on the relationship between accounting and the philosophical tradition of pragmatism, have received renewed interest in the accounting literature (Rutherford, 2013). In addition, his final contribution to the accounting discipline is now published in its entirety. I hope that he would approve that I have done the material within these covers justice.

Martin E. Persson
Ivey Business School,
Western University, London, Canada
April 2016

NOTES

1. R. J. Chambers Archive, University of Sydney, Australia. Letter from Fitzgerald to Chambers, May 17, 1955 (DOI: 10.USA P202/1/00085).
2. There is considerable accounting literature drawing on Thomas Kuhn's (1962) work on the growth of scientific knowledge to explain this change in accounting research (e.g., Cushing, 1989; Mouck, 1993; Wells, 1976). More recent research has reconsidered this change from the perspective of Graham Harman's (2011) object-oriented ontology (Persson & Napier, 2015a).

3. McMahan is also the father-in-law of James Aho, Professor Emeritus at Idaho State University and a trained sociologist with an interest in accounting and double-entry bookkeeping (Aho, 2006, p. xix).

4. Littleton published his first book, containing elementary accounting problems, while still working as an instructor in 1919.

5. R. J. Chambers Archive, University of Sydney, Australia. Letter from May to Chambers, August 15, 1956 (DOI: 10.USA P202/2/08373). Letter from Anthony to Chambers, October 9, 1962 (DOI: 10.USA P202/2/08478).

6. R. J. Chambers Archive, University of Sydney, Australia. Letter from Chambers to Weinwurm, September 18, 1956 (DOI: 10.USA P202/1/00235).

7. I inserted such a dedication in this edited version.

PART I
EVEN WITH CHANGE, PATTERNS REMAIN

1

PREFACE

It has been said that philosophy is a stubborn effort to think clearly. These pages attempt this kind of approach to the area of accounting theory. The intention has been in various separate essays to seek to penetrate beneath known accounting actions toward compelling ideas that could constitute conceptual foundations. A need exists for understanding the motivations that influence enterprise accounting, so ineptly called "double-entry bookkeeping" in its earlier days.

Aristotle believed that all men by nature desire to know. Accounting's evolutionary development reflects influences like the prompting of such desire to know. It has grown in technical capability and service capacity to an extent that suggests the same desire still acts as a motivating force. For centuries, accounting has provided a way to learn much about a business enterprise and its management through study of that unit's transaction experience. The service accounting renders to society comes largely from the way knowledge thus derived can aid future decisions by management within the enterprise and by investors outside in the money market.

It seems reasonable to consider it possible to construct a body of interrelated accounting doctrine. These pages do not attempt to reach that goal. But the ultimate usefulness of an integration of basic ideas can itself stimulate thought in that direction.

Long use has given technology a splendid capability for rendering effective analytical services. The pattern of its techniques demonstrates some persistent and vital logic. Beneath its methods, there would have been influential, motivating ideas, and intentions. Some aspects of accounting theory have been examined in a historical context in one of my previous books (Littleton & Zimmerman, 1962).

In the present essays, some aspects of accounting are examined in search of elements of implicit logic capable of convincingly demonstrating the existence of natural interrelations between accounting actions and ideas. These pages therefore present an excursion into accounting theory.

If an "equation" can compactly represent a theory about accounting theory, it might take this form: theory + logic = interrelations + explanations.

The third term can be directly related to the second. For one aspect of this logic (often called pragmatism) involves a testing of the interrelation of ends and means. While accounting can scarcely be considered an end in and of itself, it could prove to be a suitable means toward specific desirable ends. The "equation" therefore points thought in two directions: to ideas regarding the objectives of accounting itself and to relevant techniques capable of serving as means to achieve those objectives.

2

COMMENTARY IN RETROSPECT

On the occasion of his retirement, a teacher of law made this comparison: whereas old soldiers just fade away (as General MacArthur said), old lawyers just linger longer at the bar. And the old accounting teacher? Perhaps his pen just slowly runs dry. One teacher would like to use the last of his work to state the opinion that the opportunity to study and teach, and to write as part of teaching, can have much more significance for an individual than could be implied by his publications.

The materials in *Essays on Accountancy* (1961a) present some glimpses of one teacher's thoughts about the growth of accountancy as a technology, as a profession, and as subject matter for college education at both undergraduate and postgraduate levels. In the literature of our area of knowledge and of practical service (accountancy), some idea patterns are discernible. That literature came in response to a recognized need – that of making understandable some of the reasons why a growing capability in accounting technology could serve society well. Beneath its practical methodology, there should be a body of theory capable of serving as ideological underpinning. In the areas of both actions and ideas, there have been historical developments that illuminate the way.

In the years following classroom teaching, as if out of nowhere, came an interest in reading about philosophy and science. Perhaps it was because this was unfamiliar ground; it surprisingly stimulated thoughts, which seemed relevant to the nature and function of accountancy and to the reasons underlying its evident service capacity. Accounting technology seemed soundly and logically based. Its action structures seemed to be resting on a philosophy particularly well suited to giving its techniques added significance. Its methodology is more than accumulated custom. Those actions, both early and modern, are examples of well-conceived means capable of serving clearly desirable ends.

The philosopher, Whitehead (1960, p. 19) said, in effect, that ideas about concrete facts are ultimately supported by abstract ideas. Perhaps, if we look deeply enough, this thought might also apply to the relation of the concrete facts of enterprise transaction experience and abstract but compelling concepts, which become increasingly evident in the literature of accounting history and theory.

The present volume has been assembled out of that kind of recent background, and follows the earlier essays on accountancy, which grows out of the experience of teaching at the graduate level. There is no "truth machine," which can erase any of the author's previously expressed views, or make over any that might now seem to need it. Whatever the bias, it will therefore, remain; faulty choice of topic or treatment will be unchanged. If some of the patterns of accountancy's development may have become more discernible, this may usefully help to associate the past with the growth into the future. For the past is but a prelude, an introduction. Whatever follows probably will have been foreshadowed in some measure.

3

A BACKGROUND NOTE FOR THE 1920S

Accountants created a professional organization in Scotland in 1854. Accountants in England created professional organizations during the period 1870–1880. The latter development was directly influenced by legislation in the 1850s and 1860s, which placed business companies under requirements to report fully to shareholders. In France in 1881 and Italy in 1879, similar developments of professional groups took place. In the United States, CPA legislation was introduced by the state of New York in 1896. By 1925, CPA laws had been passed in 25 states.

The American Association of Public Accountants was formed in 1887, and in 1916 was converted into the American Institute of Accountants – now the American Institute of Certified Public Accountants. In the next year, a nation-wide CPA examination was made available to state examination boards. *The Journal of Accountancy* began publication in 1905. *The Accounting Review* sponsored by the teachers of accounting began publication in 1926.

For a brief period American education used British textbooks on accounting, particularly Bixley's *Auditing*, which was published in 1881.[1] In the United States, Robert Montgomery (1909) published an American edition of Lawrence Dicksee's *Auditing*, and in 1912 published his own text. Professor Henry Hatfield, in (1909), published *Modern Accounting*, an early book on accounting theory.

By the 1920s, formal education had become a feature of the CPA laws. By 1925, 44 states required graduation from high school. At the college level, New York University offered work in 1900 with professional accountants as teachers. By 1901, courses were available at Ohio University, Wisconsin, Dartmouth, Harvard, and Vermont. The University of Illinois offered a four-year program beginning in 1915, a Master's degree in accountancy in 1925, and in 1937, a Ph. D. degree with accountancy as a major subject.

In several of the following pages the leading ideas in the items in *Essays on Accountancy* (1961a) have been abstracted by decades in order to provide the present reader with a compact view of the earlier volume.[2] Following those abstracts, the author's writing in the 1960s is presented in full. Some have been published as indicated, while others are items that have not been submitted for prior publication.

NOTES

1. Markings from the original manuscript indicate that Littleton was unable to locate the reference for this publication.
2. In the original draft of "Part 1: Even with Change, Patterns Remain," Littleton referenced articles and conference proceedings republished in *Essays on Accountancy* (1961a) using the page number in which those items appear in the volume. These "page references" have been replaced with references to Littleton's original articles. The exceptions to this rule are references to items that appear in journals and proceedings that are no longer in print, in which case the original citation has been kept. The intention is to aid the reader who does not have access to Littleton's prior volume.

4

ABSTRACT OF ESSAYS IN THE 1920S

In the modern accounting literature, it is commonplace to distinguish between theory and practice, between ideology and methodology. But theory (as explanation) was slow to appear. For a long time after Luca Pacioli's book (1494), texts continued to describe bookkeeping actions.

Pacioli provided a practical description of the contemporary way of making accounting records "according to the method of Venice" (Littleton, 1961a, p. 562). The techniques the author described seem to reflect the results of recognition, evidenced by earlier businessmen's actions, that the transaction experience of a specific enterprise was a homogeneous whole, and that the underlying details need to be systematically organized in aid of management's understanding, by review, the significance of prior business decisions.

Some glimpses of emerging theory appeared in the 1800s. In 1818, an English author, Frederick Cronhelm, considered the basis of bookkeeping to be equality between the proprietor's capital account as the whole and all other accounts – the latter expressing sub-parts of the whole. Beneath such a concept we can detect evidence of the analytical and reporting function of accounting (Littleton, 1961a, p. 55).

In 1841, an American author, Thomas Jones, considered bookkeeping as reflective of two distinct plans for arranging transaction data: one set of accounts (resources and liabilities) would show the position of enterprise affairs; another group of accounts (losses and gains) would show the changes between enterprise position as of two different dates (Littleton, 1927b).

Now, more than 120 years later, questions are being raised indicating doubt that nominal accounts, being confined to recording historical costs only, can completely report the changes in enterprise financial position between two dates. The implication of such questions is that conditions not associated with consummated transaction experience of the given enterprise will also have affected the real pattern of financial position.

In the 1850s, two German authors, although borrowing the concept of "two series of accounts," used certain clarifying phases about the essence of account reporting. They spoke of "results bookkeeping" and "possessions bookkeeping." One of these terms is clearly close to the modern term "nominal accounts," the other close to "real accounts." As a matter of clear terminology, the German expressions seem, in translation, more realistic than the English terms a generation earlier (Littleton, 1927b, 1927c, 1928b).

Underlying these and later theories about the nature of accounting processes lay practical matters, which affected early developments. These influences are still strong in the modern technology of accounting. For example, the need persists for a method of mentally translate known transactions events into quantitative entries in a scheme of classification categories. Today this would be called "transaction analysis," and would refer to the process of reasoning events into account data.

A variety of methods has been advocated. Very early transaction records, before the century, were those kept by Italian moneylenders. They had a clear need to review records of deposits later to be returned and of loans later to be repaid to the lender. The key words in the record were, for a borrower "he shall give" (i.e., return the sum borrowed); for a depositor, "he shall have" (i.e., have his deposit returned). The written transaction records were essentially verbally descriptive paragraphs (Littleton, 1928a).

The British thought process was quite differently expressed before the Italian methodology was adopted. Their records were related to stewardship responsibilities on the landed states of the nobility. A steward would *charge* himself with property given in his care. He would *discharge* himself for property consumed, lost, or returned to its owner. One situation would produce an increase; in the language of the day, the steward would be *debitour*. In the other situation, he would be *creditour*. Gradually, a debt responsibility came to be called "debit." A debt responsibility canceled came to be called a "credit." These two terms are still used, and they still are technical and used out of the usual sense of the real words. Today the familiar words point not to loans or stewardship as such, but to past transaction – experience as it happened, whatever its effect on the enterprise; the effects of transactions are favorable–unfavorable. The service of accounting is to make these aspects reviewable (Littleton, 1926).

Today, all transaction experience is best analyzed (1) as increase to assets or expenses, and as decrease to liabilities or revenue – that is, as *debits*; (2) as decrease to assets or expenses, and as increase to liabilities and revenues – that is, as *credits*. It is clear that the basic terms have a minimum of relation to debts as such. It is also clear that the bilateral form of all accounts fits very neatly into the data classification problems addressed by accounting technology. Some favorable effects are increases; others are decreases. Some accounts received show increases on the left, others on the right. Unfavorable effects on the business must appear on the left side of some accounts or on the right side of other accounts. In other words, it all may sound complicated, but business experience is not simple; as such, analytically recording that experience can scarcely be a simple matter.

It is obvious that "transaction experience" is a natural aspect of the active employment of capital in association with the decisions made by businessmen in order for their respective enterprises. This characteristic is as old as enterprise and the use of capital in trade. Here are the deepest roots of accountancy (Littleton, 1927a).

In the 1920s, a change in educational developments made accounting an appropriate subject for college courses. In the older approach, the study of bookkeeping was almost entirely a matter of classroom exercises in performing relevant technical actions. Transaction analysis was accomplished by matching a variety of specific rules to specific transaction types. Model illustrations were closely followed. A trial balance was first rearranged into a calendar sheet with assets, liabilities, expenses, and revenues and then converted (following the textbook model) into a simple balance sheet and a profit-and-loss statement (see Chapter 4, Littleton, 1933).

Courses at the college level could not be well served by an almost mechanical method of instruction. Modern educational purposes are not clerical in intention; it would appear worthwhile to point instruction toward fulfilling a function of passing accumulated knowledge and in the process stimulate thought processes and to broaden the powers of penetrating to understanding and of clearly expressing the significance of observed changes in accounting data. The printed page provides contact for the student with the accounting thoughts of other minds. Problems having an accounting content can provide difficulties to be faced, analyzed, and rationally resolved. Thoughtful penetration into specific situations can have a general educational effect. Critical examinations of the ideas of other people could develop one's ability to exercise one's own ideas critically (Littleton, 1961a, p. 536).

This sort of educational theory may well have sponsored "the balance sheet approach" to elementary accounting at the college level. Perhaps this could be considered as a starting point for "theory." Reasons for transactions were summarized in enterprise experience (financial statements) and this organized experience data could then have significance for the statement user's own problems. With this as foundation, the study of the means for producing "experienced reports" would be more beneficial, more educational from its relation to ultimate use-objectives. The groups of accounts would then have more meaning; the nature of transaction events would be related to specific account types (Littleton, 1961a, p. 568).

In the study of procedures, it is desirable to consider the reason for their being. An objective of accounting is to make a business enterprise understandable. The best way to understand an enterprise, and the results of its management's decisions, is to study data reflecting those results. This data come from enterprise transaction experience. The theory of the accounting function is that its technical features guide the procedures by which transaction experience data can be assembled, organized, and compactly communicated to interested parties.

When theory and practical actions are welded together in the introductory courses, a firm foundation is laid for subsequent courses, which will gradually advance the student's education for a career in accounting. With benefit, the interrelation of theory and practice could be continued into the work for a Master's degree. It would also be beneficial if advanced work (undergraduate and postgraduate) included integrated study of enterprise economics, economic statistics, and business finance. As such, a continued emphasis on interrelations among different course materials can be highly educational. It can foster independent thinking about interrelations in general throughout life. Specialization can be overdone; accounting exists in the midst of an economy; its data serves a wide area of varied interest (Littleton, 1961a, pp. 578–583).

In the last half of the 1920s, economic issues were clearly in evidence as matters of concern in accounting education. The economic nature of enterprises and the role of management became increasingly important aspects of accounting education. Management needs to be aware of the results of enterprise's prior experience. But this knowledge should be considered against equal awareness of economic conditions and movements. Misjudging the possible impact of change could affect enterprise achievements. So too could a failure to study the significance readable in enterprise account data (Littleton, 1928c, 1938b).

Even 40 years ago, price level changes were a matter of concern. In the middle 1960s, price level changes were also still under discussion in the accounting literature. The adequacy of account data is still debated; the relative significance of data as to *value* and *price* is not yet settled. If there was need for study of enterprise economics (microeconomics) when graduate work in accounting was young, there is more need for such a study now. And particularly for two reasons: (1) because monetary inflation continues to raise difficult problems; (2) because ideas rooted in economic theories about *value* have tended to obscure an essential fact about enterprise accounting function.

That essential fact is that functions should be considered as clearly limited to reporting on the results of actual transaction experience of the given enterprise. That function would therefore be concerned with reported data from the company's own exchange-priced transactions, not with reporting on the current *value* of the residuals of prior transaction experience. When *value* is a matter of importance, as of course it often is, it should be separately judged on the basis of collateral, non-account, information. Generalized price levels (statistical index series) are not part of enterprise transaction experience. Those data, however, can be very useful as interrelated supplements outside of the enterprise's own experience.

5

ABSTRACT OF ESSAYS IN THE 1930S

Theory, in the sense of principles capable of guiding practice, could be deduced from a selected group of assumptions, which would be accepted as valid without proof. The asserted conclusions, derived from the assumptions, would rest on foundations, which may have a hidden weakness and unclear basic concepts.

The function of accounting theory should be to set a foundation of basic concepts beneath practical actions. These concepts would come from ideas distilled by an induction process, out of knowledge of the information and services of enterprise accounting. Such concepts, upon being analyzed and interrelated, could convincingly explain enterprise accounting objectives, techniques, and limitations. Theories of this kind, therefore, could help practices; ideas could guide actions, because they would be able to exercise influence through persuasive reasons for preferring one type of action to another. Here is the function of theory. The practical arts of accounting came out of deductive reasoning from assumptions. They came as means serving conceived objectives. Their modern justification could well be sought in recognizing existing objectives and in appraising existing technical limitations inherent in effective accounting actions (Littleton, 1939b).

It may be necessary to test customary actions; and proposed actions, against basic concepts of limited accounting functions and *supplementary* types of non-accounting actions. Out of a consistent body of functional theory could come standards, which would be able to critically judge the acceptability of variations in accounting actions (Littleton, 1939b).

College education in accounting should not be expected by itself to produce professionals. It could and should train individuals to think rationally in this area. Theory would be helpful here. It could provide experience in organizing account data in analytical ways to support interpretation.

The content of the CPA examination does not reach directly into the non-accounting instructional materials in a college curriculum. Nevertheless, non-accounting courses can usefully improve mental grasp of ideas and relations. The results of CPA examinations in recent years indicate a direct relation between a college degree and examination success. The reported experience in one state, Colorado, covered six examinations in the 1960s. The results showed that 56 percent of the successful candidates had a college degree that included accounting. Twenty percent had taken graduate courses. But an intention toward an accounting career should not downgrade the value of solid work in business economics, management, finance, and selected courses from the liberal arts.

An accounting curriculum, especially one including graduate work, might well be aimed at preparing students to grow into professionals by their own efforts in the context of their employment. No doubt, this kind of development takes place after graduation in law or in medicine. There, as in accounting, classroom study alone does not make a successful practitioner. Nor do passing license examinations demonstrate professional competence. As such, it is not the CPA examination that makes the candidate a professional (Littleton, 1936a). He becomes a professional by his development after his formal education. The means to that end is his capacity to learn by experience; he should have been developing this capacity throughout all of his schooling.

In law and medicine, general education proceeds education toward a profession. The concentration in the later parts of this education deals with great bodies of complex materials, and specific knowledge of these is essential to becoming a professional. Occasionally, the idea is therefore advanced that preparation for a career in professional accounting might well be offered in its own kind of professional (postgraduate) college. It is still questionable whether this would be a constructive step. The study materials now involved may seem extensive and complex, but such a postgraduate course of study would be even more ambitious and include much more than coursework on accounting, auditing, and professional responsibilities. Large areas of education for business would be involved. What physics, chemistry, biology and anatomy are to the education of a physician, economics, finance, and management are to the education of professional accountants (Littleton, 1936a, 1947a).

The school of business is the natural and most appropriate place for accounting education. If graduate work in accounting continues to grow, it should never be exclusively focused on accounting material alone. There will always be opportunities in the professional practice of accounting to draw upon non-accounting material to understand the problems of businesses. There is also much to be learned in the course of the day's work in the field. There is a steadily growing literature, which one has to browse systematically. It is simply not enough to keep up with the day's assignments with clients. Keeping up to date in relevant literature is also a part of learning to be a professional. Educational development needs to be continuous, but it can either be neglected or directed. The individual makes the choice (Littleton, 1961a, p. 625).

College study of accounting is carried on in the midst of other subjects in the business curriculum. Of particular significance are the neighboring areas of economics and finance. These are broad fields, and some of the subdivisions have quite specific objectives rather remote from accounting. Understanding the economics of the firm is indispensable because it is closely associated with business enterprise—indeed as closely as is accountancy itself. The two are natural companions.

An increased study of accountancy in association with economics has broadened professional education. Conceivably, accounting could be studied in isolation, that is, simply as a variety of techniques to be learned. Bookkeeping used to be taught that way. It is necessary that accounting study involve learning to deal with technical details. This approach, however, is educationally beneficial only in a limited way. It could scarcely be considered as sufficient by itself as preparation for a professional career.

There is good reason in support of accounting education within a context of business education. Business is deeply concerned with *capital* and with *income*. These important terms do not refer merely to elements in accounting reports. They speak of very large concepts indeed. Those terms can be used broadly, as in "capital markets" and "national income." The same words, however, have a very special significance for a specific business entity. For accounting, an entity is not a proprietor, corporation, nor management. It is an organizational unit having legal status; it is a working unit closely associated with managers and investors. It is an owner and user of assets (i.e., capital); it is indebted to creditors and security holders; it is subject to taxation; it functions in the service of society (see Chapter 12, Littleton, 1933).

The subject matter of accounting is related to this conceptual entity. The conceptual boundary of the enterprise necessarily forms a conceptual boundary for enterprise accounting, for only the transaction experience of a given enterprise enters the account-recorded experience of that entity. These two elements (enterprise capital and income) are of great interest to management, investors, and taxation authorities. Moreover, they provide the key concepts for the two basic financial statements. The balance sheet would be more appropriately named "Capital Statement," to pair with the "Income Statement," both reporting on essential aspects of a business enterprise.

It might be suggested that the generation of income was the objective of a business enterprise; that income determination was the chief objective of enterprise accounting. Actually, the enterprise objective is to create effective and acceptable service. That being the case, net income becomes a readable sign of effective management. The chief objective of enterprise accounting is to summarize in a meaningful manner the results of the enterprise's transaction experience. An important aspect of that intention is that of making understandable the inevitable interrelation of enterprise capital and enterprise income (Littleton, 1937).

The capital statement must report in two parts: capital kind (i.e., capital having productive potential) and capital sources. Some sources will have legal status as repayable indebtedness; other sources of capital represent residual claimants to enterprise income and enterprise property in the event of dissolution (Littleton, 1932, 1955). Whereas the capital statement derives from real accounts, the income statement derives from nominal accounts. The nominal accounts reflect two differing streams of data flow. Revenue inflow speaks of accepted service performance; applicable expense (converted assets) speaks of an outflow of enterprise efforts to perform to the satisfactions of customers. The income statement represents a periodic matching of account data reflecting efforts to perform and account data reflecting performance achievements (Littleton, 1939a).

In essence, the capital statement is an implement for carrying forward (1) capital kinds toward later productive use and (2) capital sources toward potential and ultimate liquidation. This statement, therefore, does not report on values.

In essence, the income statement is a report on management effectiveness in producing performance acceptable to customers and in keeping total costs below revenue inflow. This report, therefore, tells of managerial skill; it does not undertake to explore or reveal causation. People buy for their own reasons; prices rise or fall because of intricate interplays of causation. Neither customer demand nor actual sale makes the profits. Sale only provides an opportunity to profit, if management is wise, skillful, and experienced (Littleton, 1937).

Businessmen are living a theory of profit. Some of their experience enables them to sense probable near future conditions and to react accordingly. This must necessitate valuation judgments; and these may well influence the results reported by the accounting. The reported profits have come about because of the use of capital, prevailing economic conditions, and varying degrees of managerial judgment. Accounting is a limited technology, because of its necessary association with the details of the prior transaction experience of a specific enterprise. It is not technically qualified to deal with values of the moment or of the possible future. It is even less qualified to explore economic causation or human motivation.

Surely, the interpretation of the significance of accounting data for its users is beyond the competence of such a technology to indicate. Accounting can perhaps be considered as analytical in exercising its reporting function. It can properly try to realistically and dependably assemble and report on enterprise prior expense. Beyond that, it would seem necessary for separate techniques of interpretation to take over. This necessity is no less significant because the needed separate technology has not yet been clearly conceived or developed.

The 1930s brought into evidence circumstances that stimulated and frequently challenged accounting thought. In Europe, it was the aftermath of war, especially the great monetary inflation in Germany. In the United States, the aftermath followed the speculative fever of the 1920s. Certain financial practices of the speculative days led to turning a spotlight of inquiry on the dividend laws of some states and on some deficiencies in financial statement integrity (Littleton, 1934). Under some states, cash dividends could be based on the existence of "surplus"; in other states the existence of "profit" was the key. In the first situation, company solvency was the test; that is, its assets had to be in excess of its liabilities. In the second situation, the test was whether the company had earned profits from its operating activities.

The speculative period produced many mergers, consolidations, and reorganizations among companies. Under the then-allowed conditions of valuation changes, surplus accounts were created from these activities. Their balances rose substantially. This precipitated the question whether appreciation in asset values, as reflected in new credits to surplus, would be counted as profit available for cash dividends (Littleton & Staub, 1936). A collateral problem, largely related to use of stock without par value, raised questions about capital surplus. Could it absorb taxes? Could it support dividend declarations (Littleton, 1961a, p. 280)?

Because of extended critique and debate, dividend laws of several states were changed to exclude cash dividends based on appreciation or appraisal surplus. Another collateral result was the clarification by the American Institute of Accountants on the nature of financial reporting. The clear separation in the financial reports of earned surplus, appreciation surplus, and paid-in surplus, advocated as generally accepted accounting principles, was in direct harmony with the legal actions taken to place statutory limits that excluded appreciation or appraisal surplus from use as a base for cash dividends.

The literature of accounting was also broadened in the 1930s by the impact of the speculative crisis of the late 1920s. The depressed conditions of the economy, so evident thereafter, were influenced by post-war economic conditions in Europe. The roots there planted grew into deep concern over inflation, over its causes, and possible controls of its effects. Accounting would inescapably become involved because its data derived directly from exchange-priced transactions. Inflation, whether called price inflation, monetary inflation, or interacting combinations of the two, would affect business actions and plans. Financial statements would be constructed from actual transactions data accumulated in the accounts. After price levels had markedly risen, the truthfulness of account data expressed in the substantially lower prices of the time of the original transaction was questioned.

Economic theory had now begun to interact with accounting technology. *Changing Purchasing Power of Money* (1922) was the title of a book by Professor Irving Fisher, reflecting on the impact on economic thought of price changes associated with the war of 1914–1918. Several articles by accounting teachers picked up on similar themes in 1918–1920 (Littleton, 1961a, p. 177; Littleton & Zimmerman, 1962). A consensus was emerging that financial statements should in some way prompt users to consider the significance of their own problems stemming from price-level changes of the times. The issue was whether the financial statements themselves should report the impact on matters of fact, or whether the companies should supplement the published financial statements with additional statistical data, reflecting general movements in the price level.

The post-war economic collapse in European countries precipitated such a great price inflation that accounts in actual transaction prices became meaningless. In attempts to make it possible to use account data in aid of rational decisions, the original information was systematically modified by adjusting the figures by applications of statistical index series for general prices. The resulting "new" account data were believed to exclude the effect on the enterprise of monetary inflation, which otherwise might have been overlooked or misjudged. The technical features of this non-accounting statistical procedure were known in the United States in the 1930s as "stabilized accounting." Its use was expected to increase the comparability of financial statements for successive years. Presumably, the adjusted figures were to be considered as reflecting the results of management decisions cleared of the effects of monetary inflation (Littleton, 1936b).

The phrase "purchasing power of money" can frequently be seen in the literature (Littleton, 1931). Account data, however, had long been based on the concept that assets were "valuable" because of their usefulness for enterprise purposes (i.e., their value-in-use). Under the impact of price-level change, something approaching value-in-exchange seemed about to replace the earlier concept (Littleton, 1935). A middle-of-the-road modification provided a separate column beside the figures for exchange-priced data, where these figures could be observed as modified by applications of prices index services. This technique could alert users to the need to consider contemporary conditions along with account data in making decisions (Littleton & Staub, 1936).

Evident in these developments is a new aspect of accounting theory. The users of account data must be made increasingly aware of the influences of changing economic conditions on a business enterprise and on its management decisions. Associated with this interpretative awareness, there should be a clear realization that enterprise account data, whether under normal economic conditions or conditions of monetary inflation, cannot alone be all things to all people. Out of such a context, it is clear that a sharp distinction is necessary between accounting as a technology for reporting on the actual transaction experiences of an enterprise, and a still imperfectly developed separate technology of interpreting meaning out of the reported and actual transaction experience. The latter would provide significant aid to people having business decisions to make.

Separation of these two technologies is needed today. Inherent in much of the contemporary discussion is a failure to recognize or accept the appropriateness of two separate types of decision-useful data. Acceptance of the two would negate proposals that would intermingle, in the financial statements, data from the prior history (historical cost) of an enterprise and data reflecting current conditions that have not yet become actual elements in its reportable experience. There is reason for separating, carefully and clearly, interpretatively useful supplementary data from the data of actual enterprise experience. There are grounds for believing that the United States is faced with a "creeping inflation," based primarily on a policy of low interest rates, deficit spending, increased money supply, raising prices, and high wages.

A concurrent feature in the 1960s is the persistence of economic doctrines, which arose in the midst of the deflation (depression) experienced a generation ago, and were proposed and used to bring about recovery. A variety of policies was initiated to stimulate demand by government action. It may be significant for the economy, and collaterally to accounting under the impact of continuing rise in price levels, that many of the measures taken to pull the economy up from the depression of the 1930s are still exerting the same kind of upward influence. The result seems to be a planned support for a slow-moving type of monetary inflation associated with deficit spending.

Professional accountants in the early 1930s recognized a challenge to accounting logic arising in the freedom to use one general surplus account for both earnings and appreciation credits, thus working both into sources for cash dividends (Littleton & Staub, 1936). Such use was a violation of sound principle. It disregarded the logical relation between the basic concept of "dividend" and another basic concept: an unmistakable distinction between capital and earnings. Classifying surplus into earned surplus, appreciation surplus, paid-in surplus, can therefore be seen as advocacy of logic as the bedrock for accounting actions. That advocacy reflected the influence of a principle. It now could be called the principle of full disclosure, an ethical responsibility inherent in the communication function of financial statements.

Some thirty years later, principles were brought under close research, examination, and debate. Earlier discussions of rules and standards were also concerned with differentiations (Littleton, 1938a). "Rules" seemed associated with authority; "standards" seemed to identify with policies of truthfulness that would serve as guides to high quality actions. At times, departures from standards might become necessary because of special circumstances that could strongly support a variation. There was indicated some areas of flexibility, but only to the extent that this could be associated with rationally convincing justifications.

Certain aspects of persuasive logic have long been associated with enterprise accounting. For example, the bilateral form of a ledger account is a logical consequence of the combination of favorable and unfavorable effects, which occur in every exchange transaction of every enterprise. Surely, "logic" and "principle" will be related. Custom, convention, and consensus have long influenced accounting actions. But their strength comes more from rules than from logic (Littleton, 1939b).

A simple way of thinking of a logic for accounting is to identify it with rational good sense (Littleton, 1947b). This may not seem "scientific" enough. It may seem to give more support than is desirable to convention and consensus as dependable bases. Rational good sense, however, has the advantage of being related to an inductive type of reasoning. Inductive inferences derive their strength from association with actual experience, whereas deductive conclusions have only the support of very broad assumptions and postulates (Littleton, 1938c).

A tentative statement of accounting principles reflecting an inductive approach was prepared in 1936. Another statement of accounting principles was prepared in the middle 1960s, which reflected a deductive approach, having been preceded by an examination of accounting postulates capable of supporting a selection of principles. This is not the place to discuss either statement or either approach in detail. It may be noted, however, that both presentations dealt with account data accumulation and data reporting. They did not present principles of data interpretation, although all accounting actions point toward ultimate interpretative use of the emerging data. Indeed, there seems to be emerging a theory that that non-transaction data might well be incorporated into the technical structure of enterprise accounting (Littleton, 1938b).

If accounting reports can depart at will from objective data associated with the flow of enterprise actual transaction experience, such precedents will open a wide door. If wishful thinking and fanciful valuations were then to enter, this may undermine the messages of management effectiveness that must have been readable out of reported real transaction experience. This is not to argue that a web of cause and effect does not lay on the back of accumulated account data from transaction experience, but it is questionable whether accounting technology can hope to cope with these causes and effects regardless of their influence on prior transaction decisions. As an example, consider the matching of revenue and applicable cost in preparing an income statement. Is this expression of a principle, or merely a necessary technical function (Littleton, 1939a)?

The technical action has a reason: in order that management's effectiveness may be understood, it is necessary periodically to cut through two streams of continuing experience in cost and revenues. Cost tells of creative efforts, by management's judgments and decisions, to induce customers to produce a flow of revenue for the enterprise. Revenue tells of the achievement management has made through salesmanship. These two may seem to represent cause and effect; and, in a sense, they do. Without planning, investing and making other efforts (the apparent causes) there would be no acceptance by customers (the desired results) (Littleton, 1937).

Yet, this analysis does not penetrate far enough. Underlying costs as "causes" were the economic conditions of the day, the types, and varieties of competitive goods, prices in the purchase markets and the price of labor. Underlying revenues as "effects" were economic conditions represented by competition in selling, variations in customer acceptance influenced by his own financial condition and his price judgments. On both sides of the line, the influence of these factors on actual transactions is very real. These cannot be directly reflected by accounting actions, and yet their influence generate the transaction experience that accounting records.

A conclusion emerges. Accounting should hold fast to a realistic and limited function – that of reporting trustworthy data from transaction experience originating in the overt actions of the management of the specific enterprise. If this accounting data does not give an accurate picture of influential economic conditions of interest to investor's decisions, supplementary information should be made available, not within the financial statements but as collateral material.

6

ABSTRACT OF ESSAYS IN THE 1940S

This decade reflected growing recognition of the significance of thorough educational preparation for a career in professional or administrative accounting. Consideration of the function of education will reinforce the convention that a broad approach will be preferable to a purely technical emphasis – provided the chosen aspects of general education shall be carefully integrated with the study of accounting.

In all education, and accounting education in particular, the chief objective should point students toward developing a capacity for and an interest in continuing to learn (Littleton, 1944a). Increased understanding can be pleasurable; ability to communicate effectively by organizing words or organizing figures can be rewarding. Accordingly, it should be the teacher's obligation to help students to realize that learning is more than remembering. Education is itself a part of an expanding experience (Littleton, 1942). It is more than learning facts. The techniques of doing are merely suitable means for attaining ends for which there are strong supporting reasons (Littleton, 1945b). The teacher should persist in asking for reasons, in suggesting reasons, and in explaining reasons.

Education, especially in accountancy, should aim to develop analytical ability. Perceived relations among account data invite thinking into the significance hidden there, thinking of the possible meaning of change, or of no change, over time (Littleton, 1961a, p. 544). But education, in all its phases, can contribute to professional competence. Interrelations among ideas are as significant as interrelated data. Indeed, related data speak of related ideas. Account data reflect transaction experience; they speak of prior decisions and actions of management, whose decisions have been strongly influenced by non-quantitative and non-account considerations. They have been made and must continue to be made in an atmosphere of business objectives and economic conditions.

Education has a role beyond preparation to enter professional accounting as well. The need to develop, to grow in capacity, is not satisfied with formal education, or by passing the CPA examination. Accumulated field experience is highly educational. But it alone, though indispensable, may not suffice to support desired growth in competence. Adult education beyond college is practicable, stimulating, and rewarding. An example is offered in junior executive programs provided by numerous universities. These usually include guided reading. Similar materials adapted to the needs of accountants are also available. If they are not convenient, a small personal library, faithfully used, can be very helpful.

Perhaps "upper staff schools" could be organized in cities having sufficient professional accountant firms. The objective would be to correlate advanced study with increased field experience (Littleton, 1947a). Similar activities now found within the larger firms could provide outlines, objectives, and techniques. Out of this might come a high-level and truly professional school program for staff men of senior grade possessing a prior college degree and CPA certificate. Courses could be taken during a series of slack or summer sessions. A suggestion was made at the 1964 meeting of the AICPA that the profession in the future could benefit from special accreditation by the Institute for certain types of specialized professional services supported by relevant continued education and experience.

In the 1940s, college preparation for accounting careers was moving into postgraduate work. In this way, preparation could reach beneath and beyond accounting problem solving. Opportunity would then exist to deepen the student's grasp of the relation of accounting to good managerial decisions and to better investment judgment. The expanded availability of a Ph.D. degree with accounting as a major subject reflects the increase in teaching materials and the desirability of having teachers in the subject with that kind of advanced preparation.

The CPA examination is designed as a test of technical fitness. These exams, in association with college education, have grown with the growth of the profession. The results over the years indicate improvements in testing procedures as well as educational efforts. Moreover, successful candidates in the nation-wide examinations have given a good account of themselves in services rendered. Such examinations can also test several significant capabilities (Littleton, 1961a, p. 426). These include ability to work through a mass of related data, to follow appropriate procedures for reaching professional judgments, to think rationally, and to call up supporting reasons.

There was a time when a high proportion of failures may have seemed to constitute a handicap to growth of the profession. And the difficulty of the problems was often criticized. A nation-wide examination controlled by the Institute and wider opportunities for college education has changed the picture. Yet, a relatively small proportion of the candidates pass the problems section; a larger proportion passes the other sections. The present rules permitting re-examination of sections can do much to balance the results fairly. This approach is perhaps better than offering problems as a "final examination." Practical experience for admission to the tests is also being replaced by educational requirements (Littleton, 1945a). This can increase public confidence in the examination and in the profession. If experience is held to be important, perhaps certification could be held back until a moderate amount of field experience was obtained after the examination. But this might need to be broader, by accepting teaching or managerial accounting experience as satisfying the requirement.

Late in 1943, a study was made of 2,500 audit questions from the CPA examinations from 1896 through 1941 (Littleton, 1943b). In the latter half of the period under investigation, questions on procedure were reduced about twenty percent while audit theory and non-audit topics were increased. The literature of the time generally dealt with procedure, thus following earlier patterns. In a sample from an eastern state, questions on audit procedure accounted for forty percent, non-audit forty-one percent, and audit theory fifteen percent. In total, tests in auditing were allotted no more time than tests in commercial law. This would seem to imply a peculiar image of relative importance. Today, commercial law is a very broad area. It may be questionable whether it still deserves the prominence assigned. Questions about corporate finance or financial statement analysis would be closer to the work of professional accountants.

It is proper that several hurdles should precede admission to the profession (Littleton, 1943a). In the early days, practical experience was an important prerequisite. As educational programs improved, a college degree began to receive acceptance as one of the hurdles. As an adjunct to college work, aptitude tests were later made available. The results of these could provide aid in counseling at the college level and to recruiting. Tests were made available for use at the end of the first year of accounting study; others at the end of a sequence of accounting courses (Littleton, 1946b). Beyond these, the CPA examination, and the college examinations, testing became less formal. Demonstrated competence in fieldwork and tested evidence of ability to absorb new ideas in specific areas became the means of judging continued growth in professional capacities.

CPA examinations have been given since the 1890s. They still serve to screen admissions into a profession where technical preparation and ethical principle control. This is clearly in the public interest, especially that of the financial community.

The examination characteristics as well the types of public service are different here from those in Great Britain. There the audit was a statutory requirement from the middle 1800s. Where examinations were required in Great Britain, they included a considerable amount of questions about law and were entered into through accumulated practical experience in accounting. The characteristic British audit was centered on the social objective of examining the management's stewardship of the resources entrusted to the company (see Chapter 18, Littleton, 1933). The American audit developed out of the pressure of different conditions. Here a "balance sheet audit" served the needs better than an examination to discover errors and uncover possible fraud.

The American type of audit was closely related to contemporary merchandising practice (Littleton, 1961a, pp. 103–108). It was the custom of wholesalers to offer merchants an attractive discount for prompt cash payment of purchase invoices. This was advantageous to the seller and buyer. The usual implicit interest rate was greater than the interest cost of a loan from a local banker. Local bankers initially asked borrowing merchants for a balance sheet; later they asked for a balance sheet signed by an independent accountant. The latter's assignment therefore was more in the nature of a credit audit than a general audit aimed at detecting concealed fraud.

In the early 1960s prominent professional accountants were already going to classrooms and helping students prepare for CPA examinations (Littleton, 1949). Out of this experience came the first fully American audit test. There the first objective of an audit was indicated as that of passing judgment on the statement of financial condition and earnings of the enterprise. Detection of bookkeeping errors and evidence of possible fraud were secondary considerations (Littleton, 1961a, p. 101).

Further clues to the characteristics of the American audit will be evident in an examination of audit verbs (Littleton, 1961a, p. 478). Those words of action could point thought toward the auditor's ends and aims. Some 1,700 papers of auditing literature yielded a core of 475 verbs used 6,500 times. Three percent of the verbs were used forty percent of the time. The highest frequency of use was "examine" with 532 uses. The next four verbs accounted for nearly 900 uses. Averaging between 206 and 249 uses were the verbs "verify," "determine," "ascertain," and "test." These four verbs representing 1,400 uses can be arranged in two groups. The words in one list are related in various degrees to "find out." Examples: examine, determine, ascertain, investigate, inquire, inspect, and obtain. In the other list, the verbs are related to "critical examination:" test, verify, check, review, compare, consider, and prepare.

Table 1. Change of Verb Usage in Montgomery's Auditing.

1912	1940
Ascertain	Examine
Verify	Ascertain
Audit	Compare
Examine	Review
Test	Investigate
Certify	Test

Source: The 1912 and 1940 Edition of Montgomery, R. H. *Auditing Theory and Practice*. New York: Ronald Press Company.

Furthermore, some indication of the small amount of change in word preference can be noted in the choice and sequence of verbs used in two editions of Montgomery's *Auditing* (Littleton, 1961a, p. 478) (Table 1).

Considering the fourteen different verbs first indicated above produces this functional essence: ascertain by examination in order to report (Littleton, 1961a, p. 483). Related to the duty to prepare to report is the duty to disclose and to certify.

Other qualities for a professional accountant are as significant as his technical abilities. These are mental qualities such as alertness, thoroughness, perseverance, quick comprehension, and clarity of thought (Littleton, 1944b). There is also the quality of being a discerning critic. Deep understanding of the accounting functions and limitations enhances this quality. This quality is kept responsive by continuous study of the lessons from practical experience and lessons readable out of the literature on accounting theory.

Sometimes customs may be rationalized into a rule (scarcely a principle). An example is the inventory-pricing rule of "the lower of cost or market." Actions in response to this rule tend to wedge open a precedent-door to broader re-pricing of recorded transaction experience. Although this modern rule has a long historical background, it is not clear how the early custom was transmitted into the twentieth century or why its usage should be considered appropriate.

In 1408, this pricing practice was associated with heavy property taxes. The practice was also associated with the fact that spoilage was at times significant. In a French textbook from 1675, the author advocated reduction of inventory pricing for goods fallen out of style. The same author went further: he advised reduction of inventory pricing if similar goods were available "at the factory" for less than the prior cost. The problem with this advice is that the reaction to high property taxes would seem likely to encourage *any* pricing usage that would be accepted by the authorities. In this connection, evident deterioration could be persuasive. There is reason to believe, however, that the French practice was related to statutes of 1673, which were concerned with enterprise bankruptcy. In such a situation, questions could arise out of litigation regarding "overvalued" assets tending to conceal an approach to insolvency thereby constituting a species of fraud. As advance protection against such a charge, lower than cost presentation could be considered a reasonable and conservative policy. Is a comparable explanation persuasive today (Littleton, 1941)?

Here two differing conditions are identified with one accounting treatment: (1) revaluation due to *probable* present need to reduce selling price because of deteriorated goods; (2) by reason of a desire to bend the figures as to demonstrate a cautious approach to a *possible* charge of overstating the relation of assets to debts.

In regards to the second condition, it is understandable that traditional usage would be carried forward almost mechanically. And it is perhaps equally understandable that "conservatism" would become acceptable as justification. It is questionable; however, that "conservatism" should be elevated to the status of an accounting principle. Why should "conservatism" alone justify changing the record of a prior transaction experience to reflect a non-transaction current-value figure? It would seem quite persuasive to consider the accounting function as tied to recording the reality associated with management's prior actual transaction experience.

Conservatism can readily be accepted as a factor in business decisions. American use of the old inventory rule seems to reflect acceptance of price restatement as a matter of principle. This "conversion" would seem rather difficult to justify. The reprising actions indicated above really reflect only subjective policy judgments and expectations. These have not come out of new inventory items acquired at lower costs. Rationally, inventory figures should reflect only enterprise transaction experience in actual purchases in the markets by the specific enterprise. Expectations, so well illustrated by the reserve for uncollectible accounts, could also quite clearly be communicated by use of appropriate reserves. The conclusion is that the American background of inventory pricing affords an example of custom being adapted to local conditions. This has added prestige to a rule that originated under quite different circumstances.

In regards to the first condition, the method of financing retail purchases of merchandise, associated with the "balance sheet audit" (see above), produced an interest in the pricing of inventories. The wholesaler would prefer cash payment to extending credit. Therefore, He could offer an attractive discount for prompt payment. The retailer would be well-known to his local banker. And the interest on a short-term loan there would be less than the invoice discount. The banker would realize that local sales from inventory could presently provide cash to apply on the loan.

It was not unusual for the banker to ask for a balance sheet statement of the merchant's financial condition. The need for an audited statement grew out of some experiences with some self-prepared and untrustworthy statements. The lender would be particularly interested in the dependability of the current asset and liability figures as evidence of ability to discharge the debt in due time.

If the merchant's accounts receivable had not been screened for bad debts or if his inventory figures had been to some degree overstated, the banker's risk would be increased. He might even be interested in the possibility that falling replacement prices and competition could press the merchant to lower his prices, and thus reduce cash inflow available to make payment on the note at the bank. As such, the lender bank would be interested in a "conservative" statement of financial condition. The auditor, being aware of this natural attitude on the part of the lender, could serve the merchant, the banker, and through them the economy as well, by attesting to conservatively priced figures for inventory and receivables.

The result was that the "conservatism" of the nineteenth century local banker was influenced by a desire for a fair indication of his ability to repay the loan. The "conservatism" of the auditor reflected a belief, (1) that a lender needed something approaching a *valuation* of the borrower's current assets; (2) that the traditional custom of inventory pricing could provide a reasonable substitute for a complete evaluation of the borrower's financial status. This might have provided a practical approach. Yet, the "expediency" of the matter deserves attention, for accounting theory is the place for critical examination of the persuasiveness of reasons advanced in support of specific types of accounting actions. Theory need not seek to overthrow established practice, but it should open to view the strength and the weakness of the supporting reasons.

In this connection, it might be significant that accounting calculations do not *make* profits and cannot *make* asset values (Littleton, 1946a). Accounting can only attempt, within its natural limitations, to reveal the results of actual transactions created in the markets by management decision-actions. Its function is that of reporting on demonstrable experience. Accounting therefore cannot take over the responsibility of enterprise management (Littleton, 1961a, p. 312). Weighing economic currents against a background of past enterprise experience and present policies are a function of management, not the auditor. Accounting cannot rationally be made into a system of keeping experience data in close accord with changing values.

7

ABSTRACT OF ESSAYS IN THE 1950S

Textbooks play an important part in education. Accounting education is no exception. The profession of public accounting in the United States began under the direct influence of professional accountants from Great Britain, who established practices here, and, less directly, from British textbooks (Littleton, 1952a). Dicksee's *Auditing* (1900) is a case in point. The first edition appeared in 1891, sixty years later, the seventeenth edition was published. The influence of this is clear. It was the basis for an American edition in 1905, by Robert Montgomery. This work was entirely faithful to the original text, except for changed money figures and elimination of British case law and statutory rules. But already in the working was a basis for an American literature on auditing. A paper on American audit procedure was prepared by Walter Staub – later a partner with Montgomery – and delivered in 1904 before the first International Conference of Accountants meeting in St. Louis.

In the then new *Journal of Accountancy*, an article in 1905 by Montgomery also dealt with the work of the professional auditors. From these papers, it was evident that an American type of audit was getting under way. Montgomery's *Auditing Theory and Practice* (1912) was distinctly American in content and point of view (Littleton, 1952a). Characteristically American types of financial transactions made necessary a different audit approach. In particular, certification of financial statements was desired by bankers who made a practice of loaning local merchants the funds they needed to pay for merchandise invoices with cash in order to benefit from an offered discount for prompt payment. That discount usually would be in excess of the interest on a local loan. Hence, the merchant and the wholesaler would benefit.

Before long, courses looking toward the profession of public accounting were offered in American universities. In 1900, New York University – the state had passed the first CPA law a few years earlier – offered preparation for the CPA examination. In 1907, Northwestern University also offered evening courses in accounting (Littleton, 1961a, p. 531). Today, numerous university programs are available leading to a master's and a doctoral degree in accounting. As shown by the later achievements of graduates of such programs, college work in accounting and relevant collateral subjects have made definite contributions to the capability of accountants and to the prestige of the profession (Littleton, 1961a, p. 533). A factor in this result has been the fact that the practice of public accounting is not all a matter of figures. Account data constitute a medium for expressing relations among overt actions. Verbal language provides another medium for expressing relations among ideas. Proficiency in the use of one of these arts helps proficiency in the use of the other.

It is noteworthy too, that a college program in various ways gives students practice in learning to learn and practice in developing powers of analysis. It can also increase awareness of the existence of the significance of relationships within very diverse situations and between different situations (Littleton, 1961a, p. 543). These matters have not escaped the attention of the profession. In 1956, the AICPA published a report prepared by a large commission of practitioners and teachers (i.e., the Commission on Standards of Education and Experience for Certified Public Accountants). An increasing proportion of people entering the profession have now had college training (see Chapter 12, Littleton, 1933). Benefits from advanced study are made evident in some of the correlations between education and examination results for 1952 and 1955 (see p. 58 of the report) (Table 2).

From this data, several conclusions emerge: (1) These calculations speak of results in CPA examinations only, (2) The benefits of college work do

Table 2. Percentage of Candidates Passing, by Examinations and by Educational Background.

	Nov. 52	May 53	Nov. 53	May 54	Nov. 54	May 55
High school only	21.34	22.81	18.03	26.47	26.98	34.00
High school & junior college	20.59	15.36	9.30	17.07	9.43	26.64
High school & business college	24.52	20.45	26.01	18.75	20.65	21.05
High school & college (non-graduate)	27.83	30.72	35.40	19.46	24.42	27.32
College graduates	33.84	36.16	40.50	31.35	32.25	37.06
College graduates & postgraduate study	39.03	36.63	43.39	36.20	38.27	39.88

Source: Commission on Standards of Education and Experience for Certified Public Accountants (1956).

not come merely from increased contact with accounting courses, (3) Mental capabilities are also developed by contact with courses in economics, business, and various areas of the liberal arts.

Advances in accounting education and practice have had social significance as well. Statistics of nation-wide economic activities have been arranged as tabulations, variously named economic, social, and national income accounting. These reports do not present a "net-income" figure but a Gross National Product (GNP). Useful as this data may be, a question remains: do the data emerge from accounting methodology or from statistical procedures (Littleton, 1961a, p. 131)? The word "accounting" has long been identified with business enterprises under management. In that use, it has dealt with enterprise transaction experience generated by managerial decisions. In the national economy, and in the national government, there is no counterpart to management in a business enterprise – unless indeed one were to predicate a "managed economy" (Littleton, 1961a, p. 130).

Helpful as knowledge of nation-wide economic conditions can be, the significance of a compressed essence, such as GNP, can be overemphasized. To the extent this may be so, decisions tied to these compressed digits would have much the same weakness as a specific security investment decision tied to a reported average price change in the two hundred most active shares in the stock market.

The social significance of enterprise accounting as such lies deeper than a bilateral accumulation of inflows and outflows expressed in terms of money price. The central theme of this technology, the chief social service of enterprise accounting, is that of making generally visible and open to interpretative analysis the inescapable interrelation of enterprise capital under productive use and enterprise income earned by that use under management decisions (Littleton, 1961a, p. 165). The interpretative significance of account data is focused on management; the chief interest of all parties concerned is in the effectiveness of the management of the given enterprise under the conditions then prevalent.

National governments have wide responsibilities, and they should be politically accountable for the results of their actions. But the extent of those responsibilities are so varied and so vast, and the figures for gross national product are so greatly compacted from a great mass of statistical data, that comparison fails when, in contrast, we try to appraise the social service of enterprise accounting used in all levels of business. There, account data can speak separately for a multitude of different enterprises. Those data emerge out of the independent, judgmental decisions of a great many individuals. The mistakes of some will not affect the overall results.

Individual mistakes, when recognized, will stimulate better efforts on the part of the people most directly concerned. In the end, this recognition exerts a socially desirable influence.

It is not accidental that account data deserve to be recognized as having three important use-values (Littleton, 1950a, 1950b). The first is to provide internal information about prior transaction experience, which, under review and analysis, can provide a springboard toward management's next decisions. The second is to provide dependable account data in certified financial statements that are directly useful to decisions in the investment markets. The third is to provide factual data that can improve the analytical ability of its user.

Good managerial decisions, based on accounting data, are therefore good for society as a whole. Evidence of managerial effectiveness is also an important clue to good investment decisions. In fact, disciplined thinking in any context opens the way toward good judgments. But knowledge of accounting techniques and problem solving is not adequate preparation for a professional career. Emphasis should also be given to accounting theory and professional standards, for these provide the ideological base and the clues to the professional attitudes that underlay this technical methodology.

The conclusion that emerges is that the accounting function is what it is because business enterprise is what it is (see Chapter 2, Littleton, 1953b). The purpose of enterprise is that of serving society so the unit can "live within its income," and thus survive to continue to serve. Since accounting is firmly tied to the business enterprise, its purpose will be concerned with the dependable determinations of enterprise earned income. This is so because income is the interpretive signal of management's effectiveness and enterprise well-being.

The large significance enterprise income has for accounting, and the significance accounting data have for parties interested in management effectiveness, are related to the concepts of enterprise earning power and enterprise solvency. These concepts lie at the heart of accounting theory. Moreover, these two concepts tend to foster some rather sharply differing views. A solvency test of enterprise well-being would tend to identify with a contrast of revalued assets and enterprise liabilities. An earnings test would identify with current and accumulated earnings, as these have been computed from a realistic association of revenue "accomplishments" and applicable cost-expense "efforts" to serve effectively (Littleton, 1961a, p. 248).

A workable concept of enterprise income will, therefore, be a necessary part of enterprise accounting (Littleton, 1961a, p. 289). An enlightening clue to the income concept can be noted in a phrase from Adam Smith's

Wealth of Nations (1776), published nearly two centuries ago. Profit, he said, arise "if goods changed masters." Clearly, this phrase rests on a concept of earnings from enterprise actual transaction experience rather than on calculated asset revaluations, on estimated replacement costs, or on adjustments pressed into the accounts to reflect rising price levels.

Rising price levels alone may not conclusively indicate inflation. Expansion of the currency is another sign, and price levels will surely feel that effect. Yet, enterprise prior transaction experience will already have been expressed in the accounts in terms of the prices of specific, bargained, transactions. Accounting data will indeed speak of prices, but only of exchange prices specifically identified with the given enterprise. Under conditions indicating inflationary tendencies, specific recorded transaction prices, although firmly logged in the accounts, may nevertheless seem open to criticism as being "unrealistic" and the resulting financial statements may be thought "misleading." It would be difficult not to believe that such criticism could only rest on a conviction held, perhaps unconsciously, that accounting should function toward reporting not actual prior transaction price experience but *values* as of the moment of reporting.

To the extent that seeds of inflation lie in national fiscal and monetary policies, responsibility will rest with government, even though conditions beyond immediate governmental control may have been prime movers of the actions taken. Changes in enterprise accounting reports cannot help control a growing expansion of the circulating medium. Changes in accounting technology could no more mitigate an inflation spiral than prior exchange-priced transactions already resting in the accounts could have responsibility for starting inflationary movements. As such, appraisal write-up of company assets in the 1920s, and subsequent write-down in the 1930s, can hardly be considered as exercising an influence toward either inflation or deflation (Littleton, 1952b). Such modifications no doubt were prompted by desires to bring financial statements closer in accord with contemporary conditions.

Yet, this kind of reasoning and the resulting actions combine to indicate an urge to make financial statements report on values. To accept this as a compelling objective necessitates turning away from the only realistic source accounting has for its raw data – the price figures attached to enterprise transactions actually consummated in its particular markets. It would seem wise to conclude that bargained *cost* and estimated *value* are neither equivalent nor alternative terms. It would seem clear that cost, concepts, and value concepts must somehow continue to live together, but separately (Littleton, 1952b).

Since the concepts represented by these two terms cannot be rationally associated in tabulations of enterprise transaction experience, cost should be accepted and used to speak of the basic data of accounting. The historical fact of a specific transaction event and the estimated current value should be used only collaterally, as interpretatively useful but supplementary information.

There has been considerable evidence supporting this position. A survey of opinion (Bailey, 1948) revealed that a wide variety of informed people were opposed to changing corporation income reporting in order to reflect the effects of price level fluctuations. Bankers, for example, were nine to one of this opinion (Littleton, 1952b). In the middle 1960s, almost 20 years later, with price levels still rising, the trend of contemporary opinion had not been similarly examined. Supplementary relevant price level impacts have only been mildly supported in the literature and relatively little evidence is available indicating that corporation annual reports make effective use of supplementary and interpretatively schedules in general.

There is a distinct difference between advocating wider use of account data for its interpretative significance and becoming evangelists for a "new accountancy." Accounting technology has an obligation to guard the integrity of its data. It has a functional responsibility to record and report enterprise actual transaction experience, not on a matter of convention or tradition, but as an important, specific, service necessity (Littleton, 1952b). The profession of public accounting could make a notable contribution to enterprise management and to investment management by persisting to give support for inclusion of supplementary and interpretative schedules in company annual reports (Littleton, 1953a).

Some of the impetus for adjusting accounts for price level changes appears to stem from economic theory. It is understandable that economists, as social scientists, would be concerned with a concept of *real income*. It is natural that this concept, *if accepted in accounting*, would favor correction of accounting net income as an attempt to eliminate from the data the effect of change in the "value of money." It is not as clear, however, whether economists and financial statement analysts would prefer (1) supplementary disclosures in financial statements in this regard or (2) direct modification of the recorded account data from enterprise transaction experience. Perhaps economists and analysts would be merely interested in getting investors interested in developing their own skills for interpreting financial statements against a contemporary background of monetary inflation and changing prices (Littleton, 1961a, p. 364).

A rising interest in the precise formulation of accounting principles is rather directly related to the usefulness such "guidelines" might have for professional accountants and corporate financial reporting. That interest, therefore, is not a direct derivative of monetary inflation, although contemporary conditions are part of the background.

The significance of the impact on decisions of existing monetary inflation and rising prices has grown rapidly since the 1940s. Much of the impulse to deal with these matters in the accounting literature no doubt arises from criticisms of the "inadequacy" of financial statements as failing to alert users of the impact of inflation. The element criticized has not been the reality of historical cost accounting being able to reflect the transaction experience of a given enterprise. Rather, criticism derives from an assumption, belief, or desire that company financial statements should offer more help than they do to the formation of investment decisions. This attitude has probably been strongly influenced by awareness of continuing inflation and of the asserted instability of the dollar's purchasing power. Those influences seem to have fostered belief that accounting technology has persisted in reflecting hidden assumption of stability in the monetary unit in which the accounts are expressed (Littleton, 1961a, p. 405). Such a belief can easily cumulate into conviction that this assumption lies at the heart of a subtle deception, buried in financial statements and beyond users' detection.

Accounting actions do involve an assumption of this kind. It is not that the purchasing power of the dollar is stable. Nor is it that managerial actions are solely responsible for the calculated amount of enterprise net income. Accountants know that enterprise profits result from interactions between management decisions and economic change. The real assumption in the thinking of professional accountants is that an attempted separate calculation of those two causative forces is not warranted as an accounting objective (Littleton, 1961a, p. 406). Indeed, it seems clear that the functional limitations, building on enterprise accounting, preclude attempts to compute a part of annual company profit that should be attributed solely to changing economic conditions, as expressed by statistical averages of changing price levels or by an index of monetary inflation.

Another way to think about the problem described is to ask the following question: Does a successful decision by management to sell at the present high price have nothing to do with the resulting calculated profit? Does the greater profit from an even later sale, at a still higher price, derive not at all from management's prior decision not to sell earlier? If management does not sell then or later, is an "inflation gain" nevertheless a reportable item within the functional limits of enterprise accounting?

It would seem highly desirable that accounting technology should not be charged with responsibility for apportioning the positive and negative fruits of managerial decisions among a variety of *possible courses*.

The introduction of replacement prices or index adjustments into the structure of accounts or financial statements would constitute a revolutionary modification that might ultimately produce more confusion than clarification (Littleton, 1961a, p. 411). It is not necessary to revolutionize accounting in order to increase the usefulness of its data. It would be a complete answer to contemporary criticisms of financial statements, if accountants developed collateral interpretative techniques and persuaded business management to include in company reports the resulting supplementary schedules (Littleton, 1961a, p. 410). Of less importance is the question whether interpretive supplementary schedules as well as the usual financial statements should be covered by the professional accountant's certificate.

On the other hand, it would be very regrettable if the logic – that which ties enterprise account data tightly to data derived from overt transactions in the market – were lost, as these transactions were decided by management in and for that enterprise (Littleton, 1961a, p. 414). Transactions generated by other enterprises, at whatever price, (except in direct association with the given enterprise) cannot constitute actual transaction experience of a different enterprise. If accounting actions are to be faithful to functional objectives, the data used in the preparation of the financial statements must be restricted to the experience of that specific business enterprise.

"Logic" is a word that usually needs a qualifying objective such as "inductive" or "deductive." A conclusion, if reached by reasoning deductively from broad assumptions, may differ from one reached from following a path of induction related to enterprise specific experience. Logical and defensible decisions in business are likely to depend less on syllogistic and deductive reasoning and more likely to rely on judgmental and inductive reasoning, based on relevant and convincing facts related to clearly perceived objectives. Decisions, thus generated, are likely "to be sane, prudent, fair, and to commend themselves to the normal, average good mind (Webster, 1951, p. 737)." A decision of this type is not irrevocable. Indeed, its strength lies in two characteristics: (1) It is not tied to some specific hypothetical postulate; (2) Later evidence may lead to corrective actions in the markets modifying the results of previous actions.

The impact of inflation and changing price levels in the 1950s and 1960s greatly stimulated interest in accounting principles. But principles that grow out of postulated assumptions are unlikely to be any stronger than their root system. Inflation provided fertile soil for "assumptions." An example is a "money postulate." That kind of pronouncement would consider accounting technical actions to be seriously flawed from failure to reflect the economic fact that the value (purchasing power) of the monetary unit was demonstrable unstable. In light of this, accountants have been said to assume that the dollar was a "stable unit of measure." Actually, accounting actions have always been more soundly based than on a presumed assumption as to the stability of the dollar. They are based on the concept that the reviewable facts of an enterprise's prior experience are the most informative. As such, accountants know that the purchasing power of money is influenced by the purchasing power of goods and services, and vice versa. Accounting actions are necessarily tied to goods actually priced in overt transactions consummated by the given enterprise. A known fact that these prices had earlier been different, or later had proved to be different, could not change the historical event which caused the recorded data (Littleton, 1961a, p. 181).

We reach toward a principle in order that it may either serve as a guideline to an accounting action or help explain an accounting type of action. A hypothetical assumption could scarcely afford the best foundations for strong guidance. Since adequacy of disclosure has stimulated consideration of accounting principles, there should be, in a guideline to action, some clue toward a rational, justifiable, choice between alternatives. A choice, for example, between (1) reporting account data adjusted by price level statistical averages and (2) reporting data as to the significance of inflation in the form of supplementary and collateral information useful to interested parties. Accounting principles as such could usefully be limited to (a) providing guidelines tending to foster narrowing of available alternative treatment of key items and (b) making more widely understood the functions and the limits inherent in accounting itself and in the profession.

"Full disclosure" provides a compact title for a good example of a well-founded accounting principle. It clearly is in the public interest. For this reason, it deserves to be a guide to company reports and as such to be supported by the profession of public accounting. It would directly support the need for and use of interpretative information supplementing certified financial statements (Littleton, 1961a, p. 342). The distinction between certified statements and supplementary and interpretative information is not unlike the distinction between money wages and real wages. In both cases, two concepts illuminate each other; but only one of the pairs is a realistic fact specifically identified with the particular party involved. The other only supplies *additional* information.

The general characteristics of a principle should place accounting principles in the area of accounting theory. Theory can be considered as a body of doctrine, an area of explanation and justification, of a relevant and definable area of practical actions (Littleton, 1947b). Theory would usually include elements of descriptions, definitions, explanations, and, more importantly, reasons relative to action types. The supporting reasons might well be molded into convincing principles, since reasons would stand close to objectives. But rules and conventions can scarcely be considered principles (Littleton, 1961a, p. 402). A rule is essentially a directive for practical action. A convention (e.g., lower of cost or market) is essentially a rule that has achieved modern acceptance from the force of early precedent and present convenience.

My proposition is that principles should have more vitality, more depth, than rules. Many practical actions could benefit from becoming less and less under the influence of custom and weak justifications. Practical actions could benefit from closer and closer association with influential ends and objectives. Thus, to become useful means to become dedicated to the fulfillment of known ends in spite of known limits as to their full effectiveness (Littleton, 1947b). And, to accomplish this, new terminology might be helpful. The word "principles" implies a range of ideas so broad as to invite conflicts of interpretation. Perhaps a more useful substitute, in accounting, could be *compelling concepts* or *persuasive truths*. The two objectives used here will suggest two degrees of influence, each of which might at times provide a preference. The two nouns, conflict and truths, while having broad significance, would nevertheless serve more closely the needs of accounting theory than would the word "principles."

Extensive discussion of inflation and price level changes has had a strong influence on the accounting literature. In this is reflected a desire to explore the possible expansion of the accounting function. Such a desire should also inspire consideration of significant aspects of functional limitations. The literature also reflects the impact of ideas around management service – a term focused toward the arts of decision-making in and for a business enterprise. This development is taking place along with a growing theory that statistical and economic data have wide interpretative usefulness (e.g., using an index series for picturing trends and change over time). When these influences come in contact with accounting, it becomes increasingly necessary to recognize that the same account data serve both enterprise management and investors in enterprise securities and also to recognize that the decision needs of these differing parties will call for information that will be different in some respects.

Out of this situation come certain questions. For example, can accounting technology, with equal adequacy, satisfy the needs of both parties and still live within its natural limitations? Can the professional attest function associated with financial statements be properly extended beyond its specific contact with data from the actual transaction experience of the specific enterprise? Shall the attest function cover enterprise prior transaction experience, as modified by contemporary price level changes? Shall separate certification be given to reports of transaction experience and to interpretatively significant supplementary data? If so, what is the basis for attesting the latter and what is its relationship to the former (arithmetically and otherwise)?

Inherent in these emerging aspects of the accounting literature is a broadening concept of the accounting service function and of the professional accountant's responsibilities. And this, in turn, heightens the need closely to examine the natural, rational limits, of enterprise accounting against a setting of increased complexity of contemporary decision-making. An issue may well be in the making. That of a choice between (1) trying to bring accounting closer to being all things to all men and (2) recognizing and improving accounting technological capability for management and for the reporting of enterprise's actual transaction experience. The latter would also entail hastening the development of a separate but connected technology for interpreting, from reports of transaction experience, information meaningful to both management and investor's decisions. (Littleton, 1958). I prefer the latter, as it is difficult to see how actual experience data could be adequately modified for the second use and still make clear the effectiveness of management's use of enterprise resources – a matter of large significance for investors.

PART II

1

THE PURPOSE OF ACCOUNTING EDUCATION☆

ABSTRACT

Accounting education can be considered as experience, as practice in learning to learn, and as part of education for business. Accounting techniques are important as parts of a data-processing apparatus, providing deeply significant data regarding enterprise prior experience. The objective of accounting is to provide insight into the results of management decisions. The aim of accounting education is to help students learn to learn to become professional accountants. The teacher should often mix theory with practice (the why and the how), and often indicate the contact of the course with non-accounting courses.

We may well consider all formal education as a kind of experience. Textbooks reflect someone's experience, or the organized experience and judgment of many people. The thoughtful student will realize he is gathering experiences in a very convenient way.

Above all else, formal education provides practice in learning to learn. Because this is so, the effect of education continues long after its details are forgotten. Teachers need to recognize that their purpose is to help learners to learn to learn, that is, to learn to grow by their own directed efforts.

☆This chapter has previously been presented as a paper at the International Conference on Accounting Research and Education, held on October 1962 at the University of Illinois at Urbana–Champaign.

It can be a lifelong asset to have learned to perceive questions, to reason from this point to that point, and to seek a basis from which to choose among alternatives.

It is important to recognize that accounting education is education in business. It is a characteristic of account data to provide insight into a business enterprise. Accounting can do this, because its data open to review the factual experience of that enterprise. These account data expose to analysis the results of management's prior decision-actions. This has become a valuable source of knowledge. Accounting encourages self-knowledge on the part of management; it supplies decision-makers in the money market with dependable indications of the results of management's prior decisions. Both parties therefore are in position to make more firmly based future decisions. It is evident that accounting serves society well in this way.

Through the study of accounting our own thinking is put in contact with business and with management and through these, we become aware of important services rendered to society. Clearly, the purpose of accounting education should be broader than that of presenting procedures to remember.

The characteristic technical features of accounting are not important from the fact that they are technical. They are significant because of their reasons for being and because of the services rendered by accounting actions. Accounting techniques are pointed toward marshaling, into intelligible form, the factual data related to enterprise experience, which has originated in management's decisions. Accounting, therefore, is an early type of data-processing apparatus still widely used. The bilateral form of ledger accounts is part of the technique of marshaling data derived from exchange-priced transactions. That simple technical arrangement helps make enterprise experience data more understandable.

Too often, an emphasis on the mechanics of transaction analysis will obscure the logic within the bilateral account. Unilateral statistical-types of categories could not serve accounting needs very well. Accounts, with their left and right sides, facilitate a report of data movement in and out of the enterprise and between accounts. This arrangement also enables us to report, clearly, on the effects the authorized transactions were intended to have on the enterprise. Some effects are favorable, others are unfavorable, but all are significant of management's intention.

It is the nature of exchange-priced transactions to put in contrast two elements: the effect intended by each party for his enterprise, and the persuasive consideration that induced the other party to cooperate in the exchange. It is the function of accounting to report for each party both the intention and the consideration. It is clear that each transaction will therefore involve two accounts in the records of each party. It is equally clear that equality of trial balance totals is a consequence of deep fundamentals rather than being merely a test of arithmetic.

For accounting, duality is an important and basic idea. It offers a clue to the capacity accounting has for serving management, investors, and society. It is noteworthy that duality exists within every exchange-priced transaction whether accounts are kept or not. Accounting is truly marvelous in that it converts into data facts and relationships that are inherent in the economic nature of business transactions. Since transaction events can exist regardless of accounting, this technology renders a service no less significant than that of electronic digital computers. Both are examples of data-processing apparatuses; one is old, one new; one is slow, one works with great rapidity. They are cousins by the nature of their services: each deals with experience data in a different way, but both undertake to make complex masses of data relationships more understandable.

A part of the purpose of accounting education is to help us appreciate the significance of the tight interrelation between business enterprise and enterprise management. That relationship should be constantly put before the student. This relation is an important part of industrial accounting for enterprise management use. It also is an important part of financial reporting pointed toward the money market. This relationship of management and enterprise is the focal point of the audit and the professional accountant's certificate.

The thought bears repeating that, when we look at accounting through the microscope of education, it is clear that accounting education is a way of learning about business and management. When we teach accounting, we should take time to indicate, here and there, the deeper significance back of procedures and techniques. In this context, a good knowledge of accounting theory on the part of the teacher can be an advantage. It is good for students to realize there is more to accounting than method, more than problem solving, and more than preparation for professional examinations.

Knowledge of technique is indispensable, of course. But technical procedures are actions. Back of these will be justifying reasons, some close and specific, some general and distant. Actions by managements and accountants are what they are because of the objectives that bring the actions into use. It seems clear, therefore, that accounting actions are learned best if studied against a background of the objectives that give vitality to procedures. One of the functions of theory is to contribute to a background consisting of reasons why. As such, accounting should not be studied behind self-erected walls. Important ideas and compelling concepts from neighboring fields should be a part of the pattern of accounting education. The teacher has a responsibility here and so does the author of texts. Too often, the student is left to recognize, if he can, points of contact between accounting and the subject matter of other courses. Surely, he is not as well prepared to do this as his teacher.

On this point of showing contacts between ideas in neighboring fields, I once heard a teacher say, "Well, I cannot teach everything in an accounting course." This impossibility does not justify the other extreme: that is, teaching accounting as if it existed in a vacuum. It might help us as teachers to set up an objective of helping students to think and reason, and then consciously use accounting as a subject matter to provide for them that kind of exercise. Since each teacher will have acquired a wider perspective than his students will, he could now and then share this wider view without feeling he was trespassing on the field of some other teacher.

The function of education is not that of erecting boundary walls. The total of a student's education should not represent a loose group of isolated areas shut off from each other. Unless the student is helped to see interrelations among study areas, his schooling will not prepare him well for active life or for entering professional or administrative accounting as a career.

One prepares for work in the area of his interest. But he lives and works within a complex of related and unrelated activity. Much of one's working environment has meaning for his own special activities. It is a significant fact for an accountant that his working environment is a business enterprise, which is active in the economic life of the time and is controlled by daily managerial decisions.

The courses available in a college of business administration invite, or perhaps require, a student to diversify his studies. Included are courses in arts and sciences as well as economics, finance, management, law, and accounting – administrative and professional. Concentration in some area is expected, yet excessive concentration is prevented by requiring a mixed pattern of courses outside the area of special interest. This gives some guidance toward a well-rounded education. The requirements create a mixture of subject matter, but they leave to the individual the task of interrelating the elements in the mixture. The student may receive advice as to his choice of courses. But registration time cannot provide for advice on coordinating and interweaving the various materials into an education. If the student is to receive help in coordination, it will come best from the course teachers.

It would be a definite educational contribution if teachers in all subjects in a college of business administration would help make coordination real.

Surely, each teacher could find twenty opportunities in each course to indicate a few contacts the course subject has with ideas in non-accounting courses. This action would be quite informal, and would illuminate accounting technology by the reflected light from other fields of knowledge. It would show students how to seek other overlapping ideas for themselves.

Much the same could be said in favor of mixing some accounting theory throughout the elementary courses. Brief injections of theory need not be theoretical and argumentative. Theory can be viewed as explanations, objectives, and justifications. It is a matter of my personal opinion that appropriate spots of theory (reasons why) could so enliven the routine of elementary accounting as to encourage more students to elect further courses. We may be so eager to teach *how to do* that we can fail to realize that *why to do* is equally educational in its effect.

The educational purpose should not be content with teaching ideal actions. It is more important to use the given subject matter as a vehicle for teaching people how to learn, think, and bring all of one's knowledge and experience to bear on whatever problem is at hand. Accounting, taught in this way, could be educationally useful to students not majoring in it and even to non-business students.

There are probably many ways to learn "how to think." Psychologists may not agree that exercise in thinking increases the power to think. However, as I am more of an accountant than a psychologist, I feel privileged to believe that the power to think rationally increases from well-planned and disciplined exercise in rational thought, conscientiously and earnestly entered upon. Accounting study, I am convinced, offers such an area of exercise. It does this partly because of its technical nature and partly because it performs its service in a context of enterprise, management, and economic society.

These remarks may seem to have neglected direct consideration of education toward the profession of public accounting. Yet, all that has been said here is appropriate to that end. The true professional is not a technician, although he must be technically proficient. If his education has overstressed the merely technical, it has aimed the individual toward becoming a technician. The way to avoid such emphasis is to provide a "mixed education." The way to improve a mixed education is to find ways of helping the learner to learn how to detect coordinating threads that connect a variety of subject matter.

One partner in a firm of public accountants has stated the essence of the purpose of professional accounting education in one compact sentence: the formal educational process of accounting should aim at training a man to *learn to become* a practicing professional.[a] Here is, concisely indicated, the theme of these remarks; namely, that education is an exercise in learning to learn. Neither a college education nor passing the state accounting examination creates a professional man. Study and examination prepare the man and tests him, but he still must "learn to become a practicing professional." This process of learning how to learn continues for as long as the professional is gaining field experience.

Because the previous paragraphs have presented a considerable variety of ideas, it may perhaps be appropriate to look more closely at a few of these. One statement was this: Account data represent the factual transaction experience of a given business enterprise. This could give rise to a question: how firmly should theory resist actions that revise, up or down, the figures of prior actual experience?

Comment: professional accountants have little real power to prevent such revisions, for they cannot dictate to management. However, they can protest if the changes are ill advised, arbitrary, or misleading. They can also argue in favor of the accounting logic of holding account data close to the actual transaction experience. Through their professional organizations, accountants can urge development of ways and means of separating the functional actions of analytically marshaling enterprise transaction experience toward informative communications of that experience, and from the techniques of interpreting meaning out of those experience data.

Consider an example. The use of a reserve for uncollectible accounts is a logical action. It does not revise any account receivable itself. It puts the statement reader on notice, not of a revaluation of those accounts, but of a suspended judgment as to probable collectability. On the other hand, inventory is often repriced as to some items, if the price in repurchase markets has fallen. This lacks the logic of the reserve for bad debts. The use of cost-or-market is illogical for two clear reasons: The action injects an element of interpretation that will revise downward one item of invested cost – a real fact of actual experience. A loss from price shrinkage has not yet appeared as actual experience. That adjustment is based on little more than speculation; yet, it is treated as an accomplished fact. The second reason is that revised inventory pricing of goods not yet sold will create a revised cost of goods already sold. The latter figure will not then reflect transaction experience; it will only mix actual experience (cost of goods actually sold) with a mental forecast of loss, which may or may not take place.

Another statement is this: the student needs help in learning to see interrelations among study areas. Question: how early should one introduce such interrelations? Comment: it would seem psychologically better to avoid plunging too rapidly into the technical actions of analyzing transactions into debits and credits. This is the fallacy currently found in many texts. A chapter, or perhaps only an introduction, presents a more or less complex verbalization of the varied uses made of account data. The student has at that time no idea of what accounting is like; hence, its described service capacity is, for him, pure abstraction. Whatever has been said in the introduction about objectives is quickly submerged in the chapters by a maze of unfamiliar actions described, illustrated, and copied. A more useful approach would be one that pointed, thought quite early, toward accounting objectives.

Even so, the service of accounting – its objective of helping people toward insight into a business enterprise – could be made evident very simply. And it would indicate at once that accounting is related to other areas of action in business. My suggestion is to present, in simple two-column tabulation, a sample of enterprise property types, contrasted with debts and owner's investment. Press the class to suggest uses of such information: who would find it useful and why (i.e. relationships with investors, bankers, and other parties). Then ask for suggestions of transaction events by management that would effect changes in some items. Make it clear (1) why transaction changes would increase and/or decrease one or more items in the tabulation and (2) why knowledge of such changes would be useful to various parties at interest. Finally, present another simple two-column tabulation: a sample of enterprise expenses contrasted with enterprise revenues. Ask, as before, for suggestions of events, of effects, of reasons why people would find such information useful.

The point of this exercise is to highlight that the chief objective of accounting is not to mechanically present account data to interested parties. The real motivating objective, the reason accounting continues to grow, is that of making understandable the transaction experience of an enterprise. That objective reaches out beyond the enterprise and beyond the techniques of accounting procedure. If people do not need or wish for insight into a business enterprise, and insight into the results produced by management's decision-actions, there is no need for accounting: there never was a need for accounting. Surely, that is not too complex for beginners. Accounting serves people; it should be seen in a setting of its relation with people, especially people in management and people in the investment markets.

Another statement: the quality of the effect a transaction has on an enterprise exists in the event whether or not accounts are kept.

Question: how can we make this characteristic understandable to students? Comment: it would seem broadly educational if the inner characteristics of exchange-priced transactions were made clear quite early.

A student must see within every transaction an equivalence of an *intention*, which created the event, and a *consideration* offered that induced the other party to deal. He must learn (i.e., be taught) to find in a transaction some combination of favorable and/or unfavorable effects on his accounts. He must be taught, beyond forgetting, which side of each different type of account is designed to record the favorable and unfavorable effects. At first, he may be astonished to realize that, in accounts, the plus side is not always for the favorable effects.

To possess a reasoned approach to transaction analysis will be more educational in its effects than reliance on some rule such as the old one, "debit what comes in and credit whatever goes out." To repeat, it is more important to learn to think with the help of accounting than to copy and remember its illustrations. Even consolidated working papers are a way of thinking toward an idea-objective. As such, it would seem logical for teachers to work diligently to help students begin early to understand the theory (i.e., the various objectives) behind transactions, accounts, and financial statements. To be broadly educational, a subject matter should have an intellectual appeal. Recognizing its theory, logic, objectives, significance, and reason for being can show that accounting has a good deal of intellectual appeal.

One more statement: in teaching accounting procedure, we may fail to recognize that *why to do* is as educational in effect as *how to do*. Question: should we, therefore, teach accounting from a theoretical point of view? Comment: that would not be wise or useful. Accounting is a technology, a way for getting certain things done. Its ways of acting, its techniques of expression and communication, cannot be made clear by theory alone. Exercises in doing are indispensable to accounting education. At the same time, study of accounting should be organized to contribute to the student's intellectual development. Means should be sought to add to his mental capacities in ways that could be helpful even if his career developed outside of accounting as such.

This broad functioning of education justifies, in my opinion, giving more emphasis to matters of accounting theory than is usual today. Such emphasis on theory, on reasons why, on ends to be achieved, should be resolutely attached to the study of practices, procedures, and actions. The continuing and ultimate value of this is that accounting actions would be recognized as technical means toward knowable ends.

From this kind of study of accounting, the student would get two benefits. First, he would develop a better image of what accounting is and why it can serve society so well. Second, he would learn to recognize a broad truth that applies in all areas of active life, namely, that actions are means for achieving knowable ends, and that the means chosen are influenced by the nature of the end in view. He will grow in realization that all ends and objectives need to be examined closely, as to their desirability, and that all ways and means need to be examined closely, as to their suitability for the end in view. He will learn to look for possible alternative objectives and alternative means. This should be one effect of education in general, accounting education included.

You in this audience are teachers of men who must learn to think, not of machines that only perform. You are teachers of accounting from many countries. You are to be congratulated on your career choice. It can be a great personal satisfaction, to help young minds to recognize the wide service potential lodged in this magnificent technology. An additional source of satisfaction will be the conviction that your work is constructive and that your influence will continue long after your classroom door is closed.

NOTE

a. Paraphrased from Robert M. Trueblood, as cited in Beamer's (1962, p. 2) review of *The Future of Accounting Education – A Collection of Papers Resulting From a Conference on Accounting Education* (Bach et al., 1961).

2

SIGNIFICANCE OF EXPERIENCE

ABSTRACT

Experience is educational; education is a form of experience. Study of accounting ideology and methodology can help develop rational thinking and provide exercise in forming judgments. It is a good area in which to experience the techniques of learning to learn. Accounts themselves speak of experience, of the results from management decisions. Knowledge of such results offers a platform for rational decisions. Accounting is a special kind of information apparatus. Significant relations exist among its data; these provide definite aid for judgmental decisions. Thus, accounting provides experience in using accumulated experience.

It is often said: "experience is the best teacher." But wisdom thus reduced to brief "truths" loses much of its real usefulness. In the quoted example, a clear truth would be expressed by linking experience and education. Experience is educational in effect because education provides selected and organized experience. Although this revision may be an improvement, the significance inherent in these relations could also be examined with benefit. There would be reasons why practical experience can be a path toward improved education and, at the same time, reasons why forced education can be considered a valuable type of experience. Considerations such as these can have particular significance in connection with enterprise accounting and accounting as a profession.

A century ago, the path to public accounting as a career led through practical experience and private study. Beginners were apprenticed to practitioners. When the profession was taking form in the United States – the late years of the nineteenth century – state CPA laws required the candidate to pass a written examination and secure, before or after the examination, a specified amount of practical experience in a public accountant's office as a second prerequisite for certification.

After the turn of the century, American universities gradually developed programs of education for business. Accounting was one of the subjects. A few years after these developments, state statutes began accepting appropriate education in partial satisfaction of experience requirements. Eventually, a number of states required some college education for admission to the CPA Examination.

College study of accounting is educational in effect, because it promotes sharing the text author's experience in dealing systematically with data from enterprise transactions, and his experience in organizing knowledge in informative ways. Such texts put the student indirectly, yet beneficially, in contact with management and by investors. If these aspects are left obscure, study of procedures will lack the benefit available from clear awareness that accounting actions are not ends in themselves. As such, the study of accounting becomes more broadly educational when it is steadily presented against a context of its service functions and of the reasons its services are needed. The first accounting course is not too early to begin tying technical peculiarities to service potential. This approach is also broadly educational, because it helps one learn to think clearly toward rational decisions, through the understanding of relations among dependable and interrelated data.

Logic and philosophy can also serve an educational function of similar kind. Accounting theory is not so deeply grounded or similarly organized as these disciplines. Nevertheless, it has untried possibilities in that direction. For instance, although accounting is a less complex discipline than mathematics, its study develops some of the same analytical and interpretative powers. Its techniques are based on realistic data that, upon close analysis, offers insight into potential future rational decisions in business. I therefore argue that philosophy and mathematics do not hold a monopoly on teaching the arts of skillfully organizing and rationally interpreting data, derived from overt experience, aimed toward facilitating significant decisions.

No matter how far removed account data may be from informing action directly, the data speak realistically of actual transaction experience of a specific business firm. Because of its contact with this kind of reality, knowledge of accounting theory and technique is able to help the learner to learn to judge dependability of data and data sources. As such, the study of accounting makes a general contribution to college education by providing experience in translating judgments of data and of data significance into words, conclusions, and justifying reasons.

I argue that college courses in accounting provide students with contact with the ideas and methods of different accounting authors and teachers as well as contact with a variety of non-accounting subjects. This will expand the student's range of experience, perhaps vicarious but nevertheless strongly and cumulatively. It will open wider horizons; it will teach the recognition of interrelations among areas of knowledge; it will offer practice in appraising relative significance among ideas and alternates; and, most importantly, it will provide opportunities to learn the techniques of learning.

The results, of this latter contribution of accounting education to accumulated experience, continue long after graduation from college. The experience of having learned to learn in many different areas of subject matters will prove itself useful in staff training after employment, whether that is in public or administrative accounting. This is another reason for expanding upon the notion of the educational effects of experience. It is an expansion and a refocusing that will build new structures of experience and educational paths. Having learned to learn, the process can be continued from contact with clients; from personal study of materials out of the firm's own experience; from attending meetings; from taking part in discussions; and, by all means; from persistent reading of relevant current literature. As such, we can indeed believe that experience is educational and that education is a type of contact with expanding experience. The best result that one can achieve, from combining both elements, is this ability to continue to learn, intention to continue to learn, and persistence in that intention.

The word "experience" has another and very significant connotation pertaining to the reason for the existence of accounting. Account data themselves speak directly of experience, specifically enterprise transaction experience, and of the results of management's prior decisions and actions. The accumulated evidence of prior transaction experience is therefore informative material relevant to enterprise history and the evaluation of managerial effectiveness. The usefulness of carefully organized historical data such as this is unmistakable. The history of prior actions constitutes the springboard for next decisions, and it is clear that enterprise accounting technology is strongly committed to preparing this experience data for intensive review by management as well as outside investors.

The fact that account data speaks so directly of enterprise prior experience has profound significance for the profession, because of the relation of the public accountant's work to decisions in investment markets.

If enterprise experience were to some degree falsely reported, the enterprise function would be perverted. The profession is clearly committed to this doctrine. Nevertheless, the profession is also under some pressure to approve figures that to some degree or another fail to report actual prior experience faithfully.

It is technically easy to inject non-experience data into accounting records. Under the influence of long customary usage, some modifications of actual experience of the given enterprise have become accepted practice (e.g., the bad debts account). These have created a precedent for further modifications of the kind that possess some persuasive characteristic that is of interest to some people. I am hesitant about such developments. Accounting technology has proved over centuries of use to be well suited to reporting on enterprise actual experience. There must be fundamental reasons for this.

If accountancy were a science, perhaps its scientific aspects would provide some clues. But it is not a science; it is a technology for handling data having specific characteristics. We read about a growing "management science." This may still be considered a term somewhat in advance of the fact, but its significance is clear. Education toward managerial responsibilities ought to develop a continuing search for ways and means for achieving highly rational decisions in business. Accounting technology has an important part to play in that regard. And accounting can play its role well for a quite specific reason. Its data speak reliably of enterprise prior transaction experience. The techniques of accounting can make prior transaction history vivid and convincing. This kind of service can provide a platform from which men can move toward future decisions.

Accounting is, in fact, not even scientific and it does not have the computational or analytical power of mathematics. Properly speaking, accounting is a special kind of information system. Yet, it is firmly based upon convincing reality, and, like mathematics, it serves men well as an aid toward rational thought and well-based decisions.

The influential characteristics inherent in enterprise transaction experience exist there whether accounts are kept or not. These features are as permanent in transactions as are the relations among the elements in a triangle. Accounting began its evolutionary development out of unconscious, or, at least, unexpressed acceptance of the influential characteristics inherent in enterprise transaction experience.

It is not enough to point to the equality of the debit and credit as an indicator of the underlying capability accounting has for making prior transaction experience reviewable. That equality is merely an outward, almost mechanical, sign of deeper realities. It is not accounting that creates equivalence between the transaction proposals of bargaining parties as they come to an agreement. The basic elements exist in the differing points of view of the two parties. The same influential elements existed in the earliest barter transactions as well. Whether in barter or trade, two parties are involved. The emerging transaction has a different aspect for each party. In each record, the particular point of view of that party will determine the accounting record.

The consummation of an exchange-priced transaction expresses the natural satisfaction of independent parties. For each party the transaction produces a recognizable combination of favorable effect and of necessarily unfavorable effect on his affairs. It is clear, therefore, that the realism so strongly inherent within consummated transactions antecedes the records. It is equally clear that enterprise accounting is irrevocably tied to enterprise transaction experience, and thus is tied to reality. This fact has high significance: beyond a barter state, information as to enterprise prior experience is urgently needed to serve as a springboard toward next decisions.

The proposition that emerges is that data used for future decisions should rest on a more factual basis than personal desire, mere hope, or conservative opinion. The most realistic factual data is found where accounting modifications are not allowed to influence the dimensions of that data. The ideal such source is the pairing, within a transaction, of our intention (favorable to that enterprise) with a consideration, which would be unfavorable but nonetheless necessary for the completion of the associated decision.

Because of the duality inherent in transactions and the characteristics of enterprise accounting, two significant interpretative services emerge. First, the results of management's use of enterprise resources become reviewable. Second, the relation between kinds and amounts of debts vis-à-vis kinds and amounts of assets becomes available to provide a factual picture of an enterprise's financial position for study by investors. If we strip away or ignore these basic realities lying within the nature of exchange-priced transactions, the reportorial function of enterprise accounting would evaporate. A likely substitute would be an assortment of unilateral and statistical categories making available only loosely related data. Then the arrangement of communicative securities could be dictated by greatly diversified personal opinions and valuations. As it is, users of financial statements, based on realistic transaction experience, even now find it difficult to interpret from these communications the meanings relevant to their own decision problems. If organized reports of prior exchange-price transactions were unavailable, the interpretative difficulties of users would be compounded.

Exchange-priced transactions provide a dependable and logical source of data reflecting enterprise actual transaction experience. As a result of the combination of bilateral exchange-prices, accounting reports become convincingly analytical organizations of highly significant information. Without the availability of such basic data, tied to enterprise transaction experience, it seems quite likely that a profession of public accounting would not have emerged. Indeed, it is difficult to imagine how modern industrial society could have evolved very far toward its present form and extent. Enterprise transaction experience, logically organized toward interpretative review, has had a strong influence on society.

This leads to the conclusion that accounting is likely to remain a limited but informational technology tied to enterprise actual transaction experience. Much of science is related to controlled experimentation as an important source of experience. Accounting deals with directly available experience data, and it is not concerned with experiment. With that being said, the operation of business enterprises is experimental, although not in the laboratory sense. There is a continuing search for increasingly satisfactory ways of serving and, expecting from these results, to win satisfactory rewards.

It is in this context of enterprise transaction experience that accounting renders most useful services. Its foundations are constructed from the realities of transaction experience. Its contribution is that of marshaling enterprise prior experience toward effective communications. It is necessary to note, however, that the next decisions by management, inside the enterprise, or by investors, outside the enterprise, will not rest on account-reported prior experience alone. In both decision areas, much non-account data will also be needed.

This raises questions too extensive to be examined here. Is the concept of enterprise accounting to be so expanded as to include the interpretation of data meaning? Does marshaling and compactly communicating the results of enterprise prior transaction experience logically fulfill the enterprise accounting function? Can the professional accountant know the decision problems of managements and investors well enough to tell these parties what the accrual data mean for them?

3

ACCOUNTS RECORD EXPERIENCE

ABSTRACT

Within enterprise accounting, there is a significant degree of pragmatic logic. It is a suitable means toward the objective of making transaction-experience understandable. It is a combination of theory and practice and of ideology and methodology. The reason accounting function is so thoroughly acceptable is because of the pressing need in business to review the results of prior decisions in preparation for next decisions. Two compelling concepts for accounting are the following: (1) the reciprocal relation between its objectives and techniques that makes accounting an instrument for exploring the significance of enterprise transaction-experience and (2) accounting's duty to preserve the integrity of its recorded data for the benefit of later review by interested parties.

Five centuries of evolutionary growth through practical use of enterprise accounting would seem to guarantee the accumulation of some elements of functional logic capable of explaining its reason for being. Accounting technology, as it now exists, must have been motivated by strong objectives throughout its development. It must also have been under the influence of an unperceived philosophy much stronger than day-to-day usefulness. The key to this functional logic may lie in the fact that accounting has repeatedly demonstrated a capacity to serve acceptably as means toward particularly desirable ends. In this capability, for growth in its power to serve, may lay the key to its faintly evident philosophic content.

The strong practicability of enterprise accounting has tended to obscure the real basis of that practicality. The relation of accounting to the business enterprise and its management has been taken for granted. Yet, it is that relationship, which, by linking accounting with the ends and objectives of enterprise management, places accounting under the influence of philosophic pragmatism.[a] Accounting therefore affords an example of the natural chaining of ends and means toward new ends, each end achieved becoming a means toward further ends. As a result, accounting becomes a synthesis of theory and practice; that is, a union of ideas and actions. This kind of tight relationship is a prominent feature of the American type of philosophy called pragmatism but better described as "an instrumentalist theory of experience." Under this view, intelligent use of prior experience becomes an instrument for rationally planning further experience.[b]

In science, "experience" is basically equivalent to "experiment." Operation of a business enterprise is not a science. Nevertheless, enterprise management does "experiment" by devising ways for acceptably serving definite social needs with goods and services. Such operations can be considered as being experimental in two ways. First, an enterprise begins its life based on several hypotheses, however dimly these may have been conceived and formulated. Second, initial investments are risked in efforts to put these hypotheses to test. There are perhaps three such hypotheses: (1) certain needs of society are not yet fully met; (2) management can generate in this enterprise the ability to serve the specific need acceptably; and (3) this service can be provided by the enterprise at a cost below the amounts customers can and will pay.

For a business enterprise, testing these three hypotheses will be a continuous process so long as operations persist. Acceptance of the service by the public will be tested in various ways. Efforts to attract and maintain customer acceptance will be under constant scrutiny; change and accommodation on the part of management will be necessary. Competition, technical progress, fluctuating economic circumstances, variations in public preferences, and numerous other factors will leave no alternative to the constant accommodation and change in enterprise activity.

Science tests its hypotheses by controlled experiments. Out of these activities comes increased understanding of natural laws; that is, out of accumulated experience from science comes increased ability to live with and work with nature by conforming to its limitations.

Business management does not explore the forces of nature. Yet, management must explore, and perhaps experiment with, various possibilities. In this capacity, management systematically uses accounting technology to accumulate data reflecting enterprise transaction-experience. All such transactions are judgment-based and tentative. They can be considered exploratory actions, because the specific outcome is uncertain. Outcomes, such as acceptance by customers of enterprise efforts to serve, will tend to confirm or question management's prior transaction decisions. Analytical study of recorded prior experience can also give helpful direction to rational next decisions designed to continue and improve prior actions or to conceive and test alternatives for unsuccessful outcomes.

The chief service of accounting lies in this area. This technology helps to make knowledge of accumulated transaction-experience a duty of management. Such knowledge will help implement a broad area of the management function, such as maintaining effective control over attainment of the major enterprise objective (acceptable service) through effective control over transaction efforts, which are judged out of experience. Under these conditions, two areas of enterprise action will need intensive and interpretative analysis: (1) the conditions and prospects in relevant markets (both of purchase and sales); and (2) details of enterprise organization and factual data resulting from enterprise operations. Enterprise accounting can effectively serve only the second area of activity. The primary material for this use will necessarily be from enterprise transaction-experience, since these data will be directly relevant to changes in and actions for the enterprise as a unit. The same data will also be able to reflect the effects of decisions taken by enterprise management.

The data out of this experience will need to be assembled, organized, and communicated toward interpretative analysis of the messages inherent in that experience. It is appropriate, therefore, to stress the idea that the data lodged in enterprise accounts must speak of the actual experience of the given enterprise, and that the basic function of accounting technology should be to make enterprise experience understandable.

For a long time, beginning with Pacioli's bookkeeping text of 1494, accounting was considered a matter of technical methodology. Accounting was all practice and no theory. That attitude has slowly changed. Accounting has come to be recognized as a union of theory and practice and of ideology and methodology. But the integration of the two has not been perfected; interlocking areas have not been clearly indicated and convincingly justified. Hence, students are generally exposed to method and theory separately, and this continues to be the case despite the number of texts using "accounting principles" in the title.

It is not difficult to believe that certain developments could ultimately be as significant for accounting as they would be evolutionary. These would be, first, a strong integration of theory and practice throughout accounting study and, second, the clear separation between techniques for marshaling account data toward interpretation and techniques for extracting significant meaning from organized data of transaction-experience. Perhaps such developments might seem more revolutionary than evolutionary. It may be noted, however, that revolutionary modifications now being discussed would reach beyond valuation modifications (such as inventory pricing) and would further change recorded exchange-priced experience. In this manner, a shadow is being cast over the integrity of experience in an apparent effort to make some accounts more significant for interested parties.

The advisability of linking accounting theory and practice, as well as the separation of reviewable data out of experience, and the interpretation of the meaning of the reported experience, could be rested on philosophic grounds. Appropriate and convincing grounds can be noted in characteristically American philosophy (i.e., pragmatism). In this philosophical tradition, the reciprocal relation between ends and means becomes an avenue for exploring the significance of experience. In the context of enterprise accounting, that experience would be actual transaction-experience initiated by enterprise management in and for a given business enterprise. As such, many ideas will be found in pragmatism that, when set into a context of accounting theory, can add conviction to the thought that enterprise accounting does indeed have some philosophic content in connection with related ends and means and the integrity of experiences. Useful concepts of the function of business enterprise, its management, and its accounting, can come from these relations.

Some technical terms of philosophy, such as *empiricism* or *instrumentalism*, standing alone may seem unintelligible in this context and inapplicable to accounting. But they lose some of these qualities when the connotation is fully understood. The first of the two terms refers to practice, experimentation, and observation (i.e., experience) as a dependable basis for understanding (knowing). A particularly illuminating concept of empiricism is that presented in *The Spirit of American Philosophy* (Smith, 1963). Smith states that empiricism, as a philosophical doctrine, "is the theory of experience (p. 47–48)." William James, the author points out, considered experience as "a living stream in which destiny of the self is wrought out (p. 18)." Relations among elements of experience would be as much an experience as the items themselves, for experience includes "not only events and things, but connections between events and things (p. 18)." In referring to John Dewey, Smith states:

> His theory of empirical knowledge was aimed at overcoming the divorce between theory and practice. At the heart of instrumentalism was the idea that science is the best

> living example of cooperation between doing and knowing .... Instrumentalism is the philosophical expression of practical reason aimed at transforming the face of nature and at civilizing human nature in the process .... It means believing in human intelligence as the best instrument for mastering the instability of existence and enhancing the value of human life. [Its doctrine is that the] mind or intelligence exists as a problem-solving power and that this function is more important than pursuing the ideal of purely theoretical and comprehensive knowledge of all things ... it means that intelligence is a tool or weapon to be used for human purposes .... (1963, pp. 134–135)

Here is a strong philosophic support for giving emphasis to (1) marshaling data from enterprise transaction-experience as the basic function of enterprise accounting and (2) to a consequent duty of preserving the integrity of this recorded experience for the benefit of later review of interested parties. Accounting technology is indeed an instrument in aid of problem solving. Its "instrumentalism" is directed toward aiding human intelligence – particularly that of enterprise management – in using prior transaction-experience to control new experience (i.e., to master the instability of existence). It may well be appropriate to add that an important aspect of the function of enterprise management is to initiate enterprise experience that will further the service objectives of its enterprise. Because management has a function such as this, it also has a definite obligation to study the accumulating data of prior experience in connection with policy problems and next decisions.

The same author later makes this emphatic statement "... that experience – in its comprehensive and not in its narrow sense – is a genuine disclosure of reality that can be trusted (Smith, 1963, p. 206)." For businessmen, and hence as a matter of concern for accounting, two "realities" compete to influence decisions. One is the reality in the prior transaction-experience of the given enterprise; the other is a degree of observable reality in present conditions outside the enterprise. The second factor cannot safely be ignored. Yet, for our enterprise, that "reality" can only represent current experience-actions of other people. Our own experience, as read out of our accounts, is for us tested experience. Some of it is desirable to repeat; some could with probable benefit be changed. If we act without seeking guidance from our own recorded and interpreted experience, it surely would be at our peril.

The "reality" outside of the given enterprise cannot be fully trusted, so a judgment as to the potential future could not be adequately colored with the quality "reality" (even if the judgment later proves to be wise). This is a point that gives further significance to the review of enterprise prior experience firsthand, and then the cautious scanning of the economic skies for possible signs of weather ahead. These guides to decision, if intelligently associated with personal experience in integrating this approach to decisions, holds the potential for more effective actions when used together as opposed to separately.

It would be useful, here, to look at the nature of enterprise experience against this background. Enterprise transaction-experience will emerge from specific decision-actions on the part of management. But management's use of ideas – thinking, forming judgments, and reaching decisions – is itself a variety of experience in using experience data. Analysis and synthesis of prior experience toward further experience is a basic function of management. It is a function of enterprise accounting to help management exercise its functions.

The transaction elements of enterprise-experience supply the raw materials for the accounting record. That record will therefore speak of actual and deliberate enterprise experience. Consequently, prior experience is made available for review and opens up the possibility for analytical thinking, careful judging, and appropriate decision-making toward generating future experiences for the enterprise. Since prior experience, as well as experience-based judgment, provides a dependable basis for next decisions, the "integrity of experience" reflected in the accounts and financial statements become a matter of concern. Indeed, such a phrase would make an appropriate motto for enterprise accounting. Personal integrity, of course, is already a vital aspect of the certified public accountant. Integrity is also expected of men upon who rests the complex responsibilities of enterprise management.

In order best to serve its technical function, accounting theory and practice should combine in focusing upon careful accumulation, helpful organization, and faithful reporting of the data emerging from enterprise transaction-experience. At that point, the responsibility of accounting technology ends. After the professional accountant has performed his function of testing and attesting, the task both inside and outside the enterprise of interpreting significant meaning out of the data of enterprise experience becomes a separate responsibility.

To be sure, men trained in accounting might very well become excellent "interpretative analysts." But that service is not accounting per se. Moreover, something in addition to accounting training would be needed. Interpretation will call for use of special techniques and for a keen awareness of economic conditions, company policy, and several other factors. These can scarcely be considered aspects of marshaling account data or attesting financial statements. With that being said, experience data, the integrity of which is not open to doubt, would provide a realistic starting point for moving into the technicalities of interpreting the messages readable from the interrelations among the accumulated experience data.

Enterprise experience attains its realism from the fact that the exchange-priced transactions, those tangible expressions of enterprise experience, have emerged from two separate self-interested judgments. Both parties to a consummated transaction have separately judged the consideration to be exchanged as being fully justified by the benefit expected. For each party, this is a case of weighing the necessary means against the desired end. The transaction that finally results becomes a strongly realistic event, even though the two separate decisions may seem to have been more subjectively hopeful than objectively derived.

Transaction decisions, however, do not often arise from only an intention or mere desire. Fundamentally, they rest on the judger's prior experience in making decisions on a foundation of reviewable prior transaction-experience. Being derived from and rested on experience, future decisions gain a definite flavor of realism from these facts. And the emerging transaction data gain additional realism from the objectivity of being consummated in the markets by the actions of independent parties. Yet, the basic realism of this new transaction-experience is at this stage somewhat tentative. The ultimate results for each party will strengthen or weaken an unquestioned original realism. When the results of prior transactions prove satisfactory, the realism of those events and the validity of the proceeding decisions will have been confirmed.

On one hand, the accounting record and summaries from account categories will reflect a substantial degree of realistic and trustworthy experience. On the other hand, full realities cannot be read directly from raw data. Clues to these must be sought in study of the relations between enterprise efforts and achievements, as the latter are reflected in its receivables. Accounting technology itself cannot take this interpretative step. What accounting can and should do is to protect the integrity of enterprise-experience data and organize that data in ways likely to facilitate the subsequent application of interpretative techniques.

Within these boundaries, enterprise transaction-experience is dependably realistic. This quality makes that experience verifiable and reviewable as well as objective and convincing. The realism lodged in such experience data persists throughout the time interval during which experience-effort continues to contribute to accomplishment. The realism of that service capacity is not changed by contemporary conditions outside the enterprise, or modified by similar items currently priced differently. The reason for this is that these facts do not reflect experience of the given enterprise.

Effort, expressed by an exchange-priced transaction, continues to discharge its function, until exhausted by service rendered or until it has been judged to be lacking in service potential. In the first situation, no experience remains in the account concerned; in the second, the unused portion becomes investment abandoned. But it is to be noted that the amount abandoned still reflects part of a realistically determined investment. Under interpretative analysis, the "write-off" may be judged as recognition of a somewhat faulty original decision. Since human foresight is fallible, a "correction" is made that, theoretically but not practically, should be spread back over the recorded useful life of real contribution. Involved here is a judgmental or decision, which, as the phrase implies, should be as factually based as possible.

Consummated transactions initially express experienced reality, and this is tested as indicated above. But many efforts to generate later experience that is favorable to the enterprise do not come to fruition immediately. Hence, a judgment as to the ultimate effective reality of some transaction events cannot be convincingly made at once. The data will then stand in the accounts as a risked investment in future potential. That investment, once it has been made objective through bilateral exchange, continues to be quantitatively expressed by the bargained price involved. Transactions that exert continuing effect can be judged only over time as to the contributions made to results (often over several fiscal periods). Under these circumstances, the initial effect investment will need to be apportioned between present and future contribution. Thus, ultimate reality of such transaction-experience will be judged only piecemeal.

This may seem to open the door to valuation judgments, especially to those related to the unused portion of effort investment and to the future. A more logical approach would call for a judgment as to the present contribution and the deferment of the remainder of the original investment in transaction-experience. This is the more logical procedure, because it does not create an impression, as a valuation of the remainder would do, that the realism of the initial transaction investment was not defensible. Yet, the transaction is still as realistic as it had been when it was initially made. The only change has been in the judgment of its effective lifespan.

A new judgment in this respect will be subjective; it would be more expedient than logical. And expedient modification can scarcely have the force of a consummated transaction. But even a technology must live with the frailties of human judgment. Perhaps this is the reason accounting includes a procedure for meeting these situations in an informative way, while preserving intact toward the future the initial realism of the recorded transaction-experience. A second-thought judgment as to the contribution potential of the transaction could be disclosed by use of a reserve; thus, leaving reviewable the unused portion of the initial transaction in association with the indication of extent of the present opinion as to future contribution potential.

It is obvious that perfection is beyond the reach of accounting technology. But this will not diminish its usefulness. The data resulting from strict application of accounting techniques will be more dependable, through the force of functional logic, than would the data from presumably alternative techniques that trespass functional logic.

Financial statements and account computations created wholly by periodic revaluations of previously recorded experience data would merely substitute subjective opinion data for objective data determined by overt actions in the markets for this enterprise. Subjective second thoughts may seem attractive or even persuasive, but they only succeed in substituting opinion-modified data for confirmed and reviewable reality. This reality should be preserved to the greatest extent possible, but there are no such limitations to interpretations of the meaning and significance inherent in actual transaction-experience skillfully preserved in reviewable accounts.

A purely cash-basis accounting might seem to lead transaction-experience close to reality. But the realism of accrual accounting, even though judgmental estimates are used in periodic apportionments, would be far more informative. Indeed, one of the major evolutionary developments in this technology was the growth of periodic apportionment (i.e., accruals and deferments). This ultimately produced modern cost accounting and other aspects of administrative accounting, which has been a tremendous aid in management decision problems. As such, I believe that careful use of techniques, for rationally apportioning the contribution potential of enterprise efforts, to accomplish its objective will produce the most highly desirable results. These results are superior to any alternative in the area of providing dependable, reviewable, and significant experience data, ready to be interpretatively analyzed as a basis for new experience. This is so because the best platform from which to exercise the managerial function of forward decision-making is the actual, overt, prior transaction-experience of that management's own enterprise.

NOTES

a. "The validity of accounting depends simply and solely on its contribution to the economic world we live in; discussion of accounting theory will be more realistic if the pragmatic nature of accounting is kept firmly in mind (Littleton, 1963b, p. 38)."

b. This thought is forcefully developed in *The Spirit of American Philosophy* (1963), by Professor John E. Smith of Yale University. Many of the ideas in this paper related to the relation between accounting theory and enterprise transaction-experience have been precipitated by this book, especially through the author's analysis of the philosophies of William James, John Dewey, and Alfred North Whitehead.

4

ANALYTICAL NECESSITY

ABSTRACT

It is necessary that accounting actions should rest on accounting concepts, for these can explain so much. These concepts can speak about what our action is, about what it is not, about things to which action is related, and about the necessity for the relationship. Concepts can be compelling and many accounting actions are analytically necessary. Equivalence of experience for both parties is a necessary feature of every exchange-priced transaction consummated in the market. Equivalence of favorable and unfavorable effects is a necessary part of each party's record of a transaction. Neglect to recognize the analytical necessity could destroy the service function of accounting.

When the functions of accounting techniques are under scrutiny, as in the 1960s, it would seem appropriate also to examine the objectives and the limitations related to those techniques. Systematic inquiry into underlying theory could clarify many aspects of the realities in enterprise accounting. Recognition of this fact is indicated by the research programs of the American Institute of CPAs, by a search for a common body of knowledge, and by the ideological literature growing out of graduate level accounting education.[1]

The methods and techniques of enterprise accounting exist because they foster desirable needs, objectives, and purposes. Without this kind of foundation, accounting technology would not have been devised or developed as is known to have been the case. A conclusion would seem to follow: in order to appreciate, criticize, or change accounting actions, specific action types need first to be known and recognized as being interrelated structural elements of this limited service technology. Then these "knowns" of accounting actions should be fully analyzed in order to detect the way they have been sponsored and validated by a structure of compelling concepts.

Interrelations among actions and concepts are elements for accounting theory. Yet, interrelations have not been stressed in the literature. Theory as such should be wide and deep. It should undertake to make clear why known technical actions rest on persuasive rational reasons, and on recognition of significant purposeful objectives and of discernible limitations beneath the usual techniques. Recognition of some persuasive truths about accounting actions would write research downward, as it were, toward subordinate truths and clear limitations. Recognized concepts of accounting needs and objectives could supply foundational structures capable of supporting a structure of interrelated technical actions.

The term "concept" speaks not of degrees of usefulness but only of influence. Even when it is expanded with the phrase "compelling or basic concepts," the adjectives speak not of force but of power to persuade. The phrase can be considered suitable for ideas capable of exercising influence by their appeal to common sense and reason. It carries more conviction than a word such as "customs." And, to influence actions, one must first influence men's judgments. As such, one would do well to consider concepts as "a coordinated set of ideas about a given thing. A concept contains ideas of what a thing is, what it is not, and what its relationship is to other things (Mautz, 1965, p. 47)." It would seem reasonable to believe there are realistic concepts out there of this kind that could illustrate accounting principles.

Basic concepts can influence accounting from their power of providing appropriate support, control, and direction for appropriate accounting actions. *Appropriate* actions will be those capable of achieving *desirable* objectives. Those concepts may relate to choice of objectives or to choice of means to these ends. Higher-level goals will inform the desirability of lower level goals. The goals at each level should be supported by reasons more convincing than those advanced in support of alternative goals. A similar testing should influence choice of ways and means in use. There, too, persuasive reasons should be noted for using one alternative and convincing reasons against the others.

The idea of basic concepts also gains usefulness from the fact that it can apply to both positive factors – things to do and reasons for doing them – and negative factors – things not do and reasons for not doing them. An example of a compelling and negative concept is this: accounting actions will be strongly influenced by necessary functional limitations (i.e., its limitation to the recording of consummated exchange-priced transactions).

The influence of underlying concepts is not new. Some concepts, even though not clearly recognized, must have provided background for early bookkeeping actions and for the subsequent slow evolutionary development into accounting. The conception of enterprise as an entity, for instance, would have been evident even in the earliest partnerships as well as in individual life in business. Proprietors and partners were at the same time investors and managers. The trio of the enterprise entity, enterprise management, enterprise accounting (bookkeeping) is a very old and basic relationship. We see this in the accounting for early voyages, with the creation of separate reports of each voyage and its accumulated transaction experience. The trading actions would have been performed for known reasons, and, although concepts were not preserved in the records, the resulting actions are known to have produced transaction data recorded in some form.

Evidence such as this informs us that the concept of a business enterprise as an operating entity would have long anticipated the legal concept of a corporate entity. The concept of management, from the simplest to the most complex, is always about the human element necessary to make decisions judged suitable for known purposes. Deliberate intentions, whether by barter or otherwise, resulted in consummated transactions.

Enterprise accounting actions still take place under the influence of concepts that are compelling now because they were basic centuries ago. To be sure, accounting has grown, and new concepts have been perceived and new actions have been activated. These grew from necessity, rested back upon established foundations. The two structures of objectives and methods are still interlocked. It must always be so. And for this reason it is highly important that these relations be understood.

Consider another example: scientists studying sub-nuclear particles in an atom have formulated conceptual structures that could explain observed structural actions of the particles. An inductive approach such as this, although without benefit of comparable scientific techniques, would suggest that research in accounting theory could begin with known accounting actions. After probing deeply into these, in search for evidence of controlling objectives, the inner nature of enterprise accounting might be more clearly described.

Using inductive methods to penetrate deeply into accounting might help reveal reasons why this particular technology has power to increase men's ability to make well-conceived decisions. Perhaps such an objective is the "nucleus" of the "atom" named enterprise accounting. Perhaps the analogy could be carried further. There are other compelling concepts regarding action types, necessities, and limitations. Some of these are concepts of minor objectives, whereas others are of more distant and major objectives. All have contributions to make. Perhaps these might be considered as being held to their respective tastes and functions by strong forces of convincing relevance and demonstrated capacity to serve the accounting function effectively.

If accounting concepts are compelling or basic, they should be so considered for specific reasons. All of them indicate useful limits, significant boundaries, or necessary functions. These qualities and relations unite in fostering a similar objective, namely, that of providing data from the enterprise's prior transaction experience as a basis for decision by management and investor. In this regard, a major concept is that of analytical necessity. And it can properly be considered as compelling. Neglect to apply this concept appropriately would bankrupt the service function of accounting. A clear concept of function is essential, because business decisions toward the future will be poorly based if data from the results of prior actions are not analytically assembled. Hence, the word "necessity" is indispensable.

The equivalence for both parties involved in a consummated transaction in the market has long been a basic characteristic of accounting. This has been and still is compelling and analytically necessary because of factual realities: the separation of two parties, the two parties' different views and self-interests, and the mutual consent to the exchange. Lack of any one of these elements would stand in the way of agreement, hence would prevent a transaction from completion. This equivalence of favorable and unfavorable effects of a specific transaction is clearly reflected in the account record made by each party. This is a compelling concept for two reasons: (1) its absence would block the exchange and (2) the decisions whether to enter into a specific exchange must include an appraisal by each party of the positive and negative effects on their respective affairs. These realities will be reflected in the assignments of data to specific accounts. These accountants will have been given appropriate bilateral form and are able to faithfully to reflect the realities of consummated exchange-priced transactions.

There are persuasive reasons why this kind of data-classification techniques constitutes rational and useful actions: summaries of favorable and unfavorable effects will dependably reflect the same basic elements faced by management in approaching a specific transaction decision. If the relation of favorable and unfavorable effects has not been judged appropriate for one of the enterprises, no overt transaction would have emerged. And, as a result of these aspects of equivalence, summary reports of transaction experience can present to any reviewer data that is quite capable of operating to view the results of management decisions and the effects on the enterprise of those actions. Any interested party is able to interpret these clues in regards to the effectiveness of management.

It may be well to consider business decisions in and for enterprises as a continuous progression from known points toward known objectives. In this respect, accounting is exceptionally well equipped to serve this socially significant process by making enterprise transaction experience knowable to management, investor, and other parties at interest.

Let us return to the earlier analogy. It has become clear that natural forces have formed physical atoms, but it has been the ingenuity of men that makes the inner nature of atoms understandable. Enterprise accounting has been completely fabricated by men under pressure of their needs and intentions. Generations of men have slowly improved its techniques and capacities. No doubt, further improvement within the basic structures is possible. But perhaps the most pressing present need is for devising useful *supplementary* and interpretative techniques. The reason I am stressing *supplementary* techniques is that the functional objective of enterprise accounting could be damaged if too great modifications were made to the actual accounts, which are based on prior consummated exchange-prices.

Furthermore, the structural patterns relative to enterprise accounting offer no evidence in support of an idea that accounting is a complete information apparatus, adequate in itself to provide all information people will need in aid of business decisions. On the contrary, all of the compelling concepts point toward accounting as a limited technology. Its data will be convincing according to the degree that they are tightly tied to enterprise transaction experience. Future decisions by management, and usually those by investors as well, must rest on more than account data alone. In a manner of speaking, account data provide a strong springboard but an ample pool of relevant non-account information must also exist.

Although the accounting springboard is as complex as accountants know it to be, the pool of economic conditions is even more complex. For the latter represents both contemporary and unpredictable future conditions. These will exist within an atmosphere of changeable human judgments and actions. As such, decisions makers, contemplating a decision-plunge, need knowledge of the depth and the temperature of this pool. They will need dependable assurance that this springboard is firmly anchored by bolts of functional limitations set in a concrete of compelling concepts. One might step into the pool of contemporary conditions without using the accounting springboard, and sometimes one might just come up with a good decision. That would be a speculation, at best. Likewise, it would also involve risk if decisions were based on account data alone. One might safely enter the pool from the side. But who would use the springboard without water in the pool?

A well-organized technology, accounting, analytically organizes the data results of prior decisions. The facts from transaction experience are informative only as far as men learn to penetrate to their inward meaning and learn to judge the significance of those meanings. There is at present no well-organized technology for extracting the full meaning buried in account data. And there is no convincing procedure for the study of enterprise transaction experience against a context of non-account data identified with present or prospective economic conditions. Economic data, such as that presented in statistical form through index series of inflation, are useful aids to interpreting significance out of observed changes. Nonetheless, the use of such series directly to modify data in the accounts of financial statements would constitute a distortion of realistically determined account data. It would be trespass of the rational and functional boundaries of reported and actual experience of the specific enterprise.

The point is that data from enterprise overt experience and data reflecting changes in the overall economy are quite unalike. In one case, the data are specific to a particular enterprise. In the other case, the data are only representing large and overarching trends. Both kinds of data may be expressed in digits. Statistics of the GNP, for example, may be said to use currency units as accounting does. But assertions cannot override the gap between the overt experience of one enterprise and the statistical averages of transactions of many enterprises. The experience of one enterprise should no doubt be studied along with the data of the mass, but two different techniques of data selection and organization would be needed.

NOTE

1. Littleton appears to be referencing the AICPA commissioned report *Horizons for a Profession: The Common Body of Knowledge for Certified Public Accountants*, which was published in 1967 and led to a series of changes in the education of CPAs in the United States (for more about this report, see Persson, Radcliffe, & Stein, 2016).

PART III

1

THE HEART OF THE MATTER☆

ABSTRACT

The characteristics of accounting objectives are formed by the needs that exert pressure on its function to deal with enterprise prior experience. As such, the actions of accountants should be influenced less by postulated principles and more by understanding the compelling concepts that strongly influence accounting action.

In the introduction to Research Study No. 1, published by the American Institute of Certified Accountants, two quoted statements stand in contrast.[1] In a terminology bulletin (1953) accounting postulates were considered as being "derived from experience and reason"; after having been experience-tested and judged acceptable, these became principles of accounting. In a report in 1958 on the proposed new AICPA research program, postulates were considered as "basic assumptions on which principles rest." Research Study No. 1, by following the second concept, indicates a preference for a deductive over an inductive approach. It therefore tends to turn away from experience. If formation of guiding principles is the only objective, the deductive approach may be indicated. However, the inductive approach would seem desirable if improved professional judgment were to be the ultimate objective.

☆This chapter has been reproduced courtesy of *INSIGHT Magazine*, The Magazine of the Illinois CPA Society and the successor of *The Illinois Certified Accountant* (for the latest issue, visit www.icpas.org/insight.htm). The original citation for this article is Littleton (1963c).

Good judgment would grow best out of experience in making judgments. It may be noted that a broader base could exist for exercising good professional judgment than one consisting of postulate-based principles. Good judgment itself, and the ability to justify a given decision, could be facilitated greatly by a thorough understanding of the varied conceptual objectives back of accounting actions, and recognition of the compelling limitations that circumscribe those actions.

Professional men cannot escape the need for capacity to exercise good judgment. Accepting guidance from custom or rules, and no doubt from principles as well, will not avoid the exercise of judgment in each situation faced. Yet, the roots of these judgments will lie deeper than postulates can reach. They will reach down into a comprehensive understanding (1) into the capabilities and limitations of accounting ideology and techniques, (2) into clear comprehension of the influence on actions of objectives, both close up and distant, and (3) into awareness of the relation of enterprise management to the efforts and accomplishments made factually evident through account data.

The superstructure of actions is readily perceived, but the necessary foundation piers of a complex and rational ideology are not so easily detected. Yet, if one is to understand the capacity of the structure, the service functions of the foundations must be understood. Those supporting piers – the basic objectives of accounting – have been strongly influenced by the evolving service function of the superstructure. In other words, the character of the objectives supporting accounting actions have been fashioned, not by definition or assumption but from the needs of the times, early and modern, which pressed for creation and development of accounting as a means toward recognized goals.

Because technical actions and influential objectives are inseparable, understanding of both separately and in their interrelations becomes essential to the exercise of good judgment in the presence of situations involving aspects of accounting.

Basic concepts and compelling limitations give accounting actions their capacity to serve; the concepts invite inclusions, the limitations direct exclusions. Both of these areas of effects may be illustrated by regrouping the several postulates summarized on pages 21–22 and 36–37 of the research study. It will be evident that some interrelated postulates reflect certain basic concepts, and that these reveal certain inherent limitations capable of giving accounting significant aspects of internal integrity.

These propositions point toward business entities operating as separate organizational units engaged in economic activities. Accounting actions take place in these units, and postulates A3 and B3 together imply a social service function for accounting.

It is significant, in this connection, that enterprise entities could exist, and have existed in simple forms, without aid from systematic accounting. But it is difficult to conceive of an enterprise entity functioning without a human decision center, such as a proprietor, manager or management. Hence, management of some sort must be considered an indispensable aspect of an enterprise entity.

Accounting actions take place within this complex of organization entity and human management. It is difficult to conceive of accounting as having evolved outside of such a framework. It will be logical, therefore, to recognize enterprise accounting as foremost a technical means toward the broad end of aiding enterprise management to operate an enterprise capable of generating services acceptable to society.

Enterprise accounting is explained and supported by the functional logic inherent in the relation of a suitable means serving a desirable end. If this logic is to be defeated, either the overall end must be shown to be undesirable in itself, or the overall character of accounting must be convincingly shown to be unsuited to render its service in aid of management decisions.

It is evident that the ideas imbedded in postulates A3 and B3 can have deeper explanatory significance than that of headlining certain assumptions. Perhaps postulates, as such, are not indispensable. There may be other ways of breathing life into fundamental concepts. It may well be that the conceptual structure beneath enterprise accounting could do as much as postulates to make this complex technology understandable. Whatever can be known with conviction about accounting will have little need for being assumed.

A handful of basic concepts could be woven into a more convincing pattern of related ideas than that from a hatful of assumptions. Surely, interpretative judgments, rational convictions, and accumulated experience should be involved in the application of interrelated ideas to specific situations.

The central idea in postulate A1 is also related to the concept of enterprise entity. It deals with making rational economic decisions and effective choices among alternatives. To this objective, the helpfulness of quantitative data is joined. Here, "quantitative data," by implication the helpfulness of quantitative data, is joined. Here, "quantitative data," by implication rather than direct statement, refers to figure symbols produced by the typical accounting action of translating enterprise transaction events into account data.

Since this elementary action is clearly knowable, it need not be assumed. Indeed transaction analysis is itself a sub-means toward the desirable objectives of accounting. A concept of need served by an action is quite influential in bringing that type of action into existence. A single sentence cannot even headline all of the antecedent objectives and motives that underwrite the conversion of events into account data.

A few of these antecedents include the concept of a business entity and a concept of its function in society. A concept of management function is also an antecedent – the function of generating transaction events and getting these expressed by agreement in terms of exchange price. Without transactions as the substance of accounting, reflecting as it does management's prior decision-actions, there would be no accounting, as we know it. These relationships would seem to embrace fundamental concepts "so necessary as to be unavoidable." If we are to see deeply into the nature of accounting as a prelude to justifying the application of accounting to specific situations, such relationship will have important significance.

The quoted phrase has been used to indicate one aspect of a postulate. Associated with it has been another phrase–"so obvious as to be undeniable." No doubt, even the obvious may need compact verbalization. And the seemingly obvious may be the very element most needing rational justification, especially in its relation with other ideas and with a variety of actions. Very few ideas are undeniable under all circumstances, or can escape questioning in some situations.

An idea or concept may be strongly necessary in a given situation. Yet, it may be effective in varying degrees of necessity in other situations. To be significant is not identical with being necessary; "impossible to do without" may prove, under stress, to be something less than necessary. In this day of synthetic products and nuclear adventuring, many preconceived concepts have been brought under question, if not refutation. There is a suggestion herein for accounting research: resist the temptation to act quickly on the apparently obvious; concede the apparently necessary only after alternatives, existing, or prospective, have been thoroughly examined.

These propositions state that economic activities are carried on during time periods. It is scarcely necessary to assume the continuity of time, or that various units of continuous time may suit different purposes. The more significant fact is that economic activities are accomplished through identifiable, separate events occurring in practically unending sequence, hour by hour, day by day, and year by year. Only when economic events become identified with a given business enterprise are they voluntarily and purposefully assigned to particular categories of time.

A business enterprise is such a category. As a category, the enterprise should include the relevant and exclude the irrelevant in recording the results of management decision-actions. A fiscal period is another conceptual category; it comes into use as a means only under the influence of distant intentions and objectives. It can, if desired, be avoided; hence, it is necessary only under prescribed circumstances. The key to the use of time periods is intention, objective judgment of need.

This group of postulates also indicates that operating results are allocated among successive periods of time, and that these assignments are tentative. Such allocation stems from tacit acceptance of a concept of improved data significance from being assigned among categories. A time period works as a subdivision of the experience of the more basic category, the enterprise entity.

The critical element in both of these postulates is not the fact of categorizing. The important aspect is the reason for the category type, for its relation with other categories, and for the relation of all categories to knowable and desirable objectives. Categories of whatever type are means toward ends. And they take special forms because these initially hold promise for fostering improved understanding and, under use, of continuing to develop capacity to serve that end effectively.

These propositions, like A1 previously discussed, are concerned with the usefulness of quantitative data as a decision base. In essence, these three postulates point toward two concepts: (1) the idea that account data derive from exchange-priced transactions; (2) the idea that those transactions are priced in money used as a common denominator.

It is significant that these concepts are intimately related with those in other groups of postulates. Accounts, being categories, will be used to include the relevant and exclude the irrelevant. Without antecedent enterprise entities, and antecedent exchange-priced transactions, account categories would lose their reason for being. There would be no accounting, as we know it. This relationship is inseparable from accounting since it lies at the base of the account function.

In order to grasp fully the significance of one of a group in interrelated concepts, it is necessary to understand all others in that pattern of relationships. And in each case, a grasp of the intricate reasons for being, the ends and objectives involved, will be more enlightening than familiarity with typical actions, procedures, and uses.

In order to understand accounts, it is necessary to see them in relation to each other, in relation to the particular enterprise and its management, and in relation to the intentions inherent in the unending flow of individual transactions. Like other categories related to accounting, all account categories are technical means toward desirable ends. Hence, accounts perform their service under the influence of functional logic.

Each exchange-priced transaction is a tiny unit (category) of enterprise experience. Each transaction is a result of decisions by management, and it is entered upon with intent to affect that enterprise in certain ways. These intentions lie at the heart of transactions. When implemented in fact, the intended effects become elements in enterprise experience and tangible evidence of management's actions. By representing elements of actual experience, account data provide a platform from which to begin to plan toward next decisions.

It is not difficult to believe that a platform of prior experience is necessary to decisions. To be sure, judgment and a sense of timing and informed opinions as to the probable shape of things to come will also be elements in a final decision to act in and for the enterprise in certain ways. But it is significant that many of these factors are not aspects of accounting. They do not modify or justify modifying past transaction experience. However, they do influence management's appraisal of the results of prior actions taken for the enterprise. And this may stimulate corrective action through policy change or change in transaction types. But review of results of prior actions cannot provide a logical base for directly modifying recorded historical facts resulting from overt transactions entered upon in good faith.

From the accounting point of view, the money figures associated with a transaction event merely provide one of two elements needed as a basis for recording a transaction in the accounting manner. One element to be recognized is the nature of the effects of the events on the enterprise; the other is a quantitative representation of the same event – a necessary element for making informative arithmetic calculations closely tied to the accumulating experience of that enterprise.

Each transaction acquires the characteristics of an individual category having a relation to all other categories involved in accounting. It is evident that recognized interrelation among all these categories is an indispensable prerequisite for rationally operating this technology toward its objectives. Such a complex of interrelations can scarcely be effectively compressed into a few one-sentence postulates. And it is doubtful that these interrelations are in any degree assumptions.

They exist as evolutionary facts. They have not been blueprinted toward construction of a technology. They evolved out of the interplay (1) of men's sensing of a need for knowledge of enterprise transactions' experience and (2) of the ingenuity of the same men for conceiving, little by little, suitable techniques to serve this need and by their recognizing the key significance of weaving elements of techniques into interlocked patterns of actions. This is "accounting." This is part of the marvel that is enterprise accounting.

Some other highlights can be noted in the integration of real accounts (the tree) and nominal accounts (the fruit). Another part can be seen in the significant and very early recognition of the dualism inherent in every transaction: an intention to affect the enterprise and a persuasive consideration enlisting another's help in generating that effect.

These aspects of transactions are not accounting. Accounting has been created to make effective use of these antecedent characteristics. It is an oversimplification to tie these phenomena of exchange to the phrase "give and receive." This is too small a window to permit real insight into accounting. And perhaps it is rather unnecessary to postulate economic exchange as part of the environment of accounting. Exchanges have been known facts over centuries. Exchange as a fact of economic life is far older than the simplest aspects of accounting technology.

A current tendency is to emphasize the quantitative side of transaction events. The money aspect is permitted to overshadow the intended effect of the event. The latter is much more significant; the effect, not the money figures, speaks of the intention, the decisions, and the action. The transaction effect, not the money symbols, becomes enterprise experience. Money is a lubricant facilitating exchange. For accounting, money is a medium of exchange; in accounting, it can be confusing to think of money as measuring value. The various economic concepts of money can seldom illuminate accounting actions or point toward its objectives.

It is the present fashion to stress dollars as being "units of measure." Some readers of the phrase and some users of account data may interpret words and the figures as referring to measuring "price;" others may interpret them toward measuring "value." To call units of money units of measure can generate confusion from being open to different interpretations.

This dilemma is close to the heart of the matter. At issue is the question whether account data should express enterprise transaction experience in terms of exchange-priced costs, or in some variation from such cost in the direction of current values.

In a few situations valuations become necessary – purchase and sale of a business, bargaining a merger into existence, and liquidating a going concern in bankruptcy. In the absence of enterprise capital-income accounting, comparison of successive statements of resources and debts can suggest "change in enterprise well-being." Such a calculated change in status could be produced by two appraisal statements of a continuing enterprise without use of nominal accounts. The great contribution made by the introduction of nominal accounts was that of presenting factors capable of suggesting how management decisions in the aggregate contributed to a "change of status." This still contributes greatly to insight into management effectiveness – an aspect of business of higher significance than any estimated (appraised) change in enterprise welfare could be. No doubt, "change in well-being" can be influenced by changing economic conditions since these in turn will influence management's next decisions. But is seems reasonable to place the greater emphasis on management's contribution. The results of prior decisions can be known, identified, documented, and reviewed in far greater degree than effects attributed, hypothetically, to changing price levels, and decreased purchasing power of the dollar.

Valuations toward a present state of well-being are at best suitable for an exceptional situation. But the exceptions should not dominate accounting ideology. Evidently, pressure from value concepts on one side and concepts of experience-costs on the other have generated a gray area between them. This mixing of costs and values in accounts lies close to the heart of the matter. The growing issue is: shall the gray area be preserved as it is, expanded, or contracted?

If the present mixture of cost and modified cost is unsatisfactory, a choice seems necessary between the alternatives of pure or freely modified account data. Problems would emerge whatever the choice. Careful appraisals of differences in the emerging problems would seem indicated. The chief question would not be how to act, but why to act toward one choice or the other – a study of comparative consequences. Account data could be held tightly to invested, historical cost experience; or account data could be infinitely modified by extensive applications of index series. Techniques are available to implement either kind of action. A decision should rest on full exploration of why the consequences of one line of action should be judged superior to consequences from the other.

This would call for careful examination into the pragmatic relations (consequences) in two contrasting sets of means and ends: (1) account data from strict cost, serving as a technical means toward accounting objectives; (2) account data extensively modified by unilateral judgmental decisions in the direction of reflecting values – these actions being designed for use as technical means toward objectives. The same objectives can scarcely support both action types.

The starting point therefore is the formulation of accounting objectives, for these provides the key to appraising the consequences from use of alternative means. If differing objectives are visualized for the two differing techniques, a convincing judgment is necessary as to the relative desirability of each type of objective. Such problems of judgment quickly make it evident that accounting objectives must be limited. Account data cannot be all things to all people.

The inner nature of accounting technology lies close to the heart of the matter. As this becomes clearer, rationally limited objectives could inspire logically limited techniques within the framework of one technical system. Outside of the system, there would be no logical limit to the variety of types of data communication. Here is a basis for close examination toward sharply distinguishing (1) techniques of marshaling enterprise transaction experience and (2) techniques for extracting meaning from communicated data expressive of enterprise actual experience.

If these two ways of dealing with account data continue mixed within the accounting system, pressures for more and more information will tend to push accounting technology out of its natural area of service and in the direction of evolving into a special type of statistical operation. If the two techniques were suitably differentiated, marshaling would be accepted as the basic objective of accounting technology. If that limited function were recognized and implemented, the field of collateral, supplementary, and interpretative arrangements of account data would still be available and unlimited.

In addition to the analysis made earlier of several postulates, mention should be made here of postulate B1, financial statements. These are technical means for compactly communicating quantitatively the results of management's prior decision-actions. Such reports compact "the results of the accounting process"; the two statements (i.e., the balance and income sheet) "rest on the same underlying data" and they are "fundamentally related" to each other. Yet, other significant aspects may be noted.

Earlier mention was made of the integration of real and nominal accounts as reflecting a very ingenious implementation of the inescapable interrelation of enterprise capital productively employed and the income generated by that employment under management. This relationship, which exists whether or not accounts are kept, is nevertheless deeply significant for accounting.

Financial statements, the balance and income sheet, constitute a forceful epitome of the conceptual patterns lying back of them. These two statements can communicate insight because of the relationships that interrelate enterprise entity, enterprise management, management-generated transaction-experience, and the inner characteristics of all individual, exchange-priced transactions, and the functional character of bilateral categories.

The significance of these interrelations is important; they therefore might well become the focal center of a very practical evolutionary development – that of separating the actions of marshaling and of interpreting. When accomplished, this would seem to promise such an expansion of the arts of interpretive use of account data as to constitute a step toward some of the characteristics of scientific use of data.

It seems quite reasonable to believe the profession of public accounting would be strengthened by such an evolutionary development. The ethical, procedural, and judgmental features supporting the attest function would be strengthened by being initially concentrated toward the integrity of enterprise experience data. Non-attest activities of accountants in public practice could be, as they are already, services rendered on the basis of knowledge, experience and judgment related to collateral areas of service. Experienced professionals would be well equipped by those same factors to extend their collateral services to include use of various interpretative techniques for extracting meaning from inanimate account figures. This kind of interpretive action is already implied in such terms as "techniques toward decision" and "operations research." Frequently, such exploratory actions combine the use of account data and non-account data. This fact, however, does not convert the actions into accounting. On the other hand, an understanding of the nature and limits of account data would seem a necessary factor toward the judgments emerging from interpretive studies.

It is the theme of these pages that exploration in depth of the inner nature of accounting ideology and technology can contribute to the continued growth of professional service. A compelling concept emerges; the factual integrity of enterprise transaction experience should have discernible support from the functional logic inherent in accounting. If such a concept is indeed compelling, as a desirable objective associated with accounting techniques as suitable means, it should be accompanied by a corollary: reported account data, compiled under guidance from this concept, should be supplemented by appropriate, non-account data, in aid of deepening and clarifying the insight now provided by the usual balance sheet and income statement.

NOTE

1. Littleton is referring to Moonitz' research monograph, *The Basic Postulates of Accounting*, which was published on behalf of the AICPA in 1961. The postulates presented in this monograph are reproduced in Table 3 at the end of this chapter (for more about the controversy surrounding the postulates, see Chambers, 1963; Persson & Napier, 2015b; Zeff, 1982).

Table 3: Maurice Moonitz' Postulates of Accounting.

Postulates Related to the Environment of Accounting

Postulate A-1. Quantification. Quantitative data are helpful in making rational economic decisions, i.e. in making choices among alternatives so that actions are correctly related to consequences.

Postulate A-2. Exchange. Most of the goods and services that are produced are distributed through exchange, and are not directly consumed by the producers.

Postulate A-3. Entities (including identification of the entity). Economic activity is carried on through specific units or entities. Any report on the activity must identify clearly the particular unit or entity involved.

Postulate A-4. Time Period (including specification of the time period). Economic activity is carried on during specifiable periods of time. Any report on that activity must identify clearly the period of time involved.

Postulate A-5. Unit of Measure (including identification of the monetary unit). Money is the common denominator in terms of which goods and services, including labor, natural resources, and capital are measured. Any report must clearly indicate which money (e.g., dollars, francs, and pounds) is being used.

Postulates Related to Aspects of Accounting

Postulate B-1. Financial Statements. (Related to A-1) The results of the accounting process are expressed in a set of fundamentally related financial statements which articulate with each other and rest upon the same underlying data.

Postulate B-2. Market Prices. (Related to A-2) Accounting data are based on prices generated by past, present or future exchanges which have actually taken place or are expected to.

Postulate B-3. Entities. (Related to A-3) The result of the accounting process are expressed in terms of specific units or entities.

Postulate B-4. Tentativeness. (Related to A-4) The results of operations for relatively short periods of time are tentative whenever allocations between past, present, and future periods are required.

Postulates Related to the Imperatives of Accounting

Postulate C-1. Continuity (including the correlative concept of limited life). In the absence of evidence to the contrary, the entity should be viewed as remaining in operation indefinitely. In the presence of evidence that the entity has a limited life, it should not be viewed as remaining in operation indefinitely.

Postulate C-2. Objectivity. Changes in assets and liabilities and the related effects (if any) on revenue, expenses, retained earnings, and the like, should not be given formal recognition in the accounts earlier than the point of time at which they can be measured in objective terms.

Postulate C-3. Consistency. The procedures used in accounting for a given entity should be appropriate for the measurement of its position and its activities and should be followed consistently from period to period.

Postulate C-4. Stable Unit. Accounting reports should be based on a stable measuring unit.

Postulate C-5. Disclosure. Accounting reports should disclose that which is necessary to make them not misleading.

Source: Moonitz (1961, pp 52–53).

2

INADEQUATE NAMES

ABSTRACT

When early Italian accounting methods were translated into English text, they sometimes were titled Records in the Italian Manner. *Later the term "double-entry bookkeeping" was used; this gave some notice to the reader that duality was a characteristic feature of this record system. Still later, taking as a clue the term "account" (the basic category for data classification) the title "accounting" emphasized a shift from the journal entry form to the classification of categories – a distant movement closer to the essence. A more significant descriptive phase could be "a data-organizing technology for enterprise transaction experience." In an expanded form, this could clearly justify accounting as realistic because of its inseparable association with the realities of an enterprise's actual experience.*

Children learn names of things first and are taught to build on that framework. As their education continues, many of the names for things take on new significance and complexities. For one thing, they learn to use non-name words to form sentences. The meaning of specific nouns gradually broadens; some of them become compact symbols for complex ideas. Some well-known words for things eventually become so much a symbol that the elements symbolized need to be closely examined. Frequently, a noun may need to be changed in order to more strongly indicate changes in its meaning. This is also true for accounting.

Various names have been associated with this technology, during its long and useful existence. When Italian usage of the fourteenth century was reproduced for English texts, the newer method represented a change from the established charge-and-discharge records of individual accountability. Some of those early translations were simply named *Records in the Italian Manner*. Such a book title would provide few clues to the nature of the "record." Learning to use the imported method was largely a matter of making entries in typical record books in the manner illustrated in the translated texts. And the latter included no theory offering explanations for the technical peculiarities.

As Pacioli's (1494) Italian text was translated into German and English, the most striking feature clearly visible in the illustrations was quickly recognized and considered as the "key" to the methodology. The dual presentation in the records of the details of a transaction became the basis for a different wording of the book title: *Keeping Books by Double-entry* or *Double-entry Bookkeeping*. These titles were more descriptive than that using the phrase "in the Italian manner." The new phrases "keeping books" and "bookkeeping" meant making records of transaction events. In the French and German languages, the root concept of the technology is revealed in words related to counting in the sense of calculations (e.g., the German verb "*berechnen*" meaning "to calculate").

The familiar noun "account" can be identified with *a count*, that is, with the enumeration of quantities (recording digits derived from transactions in the markets). The English word "account" carried the basic connotation of a personal reckoning (calculation report) of a debt owed or owing. Very early, the only transaction records were those of moneylenders for their deposits subject to withdrawal and for loans subject to repayment (hence, a cash-basis accounting). From that background, every category in the ledger came to be cast in the same bilateral form as of a debt owed and discharged, even though, presently, many transactions were not debts but other types of enterprise experience.

If bookkeeping is to be taught by precept and example, as it was for a long time, then simple rules and illustrations to copy might be sufficient for that level of objective. However, at today's college level – with the integration of the subject of accounting with other subjects such as business management, finance, and auditing – such a simple approach will be too slow and inadequate. As such, while the technical framework of modern accounting records is clearly visible in the early textbooks, the ideological support for the usage is still almost as inadequate as earlier.

Perhaps no single word or short phrase can convey the real meaning of the word "accounting" for use in a broader context. A scrutiny of the known aspects of the nature and function of enterprise accounting would support a more descriptive approach, one that could attempt to suggest the real essence. This might need a dozen words or more, for example: a technical methodology for organizing the exchange-priced transaction experience of a specific business enterprise.

An explanation of this length would not be very appropriate for repeated use in the literature in place of the often needed, single word, "accounting." Nevertheless, this kind of phraseology could invite expansion; this would substantially clarify understanding of inner meaning, which the single-word symbol was intended to suggest. An explanation of the significance of each of the terms used would elaborate on the concept described. It could be more enlightening in the end to explore early in this manner a concept rather than to depend on dictionaries to expand upon a brief title. The approach indicated could at once open up the essence of the technology as no dictionary definition of "accounting" could do. Moreover, an early grasp of the essence, function, and limitations of enterprise accounting would enlighten any aspects of the technology and the related ideology as these emerge as study progresses.

The name "double-entry bookkeeping" does not, and perhaps never did, touch the real essence of enterprise accounting. Again, the phrase "data organizing technology for enterprise transaction experience" comes much closer. Two aspects underlying these phrases deserve comment. These may offer justification for the use of "double" in the older phrase that mere rules of thumb for analyzing transactions could not reveal.

The first aspect is that every transaction in the markets – the initial source of account data – have specific effects on the two enterprises involved. The actions of the two parties are sponsored by differing intentions to produce effects. It is also significant that both parties have a desired favorable effect in mind. Moreover, in each case, the opposite parties will need to offer a persuasive consideration likely to be attractive to the other. The result is that, for each party, the consideration he would offer would have, for him, an unfavorable effect. This result is unavoidable if the desired favorable effect is to be attained. The transaction aspect that was unfavorable to the seller (as a decrease in his inventory) would be favorable to the buyer (as an increase in his inventory).

By this realistic process of reaching transaction agreements, each party makes a specific judgment as to his own self-interest. The transaction experience of each is mutually satisfactory, and for each is obviously factual and quite rational. No record of such an item of actual experience would be adequately informative unless both the favorable and the unfavorable aspects were included. The duality so often met in accounting, therefore, is rational; and, for that reason, the account categories will reflect real circumstances. And, because duality was an inherent aspect of transactions, duality in bilateral accounts would logically follow. Accounts, therefore, were a convenient and very useful device for separating and contrasting favorable and unfavorable effects worked upon the given enterprise as results of decision-actions by its management.

The impulse for such a systematic recording arises in the need for each party to review the results of his own decisions. The experience data of each party will be assigned in his accounts only according to his own position in the bargained exchanges. Furthermore, an enterprise is many times a buyer and many times a seller. All transactions in their many variations will be translated into data entries in various accounts. When management or investor studies summaries this data, the reader is looking at a section of enterprise history. The story is readable, because elements of that history have been analytically marshaled for the express purpose of making that history more readily understood.

It is evident that account data should be restricted to that actual experience of that enterprise. The reason is clear. Only through agreement between independent parties can transaction data speak authoritatively of consummated experience. On the other hand, data included in accounts, which do not reflect such an experience, will cast a shadow over the interpretative value of accumulated experience.

The other aspect of the phrase "data from enterprise transaction experience" is related to the interpretative usefulness of summarized data. Those data are vital to both the management and the investor, for both seek to understand the results of activities that have been initiated by management decisions. Because of these facts, prior experience will have significance for management. The future of that enterprise will be influenced, perhaps dominated, by decision results opened to review. It will be equally clear that account data alone cannot provide answers to future decision problems of management and investors. All parties at interest have always needed more information than account data could rationally provide.

An investor today is one unit in greatly expanded investment markets. And the complexities of making decisions to invest or dis-invest have led to an increase in technical advisors and financial analysts. Financial statements provide needed basic information. At best, these reports can be no more than compact summaries of relevant totals that have emerged out of the technical actions of enterprise accounting. Consequently, investment decisions should also consider a great deal of non-account information.

The technical actions and the limitations inherent in accounting are not widely understood. From the point of view of investment analysis, a summary of past results alone will not be adequate. Yet, reporting on the unknown future and on innumerable current non-account data cannot rationally be made part of the basic function of enterprise accounting. Indeed, this must be an accepted limitation of accounting. Its function is to satisfactorily deal with reviewable and actual experience. Data relevant to the future, and much useful data of the present, cannot be rationally considered as fully consummated experience of the given enterprise. The criticism that financial statements are inadequate reports, lacking certain vital information, is therefore unfounded. Limitations that are entirely natural and overlooked help explain so-called deficiencies.

Nonetheless, pressure has built up for modified accounting reports. This, in turn, tends to weaken full acceptance of the basis and limited function of accounting – that of reporting factually on the transaction experience of the given enterprise. A companion desire to consider management as having some aspects of science – a particular focus on forecasting the future – has also helped to produce a measure of dissatisfactions with account data limited to transaction experience. Dissatisfaction of this kind seems involved in recent amalgamation of managerial accounting and managerial economics, an end that would be expected to be achieved when accounting emerges as the incarnation of economics (for an example of this approach, see Chambers, 1957).

It is understandable that business decisions can be helped by an abundance of relevant information. Nonetheless, it does not follow that accounting, a limited technology, is the best agency to provide a full expansion of decision-useful data. The range of such information is very wide. The freedom of accounting, to incorporate more than enterprise transaction experience, is clearly limited by a behavioral concept of its technical function. This limitation is not merely an inheritance from evolutionary development as "double-entry bookkeeping." It is limited, particularly, because of the probability that non-experience data, if infused into accounts (and financial statements), would confuse more than inform the users having business decisions to make. It would be far from a simple matter of terminology and data arrangement to distinguish experience and non-experience, if both were mixed within the natural boundaries of data pictures made from accounts.

The significance of data from prior experience as a base for next decisions would be diluted by such an infusion. Harmonious progression in the continuation of enterprise experience is highly desirable. For this reason, clues to future action should be sought in knowledge of the results of prior actions. Intermingled non-experience data would inject discord in the needed evidence of continuation of action-harmony in the enterprise. As such, evolutional developments have interrelated accounting theory and information that is useful to decision-making. The trend of those developments has shown improved techniques for organizing account data and presentation. But the fact does not support a theory that accounting technology is infinitely flexible. Any weakening of its basic functional structure and limitations may do violence to accountancy's real destiny and to its reason for being.

3

LIMITATIONS AFFECTING ACCOUNTING

ABSTRACT

Accounting is a necessary but incomplete technology for providing all the decision-useful information needed by management and investors. Accounting is inseparably tied to enterprise transactions and its history. Expected future experience may be entertained but cannot be convincingly reported as established fact. Reported expectations in the midst of actual experience could be more confusing than enlightening. Instead, non-accounting technology can effectively supplement transaction enterprise data with projected expectations and interpretative data. Furthermore, accounting does not possess the qualities necessary for a science; yet accounting, as science, has an interpretative obligation to hold fast to specific realities.

It is clear that enterprise accounting must operate within some identifiable rational limits. A sample of six of these may be formulated as follows: (1) accounting is a necessarily incomplete technology for providing all the decision-useful information needed by managements and investors. (2) Accounting is so closely tied to enterprise transaction experience and the enterprise's history. (3) Expected future experience may be estimated but cannot be convincingly reported as established fact. (4) Expectation injected in the midst of actual experience data could be more confusing than enlightening. (5) Non-accounting techniques outside of accounting technology can effectively supplement data from actual transaction experience, by using projected expectations and interpretative calculations. (6) Accounting has an interpretative obligation to hold fast to specific realities.

Enterprise transaction history is but a prelude. As such, it exercises influence on whatever shall follow. History is not like water over a dam; it is more like a flow that continues in spite of dams. A dam is only an incident along the way in a river's life. Similarly, the line separating one fiscal period from the next is only analytically significant. Furthermore, the meaning of past events is easy to ignore. The present will always seem strongly relevant to current problems. It is also easy to upgrade the significance of the future. Although the future is not knowable, it nonetheless is the center of hopes and the target of plans. In this context, it would be helpful to consider enterprise transaction experience (and its account data) as a continuing stream, flowing from the past, through the present, and toward the future.

It would not be helpful to think of account data as if they were pools of water held back by year-end dams. It would be an even greater mistake to believe past account data can be made more meaningful by being modified out of its original status as reports of prior experience. The actual past cannot be undone. We can, however, act differently now because of our knowledge of that past. And, with the help of that knowledge, we can act in the present to influence the future. As such, the businessman can plan, forecast, budget, decide, and act toward the future. Yet, he can do these things only within limits. He has no special power to design his future or completely mold it. The best projections of statistical trends are not knowledge. One can play only on a foundation of knowledge from the results of prior actions and the transaction history of an enterprise. That history is a prelude.

Today and tomorrow, for an enterprise, is no more isolated from the past than a symphony is isolated from its prelude. The themes of symphonic music are first made evident in the prelude. Elements there initiated are interpreted and developed as the music progresses. To the musician, progression in the music is clearly readable. To the businessman, progression in his enterprise should also be readable. He reads, not musical notation – those symbols of sounds – but accounting notation – those symbols of enterprise prior transaction experience. The businessman, while reviewing data reflecting results of his own prior decisions, will be interpreting enterprise experience. He will be reviewing the prelude for ideas appropriate to his emerging decision-actions. In effect, he will be composing the next section of the score of his symphony; that is, the next period of enterprise history.

Whatever presently appears as enterprise actions will not be duplications of the past, although some elements will be similar and themes will remain. The themes can and should be varied, modulated, elaborated, and expanded. The new section of the symphony of enterprise activities should be vital, creative, and progressive. To accomplish this, the results must reflect recognizable continuation of themes already established. The transactions of the new fiscal period will not be identical with the past. Yet, the changes made must be harmonious with the past; they must reflect modulated continuation of the enterprise theme and its service function.

From this point of view, it is clear that financial statements will present a data picture of a compact block of enterprise transaction history. Although that history cannot itself be changed in matters of fact, the content of history should continue to be open for review. Both the volume of flow and its rate of movement may be significant, and study of these may provide clues for next decisions. Yet, if the "data symbols" for transaction experience are not read intelligently and thoughtfully, the next passage of this symphony may not be as progressively harmonious as the prelude had predicted.

Managements and investors need account data in order to review transaction experience, which informs judgment regarding the overall effectiveness of prior decisions made under the economic conditions at the time. The usefulness to future decisions of such review will be unmistakable. Next, judgments will be influenced by the harmony observed between financial statements of the past and those of the present (i.e., the prelude and its subsequent development). For the analyst, the evident continuity between the reported past and present can help the formulation of his judgments as to the possible near future. When that future becomes a recorded past, it will add one more section to the readable experience (i.e., the history of that enterprise). The last section under scrutiny, because it had been previously forecasted, will provide a test of the quality of that forecast.

The analogy of account data to musical notation cannot be perfect, no more than the analogy to a symphony. Yet, the figure of speech can help to indicate the inaptness of the old name "double-entry bookkeeping." Furthermore, it can point to some of the reasons why accounting has had the capacity to serve society so well and for so long. Accounting could not have grown in its service capacity without improvements in its techniques, and without increased understanding on the part of data users of the reasons why current knowledge of the past results of transaction experience can provide a springboard for next decisions.

This, then, seems true about enterprise accounting. Its limitations contribute substantially to its service capability. Its obligation is not that of direct interpretation. Instead, its obligation is to open experience to interpretative analyses; thus, placing experience in contact with expectation. The incompleteness of account data out of enterprise transaction experience needs to be supplemented to support its maximum service, but these supplements should not replace the traditional accounts based on exchange-priced transactions consummated in the market.

PART IV

1

LIMITS OF EXPERIENCE

ABSTRACT

Alternatives to inventory pricing and depreciation expense calculation are examples of actions beyond the limits of the actual experience of an enterprise. They tend to mix expectations (looking forward) with actual experience (looking backward). Both cannot be equally objective. The calculation of insolvency, company mergers, and secret reserves as well as the confusion between values and prices are some of the possible antecedents for the muddling of experience with expectations.

Actions are functional responses to objectives. An appropriate and effective action related to an evident and desirable objective is a logical action, because of the existing functional relationship. But it is logical only if the action is appropriately limited. It must be limited by definite relevance to the specific enterprise. It must also be limited by excluding expectations from treatment as overt experience. Inventory pricing and depreciation calculations are examples of the mixing of experience and expectation. Such actions, therefore, would suggest a failure to recognize to the influence of functional logic of accounting.

Data from experience and data about expectations are necessarily quite different. Experience looks back, while expectations look forward. Decisions are made toward the future; hence, they must consider expectations. But decisions could scarcely benefit from the neglecting of recorded prior experience. And accounting technology can scarcely record expectations as if they were overt experience. If it is given the responsibility for incorporating data suggesting possible future conditions, accounting will be forced to risk over-expanding its technical framework and functional limits.

The results of taking such a risk could be to make accounting more confusing than enlightening.

Experience is concrete, actual, and reviewable, whereas expectations are necessarily subjective opinions. The latter cannot be factual as to the given enterprise or later be reviewable as enterprise history. Decisions, whether taken inside or outside the enterprise, should start from a look backward at past results and a look forward as to future intentions. The individual, having a decision to make, must then judge the combined significance of both views. This act of judgment cannot be transferred to accounting data, for data do not weigh intangibles or make decisions.

The message in account data, reflecting enterprise transaction experience, has been colored, gradually and subtly, by non-experience that has been brought into the accounts. One of the recognized compelling concepts of accounting technology emphasizes its function of accumulating and communicating data reflecting the transaction experience of a given enterprise. This objective is well-known, but it has been so broadly interpreted that it has invited the use of techniques that intermingle non-experience data with experience data originating out of exchange-priced transactions, which have been generated by the decisions and intentions of the management of that enterprise. A need exists, therefore, to appraise degrees of variations from logical patterns of reporting on experience as such; and, a need closely to judge the degree of persuasiveness of reasons advanced to support typical variations from the pattern.

The verb "to account" refers unmistakably to the past; we cannot account for or report on the unknown future. Yet, the future weighs heavily on the mind. Consideration of the possible future (i.e., expectations) will strongly influence decisions. And subsequent decision-actions may change the results of some prior actions. But it is questionable whether merely recognizing new decision-actions (as possibilities) should prompt direct and unilateral modification of recorded results already tied back to prior decisions.

Another way to state this is that the accounting record represents enterprise history. Its data were derived from intentional and overt actions by enterprise management. If this history faithfully records and summarizes the facts of specific events, these facts cannot rationally be made non-history by an act of will or wish. Disappointing effects cannot be canceled, by altering the record closer to some desired result. No more can non-history be similarly made into history.

As is the case with inventory accounting, depreciation accounting undertakes to allocate enterprise experience between a present period and future periods. In one case, transaction experience in goods is allocated in the current period. In the other case, transaction experience, represented by productive capital assets, is allocated over future fiscal periods, with the matching of those assets to their contribution to an enterprise's performance capability for generating revenue (i.e., the depreciation charge for the period). A single explanatory statement phrased in this way could very well replace the variety of meanings associated with the terms "inventory" and "depreciation." This would promote understanding rather than the current conflict of ideas.

Recognition of depreciation expense is a part of the established pattern of accounting actions. These actions, being means toward ends, would be limited by the conceptual boundaries that are characteristic of all categories related to enterprise accounting. Misclassification – whether felonious, accidental, or intentional with good motives – is always objectionable. The reason for this is that it will interfere, to some degree, with the integrity of the recorded data of enterprise experience. Any trespass on the boundaries of a category represents the wrong use of accounting's technical means; it is a perversion, so to speak, of the functional relation of that means to its clear objectives. Furthermore, a boundary violation, whether small or large, is likely to leave the data illogical and often misleading. False, untrue, distorted, and unrealistic might be too harsh words. But if any of these terms shall be applicable to any accounting category, the effect of the sponsoring action would modify actual experience data toward some degree of deceit.

In this regard, an important question to pose is how convincing the reasons advanced in support of departures from the functional logic of accounting actually are. Do the consequences of the departures tend to make it more or less difficult a review of enterprise actual experience? Can various categories, each necessary to the objectives of accounting, be safely denied the protection of limiting boundaries? Is there a compelling concept of relevancy at work in accounting? If the service of functional logic is to be denied, by acceptance of violations of conceptual boundaries, will it not be necessary to find reasons stronger and more convincing than this logic to support them?

For example, inventory pricing and depreciation expense, if adjusted for price level changes, will speak of non-experience that reflects economic causation rather than of enterprise transaction experience. Injected directly into the ledger, or incorporated directly in the financial statements, such data substitute expectation (opinion) for transaction experience (action). Clearly, the latter is the more concrete and objective; its data derive from actual decisions by management that have resulted in actual events in the markets intended to affect that specific enterprise. This is to say that the basic responsibility (objective) of accounting technology does not extend as far as searching into economic causation. Nor does it invite the mixing of non-transaction data with data from transaction experience. Potential events, causes, or conditions, which have or may influence management's past, present, or future decisions cannot be captured or measured with sufficient objectivity to replace account data as such. However, they can be useful as supplemental information.

When it comes to several aspects of accounting usage more widely utilized in practice, these should not be considered precedents in discussion of concepts basic to commercial accounting. One such example is non-profit accounting for institutions, municipalities, and other entities of this kind, which is best considered as fund accounting as opposed to commercial accounting. This is so because it relates more to fiscal responsibility than to the reporting on management's productive use of capital resources.

Another such example is corporations operating under legislated prices and heavily regulated environments; these constitute special cases influenced by the public interest. These companies supply their services under a condition that calls for what is essentially "cost-plus accounting." Regulatory commissions mediate two conflicting interests, those of the users of the service (interested in prices) and those of suppliers of capital (interested in a rate of return for their investments). Standard costs (i.e., non-transaction data) are injected in this process. Yet, this does not offer a persuasive precedent for other injections. Standards and variances will function only to provide management with an immediate and continuing view of the progress of operations throughout a fiscal period. These can be (and are) provided as supplementary statements; their usefulness would not increase with the replacement of traditional accounts. Note also that these supplementary elements differ only temporarily from actual costs.

A third such example is national income accounting, which also cannot constitute a precedent for business accounting. It does not closely conform to the compelling concepts associated with the categories of capital-income accounting or with the interrelation of the enterprise entity and enterprise management. The use and borrowing of terms such as "accounting" and "accounts" in nationwide statistics does not make the statistical treatment of data an aspect of commercial accounting technology. And the "dual entries" made in those statistical categories do not reflect, as entries in commercial accounts do, an interrelation among real and nominal accounts. These deficiencies mark a system lacking the major aspect that makes accounting an integrated technology. Furthermore, the national economy is not comparable with a business enterprise, and political government can hardly be analogous with enterprise management.

Returning to the topic of inventory pricing, the lower of cost or market method is sometimes said to reflect conservatism under conditions of falling prices. Perhaps the same kind of explanation could be advanced in support of secret reserves. Management could authorize such a reserve (i.e., revaluation downward) without disclosing it clearly in the accounts. The result, however, would reflect a private unilateral modification of a prior transaction experience, originally expressed in terms of invested cost. As such, perhaps the lower of cost or market pricing method, even under present conditions, tends to reflect a type of conservatism more acceptable and open than secret reserves. Yet, it is a departure from recorded actual experience.

One can continue this line of thought. If fixed assets were given a value treatment that created secret reserves, this too might have been done with motives of conservatism in mind. And, as in the case of inventories, the argument could be advanced that management was in a better position than anyone else to judge the *value* of the asset. Nonetheless, neither a policy of conservatism nor an ability to judge values could justify the disclosure of something that is less than complete experience.

Historically, disclosure came to be a recognized issue before the term itself was brought into use as a standard for financial reporting. With this movement of the term into the domain of accounting, concepts of value – that is, of valuing expectations about the future – came with it. This continues to cast shadows over the logical functioning of accounting technology, which is aimed at creating an open and accurate communication of marshaled enterprise transaction experience. Aspects of this effect persist in both the literature and practice. The term value (worth) is confused for price (cost). To value may mean to judge a thing or an action. The same verb may also mean to judge a thing's worth or potential usefulness under specific conditions. The latter is the usual intention of the use of the word in economics and business. To price, on the other hand, refers to the action of attaching a price to something.

The continuing influence of conflicting concepts needs to be kept in mind, when considering functional logic in relation to accounting practices of pricing inventory and of calculating depreciation of fixed assets. In thinking of functional logic in connection with depreciation, it will be helpful to take note of certain asset treatments that might seem to be based on valuation precedents capable of influencing concepts and actions related to depreciation accounting.

One such example is the adjudication of a bankrupt enterprise, which might necessitate a modification of the invested cost of the original assets. This might be considered a precedent for re-pricing the assets of solvent companies. Such a conclusion would be rather farfetched. A court for bankruptcy cases would not consider invested cost as a satisfactory measure of the security available to general creditors. If liquidation became necessary, contemporary market prices would seem closer to creditors' enforceable rights. This, it should be noted, does not represent conservatism. It rather reflects a judicial view that similar goods in the current market should reasonably compensate creditors. But, under conditions of forced sale, reasonable compensation may not prevail.

Another such example is the consolidation of several companies into a new corporation, which would again involve a modification of the invested cost of the original assets. And, perhaps, such action could be considered as creating a valuation precedent for companies that are not involved in a merger. That, too, is doubtful. In the early years of the present century, it was common for the securities of the new corporation to be entered in the accounts at face value, and for the assets acquired by that issue to be valued by the company directors as reasonably equivalent to the face value of the shares exchanged. There have even have been cases wherein the asserted value of the assets was close to the face value of the preferred stock and the bonds issued, while the common stock would represent a judgment by the parties concerned as to the future expectations (earning power) of the company.

The legal concepts involved in company mergers may not have been as naïve as they might now seem. In essence, a consolidation of several companies into one corporation is closely equivalent to purchase and sale by independent parties. Those parties would rest their ultimate decisions on negotiated values rather than on prior invested costs as shown by the accounts of the constituent companies. Inevitably, a contemplated purchase and sale of whatever size would call up considered judgments, by the several parties at interest, about reasonable expectations as to future operating results of the new venture.

Several decades later, in the 1920s, merger activities again became prominent and quasi-reorganization of individual companies was put into effect. These were years of prosperity, with rising prices and profits. On this basis, expectations seemed bright. Investment bankers, planning the underwriting of a new security issue, would wish to see a desirable protective margin of assets in relation to proposed indebtedness. Obviously, this would involve elements of valuation and these elements would be reflected in the financial statements.

Legal concepts, much like those prevailing early in the century and associated with the considered judgment of experienced businessmen, would tend to support a belief that quasi-reorganization was fundamentally similar to the constructive purchase-and-sale theory that gave support to earlier railroad consolidations. Thus, decisions to revalue company assets more closely into harmony with contemporary economic conditions would rest on plausible legal grounds and business judgment of the trend of the economy (i.e., expectations). Such actions may have seemed quite reasonable in that setting of prosperity, even though men's ability to know the future was limited. But valuation decisions of those days, it is clear from later evidence, are not suitable precedents for revaluations out of today's expectations and for a subsequent modification of balance sheet assets and income statement depreciation charges.

When the actions under the conditions of the 1920s are viewed in the perspective of the conditions of the 1930s, the situation is reversed. Yet, calls for a revaluation policy remained. If valuation upward had been acceptable under certain conditions, surely valuation downward would be acceptable, perhaps vital, under other conditions. Thus, a precedent persisted even though reversed in effect. The most powerful argument in support was that of getting in tune with the present, of undoing what had been done in the past and in so doing getting "a fresh start." It is an open question whether the concept of "a new start" is analogous with a concept of constructive purchase and sale.

These examples of modifications of invested costs illustrate situations in which value has been given precedence over cost in the accounts and financial statements. They may seem to pose acceptable exceptions, although they weaken the appeal of functional logic as a key to the inner nature of accounting technology. Yet, it may well be that such "exceptions" can put to test rather than weaken the persuasiveness of the service to accounting of functional logic. Exceptions can turn the spotlight of inquiry toward the reasons advanced on their behalf.

In contrast with ideas supporting these "exceptions," my proposed inquiry will make other reasons clearer in support of the recognition of logic. It will become clear that careful regard for conceptual boundaries can help move accounting technology farther away from the influence of tradition, expediency, and expectations. Clearly integrated techniques would be more easily recognized as logically associated with persuasive objectives, which, in turn, justify the formation and use of these techniques as appropriate means to those ends.

Each situation wherein assets have been revalued would probably include long-lived and productively useful assets. In that case, it would be necessary to recognize increased depreciation as an expression of the enterprise's efforts (i.e., cost experience) to perform to the satisfaction of customers. On the other hand, how is service to customers increased by asset revaluations? Since expensing of depreciation will create a definite type of accounting action, this technical operation, as is the case with other aspects of accounting, should be carried out under the guidance of functional logic and associated compelling concepts and not revaluation.

Asset valuations, whether up or down, are financial in nature and involve the balance sheet foremost. Here, the central question is related to the concept of enterprise position, financial status, and relative solvency. Very probably, known valuation modifications are often entered upon (unilaterally and without transactions in the markets) with the intention of affecting, to some degree, the picture of enterprise status. Status, however, is only one aspect of a business enterprise that has large significance for interested parties and for accounting technology. Indeed, the basic innovation reflected in accounting is that of tying together data of enterprise financial status and data indicating the results of management actions in the markets; that is, actions that have materially affected the data pictures of both status and operating results.

The outstanding technical contribution of this technology is evident in this connection. Comparison of two statements of property and debt, as of different dates, would produce a quantitative expression of interim increase or decrease in enterprise net worth or well-being. Yet, the way management decision actions have contributed to that overall showing is not made evident by this comparison. On the other hand, accounts that report on expense-efforts and revenue-achievements will reflect overt actions taken by management in the markets in behalf of the enterprise. This separation and interrelation of efforts and achievements, of expense and revenue, is a highly constructive accomplishment. It succeeds in directing attention toward management as the primary factor responsible for effective enterprise service to society.

Because of that interrelation, the price figures in the asset accounts, whether original or modified, will gradually be passed on into specific fiscal periods, to meet that period's revenues and be reported in the income statement. Since the costs assigned will be higher or lower, because of any modification of the asset account, a part of the modification effect will enter into the period's operating results. Yet, some parts of this kind of "depreciation" expense cannot justifiably be called an enterprise transaction experience. It also cannot realistically be part of operations or production cost. It therefore seems clear that accounting is closely oriented toward management self-knowledge. Only because this is the case can accounting serve some of the informational needs of investors outside of the enterprise. Those interested parties are as much concerned to appraise management's achievements as to be informed as to enterprise status.

The conclusion is that voluntary and unilateral modification of depreciation expense constitutes a violation of functional logic. It lies within the power of this accounting logic to guide technical actions toward rational procedures, which, under limitations, affect nominal accounts as well as real accounts. In fact, one of the focal points of accounting logic is in the interrelation of real and nominal accounts, and the tie between the balance sheet and income statement. It is necessary, therefore, to examine the effect on the income statement of mixing, in the balance sheet, those elements reflecting enterprise actual transaction experience and those elements reflecting subjective judgments about future expectations.

The thought bears repeating. The functional relation of technical means, used toward desirable ends, affords a firmer foundation for building a substantial structure of suitable accounting techniques than what could result from building upon definitions, including that of depreciation. The significance of definitions is limited. Usually, the intention is (1) to state a relationship of the item defined to a larger class and (2) to make a compact statement of characteristics that distinguish the defined element from the general characteristics of the larger class. Often, a definition undertakes to indicate what an item is like or what caused it. The use-objective of the item is seldom included in a definition. Yet, for thorough understanding, a grasp of the use-objective is in many cases quite essential.

The term "depreciation" offers an illustration of a confusing variety of definitions. Some meanings have associated the word with causation. The use of descriptive terms, such as deterioration, inadequacy, or obsolescence points to reasons why an asset may lose its effectiveness. The "fall in replacement price" points to a reason for believing the same service at a lower cost could be enjoyed if an asset at that price were now in use. From the point of view of accounting (and enterprise experience), the phrase "if an asset ..." could only indicate wishful thinking or speculating toward future expectations. A technology, dedicated to making transaction experience understandable, could not rationally be broadened in function to treat a hypothetical possibility as factual account data.

The phrase "fall in value" may often be construed as the equivalent to the fall in replacement price or the generalization of the effects of causes such as those noted above. Yet, since neither economics nor accounting is a science, causation will be a matter of conjecture, supposition, as well as informed opinion and experienced judgment. None of these approaches will produce "hard facts" comparable to enterprise transactions, which are validated in the markets and thus made suitable for accounting use in marshaling the actual experience of an enterprise.

Using the term "cost allocation" to describe the action ascribed to depreciation entries points thought toward a technical procedure of accounting related to a prime objective. The action serves as a means toward attainment of that end. All of accounting, and each of its procedures, is a means to an end. That end is to make enterprise experience understandable and to rationally report on the facts of that experience.

Depreciation accounting is a sub-means pointed toward showing results that are related to management's acquisition and productive use of an asset. If there is causation back of depreciation accounting, it is in management's intention to further the objectives of the enterprise in certain ways. The asset is acquired for the service capacity judged to be within it. The use of the asset, according to its nature and limitations, makes an intended contribution to enterprise objectives. The functional logic of accounting dictates the use of techniques suitable for marshaling transaction data in ways that will report, from time to time, on the fulfillment of management intention. The compelling concept regarding depreciation, in this context, is that the asset in question gives its service life to contributing to the furthering of enterprise objectives and management intentions over a specific period.

Furthermore, each periodic entry for depreciation brings some part of enterprise transaction experience into the important category of the fiscal period. If this action is neglected, the complex objective and the functional purpose of periodicity are, to some degree, distorted and the integrity of the category's data falls into question. Possible difficulty in computing the sum to be periodically allocated would not change the functional logic involved.

Any alternative to a *carefully formulated* basis for apportioning asset cost (its potential contribution) over asset service life would produce a less acceptable history of enterprise actual experience. Failure to depreciate a productive asset would seriously affect the integrity of operating data for all the asset's years of service. An asset fully depreciated, but still in use, would also seriously affect the integrity of periodic reports, and would modify the calculations achievements basic to accounting objectives. If depreciation were wholly a matter of personal discretion, management could manipulate the income calculation at will. In a sole proprietorship, such manipulation would result in self-deception. In a corporation, such deception would misstate enterprise earnings and, in doing so, defraud investors who trusted the communicated account data to faithfully speak of factual experience.

It seems to me that depreciation accounting cannot be very persuasively considered rational, if management can readily change the amount expensed. On the other hand, an alternative of regulated uniformity applied to all enterprises would not be acceptable within the concept of free enterprise. There remains the possibility of allowing the freedom to choose from a wide range of customary practices. However, since this would approximate the use of management discretion, it would seem appropriate to seek a guide to the most reasonable choice short of management will or regulated uniformity.

It may be noted that general acceptance of index-adjusted depreciation would have an effect on income tax calculations. Even if such a result is not a conscious factor supporting this approach to depreciation expense, advocates of index-depreciation have neglected some significant facts. Their proposals violate the functional logic inherent in accounting, by suggesting that expectations replace experience. This implicitly ignores the fact that changing prices have always been a prominent characteristic of economic life. Businessmen have lived with changing conditions, by exercising their judgment of conditions and their skill in finding ways to meet these changes. Changing conditions are still a challenge to foresighted management and can bring penalties to ineffective management. The problem of controlling or mitigating economic fluctuations has been widely debated with little in terms of results. Modifying the account data of experience could not provide a substitute for judgment.

Advocacy of index depreciation is related to fluctuations in economic conditions. The problem is that such advocacy fails to tie its proposals into economics and psychology, which act as conditioning factors. Such advocacy also seldom indicates a strong preference for use of supplementary disclosure of index depreciation (as would seem a more readily acceptable procedure) over direct injection of index depreciation into the accounts or into financial statements. In this context, some thought might well be given to searching out relevant aspects of functional logic that may be buried within established accounting technology. The logic found there would not provide a pattern for remodeling this technology. Rather, the hope would be that the search could reveal a central core of interrelated and compelling concepts useful for testing established techniques and objectives as well as proposed objectives and new techniques.

2

IMPACT OF INFLATION

ABSTRACT

The existence of statistical price index series does not persuasively support proposals to modify account data from prior transaction experience. The consequences of using accounting techniques will demonstrate whether those actions have served accounting objectives satisfactorily. Management's overt actions in the markets, rather than changes in general price-levels, are the source of enterprise earnings. Accounting objectives are either compelling or limiting elements affecting the choice and use of accounting techniques.

General depreciation, and index depreciation in particular, provides a good testing ground for functional logic. For in this area, there is a variety of examples of the mixing of data that reflect enterprise transaction experience and data that, surely, should be recognized as essentially related to subjective expectations of the present or the future.

The modern example of an inflation climax can be noted in the economic experience of post-war Germany some forty years ago. The booming years of the 1920s in the United States and the subsequent collapse into the depression of the 1930s were induced for the most part by security speculation, whereas the German collapse resulted from a flood of printing press "money." The European experience was well remembered and, perhaps subconsciously, an analogy has been imagined as being possible for other countries. In theory, severe depression should follow from any kind of strong price inflation, or in reverse theory, recovery from any kind of depression could be stimulated by induced price inflation. Influential economists of the time, John Maynard Keynes in particular, advocated governmental policy and action designed to speed recovery and, under other conditions, designed to prevent collapse into depression.

After the depressed 1930s, government-planned efforts slowly produced planned effects in the United States. It is significant; however, that the advantage thus created has continued its effects. These effects are now often thought to be measurable by statistical evidence of economic growth; that is, average figures for gross national product. And, increasingly, these effects seem to be thought capable of producing gradual and persistent economic growth. This concept could be interpreted as implying a belief that a "formula" exists for preventing depressions. It is interesting to note, however, that there was a belief expressed during the late 1920s that the American economy was "on a permanently high plateau."[1] By October 1929, the "plateau" had collapsed. In the 1940s and 1950s no plateau has been mentioned. In its place, a sequence of "improved conditions" and "recessions" has been evident. They, in turn, have given rise to extensive discussion of ways and means for building continuous improvement by filling in the recessions.

Economic conditions, theory, and related diagnostic or remedial techniques have come into new prominence. These have gradually tended to exert an influence on accounting thought. In the double decade of the 1940s and 1950s, price level change seemed to grow in importance; the trend seemed generally upward and, if properly coached, capable of overriding the recurring "recessions." Under these conditions, certain aspects of economic theory seemed to contact accounting through that theory's relation to the responsibilities and functions of enterprise management. The economic theory of value accretion, in its connection with the concept of income, seemed, to some people, to point toward an incompleteness in the accounting concepts, which had long shaped the customary calculation of enterprise periodic net income. Accounting concepts and its techniques seemed incomplete because they rejected value accretion as producing a measurable part of enterprise earned income.

A contrasting view is worth noting. The accounting rejection of value accretion as income gained support by the revision, in the late 1920s and early 1930s, of the dividend statutes of several states. The changes were in the direction of excluding appreciation surplus (i.e., value accretion) as a source for cash dividends – a change supported and advocated by professional accountants.

Another suspected incompleteness in accounting related to maintenance of asset capital. From the point of view of economists, asset maintenance should be provided by depreciation reserves sufficient to secure enough funds to re-establish equivalent capacity regardless of new cost prices. However, from the accountants' point of view, depreciation should be charged in amounts judged sufficient to have reflected the conversion of cost invested in productive assets into cost of production. The latter viewpoint, in times of rising price, would not meet the economic concept, since the funds in the final depreciation reserve would not cover the full cost of new equipment of comparable capacity, which would be acquired at a higher price due to inflation.

The economists' viewpoint contain two apparent assumptions: that financial policy would dictate a future-anticipating line of accounting action; and that higher charges for depreciation expense would necessarily result in similarly higher selling prices readily accepted by customers. However, as accountants know, it is customer acceptance, not accounting actions, that establishes transaction exchange price. The difference in viewpoints is not surprising. The field of economics shows a strong tendency to stress *expectations*, whereas the field of accounting tends to emphasize *experience*.

This difference in point of view reveals a belief, either expressed or implied, that account data are not as sensitive as they might be to the significance of changing economic conditions, especially those indicated by price level movements. The implication here is that accounting technology would be neglecting an important responsibility unless effort were made to alert users of account data to the impact on a given business enterprise of contemporary price movements. However, this does not necessitate the modification of accounting ideology. There already exist statistical methods for computing price index series, which are thought capable of correcting raw prices for changes in the purchasing power of money, and the mere presence of such methods does not justify creating an objective for accounting that could make use of it. As such, statistical manipulation of account data, by use of index series or otherwise, if proposed for collateral, supplementary, or interpretative explorations would not be objectionable. Such use would leave accounting free to carry out its more logical and limited responsibilities by use of techniques definitely suitable to those objectives.

Events throughout the world during the past forty years have gradually made many thoughtful people increasingly aware, even without having studied economic literature, of the impact of economic pressures. Those who have had formal training in economics are keenly aware of the complexities of economic causation. Many who have combined knowledge of economics and accounting have come to recognize the relation of economic causation and business decisions. They appreciate the service relation of enterprise accounting to management and to the investing public; and they recognize the way these services ultimately constitute service to society.

It is not a disservice to accounting that such a background could sponsor an impulse to examine accounting critically in the light of economic concepts. It is unnecessary, however, to reach a conviction that accounting could be brought closer to the patterns of economic theory in beneficial ways. Close examination will reveal insurmountable differences in basic concepts. This in itself is desirable. Cross-fertilization of understanding, on the other hand, can still be beneficial, regardless of whether or not compelling concepts or controlling objectives are modified as a result. Indeed, direct modification in either direction need not be called up. Differing points of view and types of limitations is a source of strength.

A social philosophy, such as economics, and a practical technology, like accounting, cannot exchange characteristics and remain faithful to their respective original objective and motivation. Economics is appropriately concerned about causation, as far as causes can be specifically identified in such a complex matter as economic life. Business accounting cannot be similarly concerned with causation and still be faithful to its narrower obligations. The technical actions of accounting, which have evolved over some five centuries, have proved to be appropriate means toward achieving specific, though limited, objectives. On this basis, it is possible and desirable to consider accounting as possessed of a strong strain of functional logic.

Reasoning in economics follows a different pattern. It is based on deductive reasoning, which moves from stated postulates through a chain of inferences to conclusions, which, in turn, are persuasive primarily because of their derivation. In the functional logic of accounting, the test is not in the acceptability of a distant postulate or in the close linkage of a chain of inferences. Instead, it is the emergence of consequences, from the use of accounting techniques, which demonstrate whether the actions involved have served related accounting objectives satisfactorily or unsatisfactorily.

Continuing this line of inquiry, differing points of view between economics and accounting can also be illustrated by their contrasting concepts of income and, through these, the contrasting concepts of depreciation. While a variety of concepts can be found in the literature, the most common economic view of income identifies it with an improved state of financial well-being. This concept is strongly tied to more basic concepts of value and valuation. Consequently, under a condition of increasing prices, calculated income should be expressed by a measurement of value accretion and, under falling prices, by a measurement of value decline.

This pattern of adjustments has been accepted in accounting under certain circumstances: accretion is recognized for items such as growing timber and aging liquor. Furthermore, where guaranteed prices have been established, such as is the case with certain agriculture products and precious mined metals, profit is associated with production rather than action in the selling markets. As such, it is clear that the concept "realization" has been considerably widened.

Acceptance in instances such as these invites extensions, by analogy of the accretion doctrine, to any asset in the accounts provided only that the increase could be reasonably measured. Under this doctrine, any regularly quoted price might suffice for asset re-pricing. And, once practice and eventually custom is committed to an accretion, it is similarly committed to considering fallen prices as reasonably measuring value erosion. The rule "lower of cost or market" already reflects such an acceptance. Hence, the stage is set for "realization" by both accretion and erosion as one condition follows the other.

The problem with realization, however, becomes obvious during implementation. When it is incorporated within accounting's technical structure, these innovations will tend to convert accounting, a technology for marshaling enterprise experience, into a hybrid, statistical method dedicated to trying to alert account data users to the effects of economic causation on a given business enterprise. The resulting mix of enterprise experience and economic expectations could scarcely be as usefully informative to these account data users as would a clear-cut communication of the actual results of management's real actions in real markets.

This leads me to reiterate the point that economics and accounting are at best friendly neighbors and acquaintances that are aware of their differences. Income for economics and for accounting should remain different ideas. In one case, income derives from very complex patterns of causation and human motivation. In the other, accounting technology is not equipped to search out causation or human motives. Only when underlying needs, intentions, and actions produce market transactions relevant to the given enterprise can that data be suitable to serve the functional objectives of accounting.

Enterprise income does not emerge from these accounts. Its emergence and cause lies much deeper. Accounting can only identify the evident results of complex economic causations. Its technology can only classify data representing enterprise income (or loss) or income potential. In other words, the natural limitations of accounting technology prevent it from recording cause or value as such. Its data reflect the results of market-created transactions originated by and for a specific enterprise. The quantitative aspects of these transactions have been attached to the items by actions in the markets. It should be considered as beyond the function of accounting to add to or deduct from this quantitative aspect of transaction data.

If causation comes in question, accounting cannot offer answers. If value comes in question, the initiative does not lie with accounting. Value increment or decrement call for subjective predictions. It should be considered beyond the functional limits of accounting to formally record predictions. To do so would give unilateral subjective data the impression of data bargained into existence in the markets. Internal remarshaling of exchange-priced transaction data should be carried out with the highest possible fidelity to the recorded transaction experience.

Index adjusted depreciation, injected as account data, would also be an action pressing accounting technology beyond its function. Index depreciation not pressed into the accounts, but shown as supplementary and interpretative data, would do no violence to that function. This would be a logical way of helping data users to penetrate further toward an understanding of causation and thoughts around expectations when considering future decisions. Expectations, thus viewed, need to be taken into consideration, but it is unrealistic to believe they can be adequately incorporated into the accounts or financial statements along with transaction experience.

Stated directly, in order to be faithful to its functional objectives, accounting must be dedicated to the use of data that has been determined with thorough and convincing objectivity. That dedication would be put in doubt if unrealized expectations and unilateral modifications of actual transaction experience were permitted to cloud the message lodged in experience data that reflects the results of management intentions implemented by overt actions in the markets. In fact, even unclouded experience-data carefully marshaled into the accounts cannot automatically answer the questions to be faced before future decisions are made. The data of prior transaction experience will still need to be studied against a background of mentally reviewed conditions and intentions, which influenced prior decisions toward the transactions creating the account data. The difficulty of accomplishing such a review of the intangibles underlying prior transactions is great; but outright re-pricing of account data cannot prove a substitute. Yet, pressure in that direction persists.

Two elements have been mentioned, which have brought into accounting literature various suggestions for modifying its basic techniques. One is a growing awareness of price inflation, often considered as reflecting fluctuation in the purchasing power of the dollar. The other is the existence of a statistical technique for simplifying complex price data into an index series indicating relative change in prices. Both of these concepts have been under discussion for the possible use in the calculation of depreciation expense.

A price level index begins with an averaging of prices, year by year, for a mixed variety of goods and services. These computed averages are then regrouped as percentage variations from a selected base year. The effect, probably charted as well as tabulated, is a symbolic pattern suggesting the degree and direction of change in general prices. Using such an index series to aid in calculating depreciation, however, cannot produce expense figures speaking of enterprise actual experience. The figures would be quite hypothetical; they would result from certain assumptions and would be no more factual, except in a purely mathematical sense, than its underlying assumptions. Behind an index series lies an assumption that this calculation can dependably represent a complexity of individual price movements over time. Furthermore, behind the use of an index series to calculate depreciation lies an assumption that depreciation expense is intended to represent a revenue charge expressive of contemporary asset cost, as if the productive assets had been recently acquired.

The economic environment represented by market prices is not stationary; moreover, average prices can only represent an abstract action of a changing total comprised of many differing details. Knowledge of price movements of specific goods and services relevant to a given business will influence management decisions much more directly than general price movements would. Moreover, it surely will be evident that neither new prices nor average prices can affect the prices of transactions previously consummated under previous conditions. It would therefore seem clear that only prior transaction costs could realistically represent enterprise actual quantitative experience, and that only such experience can report on enterprise transaction history. This is to say that, for accounting purposes, modified history is not trustworthy history.

The abstract character of a price index series arises in an overgeneralization of the specific into a highly compressed representation of a complex whole. Such figures brought directly or indirectly into the accounts would give the impression of being transaction-based, quantitative elements of enterprise history derived from decisions of management, but this is not the case. Any proposal for modifying the account data of actual transaction experience by application of a price index series can raise a number of questions.

Some of these questions could be stimulated by the facts of economic life related to money. For example, would a substantial increase in the supply of money, such as currency and bank deposits, affect price averages and thus influence a price index series? How can a new increase in the supply of money increase the contribution to new products made by fixed assets already possessed? Would productive assets, which are possessed and appraised upward in a time of rising replacement prices, create an increase in the cost of products derived from those assets? Could fixed asset contribution to production (i.e., chargeable depreciation) be expressed in the accounts as cost-price amortization? Could an appraised value increase be separately and gradually charged against surplus? Would the contra account to that appraisal increase in the asset account have to be a credit to some surplus account?

What belief, assumption, or hypothesis would underlie depreciation expense as a factor in income calculation if asset revaluation or index adjustment were involved? Would it be persuasive or compelling to believe that voluntary and unilateral increases in depreciation expense would be necessary to justify and secure an increase in selling prices and revenue? Can it be assumed that the market would not accept a sales price increase unless depreciation expense was first increased? Or that acceptance in the market of an increased selling price would affect the recapture, for the enterprise, of a part of the replacement price of the asset being consumed? Or that such recapture could not take place from a new selling price without an accompanying increase in depreciation expense? Is it assumed that index depreciation, in a time of rising price-levels, would realistically reduce calculated net income or taxable income? Would the Internal Revenue Service accept index-based depreciation if such calculation was generally accepted among businesses? Would this hold true both when pricings are rising *and* falling?

It is difficult to believe that index depreciation, even if generally accepted and widely used, could mitigate monetary inflation. Could it mitigate inflation on the scale of the German experience in the early 1920s? Or the inflation of the type witnessed in the United States in the late 1920s? The problem is that index depreciation expense is a type of valuation action; it is related to expectations. It is therefore less realistic than depreciation expense calculated on assets, which are based on prior invested cost experience. If expectations must be made quantitative and specific, it would seem more reasonable to make disclosure through reserves out of surplus or by supplementary information, than by outright modifications of experience-data directly derived from prior transactions.

This brings the argument back to the functional logic of accounting. This logic directs a reporting of experience; it does not support mixing data from expectations with data out of actual experience. Supplementary data, because of their own broad objectives, are not bound by the limitations inherent in the functional logic of accounting technology. Hence, supplementary reporting may appropriately include data of expectations. As such, index depreciation, being related to expectations, can be reported in supplementary statements but it does not have a logical place in the accounts or in the usual financial statements.

It may be significant that index depreciation is being discussed in the literature against a background of rising price-levels and high income tax rates. If consistency is a virtue, which it is sometimes is said to be, index depreciation should also be proposed against a background of falling prices. This has not been the case. It would also be unreasonable to assume that there will be an unending upward trend of prices or that all prices are similarly affected by changing economic conditions. And it would be equally unreasonable to assume there is or should be a positive power within our government to preserve a continuous upward trend of prices and rate of growth in the economy.

Advocacy of index depreciation could be, to some degree, more persuasive if it was accompanied by proposals for another remodeling of depreciation accounting if (when) price-levels turned downward. Under falling prices, index depreciation would involve decreased charges to products and, through cost of sales, lower charges against revenue. If the revenue flow could be maintained, the lower depreciation expense would influence net income upward. But if prices in the selling market fell in proportion to declines in the price index series, then the calculated net income might not benefit from lower index depreciation. A faster fall in selling prices could further reduce profit margins. It should be noted, however, that depreciation on cost under these conditions might put profits under even greater tensions.

To the extent that depreciation expense can be adjusted at will – before, after, or concurrent with change in price-levels – depreciation accounting can become an instrument of managerial policy. Yet, the logical functioning of accounting technology would direct that depreciation expense should represent allocations to products (ultimately a charge against revenue) based on enterprise actual experience; that is, allocation against revenue of investments in cost-efforts made with the intention of generating further revenue. As such, depreciation accounting held in harmony with the functional logic of accounting would affect the pattern of earnings differently but consistently under rising *and* falling price-levels. Under extreme conditions, idle equipment, because of the lack of product sales, would not be contributing to production. At that point, calculated depreciation would represent a loss.

This would precipitate a question whether or not loss is a proper element to be matched against revenue in the revenue-production effort.

Perhaps the connotation of the older term "profit and loss accounting" still influences the modern technique of computing enterprise net income. Perhaps "loss" is still conceived as decrement and "profit" as an increment, which in turn have provided a springboard toward advocacy of recognizing in the accounts increments and decrements evidenced by current market prices alone. This is not to argue, however, that current market prices are without significance. Falling market prices for goods, which are offered by or needed by an enterprise, is indeed a warning signal to management. But it should be clear that the initial impact is upon decision-actions (managerial policy) rather than on the account data of prior experience. Enterprise transaction history has not been changed by the signal.

Let us return to the fact that index depreciation will result in mixing data from expectations with data of prior experience and, in the process, dilute the significance of both. Yet, some argue that the injection of a depreciation adjustment is a means for revealing a subdivision between profit caused by a rise in price-levels and that caused by management decision-actions. But more is inherent in this argument than a need for an analysis of causation. The argument assumes that current price changes are a direct cause of profit, even though goods in possession have not yet moved out of possession. It assumes that management actions have only moderate effects on profits. The latent argument is that profit from foresighted buying (i.e., before a rise in price-levels) is due to economic conditions rather than management judgment. Conversely, it also means that a loss from unwise buying (i.e., before a fall in price-levels) is due to economic conditions and not management ineptness.

Adjustments of the kind described above miss the point. The principal service of account data comes from the insight they can offer to the results of management's decision-actions. Both the management and the investor are interested in such insight. The results of prior market actions by management are not realistically made visible by present or future prices. This showing can be made only after prior effort-actions are systematically compared with accomplished results (revenues). Unlimited opportunity is available thereafter to analytically interpret this data.

Such an interpretation will be subjective and will vary with the interpreter. Relatively little of all the information needed by the data user can be appropriately brought within the pattern of accounting technology because of its functional limitations. This reason alone should pinpoint the central issue now facing accounting: whether the key objective is the reporting of enterprise transaction experience or the attempt to reflect enterprise expectations through use of the established techniques of this technology. And, unfortunately, some aspects of present procedure and some parts of contemporary accounting literature seem to indicate preference for mixing these two objectives. This risks pressing accounting techniques toward new patterns and, in effect, challenges the existence, significance, and influence of the functional logic for accounting.

In accounting, as elsewhere, a complex set of objectives exists and, with these, a complex of technical actions. Where concepts of ends and means fall into controversy, the easy way is to seek compromises of the resulting dilemmas. Here, expediency tends to overshadow logic by offering a seemingly attractive middle way. This is probably a mistake.

The hard way will take longer but may be more rewarding in the end. In order to reduce the pull of the expedient, several factors should be carefully explored before technical changes in accounting technology are instituted. One might explore the relative use and consequences of reporting on actual enterprise experience through presently well-established techniques, operating within limitation imposed by functional logic and supplemented with collateral analytical non-experience information. One might then contrast such an approach to one that mixes, in the accounts and reports, enterprise experience together with present expectations and forecasted possible future scenarios. After the probable consequences of each approach have been thoroughly explored, other approaches might also be examined.

Several factors would be involved in evaluating these different approaches. One would have to consider the relative persuasiveness of accounting, working within the limits of its functional logic, its customary usage, as well as its greater freedom to include interpretative valuations. One would also have to consider the relative ability of users of enterprise data to extract significant meaning from functionally logical account data and from interpretative valuation data as well as the relative flexibility of accounting concepts and techniques and of statistical concepts and techniques to individual intentions.

The major objective of both accounting and statistics is to make data more understandable. Yet, each undertakes to accomplish this end in different ways. If the technical actions of one are borrowed into the other, a dilution of effectiveness is likely to follow. The injection of statistical averages into accounting offers one such example. Averages generalize and compact the relevant facts. But correctness of classification rather than generalization is a necessary characteristic of accounting; whereas, offering an aid for generalizations is a specific objective of statistics. As such, it becomes obvious that the two methodologies do not blend well; their individual characteristics would persist and clash.

If the influential concepts of accounting objectives are broadened to embrace some reporting on expectations, the stage will be set for further modification of existing accounting practices. In time, this may proceed far enough to contravene accounting's natural limits and its service actions. Since strongly desirable objectives provide the basis for organizing appropriate means logically toward those ends, a highly important problem in need of consideration is that of finding the most compelling major and minor objectives for accounting. These would be those objectives judged more appropriate than their alternative or subordinate objectives. After this has been established, one would have to consider the most suitable means, existing or conceivable, to reach those objectives. But here we need to be cautious. The existence of an attractive technical device, such as index series, should not dictate acceptance of an objective, such as reporting expectations through the accounts, which would be tailored, so to speak, to make use of that technical device.

The essence or functional logic of accounting is found in the fact that objectives are the compelling and limiting elements directly affecting the choice of suitable techniques. As such, a strong element of desirability inherent in particular outcomes is vital to the choice of the means to achieve those outcomes. It therefore follows that a selected means is not suitable just because of its own characteristics or perfection of pattern. It is only suitable because of the consequences emerging from its consistent use in furthering the associated objective and outcomes.

To conclude, the name "functional logic" is a useful term because of the relationship described above. Creating and preserving such a relationship in accounting may be difficult. The most desirable objectives may be difficult to formulate convincingly; the most suitable means of achieving those ends may fall into debate. Nevertheless, concentrating on high desirability as to major objectives, and on high appropriateness as to ways and means, will prove, in the end, to have provided a path well worth exploring and suggested ends and means well worth defending, because of their specific appropriateness.

NOTE

1. Littleton is presumably referencing the economist Irving Fisher, who notoriously argued that the American economy had reached "a permanently high plateau" just before the Wall Street Crash of 1929 (Tobin, 2008).

3

IDEAS MOTIVATE ACTION

ABSTRACT

Exchange-priced transactions should be recognized and treated as items of enterprise experience, which should be summarized for later review. This is so because the major objective of accounting technology is to aid men to understand the results of enterprise management's decisions. This, in turn, is based on compelling concepts that invite certain conclusions and limitations that direct certain exclusions. Intentions, purpose, and objectives lie at the heart of transactions and their nature is an aspect of the logic of accounting actions.

Not all research is experimental or related to the study of natural elements and the forces of nature. Men's ideas and ways of using ideas deserve exploration. Ideological research related to accounting should be given consideration for several reasons. When actions, in accounting or in other areas, fall into controversy, the ideas behind them need clinical examination. Scrutiny, here, may uncover persuasive logic that is a characteristic feature of enterprise capital-income accounting. This, however, does not imply an inherent logic, conscientiously built-in by early innovators. Whatever functional logic that may be found would have evolved, as did the methods, bit by bit out of contemporary circumstances and use experience and, perhaps, quite unperceived.

Central to that evolutionary development would be enterprise exchange-priced transactions, recognized as being items of experience that should be summarized for later review. In addition, central to the emerging techniques would be information-collecting categories to make accumulating enterprise experience more readily reviewable. An unpremeditated logic would be implicit in this development. Transactions were means toward achieving enterprise ends, long before that relationship was recognized as a logical association whose reason for being could be tested by the study of the significance of the results of the actions taken. Account-categories served as means toward one of management's objectives, namely to gain knowledge of the results of prior decisions and, thus, to learn from experience.

A significant characteristic of any category is indicated by the conceptual boundaries associated with it. A transaction would be recognizable as a unit of action because it is designed to differentiate itself from other transactions. An account would be even more clearly a category, whose conceptual boundaries would be constructed to both exclude and include. Those boundaries would limit classification actions constructively; that is, to serve as means toward the end of making understandable, in review, certain effects on the enterprise from management's decision to engage in specific transaction events.

Even in the early days, such conceptual boundaries would have provided discernible lines for separating effects logically associated with a given business enterprise from irrelevant effects not so associated. This is so because logic has always called for ends to be supported by appropriate means. Objectives (ends) therefore foster the use and, if necessary, invention of suitable actions. The objective of reviewing experience would logically support the creation and use of account-categories to organize transaction experience to aid that review.

The modern need for ideological research stems from controversy over accounting actions. Beneath many differences of opinion will be found some examples of illogic and some indications of disregard for the significance of category boundaries. Frequently, such violations of functional logic are considered "exceptions." A familiar expression is "exceptions prove the rule." This should only mean to "put the rule to the test of satisfactory use." Few tests would be more convincing than that outlined by functional logic. Expediency or convenience may often have appeal, but seldom can either one lend support stronger than that indicated by applicable logic.

The problem is that it is a characteristic of modern accounting that many of its conceptual boundaries are not tight enough to prevent infiltration or high enough to prevent scaling. Exceptions, variations, and deviations manage to illogically vault or squeeze under boundaries and, in so doing, mix with logical elements that do belong inside these boundaries. A considerable volume of such trespass, or significant amounts of dilution, would increase the misunderstandings to which accounting is already subjected. It is my hope that the development and use of more logically based techniques could reduce and, perhaps, eliminate illogical data from all accounting categories.

Paradoxically, the presence of exceptions and deviations in accounting actions may ultimately prove to have served a useful purpose, quite above any that could come from expediency itself. The recognition of variations also leads to the recognition of the need of improved logic. As a result, terminology and concepts increasingly filter in from economics, finance, government regulation, and law. This terminology and concepts should be closely appraised, as to their basic connotation and their service in their natural setting, before it is evaluated for its suitability when transplanted into accounting technology. Appraisals of this kind need not necessarily lead to rejection. However, it should produce clearer understanding on both sides of conceptual boundaries. In fact, such an approach is already evident in the continuing development of the literature on accounting theory and in the interest in ideological research indicated within the accounting profession. Those activities all point toward a goal of a better understanding among all interested parties.

The development of higher or broader theories (explanations) of the nature and limitations of accounting could enrich the literature, and through that literature gradually elevate accounting even further above its origin in simple bookkeeping. To accomplish this result will take continuous effort on the part of many individuals. In these undertakings, particular attention should be given to objectives, both large and small as well as broad and specific. It may seem a mere truism to say that the major objective of accounting technology is to aid men to understand a business enterprise and its management. The thought, however, is much more than a truism, definition, assumption, or postulate. It reaches deeply into an area of broad objectives. As a top objective, the idea is supported by man's natural desire to benefit from prior experience. Yet, to benefit from his experience, he must first be able to review that experience.

Although contrary opinion exists, there is good reason to believe that the technical ways and means of accounting is far from imperfect. Real issues with accounting are more likely to be found in its ideology, in particular those parts that are associated with its objectives and sub-objectives. The upside is that the mechanics of modern accounting action is well suited to adjust to whatever ideology shall be found to be rationally in tune with a gradation of rational objectives. What is holding this development back is that the ideas, concepts, and objectives of accounting have not yet been organized into an integrated and sufficient body of doctrine.

Herein lies the present challenge. Accountants have a deep understanding of their technology and the profession has a clear sense of its mission. But an organized philosophy of the mission underlying the technology of accounting is lacking (for one such example in the field of auditing, see Mautz & Sharaf, 1961). But, eventually, a clear analysis of the accounting mission has to be made. This can then be joined with a responsive philosophy of method. These studies need and should not be philosophical in form. Instead, my suggested approach to accounting ideology could, with benefit, be pointed toward the demonstration as to what accounting type of service that is needed and the consideration of the capacity of accounting to render this kind of service. This is to say that the philosophy of the mission would be best focused on concepts of the services needed; that is, services capable of mediating between the actions of enterprise management in markets and the needs men have to know the factual results of those actions.

The basic ideas of accounting objectives (mission) would be those appropriate to supporting a technology long dedicated to performing actions that dependably and systematically organize decision. This technology derives transaction data toward intelligible communication. It does not purport to be infallible, all-inclusive, or strive to provide the sole answer to men's need to understand and to act based on that understanding. But, before accounting ideology can be organized into an interrelated whole, many separate ideas, concepts, and objectives must be found, stated, justified, and classified. As such, it may prove a useful approach for basic research to look beneath a variety of objectives related to helping men to understand a business enterprise and the results of management activities.

It is part of man's nature to have capacity to know, to learn from experience, and to take present action based on this information. The early innovators of accounting must have felt such an urge to learn from the results of their prior actions in business. Out of this kind of urge have come techniques for organizing data, which derive out of and, hence, speak of enterprise experience. Decisions by enterprise management continue to create exchange-priced transactions, and these provide quantitative data regarding prior experience that is indispensable to next decisions.

A philosophy of accounting method should come for the most part from concepts underlying the accounting mission, and from the reasons why accounting techniques can serve those conceptual objectives. It is not enough to describe procedure. Every act of doing should be guided by knowledge of how that act could contribute to specific objectives and, through them, to goals that are more distant. It is therefore clear that method does not exist for its own sake. It focuses a complex set of means toward a complex set of ends. Method provides suitable means, but only to the extent that those means can satisfactorily serve specific ends. As such, to justify its existence, acceptance, and use, each type of action should contribute in recognizable ways and degrees toward fulfillment of the accounting mission.

It is desirable that basic research should look beneath different types of accounting action for clues to their reason for being. No doubt, aspects of the mission would be found reflected to some degree within each type of action. It therefore follows that each justifiable action should be able to survive the test of serving definite objectives better than an alternative action. From this study of relative persuasiveness among alternatives, reasons should emerge capable of indicating why familiar accounting actions have, or proposed actions would have, capacity to contribute to the success of the basic accounting mission; that is, the making of a business enterprise and its management's achievements understandable to interested parties.

Much exploration is needed, such as searching beneath method to uncover ideas, concepts, objectives, and achievements. I refer to this as the most basic or fundamental research and the results would be rewarding. Among other things, such research should demonstrate that accounting is at its base more logical than traditional and that its logical framework is less subject to nonsensical changes than is our own customary framework. In so doing, research of this kind would seek to make clear the significance of accounting objectives at all levels and explore its limitations. But basic research might well be extended further. Research of audit procedures, for instance, could investigate the extent to which the method of accounting, in a given case, was in close alliance with the accounting mission.

The actions of professional men are seldom routine; the exercise of good judgment is expected of them in all situations. Their education, training, and experience would equip professional accountants to engage in constructive study of the alliance of mission and method. And this good judgment would grow best out of experience in making judgments. As such, it may be noted that a broader base could exist for developing professional judgment than one consisting only of postulate-based principles. Good judgment itself, and the ability to justify a given decision, could well be associated with a deep understanding of the conceptual objectives behind the technical actions of accounting and with clear recognition of the compelling limitations that circumscribe these actions, both at the recording and professional level.

On the other hand, a capacity to exercise good judgment is not expanded by accepting guidance from custom or rules. And the roots of these judgments lie deeper than assumptions and postulates can reach. First, good judgment will need to draw upon a comprehensive understanding of the capabilities and limitations of accounting ideology and techniques. Second, it needs to rest on a clear comprehension of the influence on actions of both close and distant objectives. Third, it must utilize awareness of the significance for enterprise management of events and accomplishments, which can best be made factually evident through account data.

The superstructure of actions is readily perceived, but the necessary foundational piers of complex and rational ideology are not so easily detected. Yet, if one is to understand the capacity of the structure, the service functions of the foundations must be understood. Those supporting piers – the basic objective of accounting – have been strongly influenced by the evolving service function of the superstructure. In other words, the character of the objectives, which support accounting actions, have been fortified, not by definition or assumption, but from the needs of the times, early and modern, which pressed for creation and development of accounting as a constructive means toward recognized goals. And, because technical actions and influential objectives are inseparable, understanding of both, separately and in their interrelations, becomes essential to the exercise of good judgment in the presence of situations involving aspects of accounting.

Basic concepts and compelling limitations give accounting actions their capacity to serve: the concepts invite inclusions and the limitations direct exclusions. It is, for example, difficult to conceive of an enterprise functioning without a human decision center, such as a proprietor or manager. Hence, management of some sort must be considered as an indispensable aspect of an enterprise entity. Accounting actions take place within this complex union of the organization entity and human management. In fact, it is difficult to conceive of accounting as having evolved outside of such a framework. As such, it would be logical to recognize enterprise accounting as being foremost a technical means toward the broad end of aiding enterprise management to operate an enterprise in such ways as to keep it capable of generating services acceptable to society. The relation here, as elsewhere, is a logical relationship. It is that of a desirable end and a means suitable toward achieving that goal. And such logic permeates the interrelations among enterprise, management, and accounting.

The conclusion here is that enterprise accounting is explained and supported by the functional logic inherent in the relation of suitable means serving desirable ends. If this logic is to be ignored or defeated, either the overall ends must be shown to be undesirable or the overall character of accounting technology must be convincingly shown to be unsuited to render its service in aid of management decisions and, through summary reports of the results of these decisions, to render informative service toward decisions in the investment markets.

Returning to the idea of basic research, I believe that assumptions or customs are dispensable guides. There may be other ways of breathing life into fundamental concepts. It may well be that the conceptual structure standing beneath enterprise accounting actions could do much to make this complex technology more widely understandable. This is so because whatever can be known with justifiable conviction about accounting will have little need for being assumed. A handful of basic concepts could be woven into a more convincing pattern of related ideas than that from a hatful of assumptions. Surely, interpretative judgments, rational convictions, and accumulated experience should be involved in this application of interrelated ideas to specific situations.

The concept of enterprise entity is a central idea for enterprise accounting. That concept represents the frame within which specific economic decisions and effective choices among alternatives are made. It is out of these decisions and actions that account data flow, and this data, under review, speak of the decisions-actions that gave them birth. To this objective of reviewing data, the helpfulness of quantification becomes evident. The term refers to figures and symbols produced by typical accounting thought processes, which translate enterprise events (exchange-price transactions) into account data that then become, in effect, enterprise history. Indeed, the transaction is itself a sub-means toward the clear objective of accounting, and through it, a means toward later effective review of prior experience.

Another idea, which is basic to accounting, is the concept of the management function being that of generating transaction events for the enterprise and, in so doing, bargaining these into agreed exchange-prices. In fact, without transactions that reflect managerial decision-actions to serve as the substance of accounting, there would be no accounting in its current form. These relationships would seem to embrace fundamental concepts "so necessary as to be unavoidable," and these would still not take the nature of postulates. If we are to see deeply into researching the character of accounting, as a prelude to justifying the application of accounting to specific situations, these logical relationships will have important significance.

But where does judgment fit into this reasoning? An idea or concept may be necessary in a given situation, and yet the same idea or concept may be effective under varying degrees of necessity in other situations. Hence, judgment is called into play. To be significant is not identical with benign necessary. An expression such as "impossible to do without" may prove, under stress, to be something less than impossible. In this day of synthetic products and nuclear adventuring, many preconceived concepts have been brought under question and sometimes refuted. There is a suggestion here for accounting research: resist the temptation to act on the apparently obvious and concede the apparently necessary only after alternatives, existing or prospective, have been examined thoroughly and critically.

Let us return to the idea of categories. A business enterprise under management is itself a classification category in much the same sense as is an account. Because the enterprise is a category, its transaction history would include only the relevant records of the results of management decision-actions. A fiscal period is another category, and the key to the use of time periods for data classification is found in the concepts of intention, objective, need, and use of the resulting data. As such, operating results are allocated among successive periods of time for convincing reasons. The allocation stems from a tacit acceptance of a concept of improved data significance, gained from it being apportioned over time. And, a time period, in turn, works as a subdivision of the experience of the more basic category of the enterprise entity.

An important aspect of accounting is found in the reason for each category type, their relations among categories, and the relation of all categories to knowable and desirable objectives. Categories, hence accounting of whatever type, are means toward known ends. They take special forms (i.e., have particular limitations), because of their promise of fostering improved understanding and eventually better decision-actions. As categories, accounts include the relevant and exclude the irrelevant. Yet, without association with other accounting categories, management, and exchange-priced transactions, accounts would lose their reason for being. Again, there would be no accounting of the kind that we have today. These interrelated categories are inseparable from accounting because interrelation lies at the heart of accounting function. This does not rest on assumptions, as some would argue.

The implication from this insight is that, in order to grasp the full significance of one group of concepts, it is necessary to understand all others in that pattern of relationships. Awareness of the reasons for the concepts, and recognition of the objectives involved, can be more enlightening than familiarity with typical actions, procedures, and uses. Furthermore, in order to extract the messages inherent in account data, it is necessary to study the relation of accounts to each other, the particular enterprise, and the management intentions inherent in the unending flow of individual transactions. This gets us close to the essence of the functional logic of accounting. Intention, purpose, and objectives lie at the heart of transactions. It is the function of accounting, by its technical use of a variety of categories, to help the effects intended in the transactions to become elements in enterprise experience and evidence of management's overt actions. By organizing elements of actual experience, account data will provide a platform from which to begin to plan toward next decisions.

It is clear that a platform of prior experience will be an aid to decisions. To be sure, judgment – a sense of timing and informed opinions as to the probable shape of things to come – will also be elements in a final decision to act in and for the enterprise in certain ways. But it is significant that many of these factors are not aspects of accounting. They do not modify or justify modifying past transaction experience. However, they do influence management's appraisal of the results of prior actions taken for the enterprise. Such appraisal may stimulate corrective action through policy, transaction, or product type changes. Review of results from prior action, however, will not provide a logical base for direct modification of recorded historical facts resulting from overt transactions entered upon in good faith.

4

OBJECTIVITY OF ACCOUNT DATA

ABSTRACT

Current prices, future estimates, and price statistics cannot reflect specific transaction experience generated by enterprise management. Instead, overt transaction data in accounts continue to constitute evidence of management decision-actions, even after apportioned among fiscal periods. And the interrelation of enterprise capital employed productively, and the income generated by its use, will continue whether or not accounts are kept. Yet, the significance of factual integrity for enterprise transaction experience is strongly influenced by the functional logic inherent in accounting.

For accounting, objectivity is a recognized goal and such a known goal need not be postulated. It is true; however, that objectivity is an ideal and not completely attainable nor is it clearly revealed by generally accepted practices. Even so, there are at least two reasons supporting a belief that "objectivity" has a rational connotation for accounting. First, the actual transaction experience of an enterprise provides a highly useful springboard toward next decisions. Second, in order to be most helpful, enterprise transaction experience (account data) should be kept as pure as possible and be communicated as clearly as possible in that condition. Fidelity to these two guides will serve the interpretative needs of users of account data well. The lessons made available, from the study of the actual experience of an enterprise, would also be more obscured than illuminated by intermixed non-experience.

As is the case for most terms having technical significance, "objectivity" may be variously defined. A definition of this term, suitable for treating the named concept as a postulate, would lean away from a strong to a weaker test. The realization and validation from action in the markets by a given enterprise would be replaced by available and convenient substitute price figures retrieved outside the enterprise in question.

The latter concept might use such terms as unbiased and verifiable by another competent observer. Yet, this phrasing opens a wide door. The thought is appropriate only in reference to knowable facts outside the enterprise experience. Facts within and relevant only to the given enterprise can seldom be verified by another observer. Actual prior transactions are not widely open to the view of outsiders. The same can be said of the allocation of the effects of these transactions over successive fiscal periods. The Certified Public Accountant is the only outside observer with opportunity to verify the transaction experience of the enterprise and the allocation of data among periods, together with the organized communication made through financial statements.

Yet, many outside parties have an interest in judging a given enterprise and its management. Often, they would like information that neither summarized transaction experience, accounting technology, nor an audit could supply. The reason is clear. The desired additional information is usually in the area of valuations or interpretations. But such information is not part of the experience of the enterprise. At best, it would represent a subjective opinion regarding values such as current market prices, future estimates, and average price statistics. Such data, however useful in themselves, can scarcely be as significant of management's intentions as the account data reflecting the overt transaction experience of the given enterprise.

Objectivity is indeed a vital concept for accounting, and it should not be treated lightly. Yet, the word represents a complex concept, especially within its accounting context. An idea pointing toward the development of separate techniques for interpreting reported experience data and for an organized reporting on enterprise experience, can be noted in a book chapter on income measurements by Alexander (1950). Alexander pointedly contrasted factual data, objectivity achieved by accounting, to the subjectivity of the judgments that followed, which are the responsibility of businessmen studying those data. A strongly persuasive statement made there is that the division between objective accounting data and subjective judgment is well justified. So, too, is another thought in the extract: since accounting as such seeks to avoid subjective judgments, its reported data fall short of the ideal; that is, the ideal or complete basis for managerial and investor decisions.

Here emerges a fundamental issue: can the ideal be appropriately achieved within the boundaries of a technology whose pattern of procedure strongly implements a function limited to reporting on enterprise actual transaction experience? Some ideas appearing in the literature since 1950 seem to reflect a desire to move accounting substantially closer to the ideal; that is, toward broadening the accounting function in areas indicated by terms such as *realization*, *measurement*, and *objectivity*. In order to activate this kind of intention, the usual accounting concept of realization would have to be modified and the accounting concept of measurement would have to be broadened. By implication, this would mean that the accounting concept of objectivity would also be completely redefined.

Broadening the usefulness of technical data is a praiseworthy aspiration. But a spotlight focused on "usefulness" of additional, more widely oriented data, may merely illuminate a need or an ideal. This may leave in the shadow a highly significant aspect of account data; that is, the great interpretative value of being able to study data of an enterprise's actual experience. Enterprise account data will have been generated by overt actions in the markets – actions that will reflect management's intentions – expressed in the tangible form of transaction decision-actions. Surely, it is not the most data, but the most factual, dependable, and clearly relevant data that should be preferred as a basis for the interpretative study of management effectiveness.

This is not to argue that management's carefully considered transaction decisions exist in a vacuum. Quite the opposite is true. Decisions are always influenced by non-account data as well as by account data from past actions and results. Every transaction rests on mixed motives, judgments as to the past, and the present as well as the probable trends in the future. The combination of these factors congeals intention into action. But the effects of different motives cannot be disentangled and separately disclosed in the accounts as though motives were transaction experience. This is one of the limitations binding accounting technology to certain action patterns.

In order to support reform in the concept of *objectivity*, the concept of *measurement* would need to be broadened. It is not clear how such a change could strengthen the significant service function of accounting technology; that of reporting factually, convincingly, and rationally on the *results* of management's prior intentions, judgments, and decisions made in and for its enterprise. In fact, if accounting technology were given responsibility for penetrating underneath of overt actions, confirmed in the markets, the reporting of enterprise actual experience would inevitably be in danger of infiltration by non-transaction data. Even though it is intended to provide useful and needed information, and designed to move accounting closer to an ideal, such an attempt could surely compound the difficulty that interested parties already experience in trying to appraise the evidence of enterprise management effectiveness by the examination of an enterprise's actual experience, as reported through the accounts and financial statements.

Considering this issue, it is worth recalling that it is not only the creditor who is concerned with evidence. The pattern of accounting is itself clearly dedicated to the marshaling of data, evidencing decision-actions in and for the given enterprise. The assembled data continue to be evidence even after the data have been apportioned over several fiscal periods by rational and reasonable assignment estimates. And the necessity to use estimates here does not warrant the expansion of the concept of accounting evidence so as to embrace non-transaction data, as if this, too, were from the enterprise's actual experience.

If accounting evidence, originating in overt transactions, is not intended for the use of interpreting prior experience, then the techniques of collecting and processing this data are meaningless. Furthermore, if data organized for subsequent interpretative study lose their objectivity and, thus, their contact with enterprise realities, they thereby lose their power to cooperate appropriately with separate collateral and relevant information toward fostering further rational decisions.

The concept of realization reflects some of the context of "enterprise realities." The word still has strong significance for accounting, because it bids accounting action to wait for stronger evidence than the belief that changes in the economic atmosphere, such rising and falling demand for a product, can signal current inadequacies in an enterprise's experience recorded in the accounts. The term "inadequacy" in this context asserts not error in the data's origin but a disbelief in the use of prior transaction experience as evidence. What is to replace this data derived from actual experience? Are current price movements in present markets or statistical averages valid substitutes? My argument is that such data may be significant, but they cannot possibly constitute evidence of action by the management of a particular enterprise taken.

Let us return to two other terms. "Objectivity" and "realization" are significant terms for accounting because the concepts symbolized by the two words limit the message of account data to evidence that is objective, concrete, and unmistakably made relevant to a given enterprise by actions of its management. Evidence not conceived in this way would only be a type of appraisal; that is, an example of second-guessing or a willful change of a fact of an enterprise's experience. Under pressure of subjective opinion, this change of fact might seem supported by externally created price data, statistical averages, or price level indices. But this would be a thin support at best. It could provide interpretative clues supplementing accounting evidence, but it could scarcely be a part of accounting evidence.

From the accounting point of view, money figures associated with a transaction event merely provide one of two elements needed as a basis for the record. One element to be recognized is the nature of the effect of the event on the enterprise; the other is the quantitative representation of the same event – a necessary element for making informative arithmetic calculations closely tied to the accumulating experience of that enterprise. Each transaction therefore acquires some of the characteristics of an individual category, with either a positive or a negative relation with other categories involved in accounting technology. It is evident that recognized interrelations among categories are an indispensable prerequisite for rationally operating this technology toward its objectives. Such a complexity of interrelations can scarcely be effectively represented by assumptions.

The interrelations, limitations, and characteristic of enterprise accounting exist as evolutionary facts. They have not been blueprinted toward the construction of a technology. Instead, they have evolved out of men's need for knowledge of enterprise transaction experience. They were implemented by the ingenuity of men, conceiving, little by little, suitable techniques gradually woven into interlocked patterns of actions. This marvel is enterprise accounting.

Other highlights of this pattern can be noted in the integration of real accounts – capital and the stem of the tree – and nominal accounts – income and the fruits of the three. Another part can be seen in the very early recognition of a significant dualism inherent in every transaction. Here, an intention to affect the enterprise and a persuasive consideration enlisting another party to help in generating that effect becomes associated through a transaction.

These aspects of transactions are not accounting. This technology has been created in order to make effective use of these *antecedent* characteristics. It is rash oversimplification to tie these phenomena of exchange to the phrase "give and receive." This is a window too small to permit real insight into accounting. In addition, perhaps it is rather unnecessary specifically to postulate economic exchange as part of the environment of accounting. Exchanges have been commonplace over many centuries; in fact, exchanges as facts of economic life are far older than the simplest aspects of accounting technology. As such, there is no need to postulate that people actively engaging in exchanges or the existence of exchangeable goods that are attractive to people.

In order to modify the concept of objectivity into a new accounting connotation, the concept of "measurement" will also have to be changed out of its established connotation in accounting. Two elements within the term "to measure" are significant: a concept of quantification and a concept of unit of measure (stable or changing). The resources and activities of a business enterprise are so diverse that great varieties of "quantities" are involved. As a result, the initial exchange prices of resources and services are uniformly used to reduce the varieties to a common base so each can be used in the arithmetical computations necessary in business. The marshaling of these quantitative data into totals and remainders is an important part of the contribution made by accounting technology. But this technical contribution is not without hazard.

The unit of measure is the dollar. But the quantitative accounting representation of the event is the *dollar-price* bargained into a transaction event by the independent parties of the exchange. The account record therefore reflects two concepts: that of an agreed price and that of local money. A hazard arises from the fact that the monetary sign ($ in the United States) is indicated or implied before each entry in an account. Hence, some readers of account figures will think of "price" as related to the intentions of the parties in the transactions. Some will even think, especially with respect to totals, that the digits represent present equivalent amounts of "money." The latter thought almost automatically merges into the idea of an equivalent amount of "value."

This drift in thinking is understandable but nonetheless a mistake. *Price* is seldom clearly recognized as quite different from *value*. The former is objective; its size and digits have been attached to an event by mutual agreement of the parties to the exchange. The latter term is subjective; each party has a different idea of the value the exchange has for him. If this were not so, the parties would not have engaged in an exchange to begin with. An account therefore cannot express value as such. The value of an item in possession can only be proved by an actual exchange—a newly bargained determination by independent parties. Short of this event, "valuing" will remain a unilateral and subjective judgment. On the other hand, a transaction price recorded in an account has earmarks of concrete reality; that is, of a verifiable event in enterprise history. That price has become a historical fact. It is not such a fact by unilateral opinion. This is to say that the record of the fact speaks of experience and not of opinion.

The hazard that account data must face comes from the fact that peoples will tend to think that the price tags on merchandise in a store window will express values. In that situation, the technical distinction between price and value may not be important. But the distinction for accounting can be important, particularly in its relation to the accounting function. Since value is a subjective concept and accounting functions must be definitely objective (i.e., concerned with enterprise actual experience), only data expressive of exchange-bargained prices can serve such a function. Data reflecting only value (hypothetical or other people's prices) cannot serve this technical function.

At this point, "value of money" enters the picture, for the concept represented by this phrase adds to the hazard faced by accounting. The argument for the significance to accounting of this idea is as follows: (1) accounting must use the dollar as a measuring unit for quantifying transactions. (2) If the value of the measuring unit has changed, this fact is not revealed by accounts still stated in terms of exchange-priced transaction dollars. (3) The user of the data might be misled if the accounts and/or the financial statements do not reveal this effect. (4) This result would flow from the fact that calculated income by use of historical cost will fail to show what part of that "income" was attributable to changes in the purchasing power of money and what part that was attributable to enterprise management, through policies, decisions, and actions.

Such a line of thinking seems prompted by a theory that accounting could and should be modified in the direction of clearly indicating the extent to which economic causation (especially change in conditions) was responsible for the operating results of the enterprise. This is indeed a novel proposal, and the heart of the thought lies in the concepts of money and quantification.

It is appropriate to consider a money price as a common denominator, and it can be useful in making arithmetically homogenous a diversity of goods and services. But it is questionable whether, with respect to completed transactions, this characteristic service is lost because prices in the markets have changed. The value of money may change because the supply of that "commodity" may change. Frequently, an increase in the supply of money is a consequence of policies and actions by government. It is questionable, however, whether statistics can so convincingly demonstrate changes in the value of money to justify dividing the figure for enterprise net income in order to report separately on this change in money-value and managerial effectiveness.

Money can also appropriately be called a medium of exchange. But it is questionable whether money-price symbolized in the accounts should be considered as "measuring value" within the domain of accounting. No doubt, money, as a circulating medium, does facilitate the exchange of goods. There is no question that the money price, associated with an actual exchange transaction of a given enterprise, can symbolize an economic potential, visualized by both parties engaged in that transaction. It is doubtful, however, that the subjective side of the transaction can confer on the emerging account figures the connotation of value. Those transaction figures can speak only of price.

Actions in the markets are offered and accepted as steps toward the fulfillment of specific intentions of the transaction parties. Consummated intentions become enterprise transaction history. The agreed transaction price becomes a quantitative expression of efforts to accomplish certain intentions. The *value* for each party of the originating intention, and of the resulting transaction event, is not knowable until subsequent consequences become known. Between that later time and the date of the transaction event, the figures in the accounts do not speak of *value*. They only tell of the effort applied given preliminary intentions.

This leads to the argument that figures in accounts can reveal significant factual data, but only provided that these are recognized as representing enterprise objective experience and not subjective appraisal values. As such, the strong tendency to emphasize the quantitative and measurement side of transaction events must be dampened. The money aspect has been permitted to overshadow the intended and continuing effect of the event. The latter aspects have much significance. It is the effect, not the money figure, which speaks of intentions, decisions, and actions. Measurement is secondary; accounting need not seek to match the search for refinement of measuring techniques found in the natural sciences.

The transaction effect, not money symbols, becomes enterprise experience. In the markets, money is a lubricant facilitating exchange. For accounting, money is a medium of exchange. In accounting, it can be confusing to think or to convey the impression of believing that money measures changing values. It is in economics, not in accounting, that thought turns often to judging probable values of the future. It is for management, not accounting, to direct thought toward realistic appraisal of the results of prior efforts. Toward this end, accounting can contribute by reporting factually on the cost invested in prior efforts. That cost does not speak of value but of investment. Management's own evaluation weighs the accomplishments against the costs and risks to produce results.

Let us return to another term. It is the present fashion to think of the dollar as being a "unit of measure." Some readers of that phase may interpret it toward measuring "value." This can easily introduce confusion. It would be more realistic to avoid the phrase, or at least to interpret the words and the relevant figures, as measuring "price" or "risked investment." The basic issue lies beneath two interpretations of the "unit of measure:" (1) the account data should express the transaction experience of a given enterprise in terms of exchange-priced cost; (2) the data should be modified, after the fact, away from overt cost and toward current values. This issue lies close to the heart of research in accounting theory.

In a few exceptional situations, valuations become necessary, such as during the purchase and sale of a business, bargaining a merger into existence, and liquidating a going concern in bankruptcy. But exceptional situations should not provide precedents for usual situations. The comparison of two balance sheets of appraised values could produce a net figure suggesting a measured "change in enterprise well-being." This mind of calculation may provide interesting information, but it would be merely interpretative and only suggestive of possibilities.

The great contribution made by capital-income accounting would here be ignored. The introduction of nominal accounts centuries ago replaced this technique. The results reported through nominal accounts do not tell of change in well-being or value. They present a view of factors capable of suggesting how management decisions, in the aggregate and under differing surrounding conditions, have contributed to a change in financial status that is discernible in the balance sheet along with the results of other financial decisions by management.

Data from nominal accounts contribute greatly to insight into management effectiveness. This insight is of higher significance than any estimated or appraised "change of welfare" could be. No doubt, changing conditions in the market, competition, and technology will have an impact on the enterprise. But this impact should not be represented through a manipulation of account data from prior transactions. Perceived changes in economic atmosphere may, and should, influence management's next decisions. These decisions will then affect the accounts and the enterprise. Management decision-actions would have more effect on its enterprise than can any decision-actions within other enterprises that are unallied to this concern by overt exchange-priced transactions. Moreover, the results of prior decisions can be known, identified, documented, and reviewed in far greater degree than can effects on the enterprise attributed, hypothetically and statistically, to changing price levels (e.g., decrease in the purchasing power of the dollar). It is by these characteristics that capital-income accounting justifies its mission of generating insight into a business enterprise and its management.

Pressure from money-value concepts on one side, and concepts of actual experience-cost on the other, has evidently generated a gray area between them. This mixing of cost and value in the accounts and financial statements calls for further research. As such, the issue is reaching maturity and we need to ask ourselves whether the gray area should be preserved, expanded, or contracted? If the present mixture of cost and modified cost is unsatisfactory, a choice seems necessary between the alternatives of pure cost consistently held or freely modified account data. Problems would emerge whatever the choice. Careful appraisal of differences would therefore be called for. The main question would not be how to act, but why to act toward one choice as opposed to another. This calls for study of comparative consequences and an application of pragmatic philosophy.

Account data should be held tightly to invested cost, as being fully expressive of enterprise experience and history, as poor account data would open the possibility of infinite modification by extensive application of index series and, in so doing, convert account data into statistical data. Techniques are available to implement either kind of action, but the choice should rest upon the full exploration of why the consequence of one line of action should be judged superior to consequences from the other.

Exploration of alternative consequences is an examination into pragmatic relations within two sets of means and ends. One set is account data that uses strict cost to serve as a means toward providing insight into the experience of a business enterprise. The other is account data that is extensively modified by unilateral judgmental decisions in the direction of reflecting not actual experience but values, having particular interest for decisions in the money markets. One set of objectives could scarcely support reporting experience and non-experience by use of the same technology. If there are, as it seems, two major accounting objectives and two differing major classes of account data users, it would seem advisable to evolve separate techniques to serve different data needs.

A good starting point for research in accounting theory could therefore be the determination of various accounting objectives, for these can provide the key to appraising the need for differing ways and means and to judge between alternative means conceived as possibly available toward a given end. If differing objectives are visualized for a given technique, a convincing judgment becomes necessary as to the relative desirability of each type of objective. Such problems of judgment quickly make it evident that accounting objectives must be limited. Account data cannot be all things to all people.

The basic nature and limits of accounting technology are of high significance. As these aspects become clearer, rationally limited objectives could inspire logically limited techniques within the framework of one technical system. Outside of that system, there would be no logical limit to the variety of types of data communication. This can be a reason for sharply distinguishing (1) techniques for marshaling enterprise data toward compact communications and (2) techniques for extracting meaning from communicated data expressive of enterprise actual experience. Perhaps implicit in distinguishing these two techniques is a need for two quite different types of communications for parties having differing interests and decision problems.

If the two ways of dealing with account data continue to be mixed within the accounting system, pressure for more information will tend to push accounting technology out of its natural and limited area of service and in the direction of evolving into a special type of statistical operation. If a limited function, such as the marshaling of transaction data, were recognized for accounting instead, a wide field of collateral, supplementary, and interpretative arrangements of data would still be available to users.

Mention was made of the integration of real and nominal accounts, as reflecting a very ingenuous implementation of the inescapable interrelation of enterprise capital productivity employed, and the income generated by that employment under management. This close relationship exists whether or not accounts are kept, and it has nevertheless a deep significance for accounting. The balance sheet and income statement constitute a forceful epitome of the conceptual patterns behind them. Those two statements can communicate insight precisely because of the relationships that interrelate enterprise entity, management, management-generated transaction experience, special characteristics of individuals, exchange-priced transactions, and the functional character of various categories for assembling account data.

The significance of these interrelations is so important that they might well become the focal center of a very practical evolutionary development; that is, the separation of the actions of marshaling from the actions of interpreting. Once accomplished, this would seem to promise a gradual expansion of the arts of interpretative use of account data, which, in turn, could become a step toward achieving some of the characteristic found in data used in the natural sciences. For, in the natural sciences, there is a sharp distinction between obtaining dependable data and extracting significant meaning from that data. And it seems reasonable to believe that the profession of public accounting would be strengthened by such an evolutionary development. The ethical, procedural, and judgmental features behind the attest function would all benefit from being initially concentrated toward verifying the integrity of enterprise experience data.

Non-attest activities of accountants in public practice could then be rendered based on knowledge, experience, judgment, and in relation to the collateral areas of service.

Experienced professionals would be well equipped by those same factors to extend their collateral service to include the use of various interpretative techniques for extracting meaning from inanimate data. This kind of supplementary and interpretative action is already implied in such terms as "techniques toward decisions" and "operations research." Frequently, such exploratory actions combine the use of account data and non-account data. This fact, however, does not convert interpretative actions into accounting. On the contrary, our understanding of the nature and limits of reported account data (i.e., an enterprise's actual experience) would seem to be a necessary factor aiding the judgments emerging from interpretative studies.

Exploration in depth of the inner nature of accounting ideology and technology could contribute to the continued growth of professional service as well as to administrative accounting. A compelling concept emerges here: the factual integrity of enterprise transaction experience has discernible support from the functional logic inherent in accounting. If such a concept is indeed compelling as a fundamental objective associated with accounting techniques as suitable means, the thought should be accompanied by a corollary: reported account data completed under guidance from this concept should be supplemented by appropriate non-account data in aid of deepening and clarifying the insight now provided by the usual balance sheet and income statement.

PART V

1

THE INTERPRETATIVE FUNCTION☆

ABSTRACT

The attest function of the professional accountant does not include an obligation to interpret the significance that the account data may have for various users. As auditor, he cannot attest the effect price-level changes will have on the certified statements. However, he can assist the client to prepare supplementary disclosures of the resulting changes if the historical accounting figures were modified by systematic application of a price-level index series.

There can be no question that accounting data are able to serve the interpretative needs of business. There may be reason to doubt, however, that the accountant is an interpreter searching for meaning and significance beneath account data. Considering him an analyst, who undertakes to resolve a complex representation into more understandable form, would be closer to the fact.

Accounting has performed an analytical function throughout its centuries of use. It was initially developed to make an enterprise more

☆This chapter has been reproduced courtesy of *INSIGHT Magazine*, The Magazine of the Illinois CPA Society and the successor of *The Illinois Certified Accountant* (for the latest issue, visit www.icpas.org/insight.htm). The original citation for this article is Littleton (1960).

understandable; primarily its chief forces have been, and still are, toward enterprise management. The method has been one of classifying and compressing data of prior enterprise experience. The assembled data are then organized in ways that indicate natural interrelations and contrasts. But those data still await interpretation. Even after critical examination (audit) and certification, the financial statements represent an effort to marshal data analytically.

Within an enterprise, its factual experience may be analytically organized in any way that may aid management in making decisions. This same mass of basic data, however, is not available for interpretative study outside of the enterprise. It may be that this difference in data availability, during the years while professional accounting has been developing, has stimulated a desire to organize financial statements in ways that could cue the reader toward interpretative consideration of various significant data relationships. Certainly, modern statements, in contrast to the earlier presentations, seem to point in this direction.

Is there any limit to this kind of improved communication through financial statements? Must accounting be continually innovated toward more analysis and interpretation? Has not one section of contemporary literature been critical of accounting realism because of a belief that accounting has an underdeveloped interpretative mission?

In some of the literature lies the implication that accounting has contributed to contemporary monetary inflation. To some, a collateral belief is suggested: that reform of accounting procedure (with respect to invested-cost dollars) would influence people in authority to take steps that would mitigate the inflationary trend. On the other hand, it may be that the matter really at issue is not accounting's responsibility for fostering price inflation, but rather a question of the real value of the function of accounting and of the professional accountant.

If it were merely a matter of choosing one setting or another for defining a function, this kind of choice might be thought available: (1) Accounting should be considered a classification apparatus designed to produce, by the analysis of enterprise transactions, certain arrangements of quantitative data which help make the enterprise complex understandable. (2) Accounting methodology should be developed so far as is possible in the direction of meaningful interpretations of enterprise data appropriate to the differing needs of various users. But mere definition is not conclusive.

It is unlikely that any one belief or purpose would have motivated all the contributions to the continuing debate on common-dollar accounting. Instead, a variety of reasons can be conjectured:

1. To help awaken the public to the seriousness of a continuing expansion of the currency and of the rise in price levels.
2. To stimulate constructive consideration of the effects of the ideological, financial, political, and emotional pressures that foster inflation.
3. To show that acceptance of new elements of methodology could further increase the service accounting can render the users of its data.
4. To reveal the impact of changing price levels so forcibly that the prestige of the Internal Revenue Service and the Securities and Exchange Commission would support wide acceptance of modified accounting methodology.

Conjectures, evaluating the results to date, might include such thoughts as the following:

1. Direct reform in ledger account usage was not argued explicitly in the literature, but it was seldom ruled out and sometimes implied.
2. Various types of inflation impact disclosure were suggested, the simplest being use of footnotes and the most comprehensive being use of full scale supplementary financial statements (for the latter approach, see Paton, 1920).
3. One of the simpler types of disclosure of the inflation impact upon depreciation charges has been accepted by the Securities and Exchange Commission for some recent financial statements (see Letter to the Editor, 1959). By agreeing to certain statement amendments, the Commission has shown a disposition to accept the appropriation of net income method and to disapprove depreciation adjustments in the computation of net income.

It is clear that debate can stimulate a variety of ideas; rational judgment and satisfactory choices among alternatives can follow. Therefore, it may be reasonable to believe that this debate may have played a part (though still immeasurable) in stimulating a public awareness, such as now seems to be growing, of the dangers of cumulative monetary inflation. It seems doubtful; however, whether many readers were impressed by implications, observable here and there in the literature, that accounting methodology as such possesses the power to effectively modify an inflationary trend through self-reform.

A matter less evident than the fact of present monetary inflation also lies unperceived beneath this debate. As was indicated in earlier paragraphs, this involves the question whether two techniques – that of analytically marshaling data and that of interpreting meaning from those data – have become unwisely intermixed in accounting during its significant growth over the past fifty years.

As interest in accounting research continues to grow, consideration of underlying fundamentals in addition to "postulates and conventions" would seem very appropriate. If analysis and interpretation are different, as seems quite likely, their continued intermixing seems to invite confusion concerning the limits of the accounting function. Even if the two were ultimately judged as separate phases of one function, each phase would have a distinct contribution to make. As a result, each should be separately recognized; each should become an integral part of the training for accounting careers.

Some recent thoughts by Professor William A. Paton appear to lend support to the idea of further consideration of interpretation as a technique. He writes that management may sometime find it necessary:

> ...[to] develop staffs of economic analysts who can stand between them and their accountants and do the job of converting and interpreting the raw heterogeneous data of conventional reports ... furnish certain types of interpretations of the underlying financial data. (1959, pp. 41–42)

It steadily becomes more obvious that the mere accumulations of data in ledger accounts and the communication of the compressed essence of account data (balance sheets and income statements) are not enough. The task remains for management internally, and investors externally, to extract from the total data available to them such understanding of the enterprise as may help them make wise decisions regarding their respective problems.

It is clear that accounting operates within limits; it cannot be all things to all men. Accounting is a service technology, but it is not a service in the sense of being able to furnish those figures that one would most like to see. A significant limitation lay in the fact that accounting must present dependable figure-symbols to the interpreter. Accounting cannot provide the symbols and, at the same time, penetrate the significance of the pattern made by these symbols to all interested parties.

The usual financial statements are analytical patterns of symbols; they are familiar yet in need of careful interpretation. The idea of supplementary statements, stated in terms of current dollars, is nearly forty years old and has been studied intensely in recent years; they offer a promising interpretative adjunct to the financial statements. That so little use has been made of this device in official company reports, and that no published reasons for this hesitation have appeared in the literature, is puzzling.

Some part of accounting research activities might be directed toward throwing some light on this matter of mixing the analytical marshaling of financial and operating data with the interpretative extracting of meaning from those data. Perhaps there are, in fact, two types of techniques here. Perhaps differently trained personnel should manage each technique: people trained in business and accounting and people trained in economics and statistics. Should the functions be separated, combined, or coordinated? Should people, trained in different areas, also become thoroughly trained in the technology of the other party?

The basic techniques of accounting may seem purely statistical in nature to some people. This invites the belief that its statistical operation could easily be expanded and made increasingly interpretative, but there is another side. The apparently statistical techniques of accounting deal with the preparation of data for subsequent interpretation as opposed to the actual interpretation. These accounting techniques include transaction analysis, category integration, data organization and communication, as well as audit and certification. These techniques are not necessarily statistical in nature.

The limiting controls that form part of accounting are very significant aspects of this technology. The raw data are objective if restricted to those originating from the decision-actions of the management of a given enterprise. Thus, they can tell of enterprise effort, accomplishment, and of financial status. By restricting the raw data to exchange-priced transactions with outside interests, enterprise data are rendered arithmetically homogeneous and thereby attain a needed capacity for being analytically marshaled into a variety of informative summaries.

In essence, the analytical techniques exist, not for the sake of the statistical data, but in order that an enterprise may become understandable from a study of the *integrated* data growing out of prior experience of that enterprise. The data resulting from enterprise experience are highly complex, because of the diversity of transactions and from their grouping into highly *integrated* classification categories. This complexity is only superficially visible in the financial statements. Yet, penetration to the significance beneath the marshaled figures requires knowledge of the intricate interrelationships among the data and of the enterprise changes that are reflected in them.

People within an enterprise have access to voluminous detail in the accounts and original records. People outside the enterprise, especially those working in the money market, find relatively little analytical data accessible upon which to base their studies except those disclosed in the published reports. This situation has undoubtedly influenced the evolution of financial statements. Modern data summaries are much more helpful to interpretation that those of fifty years ago. Yet, reporting seems to be approaching a limit in this respect. For, surely, it would not be constructive to recast financial statements into other arrangements of statistical data at the price of the loss of the present close integration of real and nominal accounts. Business certainly would resist the idea of publishing all of the interpretative studies completed or possible within an enterprise. There would seem to be more in the term "private enterprise" than scattered ownership of its capital securities.

Given the situation described above, what can be done going forward? Can interpretation be separated from analytical marshaling? Supplementary statement techniques seem to have been ignored. Have they been forever rejected? If so, can new interpretative elements, injected into financial statements, be successfully held separate from the data based on actual experience?

The LIFO method of inventory accounting may be mentioned as an example of an interpretative element that has gradually been promoted into general acceptance in many areas and by various authorities. Yet, this is more an expedient interpretation than a logical and analytical part or essence of prior enterprise experience; it affects the reported amount of the cost of goods sold through an arbitrary adjustment of the asset account for goods not yet sold. There is no doubt that this sort of inventory accounting performs some kind of service to some statement users and, at least in theory, it can play a role in the calculation of income taxes. The most significant point, however, is the fact that this idea permits the introduction of an interpretative element into the midst of otherwise logically marshaled enterprise-experience data.

Careful consideration of the terms "analysis" and "interpretation" will show them separate in function, with each requiring a different technique for its different function. When this is established, it would be particularly appropriate to propose a variety of supplementary disclosures to the usual financial statements, the latter being held sharply to analytical marshaling of prior enterprise experience.

The wide development and extensive use of supplementary interpretative information would have to face practical limits as well. What information would be most useful to readers of financial statements? How much of such information would it be feasible for businessmen to disclose? What kind of reasonable compromise could be found between these conflicting motives in disclosure amount? The determination of the correct response to these questions is the great task currently facing the accounting profession.

2

APPRAISING THE KNOWNS☆

ABSTRACT

Ideas of accounting already considered acceptable might well be tested by (1) identifying specific actions with specific objectives and (2) searching out the reasons why account data can serve those ends. The reasons supporting known accounting actions and objectives are seldom examined. Yet, each objective must be desirable; each action in support must be satisfactory in its effect. Whatever can be known need not be assumed. But "knowns" still need to be understood from the exploration of their significance and limitations.

Professor Henry C. Adams, writing in 1918, included this stimulating thought: "... all sound accounting rules reflect the nature of the self-determining laws of business life (p. vi)."

A generation later, we probably now would prefer to use other terms for some of the wording. But the importance of this basic concept remains. Accounting is what it is because this technology is tightly associated with business life; because its roots hold it to one enterprise entity at a time; because the substance with which it performs its function derives from the transaction experience of the associated entity; and because these roots and this substance impose functional limitations, which do much to determine the ultimate character of the service capacity of accounting.

☆This chapter has been reproduced courtesy of *INSIGHT Magazine*, The Magazine of the Illinois CPA Society and the successor of *The Illinois Certified Accountant* (for the latest issue, visit www.icpas.org/insight.htm). The original citation for this article is Littleton (1964a).

Within a core-concept such as this, so compactly indicated so long ago, lies a variety of "knowns." These could furnish the first stones for a foundation on which could be built a structure of integrated concepts and principles. As a building of steel and masonry, this ideological structure should rise from a solid foundation. Only thereafter can it reach upward to the objectives that initially motivated the undertaking – for an office building, suitable quarters; for accounting, understanding by data users of the significance of enterprise prior transaction experience. In both cases, construction begins with a foundation. Yet, the ends in view have already influenced construction activities. Planning begins at the top with objectives; construction must begin at the bottom with foundations.

In attempting to understand a puzzling phenomenon, it is legitimate to propose an assumption. Yet, an assumption would not offer a similarly persuasive basis for the direct formulation of a principle. The facts concerning the planet Uranus furnish us an illustration. Astronomers had observed that Uranus did not hold closely to its theoretical orbit. An assumption emerged; an unknown planet was affecting that orbit. Subsequently, measurements that are more refined located the influencing planet, Pluto, previously unknown. Neither the assumption of another planet's existence nor the refined measurement produced a principle. The principle, which had been previously formulated and lay deeper, pointed thought toward the force that celestial bodies exert on each other. The observed distortion of an orbit was a challenge to the principle. Discovery of another planet constituted another validation of this principle.

It is often useful to test an idea already considered acceptable. When convincing reasons in support become evident, the associated principle has been strengthened by the test. The key is *convincing reasons*. Convincing reasons associated with repeated astronomical observations had revealed measurable effects, which could have only one convincing explanation. Interplanetary influence earned the status of a principle from convincing reasons. As such, it would seem reasonable to believe that the search for accounting principles should include examination into the reasons behind known facts of enterprise accounting. A definite need exists for such principles. But postulated assumptions are not the same as known characteristics, and they are not as capable of generating principles as are the reasons for the "knowns" of accounting.

A more determined approach to reality would consider that accounting principles could be recognized from observable uniformities among accounting actions rather than directly from economic circumstances. The first inquiry needed would call for penetrating analyses of the basic types of accounting action. This would include exploring the reasons prompting such actions and examining the objectives involved in those reasons. This would constitute an approach to understanding certain "knowns" by understanding their reasons for being. As lines of rational relationships were revealed, they probably would fall into discernible and significant patterns. The reasons explaining the relationships below would support and explain those located higher in the ideological structure.

Ultimately, items, which at first seemed little more than technical actions to "close-up" results, would assume deeper significance and responsibilities that are more meaningful. At the very least, it would be apparent that behind enterprise accounting actions stands an enterprise entity. This condition has reasons for being, and these reasons inevitably influence the types of actions that have come to be called accounting actions. If there were a principle of accounting here, it would seem to be one of identifying accounting actions with the characteristic objectives of individual enterprises and, through them, with the reasons why enterprises are what they are known to be.

Inescapably associated with the business enterprise, enterprise management also exerts influence on accounting. And behind management are the varied sources of enterprise capital and the people associated with those capital sources. The characteristics, objectives, and power to exert influence are known aspects of contemporary enterprise management and the investment community. These, without the intervention of assumptions, have exerted strong influence upon the nature and limitations of enterprise and accounting. If there were a principle of accounting here, it would seem to be a principle identifying accounting actions with the informational needs of enterprise management and enterprise investors, according to the responsibilities of each.

Two principles such as these invite certain further lines of study – one directed to detecting basic reasons why data from enterprise accounting can serve far-reaching objectives; another to searching the nature and limits of accounting and thus gaining understanding of why these particular aspects help provide accounting with the capacity to accomplish the indicated objectives. Even at the eventual risk of decreasing returns, this line of thought could be further explored.

It could prove quite useful to approach the rationalization of a complex – even a complex such as accounting – by starting with knowns rather than with assumptions. Whatever we can know with assurance, we need not assume. Yet, even knowns will need to be analytically examined. This need could energize accounting research.

When we seek understanding, it will usually prove helpful to first reach back to the knowns for information as to their reasons for being and as to the reasons for their limitations. Actions and objectives should both have discernible reasons for being: reasons for actions, as means toward ends, and reasons for objectives, as ends in need for implementation. For the ends call the means into being; and the means further the ends. The test of both factors appears in the consequences of their specific association.

A known, whether it is an end or a means, may need to be tested against its definition. And a definition may need to be examined as to its adequacy. A known, even if in clear accord with a seemingly clear definition, may still need to be tested. The strength of a known action lies in the reasons for its use, and indications of its usefulness can be seen in the results of its use. Similarly, concerning known objectives, theoretical strength comes from the identifying reasons that create the aims. Validity of the initiating reasons is tested by the degree of successful attainment of that objective. If the known is an action, the related objective must itself be determined to be desirable and of a nature capable of being served by the action under study. Moreover, that action must be judged capable of appropriately implementing the associated objective.

To assume that a known could be defined, or that the usual definition is in fact definitive, is not persuasive. It is also not persuasive to assume that the named objective can be or should be undertaken. To appraise the possible, more than the desired seems advisable. It is persuasive to be content to assume that a proposed action will satisfactorily implement the chosen objective, but the result will remain tentative until it is demonstrated in fact.

If the known is an end, an intention, or an objective, its choice should first be judged as likely to prove better than a conceivable alternative – and for convincing reasons. Various possible relevant means should be weighed as to degrees of suitability and, associated with convincing reasons, influence the choice. Here, again, the possible is preferable to the desired.

The knowns of accounting have already attained significance from use. They have gained this status more from being an aspect of the art of the possible and the necessary rather than from resting on selected assumptions. For example, it is a familiar known of enterprise accounting – and, most assuredly, it is not an assumption – that this technology works with factual data arising from enterprise transaction experience. This known could of course be phrased as a definition. But that would contribute little to understanding this technology. A more helpful approach, as indicated earlier, would explore the reasons and limitations related to this known aspect of accounting.

Since accounting is a way of acting toward knowable objectives, clues to the basic reasons for the existence of this technology, and for its known limitations, should be sought in objectives, which could be identified as reasonably antecedent and impelling. The key to the usefulness of accounting will be found in the uses that can be made of the data, which the technology produces from enterprise transaction experience. The usefulness of these account data will also identify with the detailed techniques known to be characteristic of enterprise accounting. Thus, an understanding of its use-objectives will illuminate the reasons why accounting exists as well as the reasons behind its technical peculiarities.

The phrase "enterprise transaction experience" is the key to the basic actions – the knowns of accounting. The reason is that knowledge of the prior experience of an enterprise can generate clues to the effectiveness of management. Investors are interested parties outside the enterprise; inside the enterprise, management is necessarily even more a party interested in prior experience data. The breadth and depth of the needs for understanding an enterprise make it impossible for accounting technology to service these needs completely. Indispensable as account data are, other aids to understanding must also be used to supplement account data reflecting prior transaction experience.

Compelling concepts of the objectives of enterprise management are knowns as well and there are convincing reasons supporting their existence. It falls short of the essence, however, to assert "profit" as the major objective. Much more basic is the objective of attracting and holding a clientele of satisfied customers. Failure in this would be fatal to the enterprise. Evidence of success in this intention can be read from revenue accounts, for these reports actual and realistic experience. Clues to management efforts to achieve this evidence of enterprise success can also be read from the applicable expense accounts, for these too report on actual and realistic experience.

Profit enters into the theoretical picture, as part of the technical process of reporting on enterprise experience. Instead of expressing an objective for enterprise and management, the margin (net income) is identified with management's ability to keep revenues and costs in a favorable proportion. The same accounting figures also afford a clue to the ability of the enterprise to continue. Profit is the lifeblood of a living business enterprise. It is a necessary element of life but not an objective. Instead, the objective is to live and serve; profit is a means toward those ends.

Significant messages from prior experience can be discovered in the factual relation of assets and liabilities, and the relations between earned income and key items in the balance sheet. It is the areas of inter-account relationships, made evident by financial statements, which best portray management effectiveness. Perhaps a basic principle lies within these ideological boundaries.

An enterprise, its management, interested investors, consuming public, accumulated capital awaiting management, and techniques for making capital productive need not be assumed. These are knowns. These knowns need to be understood both in their interrelations and in their inescapable significance for understanding and using the service of enterprise accounting. All of the actions involved in this complex of relationships are means to definite ends. The ends have reasons for being. The means also have reasons for being. If the reasons for the ends are rational, they are significant and the actions they support are justified by that significance. This is so wholly without resort to assumptions.

3

INTEGRITY☆

ABSTRACT

Account data alone, no more than other data alone, cannot suffice as a basis for decisions. But account data seem the more significant: they come from decisions in and for the specific enterprise. They reflect specific and overt transactions experience of the enterprise. Once such experience is brought into the record, it is unrealistic to consider the data to be misleading and subject it to unilateral change. On the contrary, actual change of the record would violate the integrity of the transaction event and of the account involved.

At the heart of accounting is the nature of the exchange-priced transactions of business enterprises. Such events have several significant characteristics and, because of these, accounting is what we know it to be. These characteristics are (1) the facts are realistic and actual because of the independence of the initiating parties, (2) the events are made quantitative by a price agreeable to the parties involved, (3) both the event and the agreed price have legal status, and (4) the transaction expresses managerial decisions initiated by separate parties and, in summary with other transactions, provides a basis for reviewing the results of such managerial actions.

☆This chapter has been reproduced courtesy of *INSIGHT Magazine*, The Magazine of the Illinois CPA Society and the successor of *The Illinois Certified Accountant* (for the latest issue, visit www.icpas.org/insight.htm). The original citation for this article is Littleton (1964b).

Another particularly significant characteristic of exchange-priced transactions is a negative one: a consummated exchange-priced transaction does not quantitatively represent value, even at the time it became an event (cf. Kohler, 1963). This is so because the concepts of value and of price are quite different; the two cannot properly be used as synonyms. A transaction speaks to both parties by their own intention of one agreed price; but within the event lie two values – a different one is lodged in the differing intentions of each of the contracting parties. The parties' intentions, hopes, and expectations are necessarily subjective, as are all values. Transaction price, therefore, speaks only of planned efforts, not of values.

Subjective elements cannot express enterprise experience quantitatively, but exchange-price, bargained into existence by a transaction, can represent experience for both parties. Therefore, only exchange-price deserves formal and direct accounting recognition. Such a transaction comes into existence because both parties see differing values to themselves in the same event. Without this dual vision of possible benefit, a transaction would not emerge; there would be no quantitative event to provide accounting with substance appropriate to its function. In other words, the function of accounting has evolved from these characteristics of exchange-priced transactions. If this quantitative aspect of a transaction were modified, initially or later, that action would destroy the integrity of the event and damage the integrity of the accounting record. To approve and foster an undermining of integrity, even for laudable purposes, would furnish an example of "the end justifies the means."

There seems to be a current tendency to ignore some of the basic characteristics of enterprise transaction events, to conceive of new functions for accounting, and to expand the single belief, that price expresses value, into the thought that the entire function of accounting is to measure values. Some recent accounting writings tend to emphasize the need for information as to values, to consider accounting as a tool of measurement, and to regard the dollar as an unstable unit of measure thus necessitating changes in reporting certain account data. In the light of the undebatable nature of exchange-priced transactions, and against the historical background of the growth of an accounting methodology closely tied to such transactions, such emphasis seems quite revolutionary.

Some revolutions are evolutionary; these usually prove to be beneficial, but the one suggested for accounting seems mistakenly inspired and could be deceitful in its outcome. The fallacy seems to come from the assumption that that accounting can and should attempt to measure quantitatively something that is inherently subjective. The deceit would come from account data directly modified (not merely interpretatively analyzed) to reflect current "values," as these are determined by specific market prices or perhaps by a statistical index of general prices. However, amounts thus produced could not speak of any transaction experience, as the enterprise concerned has not generated any new transactions producing such an effect.

External users of account data often seem more concerned about the near future position of a business enterprise than about the reliable reporting on the results of enterprises management's prior decision actions. This concern is understandable; the judged future is part of present decisions. But this natural wish is not suitable grounds for remodeling the techniques of reporting factually as to the results of past actions.

It remains uncertain just how helpful remodeling could be. Including effects reflecting current price movements in the accounts of financial statements could suppress adequate disclosures of vital transaction experience of the actual enterprise. Account data modified by index adjustments would submerge, even more deeply, an enterprise's actual transaction experience. Neither the experience of other enterprises nor that of all the nation's businesses (compressed into an index series) can rationally substitute for the actual experience of the one enterprise under consideration. And integrity of account data is important in the same way that personal integrity is important for the professional accountant. As such, integrity is well worth fostering, whatever the hat it wears.

Accounting has had its "revolutions" in stages and over many years: when enterprise accounting was adapted to serve the public interest and the investing public through the British Companies Acts a century ago; when account data were marshaled in new ways capable of facilitating closer managerial control over manufacturing activities through detailed knowledge of internal operations; when a country, as the United States, having a dual system of state and national government, generated support in all of the states for laws recognizing professional accountants and for a nationwide examination to test applicants for professional status; and when educational institutions throughout the country undertook to prepare people in technical matters and in general education for careers in public and private accounting.

From this background, the conclusion emerges that the revolutionary process can produce good results in the field of accounting. Revolutions usually involve drastic action, rapid and far-reaching change, and it has often been a reaction to unbearable pressures. But where are the similar pressures for change in accountancy today?

In contrast to these revolutionary milestones, evolutionary developments come little by little. They are more helpfully fostered by calm debate, by the full exchange of ideas, and by the study of merit in alternatives including existing ways and means. In these cases, a feeling for persuasive logic can be more helpful than expediency. The results of exploring in depth *concepts* relevant to sub-areas of accountancy can be rewarding. Close examination of significant *relationships* could ultimately have more lasting influence than overly compressed rules, rulings, customs, or compactly stated principles.

The last term used above is almost as broad, in connotation, as is the word "value." And dictionary definitions afford little help to clarify either concept. This is so because concepts are too deep to be well expressed by definition, for definitions do not indicate what a term does not mean. As such, to understand a concept, one needs to recognize some of the things the item under consideration is not. The compelling concepts of accounting need analysis in depth rather than mere definition. For example, for most people words such as "principle" and "value" are so adaptable to personal interpretation that formal phrasing of a principle or a single definition of "value" is likely to be unsatisfactory.

An encouraging sign would be the results of a study of compelling concepts examined in depth. This is so because ideas (concepts) are the foundations of actions. Other hopeful signs would lie in the examination, now so infrequently noted, of ways and means for separating the basic accounting function of factually reporting enterprise transaction experience, and the less authentic service of interpreting, from reported enterprise experience, meanings which could be relevant to the problems facing specific types of data users (cf. Backer, 1963).

Accounting technology, as such, cannot possibly point its output toward all the decision problems faced by all potential users of account data. There are too many imponderables. Furthermore, imponderables are neither sensed nor observed. Instead, an approach to recognizing them can be made through interpretative analysis of reported enterprise transaction experience. By striving to sense their existence, one can assist in the understanding of imponderables. Perception of relevant imponderables, in turn, can help decisions. These can then influence actions decisively when their apparent significance for decisions has been thoughtfully weighed, even if this weighting is tentative and subject to future correction. As such, account data from enterprise transaction experience alone cannot suffice as the basis of future decisions any more than non-accounting imponderables alone can suffice.

4

MISSION AND METHOD☆

ABSTRACT

The mission of accounting is revealed by its conceptual objectives, such as servicing the need men have to review the prior transaction experience of enterprises. This mission is the basis of its method and of the means devised to service that mission. As a basis for critically examining the means, their effective association with the mission affords the starting point. Hence, the need to search beneath method for clues to its justification, appropriateness, and distinction between logic and tradition.

It may seem a mere truism to say that accounting is a technology with its service function focused upon aiding men to understand a business enterprise and its management. However, the thought is more than a trite truism, definition, assumption, or postulate. It reaches deeply into an area of broad objectives. As an objective, the idea is supported by man's natural urge to know, to benefit from experience, and to extend his understanding.

Accounting has been functioning in aid of this need for at least five centuries. Over a few recent generations, it has developed greatly increased capacity for effectively serving this need. And the limit has not yet been reached. But now a question arises: how and how fast shall growth continue?

☆This chapter has been reproduced courtesy of *INSIGHT Magazine*, The Magazine of the Illinois CPA Society and the successor of *The Illinois Certified Accountant* (for the latest issue, visit www.icpas.org/insight.htm). The original citation for this article is Littleton (1961b).

If a broad objective were needed as a springboard, the one mentioned above would seem appropriate. Research could then be directed toward sub-objectives suitably supporting the primary reason that accounting exists. This is so because relevant sub-objectives will direct the course that accounting sub-actions take.

In spite of some opinion to the contrary, there is good reason for believing that little is at fault with the ways and means of accounting. Real issues are more likely to be found in the ideology associated with its objectives and sub-objectives. Fortunately, the mechanics of modern accounting action can adjust to whatever ideology shall be found to be most rationally in tune with the furthering of rational objectives.

Accounting ideas and concepts have not yet been organized into an integrated body of doctrine capable of matching the purposeful integration of the actions that make accounting a technology. Herein lies the present challenge. Accountants have a deep understanding of their technology and they have a clear sense of their mission. But a recognizable philosophy of the mission of that technology seems lacking. Eventually, a clear analysis of the mission of accounting should be joined with a philosophy of method.

A philosophy of mission and of method need not, and should not, be philosophical in origin or form. It might very appropriately consist of an integrated body of doctrine designed to show why accounting service is needed and, in detail, why and wherein accounting has capacity to render its particular kind of service; that is, the service of making enterprise experience so knowable that understanding may grow out of that knowledge and rational action out of that understanding.

Before accounting doctrine can be organized into an integrated whole, many separate ideas, concepts, and objectives must be found, stated, justified, and assembled. It may prove a useful approach to this kind of basic research to look beneath a variety of accounting objectives related to helping men to understand a business enterprise. If we can know why men have wished to understand, it may become clear that accounting has had a long career of serving a deep-lying human need.

Mankind has been endowed with intellect beyond all other creatures. This quality includes two significant and interrelated features: (1) an urge to understand and (2) a capacity to benefit from experience. Understanding can be a goal; experience can be a means of approaching that goal. It is part of man's nature to have capacity to understand, capacity to know in order to understand, capacity to examine experience in order to know, and capacity to take present action based on experience but with the aim toward an expected future.

It must have been an urge to understand their business enterprise that motivated the early innovators of accounting. The data organized by those techniques still derive out of and speak of enterprise experience. Only decisions of enterprise management created – and still create – the exchange-priced transactions that, in turn, provided quantitative data regarding prior experience, an element indispensable to an understanding of the present.

Perhaps the most significant innovation made long ago was the integration of real and nominal accounts. It is this integration that gives accounting the capacity to use exchange-priced dollars to picture prior experience, and thus to help men convert experience into understanding and to use this in aid of rational next decision-actions. The mission of accounting still rests upon objectives such as these. Disintegration of the tight integration between real and nominal accounts would be fatal to that mission. Contrived and artificial integration, even though trial balance totals would still equal, would seriously impair the analytical message carried by financial statements.

An important limitation in accounting appears in the fact that account figures do not act automatically to generate understanding. Digits, even organized digits, are silent and inanimate. They function only as users, possessed of an urge to understand and a capacity to benefit from experience, undertake to extract meaning from account figures. This meaning, let it be noted, is also only relevant to the users' own problems and purposes.

It is important in basic research to visualize men working with accounting methods to guide raw data toward intelligible communication; to visualize other men studying communicated account data. The image of accounting should be readily recognized as that of a technology mediating between enterprise experience and men having problems of decision-actions before them. Such an image would make it clear that full communication of meaning will be affected, not only by technical methodology, but by the capacity both groups of men shall have for understanding the objectives, needs, and limitations of each other.

Human factors are inseparable from accounting. Changes in method can dilute the communication unless the user's understanding has been suitably upgraded earlier. Changes, therefore, should be evolutionary only; they should be well thought through, not only justifiable generally but also justified within the user's knowledge and understanding. The underlying sense of the well-known phrase "generally accepted" is this understanding and justification expressed in accounting terms. It is to say that accounting has progressed over several generations and increased understanding among users has progressed in tangent. As such, it would seem that explanation of ideas and justification of limitations – in a word, accounting theory – are likely to be more effective instruments towards the acceptance and use of technical advances than legislative fiat and unsupported preferences.

To one who understands accounting only superficially, its method may seem far more flexible to individual wish than is the case. This fact might very well cue an effort, on the part of accountants, to help more people to understand the limits within which accounting must function. These limits include the reasons behind the current structure of accounting, the limits to a uniformed pattern of accounting, and the limits to which accounting can accommodate economic conditions beyond the actual transaction experience of the enterprise.

With these limitations in mind, a philosophy of accounting mission would best be centered on certain concepts of needed services – services that could mediate in the markets the actions of enterprise management and the needs men have to know the factual results of those actions. Specifically, these needs are to understand enterprise status as of definite dates and to appraise enterprise management accomplishments. Therefore, the concepts of accounting services would be those of a technology dedicated to the dependable and systematic organization of decision-derived data aimed at intelligible communications. This technology does not purport to be infallible, all-inclusive, or strive to provide the sole answer to men's need to understand and to take action out of that understanding.

A philosophy of accounting method should derive from concepts involved in the accounting mission. For this, an integrated body of doctrine should include the reasons why accounting has within its method the capacity to serve men's various needs to understand a business enterprise. It is not enough to describe procedure; an act of doing should be illuminated by the knowledge of how that act was able to contribute to specific objectives and, through them, to other more distant objectives. This is so because there are illuminating ideas beneath every type of accounting action.

Method, in turn, does not exist for its own sake. Method is made up of complex means related to definite ends. Method provides a suitable means only to the extent that the means can satisfactorily serve that end. An examination into the philosophy of method should therefore undertake to tie a wide variety of accounting actions into concepts lying within the philosophy of the accounting mission. Each type of accounting, to justify its existence (that is, acceptance and use) should contribute in recognizable ways and degrees to the fulfillment of the accounting mission.

Accounting actions are many, varied, and interrelated. Their known interrelations and customary sequences may have tended to obscure the way each could play a part in fulfilling the overall mission of this technology. For these reasons, it would seem appropriate that basic research should look beneath simple types of accounting action for clues as to their reason for being. No doubt, aspects of the mission of accounting would be found reflected, to some degree, with each type of action. Each justifiable type of action should be able to survive the test of serving the objectives of accounting better than another conceivable alternative. From an ensuing study of persuasiveness among alternatives, there should emerge reasons explaining why existing actions have capacity to contribute to a successful mission – that of making a business enterprise and its management understandable to various parties.

Consider a few simple illustrative examples. A part of the theory of accounting method calls for the use of spatial arrangement of data to point up significant relationships within an enterprise. Reading meaning out of spatial arrangements requires knowledge of the ways that meaning can be expressed in this way. This aspect of analytical data organization appeared quite early in the form of two summary accounts in the ledger: the balance account and the profit and loss account. When, in later years, summaries of account data were separated from the ledger, they were copies as to both facts and form of these two bi-lateral accounts.

By processing account data in two opposite columns, informative contrasts were made of the means available in the enterprise (assets) and the sources of those means (equities) as well as (2) the means converted into efforts to please customers (expense) and the accomplished success of those efforts (revenue). Moreover, by processing account data into two integrated report-statements, an informative contrast was created of enterprise capital (the tree) and enterprise income (the fruit). Alone, neither report could be as informative as their combination, which allowed for the contrasts described above. The result is that modern financial statements skillfully expand the use of spatial arrangement to direct reader attention to relationships. The user, however, must know how these relationships reveal meaning; if he does not, the presentation is merely quantitative and confusing.

This accounting development reveals rather than makes relationships. Before data appear in accounts, relationships exist among the transactions. Relation among accounts follows as a matter of course. Enterprise capital is at work in transactions and not in the accounts. In other words, management use of capital produces results whether accounts are kept or not. The contribution made by accounts is that of converting, into intelligible computations and communications, this inherent integration of capital in action and the income produced by that action. Since financial statements integrate capital and income, they reflect and report on the interrelations among the judgments, decisions, and actions of management.

A brief excursion is insufficient to penetrate into many reasons why accounting method is capable of carrying forward the accounting mission. Much more exploring is needed. Search beneath method to uncover ideas, concepts, objectives, and achievements would seem to be, for accounting, basic research. It would lead to inquiry into the relation between the philosophy of the accounting mission and the philosophy of its method. In the end, basic research should be rewarding. As its results become widely known, accounting and accounting reports would become more understandable to more people. Such basic research would also demonstrate that accounting is more logical than it is traditional. This is important, as a logical framework is less subject to whimsical change than a purely customary framework.

To conclude, it would be a major contribution if objectives were made clear and if the existence of inherent limitations to accounting actions were forcefully presented. The benefits of this are clear. Deeper understanding of the limits affecting accounting would make financial statements more understandable to all concerned. And, to accomplish this, research might well implement the thought from professional auditing that, in effect, uses a special investigating methodology for examining the extent to which the philosophy of the accounting mission and the philosophy of method, in the given case, have been held in close alliance.

5

ENDS AND MEANS

ABSTRACT

The logical function of accounting ends is that of stimulating and directing appropriate accounting actions as means toward those ends. These ends should be tested for desirability, whereas the means should be tested for suitability. The pairing of ends and means should be based on realistic and convincing reasons. Furthermore, rather than being expressions of values, account data are symbols of quantitative pictures of overt transaction experience. As such, dual entries express the relationship of an intended effort on the enterprise and the consideration necessary to generate the transaction. A logically coordinated body of accounting theory, along these lines, should generate a logically coordinated body of technical actions.

Because technical means are designed to accomplish specific goals, the functional logic of pragmatic philosophy has considerable significance for accounting theory. Accounting objectives are desirable ends to be accomplished; accounting actions are chosen implements used to facilitate those intentions. Hence, the logical function of accounting ends is that of stimulating and directing appropriate accounting actions. The logical function of accounting techniques is that of appropriately servicing the achievement of the chosen ends.

The word "chosen" serves to indicate close relations between ends and means. It does not imply that all techniques originally were formulated specifically and consciously to implement a variety of specific antecedent objectives. Before being "chosen" (accepted), new techniques should be analyzed against a background of established accounting objectives and existing techniques. The analysis should be directed particularly toward examination of consequences emerging from new, different, or alternative techniques in comparison with known consequences of established types of actions. The question then is, if a new method of good quality passes the test as a superior means, should it be recognized as an acceptable technique?

Reference here to "consequences" may imply, erroneously it would seem, equivalence with demonstrated practicability or usefulness. A similar over-generalization often considers pragmatism as giving support to "whatever works," although this phrase could imply that the character of the means need never be questioned. However, consequences are indeed outcomes of actions and perhaps, by implication, a technique, which works well in use, is one that produces satisfactory, suitable, and acceptable consequences. Moreover, and in addition to being adequate, an accounting technique must also be ethical.

In an analytical examination of concepts and terms symbolizing them, close attention should be given to the specific nature of the consequences observed from or expected of a given action. Particular focus should be focused on the reasons why those results are appropriate or seem the most closely aligned with the necessities that have generated the ends and objectives in question. This is a broader approach than is a simple judgment that the technical action "works." In fact, a too simplified judgment gives no indication of the degree of satisfactory contribution that is attributable to that means. A judgment as to consequences, however, would include an appraisal of the quality of the results from its use.

"Usefulness," as applied to a technique, may too often seem to equate with convenience. Indeed, the expedient may be *desired*, yet it may not always be also *desirable*. A type of accounting action, which has a long background of use, may seem to have demonstrated clear usefulness. But custom or traditional actions are not persuasive in the same way as satisfactory consequences associated with recognized objectives. Although a type of action may become customary, convenient, and generally acceptable, it will still need testing by applicable functional logic. Such testing would call for examination of the meaning of *desirability* as applied to the ends in view, and of the meaning of *suitability* as applied to the specific technique involved, especially in comparison with possible alternative techniques. A judgment based on this would support, or question, the appropriateness of change, or continuation, of the action.

Practicability, like usefulness, frequently seems to be considered as a definitive goal for accounting. However, the word does convey a better sense of rational action than the phrase "the technique is suitable because it works." As such, practicability could include a weakness from seeming too close to meaning something like expediency; or for some people it might suggest qualities opposite to the ideal. Yet, the ideal and the impractical are not necessarily unrealistic. Terms such as these invite contrasting the realistic and the unrealistic, and the pairing of the practical against the impractical. It is to be noted, however, that the realistic is not necessarily the practical, and vice versa.

Related to this discussion, the pairing of such terms as realistic and idealistic can be deceptive. But whatever is realistic must deserve that designation for convincing reasons; and whatever is idealistic may, nevertheless, point toward a possible sharpened realism. In other words, ideas about relative quality within actions toward the ends they serve may well prove to offer the strongest support for or against a specific choice of means.

The quality of an action stems from the reason it has capacity to serve satisfactorily the end in view. At one point in time, those qualities may have first been tentative projections of possibilities. Over time and under use, identifiable consequences will have tended to confirm or refute the asserted qualities of suitability for serving the indicated objective. As such, the relation of *desirable* ends and *suitable* means would have become clearly identified. Both of these adjectives refer to degrees of quality; yet, there is a considerable spread between desirable and undesirable as well as between suitable and unsuitable. Simple definitions hardly suffice.

The pairing of a specific degree of the quality "desirable" and of the quality "suitable" calls for careful analysis of gradations in the objective and in the means to those ends. Moreover, a given technical action may serve a variety of close and distant ends, and a given objective may need the service of a variety of techniques in order to fulfill its function.

It is clear that a complex of objectives will influence accounting technology, and that it will consist of a complex of means toward these ends. But if these complexes are to become understandable, a tangle of interrelations must be open to penetration. It is in this connection that functional logic could demonstrate its service.

An analytical organization of accounting objectives that reveal patterns and interrelations could help theory serve this purpose. A similar analytical organization of accounting techniques to reveal patterns and interrelations would also increase the significance of each item. This is so because no technique stands alone; each is an element in a pattern. Similarly, no objective stands alone; each is part of a pattern. Moreover, the two patterns support each other. In a sense, they are reciprocals. Each pattern is in part what it is because of the influence of the other. Perhaps functional logic, having qualities like cement, can bind accounting ways and means tightly to accounting aims and ends. Pragmatic logic would then become the element that gives accounting its characteristic pattern of a coherent whole of firmly interrelated ideas and techniques.

Some ideas relevant to accounting are so strongly persuasive they deserve to be considered as compelling concepts. The existence of functional logic in accounting could be one of those basic concepts. Along with others, it could yield increased insight into the nature and limitations of accounting technology.

Tying an accounting action to the tail of an inference, hanging from the peg of an assumption, does not by itself demonstrate the particular suitability of that action toward achieving an unspecified objective. It could only offer syllogistic argument in favor of that kind of action. This would leave the desirability of an implied objective still in need of demonstration. And the suitability of the proposed means would still need to be appraised in the light of specific consequences from its use, which are then compared with consequences of other known or conceivable means toward the same ends.

The central theme of the last few pages invites clarification through illustrative details. Accounting is indeed a complex of ways and means; study of these is the activity of many college classes and material that fill many textbooks. It is significant that an undisclosed complex of ends and objectives is affecting these technical actions. It is easy to pair these two complexes in a sentence, but difficult to untangle specific means and ends. Yet, examining a number of individual pairs of accounting means and ends might provide some insight into the interrelations between the two patterns. In regards to bilateral accounts:

1. In account categories, the title headings are means to the end of indicating conceptual boundaries for the data there assembled.
2. The bilateral form of an account is a mean to an end of separately reporting data movements into and out of that category.
3. The oppositeness of the plus and minus sides of real accounts (assets and equities) is a means to an end of (a) differentiating different kinds of responsibilities and (b) separating favorable and unfavorable effects on the enterprise of the transactions that generated the entries in those accounts.
4. The oppositeness of the plus and minus sides of nominal accounts (cost-expense and revenue-gain) is a means to an end of separating evidence of management's planned efforts to perform and the performance results achieved by the enterprise.

5. The classification of transaction effects by using both real and nominal accounts as parts of one system is a means to an end of making visible, through data, the interrelation of enterprise capital under productive employment and enterprise income produced by that employment (interrelations which exist whether accounts are kept or not).
6. Figures in an account do not express values; rather, they are symbols serving as a means to an end of presenting an analytical and quantitative picture of enterprise transaction experience, as this has been generated by decision-actions of enterprise management.

It is evident that the concept of an account has many aspects that contribute to the mental image of the account function. To understand the reasons why the account form can make rational contributions to insight into enterprise experience, let us consider transactions:

1. A consummated exchange-priced transaction is a means to an end of producing management-planned changes in the enterprise.
2. An exchange-priced transaction is a means to an end of providing both of the contracting parties with similarly quantitative reports of effects intended for the respective enterprises.
3. One money price for a specific transaction is a means to an end of associating, into one event, the independent transaction decisions made by two parties agreeing in the markets.
4. The dollar sign, shown or implied before account items, is a means to an end (a) of indicating the local money used as a medium of exchange and (b) of indicating a transaction price-sum that can represent, for the two parties, the same quantity of the actual experience of the enterprise, which originates in two separate and self-interested decisions.
5. The mental aspects of transaction analysis are the means to an end (a) of translating a transaction exchange-price into account data and (b) of marshaling transaction events of enterprise experience into categories useful for reviewing and reporting on accumulating transaction experience.
6. Dual entries are a means to an end of expressing, in account categories, the inherent relationship within each enterprise exchange-priced transaction of an intended change and a "persuasive consideration."
7. Recognition of the intended favorable and/or unfavorable transaction effects on the enterprise is a means to an end of assigning data appropriately to the proper sides of accounts, in order therein to accumulate data reflecting the planned effects of changes involved in the transaction decision.

Further, let us examine the functions and effects of accounting communication:

1. Enterprise financial statements are means to an end (a) of communicating, by compact summary, the results of management's transaction decision-actions on behalf of the enterprise and (b) of creating compactly knowable data reflecting enterprise financial status and management's accomplishments in preserving and improving that status.
2. Spatial arrangement of data in financial statements is a means to an end of increasing the power of organized data to convey meaning to users.
3. Audit and certification of financial statements are means to an end (a) of critically examining the accounts as a basis for attesting to the statements as compact disclosures of enterprise transaction experience and (b) of giving added credibility to management's representations; thus, to increase user confidence in the financial status and operating results of the enterprise.

Accounting techniques of every kind are means to an end of:

1. helping to make enterprise transaction experience understandable;
2. aiding clear thinking about the significance of enterprise experience and of management's decisions taken in that connection;
3. making it possible to review the consequences of prior transaction decisions; and
4. satisfying, in part, men's need to know factual results of enterprise prior experience in order to act wisely toward the future.

More on techniques:

1. Close interrelations among account data are means to an end of making understandable the existing interrelations among management's transaction decisions.
2. Year-end adjustments (defer and accrue) are means to an end (a) of separating transaction effects on the enterprise as of the present and as to the future and (b) of apportioning an unbroken flow of transactions into analytically comparable segments (fiscal periods) for clearer presentation of transaction effects.
3. The creation of major classes of accounts (i.e., assets, equities, liabilities, expenses, and revenues) is a means to an end of making transaction experience compactly knowable and interpretatively reviewable, especially by interested parties outside the enterprise.

Theory:

1. Accounting theory is a means to an end (a) of thinking clearly about technical actions, (b) of generating awareness of rational reasons beneath technical actions, and (c) of aiding in the evaluation of management's prior actions.
2. Logically coordinated accounting theory is a means to an end of securing logically coordinated technical actions.
3. Logic in accounting theory is a means to an end of building ideology and methodology into a monolithic whole.

Management:

1. Management decision-actions in and for its enterprise are means to an end of keeping the going concern operating toward a complex of social objectives.
2. Informed judgment on the part of management is a means to an end of moving rationally toward next decision-actions.
3. Enterprise accounting is an important means to an end of securing informed managerial judgments.
4. Management-planned actions are, by intention, means to an end of producing beneficial effects upon the enterprise through exchange-priced transactions.
5. Management actions, in creating apparently unfavorable effects on the enterprise, are means to an end of carrying forward planned favorable effects.
6. Costs and expenses, incurred by management decisions, are means to an end of providing the enterprise with capability for serving its customers satisfactorily; thus, to earn revenue from performance.
7. Knowledge of the results of enterprise accounting experience is a means to an end of later appraising the effects of management's own previous decisions.
8. Study of account data, expressing transaction experience, is a means to an end of studying the relation of prior actions and their discernible results.
9. Reviewing the effect-consequences reflected in recorded transaction experience is a means to an end (a) of seeking evidence of success or deficiencies in management's prior decisions and (b) of appraising the need for continuing or changing lines of managerial action.

In various ways, sometimes directly, sometimes by indirection, the above presentation of a variety of means and ends gives repeated emphasis to management-generated transactions in the markets as representing, individually and collectively, enterprise experience.

To be the good teacher, it is said that experience needs to be knowable, understandable, and reviewable. Accounting technology undertakes to give enterprise transaction experience such qualities as these. To do this effectively, realistically, and dependably, accounting should hold its account data within boundaries indicated by actual and overt transactions in the markets, resulting from management's intentions and decisions to affect the enterprise in particular ways.

A good way to examine stated objectives critically is to test them against alternatives. Some examples of this approach follow. Society faces certain needs that press for satisfaction: the people have need for goods and services; savings need to be encouraged and channeled into productive use; and capital (i.e., savings) productively used will produce goods, employment, investor income, and taxes. Competitive business enterprises that are under private management have been generated through such needs. And servicing such needs has become the prime objective of business enterprise. We can restate this: competitive and free enterprise, together with private management, is means to an end of servicing certain desires of the society in which the related economic activities are carried on.

An alternative concept could be found where totalitarian types of government have full control over the means of satisfying the people's needs. Such a government, whatever its technical form and however its fiat is expressed, becomes a means to an end of centrally controlling the range of types of goods and services, the employment conditions, the creation and use of productive assets, the setting of wage, and the prices of goods. Attempting to choose between such alternatives can create endless argument as to why certain consequences do or should emerge. Moreover, knowledge of concrete consequences in comparable qualities may be long deferred; and differences in what the interpretation of "satisfactory" truly means can hardly be resolved. But comparison of quantitative and factual consequences, as these may become visible, would point toward judgments more rationally based than could come from "materialistic dialectic" promises for a delectable future in some distant day.

Broadly stated, the social objective in both these situations of control is that of advancing the people's welfare. The challenge of the contrasting and alternative means to that end lies in interpreting the comparative consequences. In one situation, the history of early European feudalism and the apparent modern trends of communism in various areas provide bases for partial appraisal of the consequences of tight central controls over economic activities. For the other situation, the later history of Western Europe and the nations of North America provide evidence of better consequences for the people.

Light on the reasons and benefits that flow from a free-enterprise economy can come out of a close examination of basic objectives of enterprise management in such an economy. Those objectives would include at least four elements. First is the element of freely choosing transactions that promises to provide beneficial action toward the recognized needs of an enterprise. The second is that of appropriately balancing the favorable and unfavorable effects of those transactions. The third element is that of resting on management's decisions, based on informed judgment that is systematically applied, and the fourth is that of appraising the consequences of prior decisions and making corresponding changes.

These elements can be stated more compactly: management is a means to an end of operating an enterprise effectively. In this context, effective operation includes the aims of staying in operation and of continuing to serve customer needs appropriately, providing employment, and earning a compensating return for the capital invested. Clearly, these social objectives are apportioned among innumerable independent business enterprises. The logic is strong for preferring competitive private business.

It has been stated that enterprise accounting technology is a means to an end of supplying financial data that compactly and informatively summarize the results of management's transaction decisions. Perhaps a purely verbal report might be proposed as an alternative, in the belief that interested people would understand such a report better than technically arranged financial statements. Or, perhaps, that the use of a variety of statistical tables and charts to organize enterprise action data might be prepared as an alternative to the technical aspects of capital-income accounting and reporting. These suggestions, however, do not seem persuasive. An important factual basis for the next business decisions would be lost or at least much diluted; the informational foundation for investment of savings would be weakened and, as a result, the expansion of productive use of capital would be restricted.

Two alternatives may be examined for audited and attested financial statements. A century ago, there was no audit of enterprise accounts and no certification (except the signature of someone who had checked the accounting arithmetic). The weakness of such an alternative is suggested by the fact it was replaced as soon as decisions in the money market became numerous, important, and it became evident that the public interest required protection of investors against fraudulent financial representations.

Something like a quasi-alternative may also be noted. This would either be individualized enterprise accounts or accounting and reporting methods standardized by a governmental agency. The latter line of action has shown a degree of satisfactory consequences in the case of American banks and public utility companies, but would be quite inappropriate for competitive business. Furthermore, from some points of view, bank examinations lack the scope and objectives of professional audits of industrial business. There are two reasons for this situation: the public, which is in need of protection, consists of depositors rather than investors as such and (2) the public interest is broadly conceived because modern banking is so closely tied into a country's monetary system.

The general public interest is also an element in public utility accounting. The quasi-monopoly characteristic here places the industry squarely between two areas of the public interest: the consumer public, which needs protection against excessive charges for services, and the investor public, which will be unwilling to supply needed capital if investment return is inadequate. A careful balancing of conflicting interests has created the need for regulatory powers to consider and weigh the situation of both parties. This, in turn, has necessitated a larger degree of outside control over accounting than has been necessary for other lines of business. Some of the important factors creating the need for a good deal of standardization of system and reporting are found in the problem faced by utility commissioners (and the courts) in setting service rates and the problem of a fair investment return. Careful study of sharply comparable account data from numerous companies in this area has become a necessity, in fairness to all concerned.

Special conditions often can explain variations in accounting actions. But the persuasiveness of these special conditions should not be too widely extended where analogy is weak. Among competitive industrial companies, uniform accounts and prescribed procedures could scarcely duplicate the desirable consequences flowing from certification by professional public accountants, working under enforceable ethical standards and statutory recognition of technical preparation. Moreover, standardization of accounting and reporting would likely reduce the discernible clues as to significant individual features of a particular enterprise and its management. One of the important characteristics of competitive enterprise in a free economy is that of the quality of individuality. Therefore, a doctrine favoring the highest degree of comparability in account data could be carried too far.

The social significance of the consequences from audited financial statements has been emphasized in both Great Britain and the United States. In the former, a concern for the public interest (investor protection) led the Parliament a century ago to require audits and publication of financial statements. Audits in the United States, serving similar objectives, developed with little direct statutory pressure up to the early 1930s. At that time, legislation created a Securities and Exchange Commission charged with oversight of the conditions under which new corporate securities could be issued. This legislation is pointed more toward the financial side of the operations of corporations than to the details of accounting and auditing techniques. Because a fine spirit of mutual understanding and cooperation has developed between the commission and the profession of public accounting, the functions of both supplement each other in ways definitely in the public interest.

Behind financial statements stand accounting techniques and accounting theory. These combine to create a technology. This is a technical means serving identifiable objectives, such as (1) revealing interrelations among management's transaction decisions, (2) reflecting the consequences of the decisions, and (3) in these ways serving the objective of making enterprise transaction experience more understandable. This relation of accounting means and ends, as with other such relations in functional logic, can be put to test by examining comparative consequences of conceivable alternatives. One such alternative, as has been suggested above, might be that of using purely statistical techniques for assembling data reflecting transaction effects on the enterprise. Certain difficulties seem likely to appear if this were attempted. In fact, some features of statistical techniques would be unserviceable if injected into enterprise ledger accounts; examples are averages and index numbers.

From the nature of these statistical techniques, data derived from their use would tend to obscure recognition of the effects of individual transaction events because of the process of generalizing a mass of data. Furthermore, a change in data would only result in a change in representative figures such as averages and indices. These are interpretative actions of considerable usefulness in their place. Injected into accounts, however, they would tend to suppress the significance of individual transactions accumulated into bilateral categories reflecting both similarities and opposites. Separation of similarities and opposites would make the accounting function much more difficult to achieve. As such, individual event-effects are often most informative for an enterprise when accumulated bilaterally; that is, when it brings favorable and unfavorable events of a certain kind into juxtaposition in one category. When enterprise transaction experience is initially organized in this way, the significance of the relationships inherent among the data and its sources can be more readily studied.

My conclusion is therefore that the use of averages to represent a mass of data is not appropriate for capital-income accounting. But the objectives of statistical analysis are definitely advanced by the freedom to use averages and index series. The problem is that the differing concepts prevent accounting and statistics from borrowing from each other's techniques. The concepts of "categories" are different in the two areas. In statistics, the available categories are more numerous, and they may change considerably according to the material under examination. Account categories, on the other hand, are much more limited. For example, their data elements are confined to those clearly relevant to the transaction experience of a specific enterprise. As such, accounting is basically concerned with marshaling the transaction history of one enterprise considered as a unit. That unit and its management can be understood best if non-transaction data are excluded.

With these differences in mind, it is particularly significant that accounting operates within predetermined and confirmed boundaries. It is a matter of large significance, for example, that enterprise account categories must present a pattern of interlocked real and nominal accounts. The function of accounts to distinguish data reflecting effects of expense-revenue types of actions from those reflecting asset-debit types of action is highly important. No doubt, if accounts were broken apart into two unilateral categories for each one, enterprise transaction data could still be assembled into that system. But their intimate relationships – due to the designed interrelations among the antecedent transactions – would have to be perceived by the painstaking pairing and regrouping of unilateral totals. Accounting objectives therefore call up particularly appropriate means for achieving these ends, and techniques appropriate to statistical ends cannot be suitable as means for attaining accounting objectives.

6

ALTERNATIVE MEANS

ABSTRACT

A consummated transaction indicates a clear intention of management to affect the enterprise in a specific way. Both management and investor can benefit from the same data source because both are interested in enterprise transaction experience. Enterprise expectations, on the other hand, can at best only serve as supplements to reviewable prior transaction experience. The reason for this is that transactions become enterprise experience precisely because of management's intention to implement enterprise objectives, and the service capacity of accounting stems from the objectives that prompt such actions.

Because accounting is committed to a function of marshaling enterprise transaction data, accountants do not search far and wide for data sources as is customary with statistics. Instead, accountants make a major contribution by systematically translating enterprise transaction experience into data for marshaling into categories sharply characteristic of the given enterprise. Bilateral account categories are particularly suitable for grouping data according to matters of major significance for the enterprise. The differentiation represented there, by different patterns of pluses and minuses, or minus and plus sides of accounts, proves to be very helpful to the mental process of translating events into data and to assign that data properly into the scheme of interlocked categories.

Because of the freedom to define statistical categories differently according to various analytical problems, the range of these categories can be great and the definitions unique to the problem at hand. In accounting, however, the range of categories is necessarily limited and definitions are correspondingly restricted. Consequently, a major problem of data marshaling is that of matching transaction effects with account-category definitions. Translations of events into data reflecting enterprise experience involve more than identifying an event with the definitions of two categories. An indispensable element of transaction identification is recognition of the way the event, by using definite quantitative amounts, indicates an intention to affect the enterprise in specific ways and in specific amounts. This is contrary to statistics, where the raw materials are seldom such as to permit sharp identification of effects intended at the time the data originate.

It is appropriate to note that aspects of enterprise function and management objectives strongly affect accounting actions toward reflecting, in data, the results of decision-actions taken in and for the given enterprise. The interrelations that unite the business enterprise, management, and enterprise accounting are so strong as to exclude the use of averages or other types of statistical data in the accounts. Data on Gross National Product (GNP) may provide key information helpful to governmental decisions. But changes in such a broad indicator cannot replace the accounts of individual enterprises as a primary base for next decisions of management.

On the other hand, general statistical information cannot be neglected in its entirety for it provides collateral data deserving thoughtful study in relation to pending decisions by enterprise management. But statistics reflecting the contemporary economic atmosphere can be no substitute for the organized data reflecting the results of enterprise prior transaction experience.

Transaction events are too numerous and diverse to be understood one by one. Through long evolutionary development, accounting has grown into a highly refined and systematic means for making a complex mass of transaction events intelligible. Its several techniques have slowly been sharpened toward becoming sub-instruments effectively forwarding the larger objectives of management. The action elements of accounting are therefore tightly interlocked and quite definitely specialized toward accomplishing important but limited missions. In the nature of the case, it will be difficult to find alternative techniques of better or even comparable capability for accomplishing the objectives of enterprise capital-income accounting with similar effectiveness.

It is implicit in transaction analysis that the process of translating events into account data shall use the demonstrated exchange price for expressing the quantitative effects planned for the enterprise in the related transaction decision. Since exchange by barter is now uncommon in business, barter is more an occasional or exceptional case than a true alternative to money-price recording.

By considering money as a medium for facilitating exchange, it should be possible and useful to dissociate the figures in accounts from the concept of "value." Money as a store of value is not, for accounting, an alternative for money considered as a medium of exchange. Another way to clarify the concept named "historical cost" would be to associate a transaction and its quantitative aspect with "planned effort" and "planned performance." It will be noted that this effort and performance on the part of contracting parties will produce for each an item of enterprise experience, measured by the same quantitative figures that reflect a *price* acceptable to both, not a *value* as visualized by either party.

It is difficult, therefore, to find an alternative more suitable for enterprise accounting than that of expressing account data in terms of an exchange price bargained into existence by independent parties acting in their own interest (i.e., historical cost). Nevertheless, the literature of accounting often reflects dissatisfaction with financial statements where revenues "in today's dollars" are associated, in calculating net income, with costs and expenses in unlike dollars (i.e., old dollars) particularly in connection with the calculation of depreciation expense.

The literature is in this state because emphasis is often laid on dollars as units measuring *value*. On the other hand, if dollars measure transaction *efforts*, as seems more appropriate for accounting, there is nothing unrealistic about matching earlier dollars (e.g., depreciation expense) with today's dollars (e.g., revenue). It is a statistical function, not an accounting function, to analyze the effect that economic conditions and government fiscal policies may have on the purchasing power of money in hand and on the going price of goods.

It should be clear that in business-planned efforts for tomorrow start in the past; hence, the resulting actions will be convincingly identified with that past. When planned efforts come to fruition in planned performance (such as machinery used in production), the dollars there involved are the same as those attached to the original effort made to be ready to produce. The only difference is that those dollars can express the actual cost invested in performing.

The most desired contrast in accounts is this one, between effort and the performance, which prior effects helped bring into being. The invested cost of goods acquired for sale represents effort; the cost of goods sold is part of performance. The goods and measurement are the same. It does not seem logical to act as if *repriced effort* would rationally become, by an act of will, a measured effort to perform. It would be an action *as if* the sold goods had just been acquired by current price effort. The buyer's price (seller's revenue) expresses his effort to be ready to perform later. His planned effort toward his future is an invested cost to him, but change in our purchase market does not cause our prior invested cost to change correspondingly.

A phrase like "planned effort" or "invested cost" may not be as compactly convenient as words like "cost" or "value." It is necessary to realize that one source of misunderstanding may lie in the habitual use of common words like these two in speaking of technical accounting matters. Science seems to have little difficulty in "inventing" new terms for more specific identification. But accounting is not a science, and it must communicate with non-technical people; hence, it must, as far as possible, use terms they already understand to some degree. Nonetheless, it would help if qualifying adjectives were more frequently used to sharpen the intended meaning of common words that have acquired some technical significance for accounting and management.

It was suggested above that accounting technology is strongly focused toward enterprise management. This may imply the existence, as an alternative, of an accounting function of service focused toward decisions in the investment markets. The two ideas of function, however, are not true alternatives. Accounting serves a dual purpose. Decisions within the enterprise and outside in the capital markets both have need for factual information, dependably reflecting enterprise experience resulting from management's prior decisions actions.

Until relatively modern times, manager and investor usually were the same. Later, the extensive development of corporations tended to separate the owner and the operator. The investment market became an organized adjunct of corporate business. To describe accounting service to the investment markets as a collateral outgrowth from antecedent objectives need not suggest that one objective should be considered more important than the other should. The significant fact is that both parties at interest can benefit from information drawn from the same data source: enterprise transaction experience. Differences in the types of decision problems of management and investor make it necessary to use account data in different ways and to supplement that data in different ways. And, inevitably, the full extent of the information available to internal management cannot also be furnished to investors. Throughout a century of development, the profession of public accounting has been able to attest to the dependability of financial statement communications; thus, to some degree, mitigating the unavailability of supporting internal details for investor use.

Lately, a separate literature has developed tending to stress, on one hand, administrative and managerial accounting and, on the other hand, to point more directly toward auditing and the work of professional accountants. This provides another indication of growing distinctions, even though the basic technology of preparing account data underlies both lines of activity. This leads to a problem that seems to be in the making. Perhaps it may be compactly indicated by a few questions. Is this trend likely to point toward the widening of preparation for managerial accounting and professional accounting? Does the literature, however unintentionally, point the student toward one specialization or the other? Is there need for a clear orientation of thought in both areas toward the wide usefulness of the results of technical procedures?

This is not the place to examine alternative ways of exploring such a problem. It should not be difficult, however, to see that the basic technology probably would face problems of dual accommodation when and if administrative and financial accounting continued separate paths of evolution. And, regardless of the degree of present tendency toward a separate literature, certain basic concepts can still be significant. Accounting ideology is open to a logical integration of its elements; methodology is similarly open to logical integration of elements. Accounting ideas and actions, whatever their own complexities, need to be united, interlocked, and intertwined in mutual support. The more firmly these interrelations are achieved, the more accounting technology will be recognized as a suitable means toward discernible and desirable objectives.

In judging the significance of related means and ends, and in analyzing alternative means, it is as important to be as convinced of the suitability of the means as it is to be assured of the desirability of the related ends. Perhaps objectives can be examined as to desirability without parallel consideration of available means. But means acquire significance only in relation to specific intentions and ends. Hence, it is difficult to generalize the quality of suitability. Yet, suitability of means needs to be scrutinized, even if for no other reason than in order to develop a clear mental image of the concept "suitability of means" and to develop ways of recognizing this quality.

Accounting serves as a means to the end of enabling management and others to review the effects of management's prior decision-actions. Furthermore, an objective achieved often becomes a means toward future ends. Management's review of prior decision results; therefore, becomes a means to the end of appraising the need for continuing or changing lines of managerial actions.

The suitability of accounting as a means toward ends is not fully tested by its existence as an organized system—as one type of data processing apparatus. The test of suitability comes when and if management uses account data (1) to study results of prior decisions and (2) out of such study, plus other considerations, makes decisions to change or continue certain actions. If management ignores account data reflecting enterprise experience and reaches next decisions on the basis of considering expected future conditions, as constituting an alternative guide, accounting suitability as a technical instrument has not been tested by a judgment of the consequences of its use. It has not been used; it has not produced real consequences; and it has not been permitted to fulfill its function. At best, consideration of enterprise expectations can only serve as an illuminating supplement to, rather than as a substitute for, a studied review of enterprise prior transaction experience.

The suitability of dual entries, as a technical means for marshaling transaction data, affords another example that cannot be justified separately from service objectives closely related to other features of accounting technology. Any proposed alternative to dual entries would have to overshadow (1) the peculiarly effective service of bilateral categories; (2) the analytical service provided by integration of real and nominal account data; and (3) the interrelation within each transaction of an intended effect and a necessary consideration offered to produce that effect. The equality of trial balance totals is a result of, not a reason for, dual entries. The capacity of duality to serve as an accounting technique needs to be judged according to the significance of accounting actions that follow classification actions, and on the basis of the objectives that generate these later actions.

Some alternative means and ends may seem persuasive enough to make a choice difficult. But this fact provides added reason why accounting theory should encourage and facilitate rational inquiry reaching beneath the surface of persuasiveness. Pragmatic reasoning (functional logic) is particularly useful here, because most accounting actions are means toward a variety of goals and pragmatic testing puts under analysis the interrelations among ends, means, as well as means and ends.

Over a long period of time, man's need to understand his accumulating experience has led him to devise means likely to help him to benefit from knowledge of the results of prior action decisions. Such needs have been powerful enough to be recognized. And recognition has gradually sponsored the creation of specific action-means for systematically organizing business transaction data toward the broad goal of fostering self-knowledge. As the more simple and early means proved satisfactory in use, still unsatisfied needs for information have generated the further expansion of accounting techniques.

It is clear that means and ends are closely interrelated in accounting, as they are elsewhere. It must also be evident that, as means are responses to specific needs, successful fulfillment may reveal other objectives. However, learning to execute technical procedures does not necessarily lead to full understanding of techniques as means toward a variety of ends. It should therefore be emphasized that technical actions are what they are because of the objectives that sponsor them and continue to explain, justify, and support those means as suitable.

A familiar phrase is that "the end justifies the means." This may seem to say, more compactly, what was said above; or the phrase may be thought to express the essence of functional logic. Yet, this would be incorrect; the phrase contains a fatal weakness by implying that any means is acceptable if the end is urgent. Like most over-generalizations, this one has definite limits of application, for it raises the question of the full connotation of "suitable." Instead, a logical and rational association of means and ends will start with a clearly desirable end, not with one merely desired. A clearly suitable means should have desirable qualities in its own right. Merely to further an end is not enough. In order for the end to "justify the means," the line of action used (the means) should itself be honorable and ethical as well as effective.

In a way, "compelling concepts" is more general than the terms "postulate" and "assumption." In using the word "compelling," the intention is to suggest that concepts can be noted which strongly influence accounting thought and action. By the use of the word "concepts" (ideas), it is possible to avoid the limitations implicit in "assumption" and "postulate." The first is a weak and abstract term because it points to something we cannot know. Whatever can be known, need not be assumed. The second term carries much the same implication in addition to some of its own problems. "To postulate" is analogous with "to assert." A postulate, therefore, is a proposition advanced as a basis or point of departure for drawing useful inferences. A postulate is seldom fully analyzed toward displaying its compelling relevance.

Many ideas capable of providing insight into accounting technology are "compelling" because they refer to unquestioned facts of economic life that will inescapably influence accounting actions and objectives. Such ideas point toward many elements whose presence would have been felt in the midst of early contemporary needs and circumstances; even then, they would have been capable of influencing that technology. Most of the same economic facts of life are still active and still influence the basic techniques of accounting. Modern developments do not reach deeply enough to displace basic and time-tested "compelling concepts."

One of the compelling concepts influencing the nature and limitations of enterprise capital-income accounting is this: management-generated transactions, individually and collectively, represent enterprise experience. Almost imperceptibly, contemporary economic life has fostered some disregard for this kind of limitation, and this has opened the way for non-transaction elements to be brought into the accounts.

At least, as a point of departure, it must be acknowledged that enterprise and management are tightly joined as an area for economic action and as a decision center for directing actions taken in and for the enterprise. Without this union, there would have been no capital-income enterprise accounting. Without management-created exchange-priced transactions, there would have been no material for accounting to marshal.

The concept of experience-significance is compelling in the sense that it makes clear certain conditions precedent to the existence of accounting, as we know it. It is not necessary to assume that transactions in the markets generate enterprise experience reflecting the results of management's decisions. Transactions become experience by management's intention, and management's intentions are centered upon securing appropriate means for carrying on the functions of the enterprise.

Another of the compelling concepts indicated earlier is this: the suitability of accounting as a technical means for facilitating the functions of the enterprise is tested when and if management uses account data to appraise its own prior decisions. This concept of the necessity for an interpretative use of its data is compelling as to accounting, because marshaled account data that are unused make a mockery of the technology. Moreover, management must first know how things are in order to conceive how they might have been.

It may perhaps be acceptable to restate the earlier compelling concept: elements of functional logic, by giving accounting its characteristic patterns of interrelated ideas and techniques, can provide insight into the nature and implicit limitations of accounting technology. This concept is compelling for two reasons: (1) because the service capacity of accounting as an information apparatus must of necessity act in appropriate ways to make its materials informative for users and (2) because appropriate actions will be those influenced by ideas about the informational needs of users and about the informational potential inherent in enterprise transaction experience.

Conceivably, accounting technical actions could be merely described and used in purely routine ways. The only compelling aspect here would be that of faithfully carrying out instructions. Even then, reasons why would stand behind the described actions, especially reasons why the resulting data could be informative for users. But to fully comprehend technical action requires awareness of motivating objectives. The service capacity of accounting originates from the reasons or objectives behind its actions. It is the interrelations of actions and reasons, of theory and practice, which molds accounting into a monolithic whole.

It is a figure of speech to call functional logic binding cement; yet, this is not too exaggerated. Pragmatism suggests the testing of satisfactory relations between means and ends through the critical examination of the use made of means. The pressure of recognized satisfactory consequences from the use of relevant means toward relevant objectives will support the conviction that a coordinated body of logically interrelated elements exists, which can give definite identity to a recognizable whole—a whole that is incompletely symbolized by the name "accountancy."

PART VI

1

THEORY AS ACTION EXPLANATION

ABSTRACT

Behind actions lie objectives, and behind objectives lie motives. Accounting theory undertakes to appraise intentions as goals, to explore reasons, and to see actions geared to intentions. Intentions, in turn, produce actions and the results from this confirm the initial intentions. Furthermore, interrelations among ideas can generate interrelations among actions. Interrelations among its actions and the related ideas indicate that accounting is a highly rational, thoroughly logical, and analytical technology.

Accounting actions represent determined efforts to analyze and marshal enterprise transaction data toward the general objective of making that experience more understandable. Both functional logic and accounting actions reflect relations between suitable means and desirable ends. These accounting actions, procedures, and techniques are well-known, but the reasons for their being and for their present forms are not. This lag is rooted in evolutionary developments. No blueprints exist that would have arranged a planned development of the ways and means of accounting. Nevertheless, as the original and basic aspects of accounting actions survived and evolved, they provided continuing services over the centuries. The complex structure of modern accounting was built on that foundation.

Very little theory is visible in early records and textbooks. Yet, some motivations, needs, and intentions must have existed to sponsor the early efforts and subsequent evolutionary growth. As such, an approach toward basic theory could begin with constructing a hypothetical pattern of possible objectives or with a study of known actions. In either case, the platform would have to be based on knowledge of accounting and a belief that accounting theory should be capable of explaining the nature and functions of accounting actions.

Actions in accounting and in business are efforts to accomplish. Accomplishment leads to accumulated experience. That experience will need to reflect a recognizable and reportable substance in the form of data. And that data substance, in order to speak effectively of actual experience, will need to be analytically organized in informative ways conducive to examination and to learning its significance.

Accounting theory has not been and is not likely to become philosophic. Yet, accounting theory can function in and of thinking clearly about accounting actions. Moreover, the results of these actions can help men to think clearly about the significance of enterprise transaction experience. Furthermore, the words "theory" and "accounting" have accumulated different connotations from being used in different contexts. As the context of use varies, so is the implied meaning of the term likely to vary. Thus, one meaning may be appropriate in one setting and inappropriate in another.

Perhaps the work of Egyptian scribes many centuries ago could be called "accounting." They recorded taxes received in material kinds as these came in and recorded them again as they were withdrawn from storehouses on government orders. The most recently expanded application of the word "accounting" is reflected in the terms "national income accounting" and "social accounts." The earlier actions of the scribes could now be described as those of making inflow and outflow entries as if in perpetual inventory records. The actions producing social accounts could be described as converting various statistical data into major groupings according to the origins and destinations of the inflow of receipts and outflow of payments moving through the nation's economy. And still further meanings can be found between these two widely different uses of the word "accounting."

For example, medieval bankers (moneylenders) kept personal accounts for their dealings with depositors and borrowers. The form and phrasing of the records reflected personal responsibilities reaching into the near future. The essence of the phrasing was that the borrower must repay the loan and that the depositor must receive back his deposit.

In self-sufficient medieval landed estates, the activities of making a living from the land for the local population were departmentalized. Responsible "bailiffs" used clerks to keep charge-and-discharge records indicating responsibility flowing in and responsibility given up. Grain came into the miller's responsibility; flour moving to the baker discharged the miller's responsibility.

Early manufacturers of woolen cloth kept a separate memorandum book for each process in the handicraft conversion of wool into cloth. Therein were noted the raw or semi-finished materials placed with each family and the wages later paid them for exercising their craft. The recording practice began to show some of the characteristics of recording data toward managerial control, as did the records on a nobleman's landed estate, which foreshadowed the use of accounting controls in modern manufacturing industry.

Several generations before the voyages of Christopher Columbus, the activities of overseas traders had generated systematic procedures for calculating the success of trading branches and the financial status of each. Here, as in the other situations, there was a type of "responsibility accounting." In later years, a focus upon business activities and managerial control appeared which continued and extended the essence of earlier precedents.

Each of these early uses has contributed something to the meaning of "accounting." Early use of personal accounts marks the origin of the bilateral form of account categories. Another type of procedure, charge-and-discharge reporting, was also bilateral in nature and it still forms the framework used by estate trustees in reporting to the court on their responsibilities.

Another early development, from Italy, showed an outstanding characteristic of enterprise accounting: the tight articulation of real accounts and nominal accounts (asset-equities and expense-revenue). In the latest use of the work, however, social accounts seemed but weakly tied into these evolutionary developments. Here, there is no articulation of (1) capital productively employed under responsible management and (2) of income resulting from that supervised employment. Again, by several tests, social accounts show only meager roots in accounting technology. It is not responsibility accounting in the sense of fiduciary responsibility; instead, its data come out of statistics originating in all sectors of the nation's activities. It is not control accounting, in the sense of industrial accounting, unless government is considered in control; that is, making the decisions that produce changes in the source data, which are later compacted into the calculation of gross national product. Neither is it governmental accounting; that is, the adaptations of business accounting techniques for use by entities such as cities, hospitals, and universities.

The basic modern connotation attached to the word "accounting" clearly seems to be associated with actions taken in and for business enterprises, operating under the direction of responsible management in a competitive economy. In such an economy, capital (investment funds) flows into a money market. From there, funds fan out from investors into many business enterprises as managements find uses for capital (productive assets).

The actual meaning of "accounting" is further illuminated by its technical functions and capacities in connection with this continuous process of capital movement and productive employment. Two primary areas of accounting service evolved out of the framework originally provided long ago by simple forms of enterprise capital-income accounting. One service is that of providing compacted and organized data, reflecting the results of management's efforts to produce acceptable goods and services. This is industrial, administrative, or managerial accounting. In its other service – financial accounting – the same technology, using the same data, provides audited and professionally attested summary financial statements. These, in turn, facilitate many decisions in the money markets and help to channel investment funds into productive use.

The basic connotation of the word "accounting" is capable of description. As an objective, the word becomes part of the phrase "accounting theory." The connotation of the latter term will be influenced by its relation to accounting as an area of action wherein an associated "obstinate attempt to think clearly" can be very useful. In the association indicated, the word "theory" is sometimes thought as identical with "a theory." This would seem to imply that one idea, proposition, or formulation could compactly epitomize a complex. Or, alternatively, it would imply that all controlling ideas of accounting could be deductively derived from a single proposition representing "a theory" that so thoroughly represented the nature of accounting that it would give coherence to the whole.

At times, it has seemed as if some people downgraded accounting theory, by equating "theoretical" to the opposite of "practical." In this context, theory could possibly have been unconsciously considered as rather "academic" or representing a way of looking at ideas abstractly without regard to practical limitations affecting the associated actions. Alternatively, "theory" could have been associated with purely speculative and far-fetched ideas, such that it would presumably lack contact with practical realities. Or, the term, for some people, might mean inferences drawn from broad assumptions standing remotely from things as they really are.

Another approach is available. A persuasive concept, one associated with a need to think clearly, might consider "theory" as closely related to "explanation." Accounting theory under this concept would be not a theory but a body of reasons, explanations, interrelations, and objectives making it possible for us to think more clearly about accounting's purpose and service. This resonates with higher mathematics as a technical method in aid of thinking clearly about certain kinds of relationships. Accounting is not directly comparable with mathematics. It is, however, another technical method in aid of thinking clearly about significant relationships, especially those among the varied results of enterprise transaction experience. By its aid to clear thinking, accounting can help men to appraise the factual evidence of enterprise management's accomplishments.

Under this connotation, accounting theory should undertake to explain accounting actions, to explore reasons, to interrelate ideas, to find how actions are geared to intentions, and to help appraise intentions as desirable goals. Explanations are not all on the same level. Some are plausible or improbable, convincing or unconvincing, and persuasive or unpersuasive. Interrelations may be tightly or loosely associated; some may be negative, that is, opposites. The latter are often highly significant of movement and change; and accounting is strongly associated with data reflecting movement and change.

Accounting theory therefore exercises a degree of control over accounting actions, but not by directing the action to be taken. Rather, it exercises control by establishing rational bases for necessary actions associated with desirable ends. This characteristic will disassociate any item of accounting theory from the characteristics of scientific laws, which describe some action as controlled by forces of nature.

Contrary to scientific laws, accounting has deep within it a large measure of common sense. That faculty is not highly rated in philosophy. Yet, when the phrase is closely considered, as in Webster's *Dictionary of Synonyms* (1951), it can add an acceptable connotation to "accounting theory." Common sense is described as "seeing things as they are and without illusion or emotional bias, as an aid to making practical choices and decisions that are sane, prudent, fair, reasonable, and that commend themselves to the normal or average good mind." Choices and decisions of this type will possess many desirable qualities, whether they reflect accounting actions or business decisions resting on account data derived from enterprise prior transaction experience.

Since controlled experimentation, which is incredibly valuable in science, is seldom available for testing business decisions, the substitute must be observation and judgmental appraisal of the results of prior decisions. Accounting can play a part in this procedure, because it actively organizes the factual results of the prior experience of enterprise, as the decided events become established and reviewable facts. Known actions (implemented decisions) produce results that can be organized into data groups. In so doing, such data become available for interpretative study of significant interrelations and changes (data movements). Such study would be a way of exploring enterprise experience; that is, a way of appraising the results of prior decisions for clues toward later decision actions. Accounting theory would be useful in this connection, because it can explain how accounting organization and action is able to illuminate accumulating transaction experience.

It should be noted that theories as explanations are not all of the same quality. Explanation of some facets of accounting can be thoroughly convincing. Other aspects of theory gain strength from ties with similarly convincing explanations and justifications of other technical aspects of accounting. If a desirable degree of conviction seems directly unattainable, a plausible surmise may be conceived as a possible explanation of a condition or action or result. Or several alternative explanations may be studied for relative appeal as being "sane, prudent, fair, reasonable, and rational."

For example, perhaps the best explanation (theory) may lack conviction and plausibility, and thus fall short of acceptance as reasonable and rational support for the action in question. Such a result could suggest weakness in the action itself. Consideration of another action toward the recognized objectives might seem indicated. A clue to a trial acceptance would lie in the probably consequences of new action in comparison with the consequences of the action it was to replace. It would then be clear that the explanation of the action in the first case had failed to carry conviction, because the consequences were in some way relatively unsatisfactory even though not entirely undesirable. The explanation of the proposed substitute action would gain its plausibility from a judgment that the results in use would be more satisfactory. Action may also be justified if theory can make the action understandable and acceptable in the light of the ends in view. Where theory (an idea about acceptable action) is put in use through action, satisfactory action-results (consequences) will confirm the theory.

Accounting has had a long development as a type of action. A clue to the explanation of this fact may be found in the thought that, as a result of using accounting, men can gain insight into a business enterprise and into the patterns of its management's prior decisions. If we seek explanation (theory) as to why accounting has capacity to yield insight, clues may be found in the interrelation of its ideology and methodology (theory and practice as well as action and explanation). Further clues can be sought in the patterns of accounting objectives at different levels of action, as these interrelate with patterns of means for attaining those various ends.

A keen observer has stated: "The aim of accounting is not so much to arrive at eternal truth as to present a useful tool, a guide to judgment (Knauth, 1957, p. 62)." This idea supports the thought that accounting theory is a necessary adjutant to accounting action. For theory explains how inherent technical characteristics can make of accounting a useful tool in aid of decisions, and how its data about enterprise experience can help guide judgment. It should perhaps be added that accounting could no more be a complete and perfect guide than it can be an all-purpose tool.

Coming back to the term, theory means to explain even in science. There, it undertakes to make understandable the way observed facts, actions, and results begin, continue, and end. Some facts and results form a basis for wondering why they exist as they are. Experimentation may indicate that some factors are influencing the results; thus, convincingly extending our understanding. In the absence of available experiments, reasonable and plausible explanations of actions may be persuasive, even though not conclusive, and may therefore expand understanding usefully, even if not positively.

For example, Newton's theory of gravity was a persuasive explanation of observed phenomena for a long time. Einstein's theory, which was different, later led men to devise tests in the hope of securing factual evidence supporting one theory or the other. These tests have shown that the later theory agrees more closely with results from nuclear experiments in space. Accounting research, however, cannot call on nuclear physics or radar telescopes to assist in making choices between alternative explanations. Resort must be had to the analysis of ideas in order to uncover the reasons why accounting began, continued, and increased its capability for rendering its type of contribution to men's need to understand a business enterprise and the effectiveness of its management.

The result of this is that accounting has come to be increasingly understandable out of experience in use rather than out of experimentation. Its technical actions have demonstrated, over time, the qualities of being "sane, prudent, fair, reasonable" and, above all, usefully practical with a minimum of expedience. And its loosely organized theory has persisted in commending itself "to the normal or average good mind," which is at the same time reasonably informed as to accounting objectives and limitations.

In spite of our lack of experimental techniques, we must concede that accounting has developed quite remarkably from a very modest beginning. The knowledge of relationships among the factors, which evidently fostered this continued development, could conceivably also reveal limitations and clarify objectives. Here, one might want to draw on philosophy and its application to accounting theory. This relationship may be expressed in various ways, but a consistent theme would become evident that would be no more difficult to distinguish than is a melody that permeates and characterizes a musical composition. A few phrases may serve to compress this essence: interrelation, interaction, and integration, first among ideas and actions, ends and means, theory and practice, questions and answers, parts and whole, and secondly among rational inquiry, logical insight, coherent understanding, and interpretative judgment.

All of the elements suggested here contain clues to the functions and objectives of accounting, but they lack organization. The multitude of transactions entered into by a business enterprise also lack organization. The lack in the latter case is remedied by the use of accounting techniques. The functioning objectives of accounting could also be made more visible and effective by organization. And various methods could introduce organization into accounting theory. Ideas that explain and justify could be associated with accounting actions to which they were relevant. Ideas, well-known from acquaintance with accounting actions, could be traced from initial innovation and through years or centuries of expansion in use and usefulness. Ideas reasonably generalized out of early practices and distilled out of later literature could also be assembled and arranged into a connected discourse, which could reveal significant interrelations among ideas and between ideas and actions.

Each of these methods might yield useful results, but none has been given a thorough trial. Explanations there are, but these are brief, unorganized, and scattered throughout the literature on procedures. Yet, a few relatively recent treatises have dealt effectively with topical sections of a theory. An expanding current literature has included numerous penetrating exploratory articles. And the growth of graduate accounting instruction has stimulated ideas about theory and encouraged their presentation. The brief sample of thoughts from philosophy indicated here can perhaps lend encouragement to introducing greater organization into accounting theory. For, with a certain amount of adaptation, many thoughts from philosophy can offer us great opportunities to think deeply.

In the several thoughts tabulated above, the chief clue to theory organization is perhaps that afforded by the words *interrelation*, *interaction*, and *integration*. These, plus the phrase "parts and whole," suggest that accountancy is a complex of many distinguishable parts. Some degree of cross relation must exist among the parts and between these and the whole.

Perhaps, then, the elements of accounting ideology could be organized in ways to reveal interrelations among concepts and, thus, suggest that concept integration can be a force capable of binding action parts into their own conceptual whole. Perhaps a starting point may be found in a layman's notion of nuclear physics. It would seem that scientists draw a significant analogy between the wide universe of interacting planets, stars, galaxies, and an atom of physical matter as being a fantastically tiny universe of interacting electrons and protons.

This lay facsimile of scientific opinion may offer a springboard for searching out interrelations among accounting concepts. The idea of an atom nucleus suggests the possible existence of a core of central concepts within accounting theory. Gravitational interactions among planets, and electronic interaction among neutrons and protons, could suggest for accounting theory interactions between a possible core of concepts and other theory ideas of lesser mass. As such, close examination of interrelation among ideas and actions may indicate that accounting is less an expansion of "double-entry bookkeeping" than it is a highly rational, thoroughly logical, and analytical technology capable of serving society in many important ways.

2

RELATED FORM AND SUBSTANCE

ABSTRACT

Each exchange-priced transaction will present some combination of favorable and/or unfavorable effects on the enterprise concerned. In order to segregate unlike transaction effects and to aggregate like transaction effects, account categories are named and given bilateral form. Each transaction, in turn, speaks of the experience of that enterprise.

Accounting has become a technology from having definite characteristics. In its most basic aspects, accounting shows a special *form* (a characteristic way of working) and it makes use of a special *substance* (a characteristic material to marshal). Both form and substance are strongly influenced by basic objectives. These, together with the users need for limited but specific kinds of information, make accounting what it is.

The basic substance consists of factual data, originating in the exchange-priced transactions of the specific enterprise. Such data, by intention, tell of enterprise experience. The basic form used to make the data intelligible is the bilateral account. This is an arrangement capable of separating the increasing and decreasing effects of transactions, and bringing related data to a residual balance of opposing effects. Yet, form has much more to contribute than the structural outline suggests. The bilateral form is a definite aid to thinking clearly about the effects transactions are intended to have on the enterprise. This form is also an aid to recording the conclusions (e.g., totals) reached by the use of this type of organizing transaction effects.

It is by a skillful welding of form and substance—account categories and transaction facts – that accounting approaches its underlying objective, which is that of making a business enterprise understandable through organized factual data from enterprise transaction experience. We know that this particular welding of form and substance into a useful means toward a definite end does succeed in serving the indicated broad objective. It is clear therefore that accounting is an example of pragmatic relationships, for this phrase refers to the association of a desirable end and an appropriate means toward attaining that objective.

Relationship between ends and means are important aspects of science, economics, and philosophy, as well as accounting. There is, on this basis at least, some kinship between accounting and these other disciplines. Science is concerned with increasing our understanding of the forces of nature. Economics is concerned with the influences affecting man's wants and his actions to supply those wants. Accounting, however, is not directly similar. Yet, like economics, it deals in its own way with men's efforts to supply their needs. In addition, like science, it works with verifiable and objective data, which are organized in order for it to reveal interrelations. Philosophy is concerned with broad systems of knowledge; that is, with ideas about ways of knowing. Again, accounting is not directly similar. Yet, like philosophy, it is necessarily concerned with interrelations among relevant ideas and with awareness of rational reasons beneath its technical actions in dealing with appropriate data.

This leads one to believe that accounting stands somewhere between economics and philosophy, having some kinship to both. Its methods are orderly and focused toward practical results. Its technical methodology has had a long evolutionary development toward refining and revealing interrelations within enterprise transaction data. Its supporting ideology has had slower growth. Nevertheless, accounting theory has made definite progress toward becoming an integrated body of doctrine.

The characteristic bilateral form of an account category was not invented as a whole or previously designed for uses that later developed. It came into being very gradually, out of specific and simple needs. The present significance of the bilateral form suggests a closer look at possible reasons prompting its appearance. Even the transactions recorded by early moneylenders pointed toward the future. Initially, the record of each transaction was made in a written paragraph stating in detail persons, places, amounts, as well as dates current and dates as to the future. Frequently, both parties also signed the book record.

No special organization of recording was necessary as long as transactions were few. Later, the intermixed records of loans and repayments as well as of deposits and withdrawals proved inconvenient and perhaps confusing. Improvement was needed. Old manuscript books reveal the changes. Records for depositors and for borrowers were segregated; front pages of the book were reserved for one use, whereas the later pages were reserved for the other. This reorganization of initial paragraph recording gave very early recognition to distinctions inherent in these two kinds of personal responsibility.

Mixed entries of an individual (e.g., his deposits and withdrawals) later created much of the same kind of confusion of information. To overcome this condition, more space was assigned to each person: two facing pages of an open book. The result was the beginning of the bilateral form. For a borrower, loans and repayments were written on opposite pages, whereas, for a depositor, deposits and withdrawals on opposite pages.

It does not seem significant whether loans were in the front pages, deposits in the back pages, vice versa, or whether loans were recorded on a right page and repayments on the facing left page. Certain facts, however, persist as characteristics of modern account categories: the recognition of the oppositeness of borrower and depositor, the oppositeness of a loan made and the repayments, as well as the oppositeness of a deposit and its withdrawal. In fact, "oppositeness" permeates modern accounting: in every account, in the arrangement of balance sheet items, and in subtracting expense from revenue. The names of the accounts and the characteristics given the opposite sides of each account have a particular significance for analyzing transactions and for the understanding of messages lodged in account data.

From the earliest recorded experience with bilateral accounts, it is clear that one side of a personal account would record increases, the other decreases, and the two in combination would result in a significant remainder. The early names for each side of a bilateral account derived from the principal verb used in the verbal statement of the transaction record. In Italian, and later in French and German, a loose translation of the verb characteristic of the left side would be "he must give" and, for the right side, "he must have." A borrower's account would verbally state that he must give back a sum equivalent to the loan plus interest. A depositor's account would verbally state that he must have back from the banker the sum deposited earlier.

In several languages, the rough equivalent of "give" and "have" became technical terms, designating the left and right side respectively of an account. No doubt, there was little real logic in such specific assignments, just as there would be little logic to making loan records in the early pages of a book rather than in later pages. Either location, either side of an account, could adequately serve the purpose once the procedure had been firmly established. What it does demonstrate, however, is the power of survival that became attached to the method that proved satisfactory in use, even with little support from logic. This is not so much an evidence of continuity for the traditional as it is an indication of a continuing preference for known usefulness.

English usage has taken the name for the left side and the right side of an account from two other verbs: he owes (for the left side) and he trusts (for the right side); the Latin verbs are "debit" and "credit." These terms, like their technical equivalents in other languages, have become purely technical names for *left* and *right* in accounts. Account sides could just as usefully be named merely "left" and "right." The major handicap would be that of making verbs out of "left" and "right." However, as long as the noun "debit" and the verb "to debit" are understood as purely technical accounting terms for "left," as opposed to the translated meaning from the Latin equivalent (he owes), the traditional words in each language can serve this technical purpose quite well.

The idea that oppositeness has interpretative significance is an important part of the basic ideology of accounting. So, too, is the idea that a category, subdivided into separate and opposing effects of increases and decreases, can help make organized transaction data more meaningful. Other aspects of *form* also show that carefully planned spatial arrangements within a limited area of factual data can increase the power of organized data to convey ideas. This, after all, is the function of data and organization improves that functioning. The arrangement of data in financial statements makes effective use of opposites and other spatial placements to make the communications more informative. Several characteristics of the bilateral form may be listed, as these can explain why account data have capacity to serve interpretative purposes.

1. Accounts are classification categories named to segregate into informative groups the effects that transactions have on the enterprise concerned. Segregation by categories can compress a mass of detail into more intelligible totals or remainders. Each transaction is an event authorized by management for its effect on the enterprise. In the mass and in the various accounts, transactions will therefore reflect enterprise experience and the results of managerial decisions.
2. The bilateral form is well adapted to bring together related data that are at the same time opposite in their effects. By this means, an account can report on both increasing and decreasing effects that transactions have on a given category; thus, revealing the results (transaction history) of

changes and movements of capital within the enterprise, which, in turn, have originated in managerial intentions and decisions.

3. No single transaction could have a favorable and unfavorable effect on one account at the same time. Yet, each transaction will present some combination of favorable and/or unfavorable effects on the enterprise. Hence, more than one account will always be involved in recording each transaction.
4. Where accounts are appropriately named, they will by that fact reflect the type of enterprise and the kind of data its management considers necessary for reporting enterprise experience. Hence, systems of accounts will be individualistic, at least to some degree, and one system could not appropriately serve all types of enterprise.
5. Data in accounts are mobile and can be transferred from account to account as summarization needs may indicate. Thus, various accounts may yield up their data so those facts may be reassembled into major groups according to known aspects of data kinship. Accounts representing various kinds of assets may usefully be brought together; others representing sources of assets may be similarly associated; and accounts for various kinds of expenses and those for various sources of revenue may be brought together in two groups, to further compress data masses toward greater intelligibility.

Because of the mobility fostered by the bilateral form, compact reports of the financial status of the enterprise (balance sheet) and of its operating results (income statement) become concentrated communications about its experience, which is of high significance to internal management and to investors in the money markets.

A clear interrelation is evident between accounting substance and accounting form. If this were not the case, the service capability of accounting would be destroyed. The account categories (form) are named so as to segregate unlike transaction effects (substance) and to aggregate like transaction effects. The quantitative aspect of transactions – price in terms of local money used as a medium of exchange – requires use of categories that can arithmetically assemble, total, and contrast quantitative data. And each transaction involves an inflow and outflow: these movements stem from a combination of intended effect and a justifying consideration. These aspects of transactions require use of a technical form having certain capabilities. Bilateral accounts accommodate to these needs very well through their scheme of assigning increasing and decreasing effect to specific sides of related categories (i.e., not always to the same side in different accounts).

Each account is given conceptual boundaries as indicated by its title; thus, specifically limiting the data admitted. And the creation of a business enterprise sets up conceptual boundaries that will separate transactions clearly relevant to the given enterprise from transactions not relevant to its own actual experience. As such, enterprise data, because of these conceptual boundaries, must be strictly limited and account data must logically conform to the title limits. Transactions to which this enterprise was not a party could not speak of the experience of this enterprise or of data originating in decisions of this management. Only a thin line separates an imaginary transaction, expressing merely helpful desires, and a real transaction that involves a counterpart action on the part of a different enterprise.

This kind of conceptual boundary, by making an enterprise a limited and compact accounting and management unit (entity), opens the way for making interpretative comparisons of different enterprises and of the results of the judgments of different managements. Extensive disregard for enterprise transaction boundaries, in creating account data, could undermine the inherent confidence that the financial statements speak truly of the transaction experience of the given enterprise.

3

THE SUBSTANCE OF TRANSACTIONS

ABSTRACT

The exchange of reciprocal and quantitative consideration between transaction parties rests on the independent intentions and judgments of potential benefit for each. A transaction consummated between independent parties should logically be beyond subsequent unilateral modification. And, because "duality" is inherent in every exchange-priced transaction, the account form follows the lead of transaction substance. Conditions precedent to consummation of a transaction is two affirmative value judgments by the parties as to the benefits expected.

Separateness of the contracting parties producing an exchange-priced transaction is essential to dependable account data and informative reports. The exchange of consideration between the parties must rest on independent intentions and judgments of potential benefit for each. If it were otherwise, there would be a deceptive flaw in the validation of the transaction as a realistic event and of the money price as a realistic and reviewable quantitative expression of the event.

The translation by which accounting unites form and substance is a mental process. Translating *substance* (transaction events) into *form* (bilateral accounts) is transaction analysis. Exercise in such translation can be broadly educational in effect, if the thought processes involved are recognized as controlled by reasons. The older approach to transaction analysis provided many specific rules to be followed. The student was led to repeat the results modeled in text illustrations. Gradually, by precept and example, and by more or less mechanical repetition, some facility would be developed in translating familiar transaction events into simple account data.

Later texts presented fewer and simplified rules; yet, considerable reliance was placed on the use of rules. For example, the "balance sheet equation" is a relatively recent approach to analyzing the dual effects of a transaction on the accounts of an enterprise. Furthermore, even here, the equality of dual entries and of trial balance totals is still stressed as elements of basic significance. The result is that, even though transaction analysis has now become more of a mental reaction, analysis is not quite a consciously rational and a step-by-step breakdown of the enterprise effects inherent in the transaction event. Nor is this followed by consciously logical decisions as to where in the scheme of accounts the effects of the given transactions should be lodged.

Of course, beginners could easily be confused by too much theory, which runs the risk of being presented too theoretically and quickly. *Substance* and *form* could seem rather abstract terms and the various characteristics of each, if brought in view all at once, could be confusing. Nevertheless, a more rational educational approach than is usually seen in elementary texts would not be impossible.

Whatever the learning sequence that may be chosen, it might well rest on the foundation of two convictions: (1) that convincing and understandable reasons for accounting actions can show procedures to be understandably purposeful and (2) that beginners are likely to react better than expected to rational ideas that can demonstrate how typical accounting actions are appropriate to the needs of the situation and directly related to the objective of analytically creating informative account data. Ways could be found to gradually expand on both the distant and close-up objectives that prompt accounting actions.

Because accounting form and action are influenced by the substance of accounting transaction and by accounting objectives, it will be appropriate to summarize the characteristics inherent in business transactions together with reasons for their accounting significance:

1. A transaction, by being a specific inter-enterprise event, becomes a part of the transaction experience of both parties involved in the exchange. If economic life were so simple as to preclude enterprise transactions, accounting would have no reason for being. In any economy of pure barter, for example, there is no need for an accounting technology.
2. Since a transaction is an agreed exchange, both independent parties must expect to benefit from that item of experience or no agreement

would appear. For each party, an exchange would involve an inflow of some desired service and an outflow representing a consideration justifying the inflow.

3. Expected mutual benefit from an exchange gives motive and reality to economic action and to the transaction experience of both parties. Two elements here congeal into concrete transaction facts for both parties: (a) managerially planned intentions and (b) potential usefulness in the elements exchanged. Even in primitive barter, judgment as to use potential (value) would be the key to completing an exchange.
4. A mutually acceptable money price gives concrete quantitative characteristics to an item of transaction experience. The exchange price becomes an objectively determined quantity that can be used in arithmetical calculations by each party.
5. In an exchange-priced transaction, money serves as a common medium of exchange rather than as a measure of value. "Value" is a subjective element that is personal to each party to a transaction. Since money is the element that merely facilitates an exchange, its amount does not measure the benefit expected by each party. The goods brought have value because of potential usefulness rather than because of money price; cash received by the seller is not for him a measure of value but a generalized medium of exchange available to use in acquiring goods and services still to be chosen. "Usefulness" and "value" are also not interchangeable terms.
6. A consummated transaction becomes an undeniable experience and fact for both parties, short of proven fraud or honest mistake. Data from a consummated transaction then become symbols representing enterprise experience, and these should logically be beyond arbitrary modification at a later date as if a new original fact had come into existence.
7. If an expected benefit does not materialize for either party, this will not itself negate the prior fact of transaction experience. Second thoughts about transaction benefits sometimes lead to internal modification of the prior record; thus, becoming a unilateral management-created accounting action. But such action should not be considered a validated transaction, and it would therefore need to be convincingly justified on other grounds than those objectively supporting an external exchange-priced transaction with an independent party. Change in market prices, not specifically associated with an overt transaction by this enterprise, can scarcely be considered as an objective determination relevant to this enterprise and as having logical account validity comparable with that of a mutually agreed transaction.

The various aspects of substance as they are phrased above will probably seem only to point thought toward modern transactions. Yet, essentially the same aspects can be detected in very early transactions. These transaction types pre-cast, so to speak, the basic characteristics of accounting form (i.e., the bilateral account). A brief analyses of this background can indicate how, even in that early day, choices could produce improvement if they proved "sane, prudent, fair, reasonable, and commended themselves to the normal or average good mind (Webster, 1951, p. 737)."

Management's need for decision-useful data began very early to influence accounting form and substance. Personal accounts appeared first (bankers' records). Trading ventures abroad were at first liquidated upon return home and the full proceeds, not merely the profits, were distributed to the people who had supplied capital goods. When branch houses were later established in distant countries, the principal owner at home needed frequent information. The branch could not liquidate and divide proceeds, as a single trading voyage could, and still continue operations. Here was a need for specific type of managerial information, and this need generated nominal accounts. When these expense and revenue records were coordinated with accounts for persons and property, the integration of real and nominal accounts was achieved. This tight relationship is still the outstanding characteristic of enterprise capital-income accounting.

The bilateral form, which began with personal accounts, was found to be equally useful for other types of accounts (i.e., impersonal accounts). When the application of the bilateral technique had been extended beyond personal accounts, and the integration of real and nominal accounts had been completed, the central features of modern capital-income accounting had been assembled. From that basic conception, it became possible for men to see, through the study of data, a clear representation of the results of managerial decision playing upon the forms of capital available for enterprise use.

It is significant of the technical nature of enterprise accounting that the duality (double-entry), which is so often thought to be the chief feature of accounting techniques, does not arise in the bilateral form of accounts or in the equality of totals in a trial balance. Nor does "duality" arise in the integration of real and nominal accounts or in the administrative need for factual information about the results of managerial decisions. Duality, however, would be inherent in exchange transactions themselves even if accounts were not kept. Duality, therefore, is characteristic of the substance rather than of the form of accounting. And form follows the lead of substance.

Any exchange transaction involves two independent parties; call them E_1 and E_2. In entering into a transaction, a desired and favorable effect on E_1 is intended. This must be accompanied by a related consideration persuasive to E_2. This will be, necessarily, unfavorable to E_1. An example: the *intention* is to increase E_1's inventory; the accompanying *consideration* is an increase in outstanding indebtedness (unfavorable to E_1 but necessary). On the other side, since E_2 has suitable inventory goods, a sale transaction promises a desirable *effect* on E_2; that is, a favorable increase in revenue from the sale of goods. But a necessary *consideration* is involved, one that is persuasive for E_1, namely an increase in E_2's accounts receivable. This "persuader" is also favorable to E_2. It indicates an acceptable short-run risk but assures profitable conversion of goods into debt.

Each party, viewing the transaction from his own point of view, must see duality in the two effects on his enterprise. "Double-entry" therefore is not so much an *explanation* of a basic characteristic of accounting as it is a *result* of the nature of exchange-priced transaction agreed to by both parties. Both *motivating intention* and *persuasive consideration* are inherent in offer and acceptance by bargaining parties, each active in his self-interest.

Neglect of dual entries in the accounts of either party would leave an incomplete record of transaction effects. Thus, a later administrative restudy of an enterprise's prior transaction experience would be seriously handicapped. Such misrepresentation, by omissions of some realities of enterprise experience, could only mutilate the capacity of accounts to aid men to understand a business enterprise and to appraise the results of managerial decisions.

It may be useful to elaborate somewhat upon the ideas in the above paragraph. This is so because, first, some misconceptions exist as to the elements which lie closest to the essence of accounting, and, second, because an attempt is seldom made in the literature to disclose the aspects of logic that lie within and behind accounting technology.

None of the terms – duality, dualism, and double-entry – will signal the essence of accounting service capacity. Yet, all three speak of a characteristic form of action dealing with accounting substance. Because accounting is at once a way of thinking and a way of doing, it should be recognized as a complex of means toward a complex of ends. Duality within a transaction directs a way for thinking events into data and this leads to action bringing data into account categories. This interrelation of elements of actions and elements of objectives can help to cement the logical interrelation of ends and means.

Without making a project of semantics, it may be noted that the name "double-entry bookkeeping" may predispose a reader, and many users, toward a superficial conception of what the word "accounting" shall mean. A name such as "enterprise capital-income accounting" would be more informative. The words of this phrase could call up the idea of a business enterprise as a well-known fact of economic life. Easily associated with "enterprise," in this day at least, is the idea of management as the decision center of the enterprise. Also present is the idea that an enterprise earns income through the productive use of capital.

The longer name thus directly associates accounting technology with "enterprise entity" and "decision-making management." Many decisions made by management, in and for its enterprise, generate exchange-priced transactions that are entered into with other parties with the intention of furthering this enterprise's objectives. It will at once be clear that such transactions will provide information, which should be compactly assembled and made available for the later review of accumulated enterprise experience. At that point, accounting, acting as a data processing apparatus, undertakes to make enterprise experience more understandable and, thus, to foster self-understanding on the part of enterprise management.

Self-knowledge gets help from accounting, because accounting organizes data that, by speaking compactly and informatively of the prior experience of enterprise prior, provides a springboard toward future decisions. Accounting, by serving in this fashion, acts as a technical adjutant capable of helping the union of enterprise and management to accomplish a social mission and make their joint contribution to society.

It is a clear fact of economic life that enterprises, under guidance of management, use capital to make goods and services available to customers. It is similarly a fact of economic life that acceptable performance can be produced only by efforts, which, by the use of money as a medium of exchange, will be measurable by the money price invested in them. From these economic facts of life, it becomes evident that management performance comes from being able to produce sales through effort-costs that are below what customers are able and willing to pay; thus, compensating the enterprise for services rendered.

Now emerges a highly significant aspect of these economic facts of life: the described actions of enterprise management and its customers can take place whether accounts are kept or not. It will be clear; therefore, that accounting is not responsible for the actions taken or the results of these actions. Nevertheless, accounting is able to make a significant contribution to economic life. It does this by serving as a data processing apparatus, which makes measurable, usable, and understandable many significant interrelations between capital productively employed (effort) under managerial guidance and the revenue (performance) derived from those efforts.

In a sense, accounting is like a science in its use of measurable events to make understandable those "natural forces" that are significant for a business enterprise (i.e., its transaction experience). Capital in use and the resulting income are tightly related in reality, but not through the effect of accounting actions. It is through the use of closely related real accounts, *representing* positive and negative capital, and nominal accounts, *representing* positive and negative income, that accounting technology is able to help provide insight into business enterprise experience. When and if accounting fails to contribute to such insight, it loses its basic justification and its suitability as a means toward the indicated and desirable end.

It would be unreasonable and quite illogical, however, to believe or to act as if accounting alone can be made to provide complete insight. Natural and logical limitations, those that give accounting so much of its capacity to serve, will preclude the assignment of such a broad objective. For example, the characteristic dualism of accounting is at once a limitation on technical action and a necessary aspect of accounting action. The reason: dualism is a feature of exchange transactions whether accounts are kept or not. As a result, it is not correct to consider duality in the facts of enterprise experience as an invention for accounting. An astonishing aspect of accounting history is the fact that men succeeded in evolving techniques – hand tailored, so to speak – that could make the features inherent in exchange transactions clearly visible and useful as decision-helpful data.

Exchange transactions between independent bargaining parties are well-known facts of economic life; it is not necessary to assume their connection with accounting. It is necessary, however, to recognize the reasons why enterprise transactions furnish the raw material (i.e., the data source) for accounts, and why transactions provide the key to the characteristics of accounting actions. In looking for evidence of accounting logic, it is advisable to examine early the duality inherent in exchange-priced transactions. If the quality we call logic were not present, we would find it difficult to see how duality could become an aspect of accounting. This is so because duality is not a natural aspect of statistical data, although it can be contrived as in national income statistics.

It is significant that value judgments out of self-interest will prompt both parties to work a given exchange transaction. On each side is an intention to act in a way considered beneficial for one's own enterprise. But another aspect is equally significant and inescapable: neither party can reasonably expect to be able to benefit freely, that is, without offering some acceptable and persuasive consideration as an inducement toward exchange. It is here, and here only, that valuation, dual valuation in fact, enters the transaction picture. The subjective judgments by each party of benefits expected in relation to inducements offered will lie beneath the transaction. As such, two affirmative value judgments become conditions precedent for a consummated transaction event.

It should be noted that subjective valuations lie behind of, not within, an emerging transaction. Moreover, the money amount agreed for the transaction could not effectively represent value as such. Each part sets a higher utility value on one element exchanged and a lower utility value on the other. If this were not the case, no exchange would take place. Hence, value, being a subjective judgment individual to each party, is not an aspect available for account recognition.

The conclusion is that it is price, not value, which enters the accounts of each party. And the agreed exchange price, unless the transaction is completely undone (rescinded), becomes the same quantitative fact of the enterprise-transaction history for both parties. This aspect of transactions gives rise to the term "historical cost." It also indicates that, for accounting purposes, the quantitative aspect of a transaction speaks of money as a medium facilitating exchange, a lubricant, as it were, rather than a measure of value.

The duality inherent in a given transaction is evident to both parties and will obviously be opposite in effect for each. It must also be obvious – it does not need to be assumed – that intentional effects, both favorable and unfavorable, would be involved in each party's decision to make the exchange. It is a clear fact of economic life, and no assumption, that a consummated transaction would always produce dual effects on the affairs of each participant. It therefore follows that the quantitative measurement (money used as a medium of exchange) would be the same for both parties and that the amount would need to be twice repeated, in different accounts, in the record system of each party.

This kind of duality of entry was not an invention of accountants, nor was it conceived as the keynote for a visualized system of interrelated accounts. Duality of effect for each party has always been an unmistakable aspect of each exchange transaction. Accounting evolved to deal the facts as they are, with these undeniable facts of economic life originating outside of accounts as such. In order to reflect truthfully these compelling facts of an enterprise's actual experience, accounting has never had and still has no choice but to use dual entries. It is for statistics, not accounting, to develop techniques for working with unilateral categories and single entries of data therein.

The described basic characteristics of accounting technology direct the use of certain analytical techniques for translating transaction experience into account data. Transactions analysis calls for reasoning a situation-event into a specific recording decision. This is, necessarily, a mental process best employed in three basic steps:

1. Penetrating into each transaction in order to note the dual effect, whether favorable or unfavorable, which management had intended to produce by its decision-action.
2. Mentally associating the observed dual effects and the pattern of accounts established for that enterprise.
3. Making an assignment decision that, when carried out technically, will bring the money price of the transaction to the proper side of the proper accounts, where the effects on the enterprise may be seen in review at any time.

A pre-condition to transaction analysis will therefore involve an understanding of the reporting intent of each account in the system, and an unshakable knowledge of which side of each type of account is designed to receive entries reflecting effects favorable to the enterprise and which side for each account is dedicated to recording unfavorable effects. As such, one soon learns that favorable effects are not always increases and that unfavorable effects are not always decreases to an account. The reason is clear: enterprise property and debt are obviously opposites. In summaries, they will never be added but always be contrasted. Hence, increase in property will be considered as favorable, whereas increase of debt will be considered as unfavorable.

When this kind of logical step-by-step analysis has been completed, the content of any account can be clearly explained and convincingly defended. For entries made will have come out of logical reasoning connected with (1) a desirable objective, the preparation of informative account data truthfully representing enterprise-transaction experience and (2) a suitable means for implementing that purpose; that is, analytical techniques appropriate to accounting as a technology.

This kind of action is closely in accord with the following. A philosopher, Kaplan (1961), writes: "Means and ends reciprocally determine one another: We choose the road on the basis of our destinations, but also pick the destination on the basis of the condition of the roads (p. 37)." If accounting ideology and techniques were all analyzed into constituent parts, innumerable examples would be found of reciprocal means and ends at numerous levels of importance. It may also be reassuring to note that duality and equivalence are not characteristics found reflected only in accounting. A glimpse of these qualities is offered the layman in these phrases about Albert Einstein: "... [there is a] remarkable duality which persuades all nature (Barnett, 1957, p. 28)" and "Einstein showed that mass and energy are equivalent: the property called mass is simply concentrated matter ... matter is energy and energy is matter ... (p. 64)."

The dualism observable in accounting is a resultant of certain clear facts of economic life. These facts exist beneath every consummated exchange transaction, and this is so whether accounts are kept or not. Hence, accounting serves as an instrument – a type of data processing apparatus – for marshaling and compactly representing results made concrete and actual by joint decision-actions of independent parties, each deciding in accordance with his judgment of his own self-interest. These elements have characterized accounting from its earliest days. The technical aspects of even the most modern accounting function rest on this foundation. The same kind of duality was inherent from the beginning, and it persists usefully today within the simplest and the most complex accounting. This fact is a significant aspect of its power to continue to serve.

The implication from this conclusion is that the crowning achievement of accounting in evolution took place long ago. It was reflected in actions and not in explanations. The achievement took the form of a technique of tightly interlocked real and nominal accounts. Together, these could reflect, in data, the close interrelation of enterprise capital productively employed and enterprise earnings, the latter being a result of that employment under management. And the transactions that produce earnings for one party become productive capital in the possession of the other party.

That integration of capital data and income data is a significant consequence of the logic that has long been inherent in the dualism lodged in all exchange-priced transactions. It is therefore quite appropriate to conclude: rational transaction analysis proves to be a basic and suitable means toward the end of making evident, in dependable data, the relations existing between enterprise capital (the tree) and enterprise income (the fruit), as these two work and grow under the skilled husbandry of enterprise management.

For these reasons, it would seem appropriate to replace the name "double-entry bookkeeping" with "enterprise capital-income accounting technology." It would seem equally appropriate to begin the study of accounting by viewing its basic technical features, the chief characteristics of its usual account categories, the natural sources of its data, and the simpler interpretative significance of its data in aid of next decision-actions.

PART VII

1

THE PATH OF PHILOSOPHY

ABSTRACT

Accounting opens to analytical examination many aspects of an enterprise that are not visible to direct observation. Scientific techniques foster certain techniques, just as successful accounting techniques foster managerial techniques. These basic concepts and useful techniques are integrated by a hidden logic, much as water unites aggregate and cement. Accounting analysis breaks down diverse transaction experience and, by synthesis, re-assembles the raw data into compact and informative reports. The result from this process, dollar-price data in accounts, opens for study realities lying deep beneath the figures.

A new CPA medal has been struck that will accompany each award made by the American Institute of Certified Public Accountants for outstanding service in public accounting.[1] A significant feature of the design is the use of a prism to symbolize the profession. A prism breaks a beam of light into bands of primary colors; in like manner, accounting can break down business and financial activities into components more readily subject to analysis. And as prisms in a telescope can expand human vision; in like manner, accounting expands what men can understand in business and financial practice.

In essence, the service rendered by accounting technology is that of revealing the relation of elements which would be interrelated within a business enterprise whether accounts were kept or not. This kind of service seems to reflect some of the characteristics of an instrument of science. For, like a microscope, accounting opens to interpretative examination many aspects of an enterprise that are not visible to direct observation. These are not merely fanciful metaphors. The reality within them is indicated by the service of analysis rendered by accounting in aid of interpretation and understanding. The contribution is a real one; a complex is made more intelligible; the significance among details is illuminated. Accounting has been performing this kind of service for a very long time.

Some of the many enlightening thoughts expressed by philosophers can also be applicable to some aspects of accounting. Although aimed in a different direction, those ideas can help reveal more clearly the patterns of the rational ideology that is supporting accounting techniques. Likewise, technology can be viewed as the skillful application of appropriate methodology; technique is a studied manner of performing in practical situations. Accounting, therefore, should be understood as more than routine procedure. Without being scientific (i.e., resting on experimentally proven knowledge), accounting actions are supported by some of the attributes of science, and many accounting ideas correspond closely with philosophers' thoughts.

Behind accounting, as a body of technical actions stand a variety of needs, intentions, and objectives. Behind those, we find basic motivation. Even the simple initial techniques bear fruits (ways to get to know a business enterprise) that, through the centuries, have proved useful to society. Bookkeeping may now seem a simple recording procedure; yet the original motivation was clearly rational and the essence of the underlying ideology, we now realize, was even then clearly logical. Urgent managerial needs provided motivations. Several centuries of preliminary developments, almost comparable to informal experimentation, ultimately evolved into types of action that satisfied the then motivating needs. This was an early demonstration of pragmatic logic, the compelling relation between means and the objectives, and the ends that sponsored those methods.

In this development, there was a significant sequence: recognized needs, selected actions, related results; in other words, motive, action, and consequence, which in turn produce understanding. The parties directly concerned, in using this sequence of pragmatism in action, could appraise the relation of the result to the need as being either appropriate or inappropriate, and thus place themselves in a position to continue the action or try other kinds. A scientist works that way. His techniques breed other techniques; in like manner, successful accounting techniques foster further expansion of service capacity.

The banker-traders of the early days would have been prompted by self-interest to conceive of ways of improving next decisions. They "experimented" with methods for making their prior actions reviewable and thus associated with the results attained. They succeeded in creating, over a considerable period of time, a satisfactory technology toward that end. The resulting basic scheme of accounting action is still in use and still makes enterprise past experience reviewable. Furthermore, new technical knowledge emerging from this use has steadily given accounting an increasing capacity for rendering its service.

It took centuries for the work of many practical men, without the aid of guiding light from philosophical truth, to innovate the ways and means we now recognize as enterprise capital-income accounting. Centuries of later use give evidence of the suitability of this means for achieving a desirable end: that of providing understanding of an enterprise through review of its transaction experience. It is still the purpose of accounting, by the use of data analytically marshaled, to help men to understand the structure and activities of a business enterprise and appraise the results of prior action-decisions.

The fact that accounting increasingly serves society in acceptable ways is evidenced by its widespread use and the growing prestige of the professional group of certified public accountants. And the literature reflects a clear awareness that accounting (the technology) and public accounting (the profession) serve the public interest. It is understandable, therefore, that men should wish to know how the service of both might be improved toward further growth in capacity. Powell (1961), the first chairman of the Accounting Principles Board of the American Institute of Certified Public Accountants, has said: "We believe that a firm foundation in accounting theory in necessary to the development of a sound structure of accounting practices and procedures (p. 29)."[2]

This statement concisely puts into a few words a significant relationship: accounting practices, even those of five centuries ago, would not exist as actions for their own sake alone; they were used as means for satisfying definite needs, ends, and objectives. Actions begin in ideas. These ideas permeate actions. The same article quotes an elder statesman of accountancy, George O. May, in these words: "It is no time for patching up; it is time for viewing the system as a whole and developing, if not a philosophy of accounting, at least a mode of thought that visualizes the problem as a whole (p. 31)." These words of wisdom can inspire hope that the integration of theory and practice, which long has existed beneath the surface, may presently become more visible to all concerned. Nonetheless, it is unrealistic to think that accounting could become a philosophy, in the sense of being merely a mode of thought. Accounting can never be all theory or all practice; yet, its actions and its objectives are reciprocals.

This inescapable interrelation of theory and practice raises some stimulating questions about the reasons accounting actions possess capacity to render satisfactory service and about the features that give accounting its power to function toward a large variety of goals. Questions like these seem to call for something like philosophical inquiry. Ideas out of a sample of the literature of philosophy can be stimulating. They can often direct accounting thought very usefully toward its objectives and motivation.

We can observe accounting in action, and we can examine its growing literature. We can recognize a long history of increasing capacity to serve many needs for information about a business enterprise. When we do this, it can stir us to wonder what kind of ideas could have sponsored its basic methodology; what kinds of power within its techniques continue to provide accounting with its vitality. Perhaps basic ideas (concepts) and accounting fundamental techniques (actions) have been integrated by some hidden logic, much as water unites rock aggregate and cement into concrete. Yet, that integration of theory and practice is seldom clearly described in the literature.

Actions do not sprout without seeds and soil. Ideas, motives, and needs are the antecedents; actions, methods, and techniques themselves can only be consequences that bring ideas alive with usefulness. As such, an assumption would not stand which implied that accounting technology came out of some kind of conceptual blueprints and specification that, in time, matured into a completed structure according to plan. Extended too far, the analogy to concrete may lose its significance; it might then include the image of poured foundations and walls rising in solid sections. A change of metaphor may be needed. It may therefore be more realistic to think of accounting ideas and accounting logic as warp and woof for a woven fabric of theory, which could serve accountancy as its own kind of philosophy. That fabric may let light shine through and therefore seem insubstantial. But if its patterns nevertheless become visible – patterns that make accountancy somewhat more understandable – even a thin fabric of accounting philosophy would serve a useful purpose.

The long evolutionary development of accounting began in a search on the part of the managers of early trading ventures for ways and means of understanding their enterprises. Means of moving toward such a goal were conceived little by little. After perhaps three centuries, the structural framework of enterprise capital-income accounting had been developed. By the end of the fifteenth century, it has become a well-organized instrument for providing data in aid of management's problems of decision-making. The continuing need of management for more enterprise information, up to the present day, gave continuity to those means that had proved satisfactory in use. Surely, this was logical. As a result, change along with continuity proved able to meet increased demands arising from increased complexity of enterprise operations (see Littleton & Zimmerman, 1962).

A rudimentary informational apparatus could supply rudimentary aid for understanding a simple business enterprise. The history of early accounting can provide some insight into early methodology. But the modern need to understand calls for something more than early history; it calls for insight that will reach into the ideology behind the methodology. Part of the search for insight into accounting should deal with ideas, concepts, explanations, and justifications, because these elements are related to accounting actions. We can better understand present and proposed actions if we are aware that good reasons and persuasive logic lay beneath even the early methods, and if we see these still beneath modern aspects of accounting.

It may well be that strong fibers favoring survival had developed during the early evolution of accounting methodology. It seems possible now to detect elements of unperceived pragmatic logic beneath the surface of the simple recording procedures of a much earlier day. Such fibers of logic – even though long unnoticed as such – may have provided in accounting an impulse toward continued service growth. It may have fostered a capacity to serve as an effective means for attaining desirable ends. A capacity, which was strong enough to last, could still be functioning within this technology and supporting it as metal lath supports plastered walls. Such inner logic could reasonably be expected to bind accounting ideology and methodology into a monolithic whole.

Accounting method would have developed out of its own kind of "chance variations." Some elements survived, others less suited to the "environment" disappeared. Different men, searching for effective aids to understanding a given business enterprise, would have made efforts that in effect could be "chance variations" such as those that the natural scientists believes have often been involved during the long course of evolution.

The business enterprise and the economic atmosphere that surrounds it was the environment in which capital-income accounting developed. Survival in that environment would have depended on a capacity in accounting to contribute satisfactorily to management's understanding of a given business enterprise. Selectivity would play a part when one method, upon use, proved more satisfactory than some other did. As a result of selectivity and continuity, this instrument of analysis has grown more and more capable of increasing men's ability to understand a business enterprise. As accounting grows in service capacity, better managerial decision-actions result within a complex structure of many interacting enterprises. These actions in turn contribute to a continuing evolution of the environments in which accounting functions. Therein lies the essence of the social service of accounting – a part of its reason for being.

Little is at fault with the ways and means of accounting. More important issues are likely to be found in the area of ideology, particularly where objectives and sub-objectives are involved. There is need for accounting ideas and concepts to be organized into a logical and integrated body of doctrine capable of matching the purposeful integration of accounting actions and procedures.

From its beginning, the mission of accounting has been that of providing means for understanding a business enterprise, through insight into the results of management's decision-actions. Of course, it is not enough merely to assert or define such a mission and then attach aspects of accounting method to the definition as if the latter were an assumption. It is necessary to find reasons that can explain why account data can open windows of insight into a business enterprise.

Even when accounting began its service to enterprise management many centuries ago, men had need for actual information accumulated out of prior enterprise experience. Gradually, out of the ingenuity of many individuals, various simple ways and means for satisfying existing informational needs were contrived. Experience with their use brought improvement; satisfactory means for achieving recognized ends became increasingly suitable as they were usefully expanded. All the while, the basic need remained relatively unchanged in character but progressively satisfied in fact. Each aspect of accounting method became part of a complex of means contributing to a single goal: understanding the significance of prior enterprise experience.

Thus, we come to the edge of an illuminating idea: the significant elements of accounting actions derive from deep roots in human nature. Understanding how this can be would heighten the conviction that accounting has a logically based and inherent high capacity to be of service to society.

Human nature is involved here. Living creatures are endowed with instinct for survival and are possessed of five senses as means to that end. Mankind has these endowments, and more. He also has intellect. This quality makes it possible for him to use his five senses in many complex and rewarding ways. His intellect gives him these two highly significant and interrelated characteristics: an urge to understand and a capacity to benefit from experience. This understanding is, for man, a broad goal. Experience, through trial-and-error, experimentation, and education, is a basic means for approaching that goal. Man's intellect gives him several capacities that tend to foster rational action:

1. Capacity to grow in understanding.
2. Capacity to know in order to understand.
3. Capacity to seek experience in order to learn from success and failure.
4. Capacity to take present action based on experience and aimed toward an expected future.

In essence: capacity to know, in order to understand, in order, thereafter, to act advisedly. Some significant relationships lie within these ideas: relationships between action and motivation, among aims and objectives, as well as ways and means. As to objective (motives): we try to conceive of desirable ends; to detect and justify desirable goals; and to weigh competing objectives according to known or expected consequences of ends fulfilled. As to means (actions): we try to conceive of means particularly suited to chosen objectives; to detect and justify the most suitable means; and to weigh alternative and competing means according to a judgment as to relative capacity for contributing to the realization of chosen objectives.

Making choices of alternatives calls for penetration into objectives and for critical judgments as to the best means. Experience with prior choice of objectives, and with the outcome from the use of various means, will be a valuable aid in new situations.

Thinking about the significance of interrelations among data can become a guide to rational decisions. Since accounting technology organizes naturally related data, it deals extensively with interrelations. Because of men's urge to understand, the capacity of accounting for informatively marshaling interrelated data makes of this technology a very useful tool for man's approach to many of his decisions. Herein lies one of the basic reasons for its capacity for rendering effective service: its suitability to serve the objective of making future decisions.

Behind an ultimate goal of appropriate action, in a business enterprise, stands an antecedent need for understanding the accumulating transaction experience of that given enterprise. By the analysis of the interrelation among various expense data, for example, a man's powers of decision are strengthened and a better approach is made toward successful operations. On the other hand, an effort to grasp significance may tempt the use of intuition. The result might sometimes be satisfactory to the individual, yet might be difficult to explain, even to one's self.

Another and better road would involve the conscious exercise of native intelligence. All of us have some capacity for independent thought. We may ask ourselves questions and try to answer them out of our experience. We have native capacity for wondering "why" and for asking "what then." We can be curious as to the controlling motives behind actions and as to the actions likely to follow from specific intentions. Yet, we are so habituated to learning with the aid of the printed page that we may have under-developed the capacity to penetrate toward meaning back of interrelated data, such as the data that come out of accounting. Where we seek to understand a business enterprise from the study of its financial statements, we need to be as able to read meaning from contrasted money amounts in the way we read meaning from associating a subject and a predicate in a printed sentence.

The idea of interrelations is given considerable emphasis in the above passage. Such an emphasis points toward the need for men to learn how to exact meaning, by detecting significant relations among account data. Furthermore, because enterprise accounting has evolved in ways that make data interrelations discernible, we are able to use accounting data to deepen our understanding of enterprise experience. This provides a key to the nature of accounting.

It is appropriate to think of all accounting actions, from the simplest to the most complex, as being sub-means to a distant and desirable end, namely the goal of making enterprise prior experience understandable in order that managerial actions may wisely extend enterprise experience. Through serving for a long time in this manner, accounting has evolved into an engine of analysis and synthesis. These two types of accounting action help make past experience understandable. Analysis breaks down a complex (such as an exchange-priced business transaction) into more readily understandable parts. Synthesis re-assembles separate but relevant elements into a more informative whole, such as a balance sheet. Thus, these two techniques, when applied to raw data, convert events into quantitative digits that, in turn, provide insight into a business enterprise. The result is that accounting has become a technology that can help men gain insight into a complex, and, through this insight, gain understanding.

A businessman, approaching a planned decision, will have been thinking ahead, sensing problems and seeking tentative answers. He does not think of this analytical reflection as philosophic actions. Nevertheless, enterprise management, in studying schedules of account data, and investment analysts, studying financial statements, are both seeking enlightenment. He who seeks enlightenment, as to the realities within a business enterprise, and who searches for insight, into the significance of the continuity and change he sees in the data, is in his own way following the path of philosophy. As such, inside and outside a business enterprise, men try to look through the window of account data and into enterprise experience; that is, to understand the enterprise as a whole. This is consistent with philosophy, which has been described as "... a study of experience as a whole, or of a portion of experience in relation to the whole, or the interpretation of a part in terms of its place and value for the whole (Durant, 1926, p. 14)."

The user of account data or financial statements tries to interpret figure symbols, to extract from the factual summaries some meaning related to that enterprise. He will note the significance of each part of the communication in order to comprehend the message of the report as a whole. This is a road to insight; the path leads in this direction because the gravel underfoot is the life experience of an enterprise. As such, the man who undertakes to extract meaning from financial statements, and the man who arranges data in ways that can facilitate interpretation, are trying, each in his own way, to make visible and understandable and therefore more significant and fruitful some of the experience of a business enterprise generated by the actions of its management.

Many of the thoughts of philosophers are directed toward science; their experimentation is a well-known road toward experience. Business experience, however, cannot be said to emerge from controlled experimentation. Yet, business experience is not haphazard either, for it consists of the results of planned efforts to be able to serve customers satisfactorily. Accounting can make evidence visible as to both satisfactory and unsatisfactory results of such efforts. Those "efforts" are not like scientific experiments, yet they are in a sense experimental. Out of analyzed experience come conclusions and decisions, which tend to delete those efforts that proved unsatisfactory and direct action towards those that proved satisfactory.

To analyze experience and make new decisions is part of management's practical function. This function is not philosophical. Yet, within it, there is logic. And logic is an aspect of philosophic method. Practical experience of this kind carries the philosophical name of *empiricism*. Philosophers speak of the usefulness of suggestions which derive from the past as being "... developed and matured in the light of the needs and deficiencies of the present, employed as aims and methods of specific reconstruction, and tested by success or failure in accomplishing this task of readjustment (Dewey, 1953, p. 89)." Another philosopher makes this pointed observation: "It is doubtless to one's advantage, if one is to act effectively, to think what one will do, to understand what one has done, to have a clear conception of what one might have done (Bergson, 1946, p. 42)."

It almost seems as though these writers had in mind the needs of enterprise management, of enterprise investors, and the way accounting functions on their behalf. The investor tries to understand what management has accomplished; he judges management skill in the light of his own analysis of the financial statements. Enterprise management, for its part, will need to review what has been done and think about what might have been done differently. This is logical procedure and a part of the approach to decide what to do next. As such, philosophy is a way of thinking analytically. Likewise, accounting is a way of helping management and investors to think analytically. Whoever acts rationally, logically, and effectively after taking thought of what has been, and what might have been, is following a path marked out by philosophy regardless of the coat the thought may be wearing.

Account data are important stimulators to generate thoughts, even though, on the surface, the data seem inert and too concrete from being merely quantitatively factual. Indeed figures, digits, and numbers are but symbols and abstractions. Yet, deep reality lies within an exchange-priced transaction, an economic event that originates in decision-actions by management. It is the function and service of dollar-price data in accounting to open for study realities that lie deeper than one who analyzes them.

The point is that account data must embrace that accounting is a conceptual window, through which to view the effects real transactions have on an enterprise. Philosophers present a similar thought this way: "The function of theories and abstractions ... is to extend and deepen the range of significant experience by showing what to look for in situations ... (Murphy, 1943, p. 136)." Another writer tells us: "The need for satisfying our desire to understand, to have our experience hold together logically ... is very strong among human beings (Brinton, 1963, p. 258)."

This last thought reaches deeply into the basic reason that accounting has evolved into a socially important technology. For a person analyzing financial statements, and for a person constructing them out of account data, it is important to look for evidence of change in details of enterprise status, efforts, and accomplishments. It is also important to look for changes that move together or move in opposite directions. Both are significant. Such awareness of change can serve as a means of gaining deeper understanding. It is therefore clear that accounting technology must be conceptually and structurally capable of acting in two directions: that of assembling experience data analytically and that of communicating, through these data, the essence of that experience in ways that can help an interpreter to see change. This is so because change is far more significant than instant facts. Note how clearly the above samples of philosophical thought harmonize with the next statement about managerial accounting.

> All indications, all estimates of the consequences of contemplated actions, derive from experience of past events ... the major differences between guessers and expert estimators lie in the sophistication with which each probes, analyzes, and interprets the past. (Goetz & Klein, 1960, p. 481)

Wherever understanding is involved, interrelations and changes in relations will play a part. Accounting is very active in posing relationships. So, too, is mathematics. Its equations are calculation devices using symbols composed to express conceptual ideas. Although accounting itself is not mathematical beyond arithmetic, we find some account relationship composed by symbols that are expressed in equations. For example, "Assets = Equities" is the equation of a balance sheet. More fully verbalized, the relationship means: total invested price of capital available for enterprise use will always be exactly balanced by priced-investment claims held by various types of contributors and claimants, who have legal equities in that enterprise and its operation results.[3]

The equation has significance because it can headline the verbal statement that compresses into one sentence a clear and forceful fact of business life. This is the close relation of economic, financial, and legal factors, which give a business enterprise its form and function. The balance sheet equation, therefore, can present compact meaning only to a mind previously conditioned by prior knowledge of relations existing between the basic concepts involved.[a] As mathematics provides the symbol language for science, so accounting provides the symbol language for business. The key to that language is the fact that accounting substance comes from actual transaction experience of the specific enterprise as this has been generated by decisions of its management.

Data originating in this transaction experience are basic and indispensable to understanding a specific business enterprise and for judging the effectiveness of its management. If these basic data are modified out of their natural reality and objectivity, real understanding of that experience may be affected, even though the modification of recorded actual experience were considered conservative or useful to data users. Yet, the contribution to understanding of an enterprise cannot be completed from its transaction data alone. Those data can only be organized by accounting toward user understanding. Only the user can know the questions that he hopes account data can help him to decide.

This leads to the conclusion that, like mathematics, accounting is a useful tool in aid of thinking toward understanding. Both tools are analytical; both compact a variety of messages. Yet, certain technical skills are necessary antecedents to communications. This necessitates different skills, which must be called upon to interpret the communicated data according to the type of decision problems involved.

NOTES

1. Littleton is most likely referring to the AICPA Gold Medal Award of Distinction, which was established in 1944 to recognize persons who have made a significant contribution to the accounting profession.

2. For more about the Accounting Principles Board, see Persson, Radcliffe, and Stein (2015) and Zeff (1972, 2007).

3. The more common equation of the balance sheet today is "Assets = Liabilities + Equities." The following sentence, however, does address both contributors and claimants, indicating that Littleton had both equity investors and creditors in mind.

a. Mathematics is useful to scientists for similar reasons. Einstein's famous equation ($E = mc^2$) is one such example. The relationship that the equation symbolizes is that mass (m), accelerated to an extremely high rate, will convert into energy (E). The symbol c^2 is the constant expression of very great speed; that is, the constant velocity of light (186,000 miles per second)^2. As with all equations, verbalization of relationship may illuminate a complex idea, and yet it cannot completely express the underlying complexities.

2

BROAD PATTERNS OF MISSION

ABSTRACT

Management engages in self-examination by studying the account data reporting the results of prior decision-actions. Actual transaction experience data will be more significant than data that are hypothetical. This is so because back of financial statements lie consummated transactions reflecting planned efforts on the part of the buyer and planned performance on the part of the seller. With this in mind, profit as motivation can be over emphasized, although in reality it is still a good indication of sound prior policies, plans, and decisions of management. Standardized accounting, however, is not without its limitations, as it cannot reflect the individuality of competitive enterprise and their management.

Since the objectives of accounting dictate the nature of the necessary accounting actions, the significant motives, needs, and intentions should indicate the broad patterns and some of the limitations of the accounting mission. Very broad needs, such as the urge to understand and the desire to know, could be considered as likely to produce accounting actions capable of contributing to satisfying those needs. All accounting actions and details of techniques could therefore be related to these distant ends. But the variety of accounting actions suggests the existence of intermediate objectives lying closer to detailed actions, and thus able to explain them better than could more distant and broad objectives. Those lower level ends can be perceived rather easily beneath typical actions. In mass, these various sub-objectives join in supporting the broadest ideas as to the major ends served by accounting techniques.

Some objectives point directly toward preparation of factual data significant of enterprise experience. Back of bilateral categories and transaction analysis lie justifying objectives. These are the organization of data to reflect movement and change using data derived from favorable and unfavorable transactions that affect the enterprise; the facilitation of the flowing of data in, out, and between categories; and the summarization of that enterprise transaction experience into informative and interrelated groups for use in reports.

Unilateral statistical categories would not prove as satisfactory for business enterprise data as bilateral account categories. For example, one bilateral cash account would better serve accounting purposes than would separate categories for cash received and cash paid; or one category for debt due from customers and one for customer's debt discharged. As such, an important service of an account is to reveal, by residual remainders, the net effect of numerous events, some positive, others negative. It is clear that all data movements in and out of accounts related to enterprise transactions would have to be recognized whether unilateral or bilateral categories were in use. The bilateral form, however, would greatly facilitate the thought process by which transaction data are recognized, assembled, summarized, and studied as to the significance of changes and movements indicated.

Related to category objectives are the objectives of transaction analysis. The basic purpose is one of translating events into data. The quantitative aspect is supplied by the agreed exchange price of the event; the conversion (translation) is a mental process. The objective of thought here is twofold: to see in transaction events data, which has the potential of revealing the intended effect on the enterprise, and to determine which categories must receive the data so all effects may be easily read back from data collected in a limited number of categories.

It is difficult to conceive of an acceptable alternative to this mental process. Enterprise events will need to be translated into data, whether the latter are organized as accounts (bilateral) or as statistics (unilateral). This is so because underlying decisions for analysis and classifications is the need to know the purposes and limits of the categories in the system and the need to see data potential in the event. Intelligent translation of events into data would also call for an understanding of subsequent grouping of categories toward informative and analytical communication. These actions would be based on the consideration of alternative possibilities and customs.

Any use of data categories has the general objective of making visible and more understandable an almost unintelligible mass of separate detail. The need is to reveal patterns of relations among the data. This broad purpose is aided by using bilateral categories to speed the process of systematically and logically isolating and comparing positively or negatively related data. It also facilitates the progressive movement of data among categories toward ultimate communication and interpretative study. Because of this transaction analysis, the accounts become the first resting place of classified, factual, and quantitative data derived from management-generated enterprise experience. It is a partial objective of accounting to make enterprise transaction experience reviewable as a whole, in order to place demonstrated experience at the base of management's next decisions. Indeed, it can be considered an objective of management regularly to study the results of prior transaction experience.

In planning future action patterns, the review of experience can be directly helpful, especially so if this includes recognition of the way past economic conditions influenced the earlier decisions and, thus, may be related to the resulting decisions. Such coordination after the fact can provide a backdrop for current decisions to be framed in the light of the probable impact on results of expected near future conditions.[a] Furthermore, because accounting data have been collected within the definite boundaries indicated by the account titles, they can report various aspects of favorable and unfavorable effects that transactions have worked upon the enterprise. In this way, they point thought back to previously planned efforts, which in turn can help evaluate present performance reflected in current operating results and financial ratios.

It will be useful to look at an alternative to the scenario described above. As I have argued, the objectives indicated might point toward account data held strictly to those originating in overt transactions chosen by management for the effect they will have on their enterprise. The alternative is to argue that the objectives may seem to imply the acceptance of non-experience data (i.e., data not originated in specific enterprise actions in the market) into the accounts. In such a situation, one alternative must be proven more persuasive than the other alternative. The two alternatives cannot be considered identical nor can they be logically used together.

The issue here calling for a judgment would be whether prior transaction experience data would be more revealing and helpful if kept "pure" in the accounts; that is, restricted to overt transactions as the data source or if it would be helpful to embellish this data by the interpretative injection of collateral information. Of course, the latter would bring in further questions regarding the limits, if any, to the injection of additional non-transaction based data and as to the degree to which such data could or would cloud the messages to be interpreted out of undiluted overt transaction data. Let us consider replacement prices, higher or lower, as the case in point. Accounting can scarcely be logically changed to systematically report past enterprise experience as fact and, within the same system, report on results *as if* some transaction decisions had been made as of the present moment. *Actual* experience is very likely to be quite different from *hypothetical* "experience" based on a series of "what ifs."

Enterprise management has recognizable objectives, some of which are indicated below. The influence of these will affect accounting objectives, and through them offer reasons capable of explaining the technical actions of accounting. Consider the following propositions. Management objectives: conceive of needed products and services; organize enterprises to contribute to these needs; plan operations, policies, and transactions toward making enterprise actions effective; control activities by sound decisions under existing circumstances; perform in ways satisfactory to customers and at overall costs below the price buyers are willing to pay; survive under pressure from competition and grow with the times; and adequately compensate employees for services rendered and investors for capital dedicated to the objectives of the enterprise.

Here are suggested objectives for both enterprise management and business enterprise. Both concepts continue to exist within organized society because they have demonstrated a combined capacity to serve effectively. The needs of society generated free enterprises under management. Time has demonstrated in these enterprises a capacity to make satisfactory contributions to a healthy economic atmosphere, and these contributions continue to justify their existence and growth. In fact, the same basic human need for products and services, which generated competitive enterprise, has produced examples, under dictatorships, of tight governmental control over the means of satisfying the needs of the people. Government officials and employees decide such things as production types, employment conditions, wages, and prices. But even under those conditions, there must be operating units and within them some types of decision must be made.

There, however, the similarity between enterprise and government ends. The guiding lines for lower level decisions come down from top government. If this were so for enterprises, flexibility of decision at the enterprise level would be limited. Centrally determined material prices, wage rates, and selling prices are inflexible elements until government dictates changes. The result is that the verdict of the market place is not very evident in a controlled economy. Accounting will still have services to perform, but its data could not directly tell management the real economic facts of enterprise experience from the field. The full consequences of enterprise prior activities would not be visible in account data – only variations from dictated norms. Hence, only a limited amount of guidance could come from local accounts toward correcting a trend in operation results. And there could be no guidance whatsoever for local modification of norms.

Competitive business enterprises, and their separate managements, are sometimes said to consider the guiding objective to be maximizing enterprise profit. Hidden in this concept is a sly implication that maximization will be achieved regardless of the burdens transmitted to the factors of production by management's power to decide. It is doubtful in this day that such implication is tenable. Management is no longer the owner of the capital; also, labor is far more mobile and less docile. Management has to navigate its craft through more shifting crosscurrents than in earlier days. In contrast, an enterprise in a controlled economy would not seek enterprise profit but only to produce and serve. Yet, a spread between government-set prices (cost and sales prices) would be "profit" to the government, which might be visible, if at all, only within a complex of governmental statistics.

This example demonstrates that it is not a clear-cut statement of economic life to say that enterprise profit is the chief motive in a competitive economy. Profit is closer to being a means to distant ends. Profit and loss provide evidence indicating, in its total and its relation with other elements, the degree of management's success or lack of success in effectively managing the enterprise; in making the necessary right decisions; in recognizing need for changes; and in readjusting policies, personnel and plans. Enterprise profit, and the whole body of account data behind its calculation, carries a complex message about the cumulative results of management's decision-actions. It is possible, therefore, to trace back through the data, to uncover clues pointing towards responsibility, which in turn enables investigation. If necessary, this investigation can then prompt corrective action within the enterprise.

Alternatives to accounting – tied into competitive enterprise and intelligently used by responsible management – are not very persuasive. The basic reason is simple. The accounts of competitive business tell of overt, reviewable, and factual experience, both favorable and unfavorable, of the given enterprise. The accounts reflect the results of management's judgment decisions in and for that enterprise. Such data can speak in revealing terms of managerial effectiveness. They also aid management in self-appraisal, enabling the selection of areas and ways to make corrections where needed and the continuation of demonstrated satisfactory lines of action.

All this being done locally, adjustments can be made promptly and in small units of the economy as local judgment may dictate. In a competitive economy, this promptness of individual corrective reaction usually makes a definite contribution to economic stability. Individual factors sometimes congeal into unplanned mass reaction expressed in cyclical movements of prosperity or depression. These movements tell of a congestion of unwise decisions. For a time, individual decisions do not counteract each other into stability. But the demonstrated facts of a congestion of disturbing events – such as business errors, governmental policies, speculative fever, and international crises – affords knowledge upon which to build corrective actions. In their own way, cyclical movements constitute broad action-experience, and, as such, these direct thought to the complex of economic origins in much the same way that accounting results direct thought toward the antecedent complex of transaction decision-actions. Furthermore, out of this recognition and analysis come corrective actions, by the same parties whose collective actions generated the evident results.

One of the objectives of accounting is to produce financial statements, and these have the objective of compactly communicating to interested parties the results of management's transaction decisions. A possible alternative would suggest: make no public communication. Such inaction might rest on belief that business information is private and confidential and that this information in the possession of competitors could have damaging effects. In the present era, such negative reasoning has lost its appeal. The corporation has become a "public company" in the widest sense, dependent for funds from an informed money market. Published financial statements – by statutory requirement in England and largely voluntary in the United States – are the primary basis for judgments in the investment markets. In a free-enterprise economy and in an era of mass production associated with a mass purchase market, something approaching a mass money market must exist where investment decision direct the flow of capital into appealing productive uses.

It would be a doubtful alternative to suggest the use of statistical tables for all important enterprise data. Conceivably, enterprise transaction experience could be accumulated in unilateral statistical categories. But bilateral account categories, and financial statements made from them, possess definite analytical advantages. This is so because, in their own way, accounts tabulate transaction data. Their content is strictly controlled by definition of the function of each account category. The entered facts have been objectively derived and validated by concerted actions in open markets and in agreement between independent parties. Perhaps, these characteristics could be attached to data in unilateral categories. But there is a significant distinguishing aspect in bilateral accounts: they are tightly and plainly integrated into an informative pattern of interlocked relationships.

Interrelations among statistical categories are also of high significance. Indeed, the search for relations among data is the reason statistics exists. Accounts, however, are a limited type of category. They are limited by the boundaries of a given business enterprise; the dualism inherent in each exchange-priced transaction; and the need to disclose movement and flow of data between accounts. The patterns of data interrelations are influenced by these objectives. For a business enterprise is, in a very definite sense, a self-contained unit. Its data must be clearly relevant to that unit and the interrelations among account data should reflect only interrelations which exist among enterprise transactions regardless of whether accounts are kept or not.

Conceivably, alternatives could exist to audited enterprise accounts. Audits could be non-existent, or governmental examinations of prescribed accounts could be instituted. At times and in places, where audits have not been voluntary or required, this neglect has come to ignore certain aspects of human nature. As between statutory and voluntary audits of competitive enterprises, there is little to choose under present practices in Britain and the United States. Both are usually superior in consequences to those that emerge from fully prescribed accounting regulation examined and enforced by governmental agencies. This is so because prescribed accounts could scarcely duplicate the effects of accounts reflecting the individuality of the specific enterprise, or the results of the independence, technical preparation, and enforced ethical standards that are a part of the profession of public accounting.

A broad phrasing of the accounting mission would point toward the aid its data can render enterprise management and investors. The social significance of the service to investors is in no way less significant because of its relative youth in contrast with the age of accounting service to enterprise management. Yet, considering its long history and the continuing impact of accounting service on management, it would seem that this technology has been making its greatest social contribution through the impulse given toward the well-being of well-managed business enterprises.

It is sometimes said that the explanation of most business failures has been the "lack of capital." It would seem clear that merely to supply fresh capital for inept management could only postpone financial difficulties. Enterprise accounting has grown along with skilled managements, and it has become a dependable tool to management's hand. Administrative accounting has contributed in the past, and continues to contribute today, to good operating and financial decisions of management. In this manner, it can contribute daily to the service that enterprise renders to customers, employees, and investors. And, over a period of time, accounting can contribute substantially to the competitive survival of a given enterprise. These are socially beneficial services, and they deserve to be considered valid objectives of accounting.

Every enterprise requires capital, both initially and repeatedly. An extensive money market has developed to meet this need. Because the factors of safety and an enterprise's good prospects could influence considerably the people who make decisions in the investment markets, these decision-makers will study enterprise account data carefully. The best accounting communications will be prepared with this in mind. Yet, management's use of accounting is more basic: it is management's use of investment capital that provides the "point of contact" at which account data can make important social contributions through bringing together the thinking of enterprise management and absentee investors.

Although the primary mission of accounting runs toward enterprise management's decision-actions, a modern and collateral mission runs toward investor decisions. The same data source provides evidence of enterprise experience for both interpretative uses. This tends to place some strain on the technology, for ideas differ in each area of use as to the kind of information desired and available. Investment analysts may wish for data which management does not desire to publish, perhaps because of competitive situations. Professional accountants therefore recognize that it is not possible for the two usual financial statements to supply the money market with all of the data available to internal management. Yet, the opinion is growing in the American economy that it would be in the interest of management to publish information regarding its accomplishments in the enterprise in supplementary statements.

This need not to imply that revolutionary changes in time-tested accounting techniques as such. It should not be difficult to conceive of ways for making published company reports more informative toward outside interpretative analysis, and to do this while still preserving the central objective of the usual financial statements: that of providing compact summaries (capital and income statements) reflecting the outcome of management's prior decision-actions.

The operating results of management action will be most directly presented through the income statement. The objective here is to contrast (1) the results of overt transactions expressing enterprise performance acceptable to customers (revenue) and (2) the results of overt transactions (costs, expenses, and depreciation), which can speak of efforts made in the enterprise to be able to perform to the satisfaction of customers. The financial results of management actions can be reflected to comparative balance sheets or in an application of funds statement. Although the latter summary is seldom included in published company reports, it would seem a logical companion to the income statement for revealing management in action. These summaries of account data, since they derive from and speak of enterprise experience under management decision, will almost directly reflect, perhaps even measure, management's effectiveness in two important areas of action: control over the relation between costs as efforts and revenues as performance as well as the maintenance of a financially sound relation between enterprise property and debts.

The summary of enterprise status, as of a given date, is not very persuasively named either as a statement of financial position or as a balance sheet. The first title tends to suggest a report on enterprise financial capacity to pay its debts and, if necessary, to retire its security obligations without loss to the parties concerned. The second title is a heritage from the past and has now become a technical term in bookkeeping. The name apparently originated in an early ledger account used for summarizing all real account balances remaining after closing the nominal accounts. Such an account, and later its copy used as a report, therefore assembled transaction residuals, the remainders to be carried into the next set of account books; that is, today's results into the next fiscal period. This concept has undergone a considerable modification in modern times, which also deserves examination.

The theory that residuals of exchange-priced transactions are carried forward over the boundary marked by a cut-off date has been losing favor, as the use of accounting statements in aid of decisions in the money markets has increased. Since users in these markets face decisions (value judgments) regarding investing or disinvesting, a statement of residual balances carried forward toward future application to enterprise objectives has come to be considered deficient in the kinds of information most helpful for reaching investor judgments. The pull of differing interpretative problems, internal and external, has kept alive an issue of whether accounting statements should speak of contemporary values or exchange-priced transaction costs.

The real nature of the quantitative measurement of a transaction should be associated with investment, on the part of buyer, and with disinvestment, on the part of seller. When such designations are associated with the concept of money as a medium for facilitating exchange, it should be possible to disassociate the concept of "value" from the account figures in a recorded transaction.

Another way to think clearly of the transaction basis of financial statements would be to associate a transaction and its quantitative aspects with *planned effort* on the part of the buyer and *planned performance* on the part of the seller. In some aspects, the financial statements reflect the results of planning by a seller on one side and of a buyer on the other. The use of the same medium of exchange harmonizes widely differing transaction objectives relevant to the contacting enterprises. It also harmonizes the quantitative entries in the accounts of both parties. The cross-the-boundary relation is inherent in a transaction whether accounts are kept or not.

It would be a distinct advantage to reduce sharply the use in the accounting literature of such broad terms as *value* and *valuation*, for they strongly suggest an element of subjectivity inappropriate for accounting reports of management actions. Accounting as a technology should hold its data tightly to factual objectivity. A somewhat similar contrast is visible between *analyze* and *interpret*. Accounting technology might well be considered strongly committed to *analytically marshaling* objective transaction data. Thus, it should not be charged with *valuing* data and *interpreting* meaning out of data. Its objective should, of courses, include (through the word "marshaling") a responsibility for arranging raw transaction data *toward* user interpretation for significance for him.

Under guidance from functional logic, we do not need to "prove" the indicated objectives as being desirable ends related to accounting technology and to enterprise management. We need not even assume that they are desirable. It is only necessary to ask whether objectives such as these could have sponsored, with convincing logic, this technology in its small beginning without being then clearly perceived as ends, and whether such objectives, purposes, and functions, during long application, could aid, or perhaps beneath the surface even direct, the later extensive evolutionary development of this technology.

NOTE

a. Some reviewable record, perhaps simple memoranda of the major circumstances, leading up to a former decision, could illuminate the rationale of the prior actions and help explain the results.

PART VIII

1

RELATION OF THEORY AND PRACTICE

ABSTRACT

Techniques are actions. Reasons for actions tell of objectives, such as the need men have to review the results of prior decisions. Convincing support for an orderly methodology can be sought in the orderly structure of accounting ideology, and a basis for constructive criticism lies in clear knowledge of how things are in the present. This ability to learn by experience rests on knowledge of prior experience, and knowledge means that those prior events are understood.

Within the past half century, the technical accounting literature has presented relatively little analysis of the structural relations among its ideological elements. Yet, these are the basis for the technical processing of data suitable to the needs of administrative and financial accounting.

The problematic characteristics of these two areas of accounting action might become more understandable if existing controversial ideological aspects were projected, so to speak, against a backdrop of basic techniques and their reasons for being. Techniques are actions; their existence tells of objectives. Together, actions and objectives contribute to the capability of accounting to provide its particular kind of service. Understanding the relationship between them can foster a better understanding of accounting controversies. And, although a considerable literature presents details of administrative and financial accounting separately, it would seem quite significant that differing ideologies arise even though both services use the same basic data.

All account data are logically interrelated. The ideas beneath all accounting actions, which produce those data, form observable patterns. Because of these conditions, transaction data, when analytically marshaled and fully communicated, will afford a dependable approach toward meaningful interpretation by interested parties. Furthermore, since interpretation of significant meaning will mark the contact point of account data and the potential user's need for that information, the logical characteristics involved in processing the raw data should be known and understood.

As an approach to examining the basic action characteristics of accounting, it will be desirable to consider the objective prompting the developments of these techniques and to look for ideas expressive of the accounting mission. The basic service of accounting technology, indeed its primary mission, is to aid men to understand a business enterprise and to review the effects of the actions of its management. The thought is more than truism, more than definition or assumption. It is a compact statement of rational objective. The concept is supported by man's natural urge to know. In particular, he needs to know in detail the results of his prior business decisions; and on proper occasions, other people need to gain insight into the accumulating experience of a given business enterprise.

If a broad objective were needed as a springboard toward penetrating into accounting logic, the one phrased above would seem compactly appropriate. Research in accounting theory could be directed toward interrelated sub-objectives suitably supporting the primary objective, and at the same time directing the course these sub-actions should follow.

In connection with the above concept of objectives, reference was made to "man's natural urge to know." Perhaps this urge may be the most deeply rooted motivation beneath accounting, just as it is beneath so many human activities. The long existence and continued growth of accounting can give credence to a belief that it has served a deep-lying human need from its earlier days. Mankind has been endowed beyond all other creatures with a capacity for developing an intellect. Once developed, this intellect includes two significant and interrelated features: an urge to understand and a capacity to benefit from understood experience. Understanding can be a conscious goal; experience can be a means of approaching that goal.

It must have been an urge to understand their business affairs that motivated the early innovators of accounting. They were the ones who conceived the basic techniques that became enterprise capital-income accounting. Data organized by those techniques still derive out of and tell about enterprise experience. Only decisions of enterprise management created – and continue to create – the exchange-priced transactions, which provide dependable quantitative data regarding prior enterprise experience. Thus, transactions identify with enterprise experience and constitute the substance of accounting. Accounts provide the form for organizing data toward understanding. Together these elements are able to make more comprehensible a mass of events, which, without the services of accounting, would be less comprehensible.

In order to understand, one must gain insight into that for which understanding is desired. If a business enterprise is to be understood, its accumulated experience must be open to review. That experience will consist of all the transactions that management decisions have generated in and for that enterprise. If transaction experience is the substance to be understood, the window providing insight into accumulating experience may well be account data. Accounting, therefore, would be a technical way of providing insight into a complex and, through that insight, to make a direct contribution to man's exercise of his intellect toward knowing and understanding.

To round out the pattern of accounting's major objective, some reasons should be noted indicating why understanding and insight into transaction experience is desirable.

Since management and enterprise are inseparable as to economic actions in and for that enterprise, insight into transaction experience constitutes self-knowledge. Such insight can yield understanding because it encourages a questioning examination of what has been done; thus, pointing thought toward what might have been done differently. Critical review of prior experience brings prior decisions under scrutiny. Such examination would involve: (1) comparing evidence of effects with evidence of efforts and (2) study the significance of data changes between points of time. This is so because new decisions toward new actions are constantly under consideration, and insight into the results of prior transaction decisions enables management to face specific decision problems from a platform of knowledge.

Reference has been made to certain significant relationships in accounting: between theory and practice; ends and means to these ends; efforts and effects; and experience and insight. Similar relationships are evident in the literature of philosophy. In fact, many of the thoughts of philosophers, even though taken out of context, could illuminate the context of accounting theory. It would seem particularly useful to use this insight to seek to perfect the pattern and the persuasiveness of accounting theory as such. For example, it has been said that "... history has proven again and again that nothing is so practically valuable as pure theory (Randall & Buchler, 1942, p. 3)." In this context, "practically valuable" would mean effective in furthering successful actions toward desirable objectives. In recent years, "pure theory" preceded certain later concrete actions in nuclear physics. My hope is that the development of something approaching "pure theory" for accounting might also prove "practically valuable."

The present interest in accounting research suggests awareness that the partnership of theory and practice needs strengthening. The kind of service accounting theory can render to practice is almost directly expressed by this thought from the literature of philosophy: "The function of theories and abstractions ... is to extend and deepen the range of significant experience by showing us what to look for and what is significant in situations ... (Murphy, 1943, p. 136)."

Take, for example, the phrase "what to look for." It is a phrase full of meaning, particularly for the auditor. The audit work of an assistant may be purely mechanical, unless he has been instructed in what to look for. Every item in a tailor-made audit program should be a clue to look for something, to think of something, to see the specific task as a means toward known ends, some of these being close up whereas others are distant.

Following a similar line of thought, there is also persuasive precedent for a firm partnership between accounting ideology (theory) and accounting action (practice). Writers on philosophy have found theory and practice to be closely related. Their thoughts give support for confidence that accounting actions can gain strength and direction from accounting theory; that is, from concepts and ideas that are rational, interrelated, and defensible. Dewey (1953), for example, considers that theory and practice should not be separated: "... an unreasonable exaltation of theory on the one side and an unreasonable contempt for it on the other [would precipitate] a tragic division (p. 89)."

To be sure, it would not signal tragic division if some people (e.g., professional accountants) were preoccupied with practical actions and others (e.g., accounting teachers) were deeply interested in knowing that customary actions persist for convincing and persuasive reasons. It seems entirely rational to stress reasons and justifications even in the preparatory stages of an accounting career. In fieldwork, accounting theory can aid a person to be consciously concerned to integrate "what has to be done" with understanding of the reasons beneath each separate task and back of the whole line of action. In another place, Ratner (1939) expands upon the reasons back of the interrelation between theory and practice:

> There is no inherent opposition between theory and practice; the former enlarges, releases and gives significance to the latter; while practice [doing] supplies theory [reasoning] with its materials and with the test and check which keep it sincere and vital. (p. 623)

Another philosopher, Murphy (1943), states:

> ... using experience [practice] as material for theories, and theories as guides to further observations [practice] (p. 76)." And again, "... theories [ideas] guide observation to events that unaided observation had never seen, while observation gives the basis for new theories [ideas] which mere theorizing could not have established. (p. 43)

The close relation of theory and practice, of ideas and actions, and a sharp awareness of the need each has for the other, applies in accounting as well as in science. It would indeed constitute a "tragic division" if accounting were to be taught as if it were deductive philosophy or syllogistic logic; and it would be an equally tragic misconception of this technology's complexities if learning from observations in the course of the day's work should take priority over selected formal education. As such, a combination of general and technical education has come to be a highly useful approach to a career in accounting. Such preparation constitutes a means toward a definite goal. "And if history teaches anything, it is that with intellectual order we have the surest possible promise of advancement to practical order (Ratner, 1939, p. 954)."

Formal education can accomplish a great deal in revealing the "intellectual order" that exists in many areas of thought and action. Accounting education should be increasingly strengthened in that direction, for it is actively concerned with bringing intelligible order to a mass of detail. In fact, accounting theory might well be subjected to a thorough critical analysis toward a constructive reorganization. The purpose of this would be that the resulting theory, as an area of ideas, would reveal the accounting type of "intellectual order" and in so doing contribute to an "advancement to practical order." Theory need not, indeed it should not, be exalted. But the degree of traditional disdain for accounting theory that is implied in the term "wholly impractical" could, with benefit, be counteracted.

A thought particularly appropriate for enterprise management is the following: "It is doubtless to one's advantage, if one is to act effectively, to think about what one will do, to understand what one has done, to have a clear conception of what one might have done (p. 42)." Bergson (1946), the author of the above, was writing a generation or more ago; he was thinking not of accounting or business but of knowledge in general, and about how to gain knowledge. Yet, the point admirably suggests the way accounting data, intelligently used, can help men reach decisions.

The businessman – a unit in enterprise management – surely is a person concerned to act effectively, to decide wisely, and to choose to do well in what he undertakes. As an approach to action (i.e., to next decisions), an obviously useful starting point would be the consideration of the prior experience of the enterprise. This experience is the result of previous managerial decisions; that is, "what has been done." In retrospect, this enables him to reflect upon "what might have been done" better or perhaps done worse. In using such as approach to considering next actions, various ideas probably would appear as to things to keep on doing and those to avoid repeating. When linked with experience-generated constructive imagination and with restraint in exercising good judgment, these ideas should provide a springboard for action ideas that probably could prove in use to be to the advantage of the enterprise involved.

Since accounting is an intelligible technique in aid of accumulating enterprise transaction experience – experience that, item by item, stems from managerial decisions – the accumulated data that result can be considered a primary source of information about "what has been done." The same author, Henri Bergson, provides a clue to the reason recorded enterprise experience serve these next decisions "... our distant past adheres to our present and constitutes with it a single and identical uninterrupted change ... (p. 153)."

It may therefore be appropriate to say of accounting theory, as Ratner (1939) has written of philosophic decisions, namely that, "... its primary concern is to clarify, liberate, and extend the goods which were within the naturally generated functions of experience (p. 267)." In business and accounting, ideas may be considered as good if they lead to actions that are preferred because they produce or promise to produce desirable results. The function of theory should be that of indicating reasons why an idea might be considered as a good one and why a certain result might be accepted as desirable. It will be appropriate to add that accounting theory should also be concerned to aid men to understand and, hence, to be able to avoid such business and accounting experiences as might be judged undesirable.

Another philosophical work – Ratner's (1939) thorough analysis of John Dewey's philosophy – provides this further thought: "You can know that things should be different only as a consequence of knowing how they are (p. 131)." In other words, a basis for criticism lies in clear knowledge of how things are in the present. It is clear that such knowledge could also provide a basis for approval rather than criticism. An improved basis for either criticism or approval would seem to be one that also included knowledge, or a judgment, of how and why things became what they seem to be.

Antecedent motivation and causation may still be persuasive even under new conditions. Merely to have conceived of a way to effect a change can offer very little support for making that change. Sometimes criticism of things as they are would reflect rationalization backward from desired ends. Important for either criticism or approval of a part or detail – whether these are policies, regulations, or other accounting actions – is clear knowledge of the whole that embraces the part.

It should be an aspect of the function of organized accounting theory to help create an image of the whole that is accountancy. Since the whole of such a complex is not easy to grasp, analysis of significant interrelations within accounting should help to bring the image of the whole into sharper focus. For accountancy is more than a mechanical sum of its distinguishable parts: interrelations among the constituent parts are also factors. The messages readable from these interrelations can become clouded, perhaps even distorted, from the introduction of spot changes that lack effective coordination with the parts that continue unchanged. Replacement prices would be an example of such a spot change.

Coming back to the contribution of philosophers, the term "experience" appears frequently in these pages. Philosophers have had much to say about that topic. Some speak of:

> ... the philosophic search for what is significant in experience." And again: "Sometimes it is not whether a view [a conclusion out of experience] is true or false that is the major issue, but whether it is at all intelligible or meaningful. (Randall & Buchler, 1942, p. 119)

One of the conditions for admission into the profession of public accounting has been evidence of practical accounting experience. In applying such a requirement, no guidance is given in the rule as to how to learn what had been significant in the background of experience of the given individual. It would no doubt be difficult to set an acceptable standard for "meaningful accounting experience," especially in case the rule would have to come into existence through legislation. Perhaps the recent trend, toward broadening the educational preparation, reflects the realization that a few years of employment by a public accountant might not add up to meaningful accounting experience. This development does not mean that accumulating experience in public accounting is lacking in significance. It does suggest, however, that practical experience is most beneficial when it follows adequate preparation that is in itself desirably varied.

Accountants and enterprise managers will agree with the philosopher that an important factor of progress is "... the ability to learn by experience, that is, to derive ideas from what we observe, and to correct beliefs in terms of what is found to be the case ... (Murphy, 1943, p. 311)."

The present tendency in public accounting is to look to appropriate education to provide the principal initial test, and to consider the ability to learn by field experience as the critical factor working for or against professional progress thereafter.

We cannot count on accounting or business management to make their contributions by controlled experiments. Yet, both have progressively developed their respective techniques and expanded their capacity for service. This has been accomplished by slowly building on accumulated prior experience. As a result, we are able to teach some of the arts of analytically recording enterprise prior experience and to teach some of the techniques for communicating the data resulting from that experience. There is a new need now of developing techniques for extracting significant meaning out of the organized data of enterprise prior experience.

Dewey (1953), writing of modern scientific inquiry says: "It is a method of knowing that is self-corrective in operation; that learns from failures as from successes (p. 22)." This thought can apply also to account data, which is based on enterprise transaction experience. Enterprise management can read enlightening factual evidence of success or failure of prior decision-actions. And they can do this not merely in annual financial statements, but, if desired, day-by-day. By appropriately continuing or changing the pattern of decisions and actions, prior actions can become self-correcting. And, ultimately, we know much more about early accounting methods (techniques) for keeping accounts than we know about the ideas (concepts) that lay beneath the initial formulations. More knowledge is needed of the logical base, or the rationale, of accounting.

2

A TOOL FOR THINKING

ABSTRACT

Accounting is a systematic method of providing experience-tested data as a basis for future decisions. That experience, which is much more dependable than expectations, is open to diagnosis as an approach to decisions. An analytical recording of experience can stimulate an interpretative reading of the results of prior policy. This can be a road toward learning from experience. Ratner (1939) foresees this development, stating that "[e]nds which could justify themselves to reason [should] take the place of custom as guides to conduct (p. 288)." As such, functional theory can be useful even to practical roles, as theory can improve practice and good practices can improve business decisions.

The ideas philosophers have about science may provide a sense of direction to inquiry into accounting, even though accounting is a technology rather than a science. This is so because the word "science" signifies an area of tested and authentic instances of knowledge. Ratner (1939) provides further direction:

> Knowledge means ... events understood ... it means comprehension ... what makes any proposition scientific is its power to yield understanding, insight, intellectual at-homeness, in connection with any existential state of affairs, by filling events with coherent and tested meaning. (pp. 945, 947)

Accounting data give enterprise transaction experience a "coherent and tested meaning," and, by this meaning, the data serve to increase comprehension of enterprise status and results. Events are understood and knowledge is acquired. Furthermore, a system of accounts is designed and used to facilitate inquiry through thoughtful interpretation of intelligible data. In other words, management seeks to control its enterprise "more intelligently," and account data aid this intention. Note the significance of inquiry in science:

> ... science signifies the existence of systematic methods of inquiry which, when they are brought to bear on a range of facts, enable us to understand them better and to control them more intelligently, less haphazardly and with less routine. (Ratner, 1939, p. 632)

A few sentences out of context cannot pretend to cast business in the role of science. Yet, the businessman must deal with a wide range of facts in making his decisions. He needs to control (decide upon) enterprise actions as intelligently as possible. In his accounting, he finds "a systematic method of inquiry." In the data, he finds the accumulated recorded experience of his enterprise and, in particular, the recorded results of prior managerial decisions. This may not be a typical example of scientific method, but decisions rested on such a base surely would be "less haphazard and less routine" than decisions dictated by opinions of future expectations alone.

The businessman's approach to judgmental decisions involves both the past and the future. The use of recorded experience is a diagnosis, and such a diagnosis helps prepare next decisions toward the future. Accounting cannot possibly supply all the evidence management will need to take into consideration. And accountants, with good reason, begrudge non-objective data being injected into account categories containing objectively derived data that originate in the decisions of the management of the given enterprise. In this feature, accounting shows another characteristic like those of the scientific method. But there is, of course, more to making next decisions in business than scrutinizing account results. That illusive factor, judgment, is also involved. Judgment may best be considered as an outcome of past inquiry used as background and combined with conclusions from present inquiry.

The man of science, so writes Dewey (1953) "... wants a correlation of change, an ability to detect one change occurring in correspondence with another (p. 67)." Businessmen also study interrelated account data to try to detect significant correspondence or significant lack of correspondence of degrees of change. It is to aid in this kind of study that administrative accounting includes standard cost procedures and industrial budgeting. Viewed from another angle, accounting will be seen using symbols to make it possible for men to undertake an interpretative reading of enterprise experience. This is part of the way science works out its function. A philosopher, Benjamin (1937), has expressed this thought about science:

> Knowing is not merely the being aware of events; it is also the symbolizing of them ... the scientist does not *discover* a symbolic scheme, he invents it (p. 58)." And again: "... by this process a qualitative event ... is replaced by a number corresponding to the reading on an instrument. (p. 246)

Surely, these thoughts include something that needs to be said about accounting. It too is a symbolic scheme. It is invented and not discovered. Ledger entries use dollar amounts to symbolize quantitative actions taken in behalf of enterprise – actions that grew out of enterprise management decisions. Account categories, wherein the entries are lodged, are classification symbols for associating like with like and for contrasting opposing elements. Compactly summarized into financial statements, these symbols of qualities, quantities, classes, actions, and decisions, are set in arrangements, which then symbolize realities in the form of tightly integrated capital and income and of real and nominal accounts relative to the given enterprise. These analytical uses of symbols greatly facilitate understanding a business enterprise.

Because accounting organizes experience data, it has capacity to help decision-making. In itself, accounting has no power of decision, and accountants acting as such make decisions only within the area of marshaling transaction experience and in applying the techniques of auditing. On the other hand, management and investor decisions are formed in the minds of those individuals. This mental activity calls upon the decision maker to interpret (extract meaning from) the factual interrelations among account and non-account data. Accounting acts as a "tool for thinking." And, if the study of account data does not stimulate thought about enterprise prior transaction experience, then those data have not been made usefully informative or the interpreter has failed to use appropriate techniques to extract meaning.

One must reflect upon data put under critical examination, in search of understanding and insight into enterprise experience. Philosophy points out the value of reflection; it too is a "tool for thinking." As such, thinking is often a search for the kind of understanding that can provide a base for rational action. Philosophy aims at subjecting our ideas (and experience) to critical examination; their rationality can be tested by their reasons and origins. The ability to engage in analytical reflection on the messages lodged in data is one of man's most important powers. "In its most obvious features [reflection] is the power to ask and answer questions, to set and solve problems, to look ahead and plan conduct (Cunningham, 1924, p. 4)." In summary then, we can say, that accounting marshals transaction experience data to provide material for study in connection with the decision-making involved in planning enterprise conduct.

Accounting technology is a method; yet, objectives inherent within these accounting actions indicate reasons why the actions exist. It is the function of objectives, based on known motivation, to stimulate appropriate means for implementing those intentions. The function of the means selected is to provide suitable ways for achieving related objectives. Critical appraisal of the desirability of objectives, and of the consequences of the use of selected means toward those ends, can open the way for logically based continuation or change. In effect, this is a road toward learning from experience.

Appraisals of means and their consequences, when associated with data originating in decisions and actions of a business enterprise, are appraisals of the course of enterprise experience. Enterprise accounting functions are primarily means for opening enterprise transaction experience to summary, inspection, and evaluation. For this reason, accounting may properly be considered a technical means toward the end of making the results of enterprise management's decision-actions visible and reviewable. Being an appropriate means toward recognized goals, accounting can be considered a working example of functional logic.

The philosopher's name for functional logical is pragmatism, a branch of philosophy which, as an aspect of the scientific method, offers helpful guidance toward the search for knowledge by experimentation and verification. Some thoughts from pragmatic philosophy can be associated with the above ideas about enterprise experience, and therefore can have significance for accounting, even though accounting itself is neither science nor philosophy.

Observe first some thoughts about ends, for the presence of ends calls up means for achieving them. Accounting is not alone in possessing an area of knowledge that includes theory and practice as well as ideology and methodology. In fact, the opposite is true. All social institutions have a theoretical and a practical side; and each has its own kinds of objectives along with characteristic standards of satisfactory functioning.

The accounting ways of functioning make use of well-known procedures; the related objectives are less clearly perceived. There is no orderly array of aims ranging from small and intermediate to broad and relatively distant ends. If only immediate ends control all actions, the results may not be substantial or make needed contributions to distant goals. Distant objectives are not large items to be mentioned once and not referred to again. On the contrary, they should be definable objectives deserving frequent mention in many different contexts. As such, it should be their nature to influence close-up objectives and, in so doing, influence the choice and use of appropriate detailed means. Distant objectives may also prove to be useful tests for judging the suitability of particular close-up procedures.

Ratner (1939) states that "[e]nds which could justify themselves to reason [should] take the place of customs as guides to conduct (p. 288)." Custom is a strong guide to conduct in many areas of action, and often desirably so. A philosopher's preference for reason over custom should not in itself cast a shadow over accounting actions that may reflect custom. However, a part of the function of accounting theory could be that of fostering close re-examination of the ideas supporting customary procedures. Many of those actions may be found to "justify themselves to reason." If at the same time they reflect custom, it would appear that reasonable ends had been "guides to conduct" even though never spelled out as such.

There probably are many accounting actions of this type; their persistence in use may in fact suggest they have long served satisfactorily as means toward reasonable ends. If the end were still a desirable one, its association with a satisfactory action-means would indicate a logical (pragmatic) relationship. That relationship would need to be convincingly dissolved before the particular means could be judged unsatisfactory. The clue as to dissolution would lie in the consequences emerging from the relationship.

The practical gets strong emphasis in accounting; to some people this may seem to imply that expediency is in control. Yet, in public accounting, judgment as to the best means to use, not expediency, is a characteristic of the profession. For internal accounting, on the other hand, established practice justifies itself by the services rendered. Again, and as always, the term satisfactory means that a specific way of acting continues to serve the end in view until the goal is changed or a more serviceable method becomes available. Consider the following two quotations from philosophy:

> Men act rationally in practice when they act effectively for the attainment of ends rightly judged to be good. And they will so act ... only when the ends proposed for action are those that they believe in and care greatly about. (Murphy, 1943, p. 190)

> Philosophy may be considered as deeply reflective and critical thinking ... history has proved again and again that nothing is so practically valuable as pure theory. (Randall & Buchler, 1942, p. 213)

These quotations will not support the idea that every decision by management and every action by accountants are ponderously philosophized out of concentrated reflection on the spot and item-by-item. No more is the other extreme indicated: intuitive decisions and impulsive actions. Transaction decisions and accountant reactions are practical matters of the moment. And these are practical men, not philosophers. Yet, even to practical men, theory can be useful.

Philosophy can render practical service as a background based on two conditions: (1) if accounting theory has been shown to have philosophical and logical roots and (2) if that kind of theory has been studiously associated with the study of procedures and actions. Two results should emerge: (1) an integrated understanding of useful procedures and their reasons for being and (2) a mind sharply and rationally sensitive to the elements and potentials of each situation and to interrelations involving other situations.

Theory is already inherent in accounting and, therefore, can, and often does, influence practice practically. Its service can be extended and ideas imported from philosophy can help. The man already immersed in business can fortify his practical decisions and his professional judgment, by increasing his integration of the theory, practice in making decisions, and forming considered judgments. Furthermore, with accumulated experience, these actions become easier to make and easier to press closer to rational bases.

One gradually forgets that theory has philosophic content, and that practice is colored by theory. It is, therefore, somewhat by indirection that accounting theory renders its philosophic service to the management and accountant. Directly, or indirectly, rational accounting can serve management well, and, through better managerial decision-actions, serve society. This is a practical service; and theory, even philosophy, can play a part. A philosopher quoted above has said: "nothing is so practically valuable as pure theory." One might add: providing that theory improves practice and, in our particular case, that accounting practice improves business decisions.

Throughout the philosophy that looks beneath action in science, there is strong emphasis on observation and experimentation (experience) as a road to increased knowledge. Many of these ideas are also applicable to accounting, although accounting is not an experimental science. However, its data are experience-derived, from management-determined prior transactions, and it is also focused toward later experience (i.e., management's future decisions). As such, accounting acts as a means of servicing management's need to know how things are now and how things were previously. Surely, it was not pure accident that brought the two basic financial statements into existence: one showing how things are and one summarizing the results of interactions of many events antecedent to the present status. These aspects of accounting could hardly have developed out of philosophical reflection; yet they clearly possess philosophic content:

> Something needs to be done to accomplish an end. Various devices and methods of operation are tried. Experiences of success and failure gradually improve the means used. (Ratner, 1939, p. 333)

Financial statements did not appear until after capital-income accounting had experienced a long evolutionary development. We do not know all the successes and failures that went into this evolution. Failures there must have been; inadequacies are recognizable even now in the old and incomplete records. As difficulties were gradually overcome, the integrated fabric of accounting action took systematic form. The basic structure has changed but little. Yet, within that frame, a technology grew to be used in the public interest and a profession developed.

Accounting actions are means toward the ends indicated by accounting objectives. Hence, some thoughts from philosophy directing attention toward ways and means, and to the consequences of their use, will also have something to say appropriate for accounting.

The usefulness pragmatism has for accounting is this: it directs debate toward consequences, actual and imagined, of accounting actions. It shifts argument toward the factors that characterize results (consequences) as desirable and toward the factors that characterize an accounting or managerial action (means) as suitable for the end in view. If consequences are still persuasive, then old means may be continued in use. Persuasive consequences visualized for a new proposal may well justify tentative use. Demonstrated consequences from use experience would then be more conclusive than persuasive. By keeping an idea-in-action under observation as to consequences, its continued validity or its growing inadequacy would come to attention.

It would seem useful to examine many accounting actions in the light of pragmatic logic. It could be reassuring, as to the vitality of accounting, to find that most of the accounting ways of doing things have better consequences than alternative methods would be likely to have. As new proposals appear, they too could be put under a "pragmatic microscope" to better visualize possible or probable consequences for comparison with known consequences of ideas already tested in use.

My thought is that the study of consequences, the demonstrated and the probable, should be a continuing responsibility. Such study also needs a well-formulated method of approach. And, this study of consequences, past or future, should not be expected to be at once conclusive. This is so because study alone will not produce proof of unquestioned superiority of one action over another. In fact, lack of proof is not fatal to good judgment. Instead, after careful consideration of experience and available alternatives, a basis for preference and choice sufficient for trial may be evident. The pragmatic approach leads us to review preferences after they have produced results. If we have chosen unwisely, subsequent examination of actual consequences for the enterprise can signal further use of another choice of means.

> We can perceive the meaning what exists only as we forecast the consequences it entails .... As one perceives different consequences, preference inevitably goes out to one or the other ... intelligent discrimination and choice is the first step out of confusion. (Ratner, 1939, p. 414)

Because accounting procedures have been in evolution for a long time, many kinds of actions have gained such status that they are now accepted without recognition of the persuasive logic or lack of logic supporting them. Yet, each element of system and procedure being means to an end should reflect some aspects of pragmatic logic. There must be reasons why many procedures, both simple and complex, have continued substantially unchanged. A reason could be that the action continued satisfactorily to serve the same desirable end. Neglect to search out underlying reasons such as these might be due to a tacit belief that "theory" consists of hypotheses that probably would lead to "impractical" results if closely followed. Alternatively, perhaps "theory" has been thought to be closely associated with the syllogistic type of logic. That method of reasoning, from assumptions through a chain of inferences toward a firm conclusion, would seem to have little to contribute to the practical functioning of accounting technology.

This is far from the actual state of things. In fact, accounting is able to provide insight into an enterprise precisely because its organized data can make enterprise transactions understandable in mass. Here, definite procedures lead toward definite objectives. This offers evidence of pragmatic logic at work in accounting. A "theory" that systematic data organization would be a suitable means toward the objective of making understandable a mass of heterogeneous events would not be an "impractical theory."

A satisfactory result from using a suitable (i.e., adequate or acceptable) means to attain a desirable end will always provide an example of logical relationship. The whole of accounting technology is a collection of logical means for organizing enterprise transaction experience into many significant relationships. Revealing the relationships among data is the factor that makes a mass of detail understandable. Consider the following two quotations from a philosopher of science:

> Instead of judging an idea by its origin, or by deduction from first principles, William James calls it to the test of action, asks for its practical consequences when applied, and turns the face of thought again to things. (Durant, 1926, p. 30)

Later the same author elaborates that statement.

> Instead of asking whence an idea is derived or what are its premises, pragmatism examines its results and turns the fact of thought to action and the future ... What were the truths [of pragmatism] but formulations of experience, convenient and successful in practices? (Durant, 1926, p. 553)

Many ideas like these can be associated with accounting. An element of accounting action is neither good nor bad because it still exists in a form used centuries ago. For example, consider bilateral accounts and interrelated real and nominal accounts. There is no evidence that these accounting actions were deduced from "inviolate first principles." Those early actions and later ones as well were "formulations of experience, convenient and successful in practice." That is to say, accounting appeared in response to the need to understand experience; it evolved out of study of that experience. In a word, accounting grew by *inductive* rather than *deductive thinking*.

We would today find it difficult to formulate a "first principle" that could have started this technology on its long evolutionary journey. It is doubtful whether a "felt need," such as the need to understand the significance of one's prior transaction experience, could be considered a first principle from which Italian traders long ago deduced by syllogistic reasoning a conclusion, which in use led to integrated real and nominal accounts. Considering the following passage from Ratner (1939):

> Tradition makes the tests of ideas to be their agreement with some antecedent state of things ... The test of ideas, thinking generally, is found in consequences of the acts to which the ideas lead, that is, in the new arrangements of things which are brought into existence. (p. 341)

The basic and compelling idea, which early traders must have had, was probably little more than a desire for some kind of actions on their part that could make the results (consequences) of their prior trading activities reviewable in the interest of future trading decision-actions. Their interest in past results had turned the face of thought to action and the future. And, out of that point of view, "new arrangements of things were brought into existence." This "new management" was quite rudimentary; but compelling needs would press toward further experimentation. Slowly, technical details fell into place, and an interrelation of elements became a system operated according to simple rules. Nevertheless, a desirable objective was being served: enterprise transaction experience was being marshaled into interrelated data categories that could make that experience reviewable in an interpretative search for clues toward future decisions.

PART IX

1

THE INNER NATURE OF ACCOUNTING

ABSTRACT

Searching into the inner nature of accounting can be approached by finding supporting reasons for propositions, which undertake to penetrate beneath its techniques and explain its limitations. From the understanding, thus based, it should be possible to formulate accounting's most compelling concepts and persuasive truths – ideas, which, if desired, might be assembled under the scientific sounding term "principals."

In 1918, professor Henry C. Adams suggested that "... all sound accounting rules reflect nature of the self-determining laws of business life (p. vi)." This penetrating observation touches on the limitations inherent in the nature of enterprise accounting.

Because of the intimate relations of account data for business life, it is clear that the root-source of account data identifies with one enterprise entity at a time; that the substance of account data comes from the transaction experience of that one enterprise. These roots and this substance unite to impose functional limits upon enterprise accounting technology. It is because of the effect of these inherent limitations that enterprise accounting can effectively service the basic informational needs of enterprise management and enterprise investors. Because these are persuasive truths regarding accounting, it is quite plausible to consider them as constituting the core-concept of a body of compelling concepts, which, by explaining, supporting, and limiting the characteristic features of this informational technology, give enterprise accounting its basic service capacity.

The familiar approach to examining the nature of accounting has been to describe and illustrate its techniques and usage in detail. A more recent approach has made use of asserted accounting postulates and certain related accounting principles.

It is conceivable that other paths might be worth exploring. One of these could examine the logical ties associating accounting ends and objectives with accounting ways and means. This endeavor would call for (1) judgmental determinations of strength and influence of the close-up and the more distant objectives of accounting (the ends in view) and (2) critical examination of the appropriateness or inappropriateness of technical actions used or proposed for achieving those ends.

Another path could undertake to formulate a conceptual inner nucleus indispensable to accounting service capacity, and to define the limiting outer shell enclosing that nucleus. This approach would call for judgmental determinations, the absence of which would destroy the service function and technical structure of enterprise accounting. One such determination seeks a single, ever-present, and unchanging conceptual factor that could constitute a strong inner nucleus. Another would seek a conceptual factor serving as an outer shell to form a boundary capable of confining the nucleus within interpretatively significant limits.

The latter approach to the nature of accounting offers some interesting possibilities. The outer shell confining the inner nucleus would be the specific business enterprise that accounting services. The undeniable identification of certain transaction experience with a given enterprise makes it necessary that its accounting shall work within that functional limit and restrict account data to those originating in the prior and actual transactions of the one enterprise concerned. To the extent that such a limit was violated, the interpretative purity of the data message would be diluted.

The ever-present inner core cannot be so concisely indicated, although it may perhaps be suggested by the word *equivalence*, where that term is focused upon exchange-priced transactions – the clear source of account data reflecting enterprise transaction experience.

If we penetrate into the nature of exchange-priced transactions, two types of equivalence can be noted. There is a clear equivalence, between pairs of enterprise transactions, matched in the markets into a consummated exchange between two interested and independent parties. This agreement is accomplished because of the pull of differentiated motivation within the action of the contrasting parties. Each party has his own intuition and his own idea of what may constitute an offered consideration persuasive to the other party. It is the acceptability of that differentiation that produces the consummation of an exchange-priced transaction.

There also is a clear equivalence within each one of the transaction pair. For each contracting party, the event presents a favorable aspect and an unfavorable aspect. This unmistakable characteristic has two effects: (1) it precipitates for each party's record a dual-quantity, one favorable in its effect, one unfavorable in its effect; (2) it inspires a bilateral form of category for use in data classifications – the familiar account form of two columns. The result is to set, in opposition for each category, favorable and unfavorable data.

Perhaps due emphasis on equivalence, as observed here, could provide a clue to the formulation of a basic principle. Perhaps emphasis on the relation between a conceptual nucleus within enterprise accounting and a limiting outer shell isolating that nucleus from transaction experience of other enterprises may offer further support for formulating a basic principle. That formulation could not effectively take the form of one compact sentence because two aspects would be involved:

1. Recognition of duality and equivalence as being clearly factual.
2. Recognition of recorded account data as quantitative symbols of enterprise experience.

As to aspect (1), the dualistic qualities are inevitable in the existence and action of separate parties to a transaction; the equivalence quality is rooted in the favorable-unfavorable pairs within every transaction of a given enterprise. As to aspect (2), the digits in accounts are symbols of judgments and quantitative agreement between the transaction parties rather than expressions of values exchanged. This is a very necessary distinction, because the concept of value must be different for each party or no transaction would emerge.

It is collaterally significant that the self-interest of each party strongly influences the decision to contract in those quantities, and that the need each party has to review prior experience will influence the decision to record and analytically to organize his own transaction data. In fact, without suitable two-part recognition by each party, there would be no bilateral classification categories, no integration of real and nominal accounts in the ledger, and no interconnections. As such, two necessary elements emerge: (1) rational explanations capable of offering reasons justifying account-type techniques and (2) guidelines for the use of these techniques.

A group of concepts such as this would be in accord with the concept of an inner nucleus – that inner center would be represented by conditions of equivalence found within an exchange-priced transaction, which is an integral part of the accounting function. The surrounding outer shell would be the business enterprise acting as an enclosure isolating the transaction experience of the given enterprise from the transaction experience relevant to all other enterprises.

Certain specific techniques for organizing data from prior transaction experience are expressive of this concept of a two-part root-principle. Bilateral accounts give special prominence to the balance resulting from comparing the favorable data of one side with the unfavorable data of the opposite side. This separation of data in each account category also facilitates study of interrelations among different accounts, which record differing kinds of transaction experience. It is clear that these interrelationships are very significant aids to interpreting the messages inherent in the account data.

Also expressive of this root-principle is a system of interrelated data summaries: (1) a position statement (balance sheet), contrasting kinds of resources possessed, and an earnings statement (income sheet), reporting the revenue achieved by management's use of company resources and contrasted with the cost efforts applicable to those revenue accomplishments. These two basic reports of account data, being of significance outside as well as inside the enterprise, could give contrasting ideas. As such, one must not ignore the limitations (i.e., the "shell") within which account data are assembled. Instead, one should focus on the interpretative significance, lodged in account data by the factor "equivalence." The equivalence of favorable and unfavorable effects, so evident within the "nucleus," can foster integration of related data, and at the same time set in interpretative contrast data in the form of opposites.

The superficial feature of accounting, so long labeled "double-entry," is seldom thoughtfully penetrated. As a result, the logic within accounting is not recognized as significant, or, if glimpsed, is ignored. Yet, a true technology will be made up of knowable types of actions, which are capable of servicing recognizable needs. There will be some logical relation between actions and needs. The needs will surely influence the techniques. Reasons can be discovered in support of specific needs. Reasons can be found capable of explaining why certain techniques effectively service these needs. As such, an interwoven web of needs, of techniques and of supporting reasons will make it clear that enterprise accounting is a more logical discipline than it is an aggregate of convenient customs.

The underlying nature of accounting has been considered closely related, first, to an "outer shell" – the business enterprise. It serves the function of a boundary restricting account data to those originated in the exchange-priced transactions in which the given enterprise was one party. And, second, related to the "inner nucleus" represented by the several aspects of *equivalence* inherent in every exchange-priced transaction. Together these two concepts identify, differentiate, limit, and facilitate the accounting objective of making a business enterprise more understandable to its own management and to enterprise investors.

It is not enough, however, to be satisfied by assurance that accounting must serve both of these parties with the same data out of double-entry bookkeeping. These data are indeed useful, perhaps basic, for both parties. But account data alone will be insufficient. Most business and investment decisions need the help of many non-account data. Out of this situation, a dilemma arises. Shall accounting service be limited to reporting enterprise actual transaction experience, or should it be expanded to include, within its technical structure, informative data not directly derived from specific transaction experience of the given enterprise?

The positive relation between the shell and the nucleus point toward one technique of data interrelation (will this be a principle?). Marshaling would implement the nucleus concept (while maintaining the purity of the data), by bringing exchange-priced data into suitable account categories on the way to compact factual summaries of enterprise experience. In various ways, interpreting the reported transaction experience would extract meaning significant for investors' decisions. A separate technique would be needed for interpreting collaterally useful meanings for relevant non-account data. The alternative to separate techniques is less promising: this is the incorporation of a maximum of useful non-transaction data into the structure of enterprise accounting. This could not escape diluting the purity of actual and reported experience. It might even create an impression that injected modifications were themselves expressions of enterprise transaction experience.

The lower-of-cost-or-market rule for inventories is an example of injected modification of actual transaction experience of the given enterprise. Comparatively, it may be a small modification; and, undoubtedly, it continues a long tradition. Nevertheless, it has a basic weakness in the fact that it makes no distinction between the effect of clear damage and an assumed effect of lower current prices of specific items. Moreover, use of such a modification tends to set a precedent for other interpretative modifications, which, perhaps, would not even have a long tradition to support them.

Perhaps arguments pressing for greater comparability among the financial statements of different companies could ultimately bring more uniformity to inventory reporting and hold account data closer to reporting on enterprise actual experience. It is to be noted, however, that extreme uniformity could to some degree have the effect of smothering the individuality that characterizes every business enterprise.

The problem of inventory reporting also highlights a larger problem of the logic that ties account data to the actual transaction experience of the enterprise. When the initial investment in an asset is greater than the investment consumed or sold in one fiscal year, it becomes necessary that accounting should distinguish the part relevant to the single period and the part relevant to later periodic calculations of enterprise earnings. The resulting problem of investment allocation among periods is inescapably judgmental. But this fact does not justify bringing "valuation" into the apportionment decision. This is so because the term carries a connotation of appraising (revaluing) the asset residual and carrying the rest of the recorded amount into the earnings calculation. It would not be any closer to accounting logic to appraise (decide on) the specific amount desired to represent cost of goods sold, thus determining the residual amount for the balance sheet report. If the portion charged as applicable cost in the earnings calculation is not convincingly tied to enterprise actual experience, the balance sheet item will be greater or less than unused prior transaction experience.

Allocation of fixed asset depreciation poses a similar problem of realistic apportionment of prior investment experience between present and the future reporting. In this area of accounting action, judgmental managerial decisions usually have considerable latitude. Perhaps this is desirable, yet the responsibility can be manipulated under the pressure of self-interest. This possibility is widened, even when good faith is not in question, by the theory that apportioning invested costs over a series of fiscal periods is a matter of valuation judgments.

Yet, the terms *valuation* and *apportionment* do not refer to the same process. The latter means assigning facts of a prior investment according to an orderly plan proportioned to the expected service life of the asset. The plan would necessarily be based on estimated service life. Moreover, those estimates would probably not prove in the end to have been entirely correct but only tentative. Nonetheless, where estimates have been made realistically and in good faith, corrective readjustments can later be made when new knowledge of actual service life is available.

In contrast, valuation, rather than apportionment of invested cost to the best of management's ability, is less logical than later corrections based on better knowledge. If a principle may be stated in the negative in this situation, it would disallow entry of non-transaction increments or decrements to the balance sheet picture of capital position and, similarly, disallow introduction of non-transaction increments or decrements into depreciation expense.

One financial statement would seem to report financial status improved by an individual decision. The other statement, through increased depreciation charges, would seem to report smaller net income. Verbalized, the statements would say that the assets look better because of a price level change; net income looks less attractive because of price level effect on depreciation expense. This kind of situation generates certain observations. Modified account data would not faithfully reflect the results of actual transaction experience of this enterprise in asset markets. The earnings picture does not faithfully reflect the effectiveness of management's prior decisions. In certain respects, and to some degree, these reported data would reflect disregard for the functional limits of enterprise accounting, particularly those here characterized as the *inner nucleus* and the *outer shell.*

Recognition of the confusing effects of mingling actual transaction experience and non-transaction data may have been the primary factor back of the need, some years ago, to distinguish between earned surplus and appraisal surplus. Such recognition may also have stimulated contemporary interest in searching for ways and means for bringing to attention the price level changes that should be of interest to management and investors. These thoughts reinforce the belief that data of current economic conditions can and should influence current decisions; and belief that data of that order should not be mingled in the accounts along with data expressing management-originated and actual transaction experience of the given enterprise. These conclusions derive support from the basic concepts of the limited function of accounting as indicated earlier.

2

ACCOUNTING AS SCIENCE

ABSTRACT

Mathematics is a tool of service, but the use of quantitative digits does not automatically make accounting also a tool of service. The equality of total debits and credits is not an example of scientific perfection. The close interrelation between real and nominal accounts, between balance sheet and income sheet, however, reflect near perfection. Account data from consummated transactions between independent parties also approach near perfection: there is an equivalence, for each party's transaction of favorable and unfavorable effects, although each party's intentions have been quite different.

The literature of accounting is becoming increasingly rich in theory. Some of this development reflects the impact from expanding concepts of managerial functions and of related decision problems. Some of it reflects an increasing recognition of the investor's need for interpretatively useful information. These manifestations are relatively new aspects of accounting evolution. And they deserve more thorough examination in that context than is here possible. But it is clear that functional patterns and inherent limitations relevant to this technology should continue to have a prominent place in accounting theory.

The most serviceable communication technology would not aspire to be all things to all men. Accounting actions lead to communications. To be most effective in that form, the actions should be within natural and functional boundaries. These limits will form a large basis of the authority of accounting.

The phrase "enterprise prior transaction experience" compactly indicates the most significant of these limitations. The authoritativeness of accounts will be strongest when their data can confidently be considered as derived from such experience. All other data not so derived, however interesting, useful, or informative, would best be communicated in non-account supplements to accounting reports of enterprise transaction experience. Cost-or-market choices, replacement costs, and price level indices are examples of such useful collateral information. But they cannot speak in the accounts of manifest transaction experience of the given enterprise.

Arthur Cayley, professor of mathematics at Cambridge, is quoted in Hatfield's (1924) "An Historical Defense of Bookkeeping," as having expressed the opinion in a text published in 1893 that bookkeeping is "one of two perfect sciences." As a teacher of mathematics, that author would be likely to consider his subject as the other one. As to a similar characterization for bookkeeping, we may have the speculative. Surely, the equality of debits and credits, in an entry and in a trial balance, would not speak directly of science or represent a significant type of mathematical equation.

During the intervening seventy-one years since the thought was expressed, many reasons supporting accountancy's capability to serve its limited function will have become increasingly clear. Yet, even this could not convincingly mark accountancy as a science. This is so because an inherent "perfection" can easily be observed in mathematics that runs deeper than equations. In a simple triangle, for example, the relations among the sides and the angles are inescapably realities. Any change in the length of a side, any change in the reach of an angle, will change the relation of the other components in recognizable ways. Enterprise accounting cannot reflect relations between causes and effects as closely as this. Nevertheless, accounting has inescapable and very significant relationships with business enterprises.

An enterprise is a vehicle for economic service. Enterprise management, the vehicle's pilot, controls and directs its course by specific transaction decisions. Enterprise accounting provides much needed navigation information in the form of account data. The enterprise entity and the enterprise accounting technology are as closely related as the sides of a triangle. Managerial decision-actions realistically change the size and shape of the enterprise. Enterprise accounts visually reflect those changes, by technically organizing the transaction data flowing out of management actions. Knowledge obtained from review of reports of action results will affect management next decisions. Such knowledge can also influence decisions of investors interested in judging management's effective use of enterprise resources.

Enterprise transaction experience is actual and realistic. The emergence of transactions from management decision-actions is a reality. The organization by accounting of such data is a realistic survey of realities that are inescapably related in fact, and by intent, to the deeper and basic realities of business life.

Within this pattern of relationships, there are signs of identifiable "perfection." Account data, by dealing with understandable realities, make readable and reviewable real messages about the results of the continuing association of enterprise entity and enterprise management. The technical forms of accounting also show a degree of "perfection." Data categories in bilateral form may not in themselves reflect an aspect of science. But they offer a glimpse of technological approaches reaching out toward more perfect functioning. This characteristic is interpretatively significant for a definite reason: it synchronizes so well the reviewable record and specific indisputable real facts of economic life lying back of accounting entries.

There are other realities as well. Each of the parties to an exchange-priced transaction intends to produce a realistic and favorable effect on his own affairs. But he must offer a realistic, persuasive, and favorable consideration to the other party, even though this is unfavorable to himself. As such, favorable effects for one will be unfavorable for the other. Nevertheless, the "ultimate difference" between favorable and unfavorable, as visualized by the parties, must be acceptable to both; otherwise, the specific transaction proposal will not be completed.

Bilateral accounts synchronize the opposing effects of the transaction on each party. Each party, viewing summaries of his own accounts, is therefore able to observe the degree by which the net effects have been favorable to himself. Significance, read from this account data, demonstrates real managerial effectiveness. That reading and the resulting judgments cannot be perfect in the sense that science is perfect. In fact, human decisions and judgments will never reach perfection. Yet, within the mass of experience, the essence may be entirely acceptable and interpretatively useful, almost as if the mass of experience were scientific data.

This leads me back to the proposition that enterprise accounting is not a science. It can only be considered a technology with recognizable but limited functions. And beliefs in its accomplishments are justifiable; for these accomplishments are the results of revolutionary growth in service capacity that is approaching, closer and closer, a state of perfection. But adding the word "science" after "accounting" cannot create the status suggested. Such a designation is not needed to epitomize the source of accountancy's service capacity. A "rational yet limited technology" would be a realistic term for accounting where science would not.

A modern development of considerable significance has been the fact that this technology has been called upon, not only to continue its early function but also to expand that function. As such, it has been called upon to provide data sharply focused toward internal managerial decisions; yet, at the same time, and with the same techniques, to provide data sharply pointed toward decisions by outside investors. On one hand, "administrative accounting" would seem to have characteristics of a private information service. On the other hand, the term "financial accounting" would seem to promise that this technology would also serve the public interest. That implication surely lay beneath the actions in the mid 1800s by the English Parliament in the series of Companies Acts.

For some five centuries, enterprise techniques have been slowly undergoing evolutionary development. This growth has been possible because deep root-structures had been put down, and because these have been able to sustain an upper growth that ultimately flowered into modern accountancy. Inherent limitations have tended to hold that modernization firmly to the pattern of serving management. Gradually, however, and specifically in relatively recent years, the desire has increased for improved service to the investment community. The intention has been praiseworthy and some of the results have been satisfactory. But the functional limits, which stand in the way of injecting non-transaction data, still resist further modernization in the name of improvement. There is no limit, however, to the amount of supplementary data, which might be made available for interpretative analysis, outside the framework of recorded and actual transaction experience.

Some of the impulse toward more comprehensive financial communications is no doubt fostered by a growing awareness, on the part of people concerned about accountancy, of ideas from economic theory. Study of managerial problems against a background of microeconomics is highly desirable, as preparation for a managerial career in taking the risks involved in making real decisions in and for a real business enterprise. But a binding marriage (amalgamation) of a part of economic theory (e.g., accretion as profit) and a part of accounting technology (exchange-priced actual experience) could only produce some sort of hybrid. It could scarcely be, for accounting, an "incarnation" to merge a flexible economic ideology with inductively based actions (transaction experience), which were circumscribed by limiting and realistic functions. As such, enterprise accounting can no more usefully take on (incarnate) the nature of economic philosophy than economics can usefully put on the garments (historic functions) of enterprise accounting. Good friends and neighbors have a desirably different status than newly wedded couples.

3

CONTINUING IMPORTANCE OF BASIC CONCEPTS[☆]

ABSTRACT

High significance for accounting objectives is evident from the support they provide for accounting actions. An inventory of these objectives could be very useful. In such an inventory, the integrity of all account data would be supported by tight identification with the consummated transaction experience of the related enterprise. But since enterprise economic activities are necessarily continuous, the results can only be made understandable by reporting account data periodically. Yet, this allocation to fiscal periods does not call for new measurement of the data. This is so because the center of accounting function is not measurement but that of reporting prior experience. This mistake has come about because of the emphasis on measurement as a function, which invites advocacy of using a "stabilized unit of measure." This is a useful analytical technique for statistical economics, but it can only represent a revolutionary idea for accounting where the technical function is far more limited.

The word "concepts" may often be more useful for accounting than "principles." It is closer to the meaning of an idea. Words and sentences are symbols for ideas. So too are digits and sums of digits. Words must be

[☆]This chapter has been reproduced courtesy of *The International Journal of Accounting* and the Vernon K. Zimmerman Center for International Education and Research in Accounting, University of Illinois at Urbana–Champaign. The original citation for this article is Littleton (1965b).

interpreted and understood as ideas. Account figures must be interpreted into ideas. And the resulting ideas and concepts are more important than the words and figures beneath them.

In accounting as elsewhere, professional development needs continuing attention. Technical skills can be sharpened. Action types can be rationally explained. Concepts of objectives and limitations can be clarified. In a continuing search for accounting principles, perhaps the most promising springboard could be identification of relevant and fundamental concepts. These could well serve as a basis for formulating guiding principles which, in due time, could lead to improved accounting communications.

The contemporary research program of the American Institute of Certified Public Accountants has followed a different path – a path of deduction leading toward conclusions derived from assumed or postulated premises. The degree of conviction carried by conclusions, derived by deductive process, can reflect only the powers of conviction possessed by antecedent premises. If initial assumptions are weak or inadequately justified, the associated conclusions are not likely to be strong. Instead, perhaps use of an inductive approach could prove helpful. For example, conclusions as to the nature and limits of accounting technology could be reached by reasoning from particular facts known to be characteristic of accounting. Surely, the characteristic objectives, distant and close up, would suggest principles capable of helping to resolve specific problems of accounting action.

An inductive approach would rest on the conviction that a significant aspect of accounting need not be assumed or postulated when it can be known as a fact. Starting from known facts and characteristics, research could move toward clarifying the functional limitations and objectives that condition technical actions. Back of these objectives will stand persuasive reasons justifying their existence. Thus, a chain of clarifying relations would be built: discernible reasons justify functional objectives; the latter motivate known types of technical actions; and a complex sequence of accounting actions eventually produces, for a given enterprise, certain compact accounting communications.

The financial statements that result will be technical communications of account data. But they will not be as readable as is a printed page. For this reason, they will be more difficult to interpret than the average statement. Therefore, perhaps there is also a need for research into the nature of interpretative techniques. Perhaps an inductive assumption as the base could clear a path for the formulation of principles to guide accounting actions and to improve interpretative techniques for extracting meaning from organized account data.

Assumptions and specific postulates might more usefully be brought into contact with imponderable elements not perceptible as data facts. In that association, assumptions could serve as an ideological basis for reasoning toward probabilities. Clearly, this kind of action poses a problem for management and investment analysts, but not for accounting as such. The accounting function is not an imponderable element. By the evidence of all its characteristics, accounting is equipped to deal with enterprise actual experience but not with expectations of future probabilities. Research in compelling concepts and basic objectives might lay a useful base for improved data communications and, thus, for a better understanding of the enterprise concerned.

The postulates formulated in *Accounting Research Study No. 1* could be examined against this background.[1] It is scarcely necessary to postulate or assume that business activities and the associated accounting actions are carried on by self-contained and individually controlled entities (postulate A-3). These operating units of business have long been known to be facts of business life – and for known reasons. They make possible the division of labor and the specialization of managerial skills.

The accounting technology (postulate B-3) that serves business units exists as a fact of business life parallel to the entity as a fact of life. From this relation, it is clear that enterprise account data *must* speak for one enterprise entity. The reason for the emphasis is the need to make that enterprise and the results of management's decision understandable to management itself and to other parties at interest.[a] This kind of service from enterprise accounting need no more be assumed than an "entity" need to be postulated. Yet, both concepts need to be described, explained, and justified in their relation to each other. Those relations have reasons for being explained; and these can be more enlightening than separate assumptions can be.

The mention is also made of a relation between active exchanges in the economic environment (A-2) and market prices reflected in accounts (B-2). Both items are stated as postulates, yet exchange of goods is an unquestioned fact of business life – a known and necessary characteristic, a fact. There can be no doubt that transactions recorded in the accounts arise from price bargaining by interested parties in the markets.

In postulate B-2 this clause appears: "Account data are based on prices generated by past, present, or future exchanges." There is no place for so broad a generalization within the body of concepts making up the functional logic of accounting. Look at these time segments more closely. The phrase "past exchanges" would quite properly cover all transactions generated by decisions made in the given enterprise. Acceptance of the phrase "present exchanges" would seem openly to justify extensive use of current replacement prices even though these speak of other people's transactions.

"Expected to take place in the future" is a phrase that reaches still further beyond the actual experience of the given enterprise. Apparently, the door has been opened for this postulate by the widespread acceptance of the practice of pricing inventory at the lower of cost or market – itself an expectation. Of course, expectations do influence decisions. In order to serve that purpose, however, the possible future need and should not be brought into direct and modifying contact in the accounts with data from enterprise actual experience. Expectations such as these, reported as items in the financial statements, will too often seem, to many readers, as expressing real objectivity for the given enterprise. Yet, those digits can only speak of elements that, for this enterprise, are subjective conjectures. Quantified expectations are judgmental opinions. Since these do not express actual experience, such items are best treated as interpretative data supplementary to actual experience data.

The significance for accounting of periodic reporting is unquestioned. Its orientation runs toward management and investors as users of account data. For this reason, very little real explanation of periodic allocations and reporting can come from a postulate that "economic activity is carried on during specific periods of time (A-4)." In fact, both general and enterprise economic activities are essentially continuous, even when seasonal. Despite continuity of actions, or because of continuity, interested parties need to know, dependably and periodically, the results of management's decision actions. Direct observation and memory could perhaps serve some management as a sort of alternative to data. But for the investing public, even this weak alternative is not available. Because of these informational needs in the presence of continuing activities, it is essential that recording of accumulating experience data be continuous and that reporting should be periodic. The time period used in accounting is therefore a practical necessity of business.

A postulated time period (A-4) has been linked with a postulated "tentativeness" (B-4), the latter referring to allocations over time of various operating results. Perhaps "tentative" is to mean experimental, subject to reconsideration, or to later correction. Alternatively, the term may conceivably mean to imply that accounting does not have scientific bases for its data allocations. The term may also carry certain overtones. For example, implication that allocation might be arbitrary or purely expedient; that allocations could be changed at management's discretion; and that allocations could be strongly influenced by tax considerations or by a need to present the best possible picture of financial solvency. But accounting is not that tentative.

Quantification of transaction data (A-1) is a necessary feature of business; hence, so is accounting. Financial statements (B-l) are also a necessity, particularly in order to communicate to parties outside the enterprise. Surely, these needs do not have to be assumed. The reason account data, in arithmetic digits, can be helpful to business decisions is because they are identified with and can directly reflect management-generated transaction experience. Account totals and remainders are part of the "grammar" of this figure language. It is unfortunate that this kind of communication is not as readable in the same manner as a verbal text. Few people are as well trained in figure interpretation as they are in word and sentence interpretation. Perhaps educators could work out ways for improving that condition without going so far as to make higher mathematics a required subject for everyone.

Financial statement (B-1) need no more be postulated than does data quantification. The arrangements within those statements, the experience data there disclosed, and the antecedent for account categories for data classification are all well-known communication devices. By their use, a multitude of separate events can be compacted into figure patterns of enterprise experience. Thus understood, financial statements will be seen to lack the characteristics of assumptions. The building blocks in them are data from real events definitely relevant to this enterprise; the technical structure of these reports makes effective use of special organization of account data to enhance the "readability" of that picture of a section of enterprise transaction experience. These service functions need not be assumed; they clearly are matters of technical fact.

Some postulates are named "imperatives." These are ideas, goals, standards, and objectives related to accounting "as it ought to be." To the extent that the apparent synonyms above may be represented by one word, "objective," each item in the list must be considered as referring to a guiding, limiting, and controlling concept. Four of these have particular relevance to the usual financial statements and the several imperatives named do include a number of influential objectives. But a more extensive list would be needed to cover all major objectives of varying degrees of influential significance. Beyond this would be a large number of minor objectives that influence subordinate actions. All of such objectives constitute the foundations supporting accounting technical actions and services. Apparently, no "inventory" of these objectives has even been undertaken.

An example of a broad objective influencing, perhaps dictating, accounting technical capacities could be stated this way: make understandable the actual transaction experience of a given business enterprise. Back of a compelling objective such as this, there stands a major objective of management: review the results of prior actions as part of the preparation toward next decisions. Also influential for accounting is this financial objective: compactly report to people in the investment community on enterprise financial status as of a given date, and on the operating results over a period of time insofar as status and results can be reflected by data from enterprise actual experience.

Associated with these basic objectives should be the recognition of the following as one of the compelling concepts exerting their influence upon accounting actions: the integrity of data originating from enterprise transaction experience should be preserved in the accounts to the greatest extent possible. There are at least three reasons why this concept should persistently influence accounting.

1. Unprotected reported account data cannot be depended upon faithfully to reflect enterprise actual experience or the results of transaction decision taken by enterprise management.
2. Account data of doubtful integrity in these aspects, even in association with relevant non-account data, are not a reliable basis for next decisions.
3. Non-account elements, such as economic statistics and managerial judgments, should strongly influence next decisions. But the results would be more rationally based if they were also supported by analysis of significant factors made evident by enterprise prior experience.

Both the processing and the reporting of account data from transaction experience could be justified by considering the several "imperatives" as necessary and antecedent concepts. Four of the five are of particular interest. These are continuity (C-1), objectivity (C-2), consistency (C-3), and disclosure (C-5). These forceful names can headline significant aspects, not of accounting, as it ought to be, but of the nature of accounting technology, as it is known to be.

Continuity is a reasonable expectation based on experience in an observation of business. Enterprise operations can continue if conditions are met that are largely within management's responsibility such as satisfying customers; keeping expenses plus cost below revenues; maintaining safe solvency patterns; and maintaining good relations with capital sources and employees. Since reasonable continuity can result from proper efforts, there is no need to assume it a characteristic.

Full disclosure in financial statements is an aspect of morality. *Objectivity* of account data has moral connotations as well, for subjective data will lack reviewable validity. *Consistency* is particularly related to period-to-period comparability in aid of interpreting reported experience data. It gives assurance that changes in reporting methods will be made evident to statement users. These several concepts are reasonable and rational aspects of honorable management and honest communications. As such, they may well be considered as imperatives for management as well as accounting. It is not clear, however, why convincing goals and actions such as these should be named postulates. As rational characteristics of modern enterprise accounting, they seem, along with other basic and defensible characteristics, to deserve designation as *compelling concepts* capable of exercising vital influence on accounting actions and business activities.

Two other postulates have not been discussed above because they lack qualities that would entitle them to be considered as compelling concepts. These two are the dollar as a unit of measure (A-5) and stable measuring unit (C-4). Part of the reason they are not in themselves compelling concepts is that they set up *measurement* as a key function for enterprise accounting. The major effect of this implied function is to divorce account data, at least to some degree, from enterprise actual transaction experience. To the extent that this happens, the door will be opened to use of current replacement prices –these being considered objective and readily available "measures" – or to use in the accounts of price level index adjustments – these index series being considered sufficiently objective from governmental sponsorship.

In one of those situations, measurement would use selected market prices to which this enterprise had not been a party; in the other, account data would to some degree represent everyone's prices – these having been statistically converted into a type of nationwide average. These two postulates are difficult to fit into a persuasive concept of accounting function. This is especially true if the function was considered to be that of providing dependable and reviewable data about prior actual experience of the given enterprise.

Stability of the measuring unit, however scientific the phrase may sound, is a revolutionary idea for accounting use, even though it is not new in economics and statistics. Beneath these two measurement assumptions lie another assumptions, and these may be questionable.

1. That accounting technology could expand its destiny by incorporating revolutionary charges;

2. That the digits attached to an exchange-priced transaction, once they are lodged in the accounts, no longer speak of quantitative facts out of actual and individual prior experience. Instead, they speak of an isolated item having quantitative individuality only as of a given moment of time – a mere speck in general economic price movements, which were different before and continued to be different after the specific transaction. In contrast, it is to be noted that a given expenditure makes its short or extended contribution to enterprise purpose regardless of prices before, in, or after the current market. Thus, two concepts appear to be in collision:
   1. That accounting is concerned with one consummated transaction at a time, and that these in total speak of actions (experiences) identified with the given enterprise;
   2. That accounting should undertake to function as a device for measuring (valuing) enterprise resource changes, even though these are not identified with new transaction experience of the given enterprise.

The roots of the second of these concepts reach deeply into the soil of economic theory and statistics as a tool for analysis of economic change. For accounting, this concept would carry an implication that some data in financial statements should directly reflect the effects of new changes in economic conditions originating outside of acts of the given enterprise. Yet, the basic character of accounting technology directs, not the measurement and reporting of economic equivalents, but the marshaling of data derived from specific transactions generated in and for a given enterprise by decisions of its own management.

These two postulates further imply that "to measure" includes the meaning "to value." The latter is more appropriate for economics or statistics than to accounting technology. Two quite different concepts of enterprise profit are involved here; one tied into actual transaction experience (validated realization); one related to revaluations (effects of price level changes). Some of the suggested postulates point thought toward the second concept of profit as more significant for dependable financial statement communications.

The first concept is supported not only by the functional logic of accounting but also by the fact that this early feature of accounting's power to make its technical contribution has continued as a compelling concept. As long as the right integration of real and nominal accounts continues to be a basic feature of enterprise accounting, this technology has no logical place for subjective valuations, for these would not be associated with overt action based on price bargaining in which this enterprise had been a party.

An asserted need for using "a stable measuring unit" follows from an assumption of "measurement" as the function of accounting. It is a serious matter to undertake to change a function merely by changing definitions, especially when the present definition has been inherent and evident throughout centuries of accounting growth in service capacity. Both early and modern technical aspects of accounting reflect an objective of producing an *intelligible organization* of enterprise transaction experience. This technology has evolved into the character we know because its elements proved able, under use, to provide a conceptual framework for making understandable the results of actual transaction events coming out of management decisions. The body of concepts underlying the use of that technical framework constitutes the essence of accounting theory. It would seem reasonable that this body of compelling concepts could best be derived from the empirical aspects of this technology; that is, from close examination of the historical and practical aspects of accounting actions and limitations.

This approach would be the converse of explaining accounting by starting with a controlling definition that would place measurement at the center of its function. A better springboard could be found by considering the significance of inherent limitations. If no compelling limitations affect its technical actions, accounting becomes as flexible in its use of data as is statistical methodology. This is not to argue that increased flexibility could not produce useful data, but much of it would fail to reflect the actual experience of a given enterprise. As a result, the lessons to be read out of known experience data would be obscured. To the extent this would be the case, management would lose some of its opportunities to learn from transaction experience. And investment analysts would have to try to sort out injected interpretative data in order to read the evidence of managerial effectiveness.

The action characteristics and natural limitations of enterprise accounting are logical consequences of men's needs to gain knowledge of the results of prior decisions. Recorded and organized individual prior experience can supply the basic clues. This fact indicates a limitation that should be permitted to continue to exert significant influence upon this technology. There is, of course, no limit to the use of relevant, collateral, and interpretative data outside of the formal structure of enterprise accounting technology.

It is clear that accounting is not a philosophy leaning toward a deductive or syllogistically based approach to conclusions. Nor is accounting a science where effective use is made of induction for drawing inferences from experimentation. Yet, because accounting is a technology, it stands somewhat closer to science than philosophy. Hence, an inductive approach might well be favored in its theory formulations in place of generalizations deduced from postulated assumptions. Such reasoning, based on known characteristics and clear limitations, would call for several lines of action:

1. Recognition or formulation of concepts of the most influential objectives of accounting.
2. Analysis of interrelations among concepts, objectives, actions, and among all three.
3. Search for persuasive reasons why accounting objectives can or cannot explain and justify specific types of accounting actions (both positive and negative).
4. Closely consider possible effects on accounting objectives and actions of concepts new to already established patterns.

As science aids men to understand the forces of nature, which then leads to useful applications, in like manner accounting theory should aid men to understand clearly and use accounting techniques within the boundaries of their logical limitations. Awareness would then follow of known action types in their relation to rational and justifying objectives. The essence of the functional logic of accounting lies within these relations.

Since the aim of research is to increase awareness and understanding, it would seem particularly appropriate to make use of induction in accounting research whenever possible. This approach would guide the critical examination of both known and proposed concepts, with the end goal in mind of promoting useful generalizations about accounting action types and their necessary limitations. It could be especially useful to analyze the way objectives and limits (supported by cogent reasons) can, and do, condition, or explain, accounting technical actions. Knowledge, thus derived, could serve as an excellent basis for a realistic reporting of actual experience. There is no doubt that this basis could prove more useful than one provided by chaining assumptions toward formulation of a few principles.

The problem is that principles often seem too much like headlines. This can be useful, but only if these compact statements reflect the essences from a sole body of ideas. Otherwise, headlines may detract attention from the real news back of them. For accounting discussions, the important elements are the ideas, concepts, objectives, and reasons. These motivate and direct accounting actions. And, when certain types of action seem less acceptable than others, reasons for and against should be thoroughly canvassed. When this is done properly, persuasive and convincing reasons may prove more effective than either familiar customs or compact principles.

NOTES

1. Littleton is referring to Moonitz' research monograph, *The Basic Postulates of Accounting*, which was published on behalf of the AICPA in 1961. The postulates presented in this monograph are reproduced in Table 3 at the end of the chapter "The Heart of the Matter."

a. The fact that account data do not, and could not, provide all information needed as a basis for business decisions would scarcely need elaboration.

PART X

1

BASIC POSTULATES OF ACCOUNTING☆

ABSTRACT

This well-planned research is in tune with the times.[1] *Five of the postulates are called imperatives. They are indeed persuasive objectives. The remaining postulates deal with means for attaining those goals. Another word for postulate is assumption. Both words refer to ideas that we cannot know as facts of business life, and yet are needed as a basis for discussing accounting principles. Perhaps, therefore, they may be considered as compact verbalizations of basic concepts serving as foundational stones beneath accounting technology.*

This publication by the American Institute of Certified Public Accountants demonstrates a continuation of interest in research for the profession. A beginning was made some thirty years ago in work which led to the breakdown of general surplus into informative subdivisions, and which produced a form of audit certificate emphasizing, "generally accepted accounting principles." The well-known series of *Accounting Research Bulletins* followed. They dealt with specific professional problems of that time. Based on current research, similar problems of the future can be closely examined in the light of the carefully thought-out postulates and principles now

☆This chapter has been reproduced courtesy of *The Accounting Review*, the official journal of the American Accounting Association. The original citation for this article is Littleton (1962a).

under study. Such an approach to judging alternatives is very promising of good results. For accounting is more than a technical discipline; involved along with technical actions is a structure of interrelated ideas orbiting, so to speak, in an atmosphere of compelling needs and objectives.

It seems not unreasonable to believe the ultimate results of extensive and well-planned research could produce contributions from the profession comparable in social significance to the uniform CPA examination. Viewed in the context of today's rapid developments in science, joint research, which welds professional practical experience and academic research in ideology, is clearly in tune with the times. Moreover, the future will undoubtedly show these research studies (particularly those on postulates and principles) to be as full of "seeds" as a grapefruit, and thus equipped to provide many seedlings from which new trees of understanding will grow.

Since postulates and principles naturally complement each other, they could very well be published eventually in one binding. Together they may prove to be a real breakthrough. It would be a lasting contribution if this research brought closer the integration of practice and theory; that is, the actions and the supporting ideology.

The report on principles is not yet at hand but the presentation made of postulates deserves examination in its own right. Included is a brief introduction, summary, and three and one half pages of bibliography. There are four intervening chapters, three of which deal with postulates out of the environment in which accounting and accountants perform their functions, and with postulates arising from accounting itself. The third of these four meaty chapters presents certain postulates described as "the imperatives." And, since a research study is not a mystery story, it may be permissible to look first at the last of these four chapters. All of the propositions under the heading "imperatives" use the verb "should" and deal, it is stated, with the area of things "as they ought to be," that is, as referring to "goals, objectives, standards." In contrast, the postulates stated in the other chapters "are couched as simple declarations ... conveying an impression that this is the way things are (p. 38)."

The five postulates designated as imperatives are named *continuity*, *objectivity*, *consistency*, *stable unit*, and *disclosure*. It is stated that *uniformity*, *materiality*, and *conservatism* were discussed without formulating postulates. The two latter concepts "logically do not belong in a set of basic propositions ... one being a psychological-statistical concept, the other represents merely a counsel of caution (p. 47)." If these five propositions deal with goals, it should also be appropriate to consider them as compelling concepts, which, by expressing objectives, will underlie, support, and justify postulates, principles, and eventually technical action.

Objectives (such as above) would be ends, which ways and means (such as technical actions influenced by postulates and principles) would be, designed to achieve. Such a relationship of means and ends would constitute a pragmatic way of testing the suitability of the means employed. Such a "test" is not to be explained by an asserted "usefulness" of the means. The test of pragmatic relations would come into view from examining the consequences of the use of the given means. This, in turn, would put in question (1) the desirability of the indicated goal and (2) the relative desirability of certain means to that end in comparison with alternative means.

It is not indicated in the text, yet the five imperatives seem to imply one controlling goal; namely, trustworthy and comparable financial communications. A moral obligation exists to disclose all material facts and to avoid misleading the user of the data. The concepts of continuity, objectivity, and consistency, tell of means toward the goal of producing trustworthy and comparable accounting communications. Alternatives for those means would presumably produce less satisfactory insight into the given business enterprise, or they would have been made the means.

If these propositions were to be true imperatives, it would seem logical to use verb forms of "must" rather than "should." Yet, professional accountants prefer to consider themselves independent counselors, so to speak, with no power to dictate what must, or must not be. Their research activities would therefore be educational in intention as to accountants themselves and the general public. As such, these five postulates may perhaps be considered more as persuasive concepts rather than compelling imperatives. For it must be clear that the best accounting communication will lack the power to generate the fullest possible understanding of and insight into a business enterprise. Such understanding is strangely influenced by the user's own problems and his knowledge of accounting.

One of the valuable, though indirect, services of research may well be that of directing attention to the limitations inherent in accounting and accounting communications. This kind of service could become increasingly important if a discernible present pressure continues toward ever more comparability of data. For full comparability would foster uniformity and these two factors fully grown, could together becloud the characteristic individuality of a given enterprise and its management.

Some confusion of thought may exist today from failure to see accounting as primarily serving the management of a given enterprise, and to consider outside use of data from the same account sources as an important but nevertheless collateral service. It is important therefore to distinguish clearly the analytical marshaling of enterprise transaction history and the interpretative extracting of meaning by users of the communicated data. It would seem clear also that interrelations among principles would be more significant than individual formulations. The same thought would apply to postulates and to interrelations between principles and postulates. Interrelations are necessary features if various concepts and different actions are to be recognizable as essential parts of one discipline or technology.

Relationships demonstrating a unifying force within accounting can be detected among the fourteen postulates presented in the research report. In considering this aspect, imperative postulates, C-1 to C-5 can be tied back to postulates out of accounting, B-1 to B-4, and thence to postulates out of environment, A-1 to A-5. The postulate of continuity of enterprise operation (C-1) ties back into the tentativeness of periodic allocations (B-4), thence to activities identified with time periods (A-4). Adequate disclosure (C-5) and period-to-period consistency (C-3) tie back into a set of articulated financial statement communications (B-1), thence into economic activities separated among individual entities (A-3).

The postulate of objectively measured changes (C-2) ties back into account data generated by market-priced transactions (B-2), thence into need for quantitative data as bases for rational economic decisions (A-1) and for activities that generate account data originating in exchange of goods and services (A-2). The postulate (C-4), "accounting reports should be based on a stable measuring unit," seems to be intended to tie back into data generated by market-priced transactions (B-2), thence into money as the common denomination for measuring economic exchanges (A-5).

Taken together the various postulates seem, for the most part, to describe the characteristics of accounting technology concisely and rather completely. Since the imperative postulates are presented as goals or standards to be achieved, this would seem to imply that the other postulates deal more or less directly with certain means used to attain those ends and goals.

Yet, some of the elements thus brought together appear to be strange neighbors, such as a stable measuring unit (index dollar?), exchange-priced transactions (actual contract dollars?), and economic exchanges stated in units that express quantitative measurement (money, a measure of value?). For example, index-adjusted dollars reflect statistical theory, which accepts averages as realistic measures. Adjusted dollars will therefore be reinterpreted market-originated dollars, contract dollars that have been associated with specific transactions in the markets, and thus tell of consummated and verifiable facts of enterprise experience. Any subsequent change in the accounting record of contract dollars will constitute a modification of recorded actual experience. Whether such change is necessary or merely desired, the modification would need separate justification by persuasive reasons.

It might indeed be beyond the purpose of this or any other section of the present research program to examine the reasons for the clash of two such prominent concepts as invested cost and attributed value. Reconciliation of concepts that are poles apart may be so nearly impossible as to discourage any attempt. However, some clarification might emerge from a search for ways and means of separating the analytical actions of organizing enterprise transaction data toward communication, and the actions of interpreting meaning out of the organized communication of objectively derived and professionally scrutinized account data.

A judgment of the ultimate usefulness of an exploration of postulates such as this report offers cannot be made until the immediate consequences (a report on accounting principles) and the subsequent consequences (application to field problems) can be examined.[2] For, in a very real sense, this study of postulates is a means pointed toward the goal of using principles to clarify decisions regarding field problems. Satisfactory help from guiding principles in resolving accounting dilemmas will afford a testing of those principles and of the antecedent postulates as well.

This brief viewing of a compact and necessarily complex report has brought some questions to mind, some of which may perhaps stimulate useful discussion. Are postulates also assumptions? Are assumptions something we cannot know as fact but need as a basis for discussion? Are any of the stated postulates elements that we can know to exert influence on accounting and, thus, contribute to making this technology what it is? Is accounting what it is because of the impact of the environment of only the last one-hundred years? Have evolutionary developments in prior centuries contributed lasting elements to the ability of accounting to serve modern society?

If postulates derive from experience, environment, and reason, why are they also assumptions? Could they be usefully considered as verbalizations of compelling concepts that explain accounting's reason for being and its capacity to serve society over many centuries and in the present?

Nine of the fourteen postulates deal with "the way things are" in accounting. Are the several declarations sufficiently interrelated as to form a discernible ideological pattern? Are they interrelated only from being generalized out of knowledge of accounting as it is?

A-2 (exchange of goods) and A-5 (money, the common denominator) seem precedents for B-2 (market price for transactions). Do these concepts interrelate in ways that explain the source and basic nature of enterprise experience data? Is not transaction experience the raw material for account data and the focus of people's interest in account data?

Does the phrase in B-2, "or future exchanges," propose interpolation of non-experience data into accounts consisting of experience data? Would an injection of interpretative elements into the accounts have the effect of negating the imperative postulates C-2 and C-3 (objectively and consistency) as far as interrelations among compelling concepts are concerned?

Some readers of the report may wonder whether the term "postulate" is fully descriptive of each of the propositions, and whether some of these have more substance than other postulates. Perhaps the first five postulates (Chapter 3), though drawn from the environment in which accounting functions, could be considered as expressing effective means for accomplishing definite ends, as the better choice of alternatives, or as verbal symbols compactly suggesting concepts based on facts from economic life, which can provide clues to the capacity for service that lies within accounting technology.

Quantification is clearly a necessary fact of economic life; as a familiar means, toward the end of aiding rational decisions, it need not be assumed to exist.

Exchange is another characteristic fact of economic life, one that acts as means for helping business activities to serve customer needs.

Entities are conceptual characterizations of organizational service units. A business enterprise is a grouping of people, material, and ideas. This "association" must have conceptual and contractual boundaries in order to function, in order to isolate its operation data from those the of other entities, in order to limit the scope of the decisions of its management, and in order that people outside the entity may study data telling of the results from this management's actions taken within the boundaries of an organizational unit.

Periodic reporting refers to another conceptual boundary, a sectionalization of the operating life of an enterprise. When the concept is activated by accounting procedures, periodicity becomes a means toward the end of helping management and other interested parties to gain insight into an enterprise entity.

Unit of measure (A-5) is a fact of economic life closely related to *quantification* (A-1) and to *exchange* (A-2). It is a means toward the same ends as the other two. Yet, a somewhat confusing element appears here in the use in the text of the phrase "money is the common denominator." It would seem more persuasive to think of money-price as the measure of a transaction event and hence as a quantitative experience to be stored in an account.

Money is a means toward the end of facilitating exchange of goods; it serves as a means of pricing the items exchanged. This is the connotation of "common denominator." The function of serving as a medium of exchange applies to currency money and check money. It is confusing, for accounting use at least, to think of money as a measure of value. Gold has been called a standard of value, but this designation, especially in this day, can scarcely carry over far as to justify considering money as a measure of value. Using paper money (Federal bank notes), bank checks, and credit cards as mediums of exchange leaves valuation where it has always been – in the utilities judged to reside in exchanged services, such as labor exchanged for travel by way of wages used to buy gasoline.

Occasional uses has been made here and in the report of that relationship between means and ends which is often called pragmatism. Pragmatic logic is best considered as a way of *testing* the relation of end and means. The test is not properly equated to "usefulness," or in a setting implying that "the end justifies the means." A pragmatic test calls for careful appraisal as to the desirability of the end. The means used or proposed will need to be judged as to their suitability, according to the consequences, known or expected, emerging from this use. Opinions of "usefulness" could scarcely be equivalent to rational and separate judgments as to desirability of ends and to suitability of the associated means.

A questioning attitude of mind can often be a useful stimulant toward deeper insight. Hence, questions need not be considered as critical in purpose. Certainly, the questions raised above have no such intent. Much of the ultimate benefit from this extensive research program is very likely to stem from the discussion generated. Ultimately, accounting will become more widely and much better understood for what it is and why it is able to serve effectively. The effects of earlier research activities of the American Institute of Certified Public Accountants offer persuasive precedents pointing in this direction.

NOTES

1. Littleton is referring to Moonitz' research monograph, *The Basic Postulates of Accounting*, which was published on behalf of the AICPA in 1961. The postulates

presented in this monograph are reproduced in Table 3 at the end of the chapter "The Heart of the Matter."

2. Littleton is here anticipating the second research monograph, *A Tentative Set of Broad Accounting Principles for Business Enterprises*, written by Sprouse and Moonitz and published in 1962. Littleton would not, however, have been able to ever observe the consequences of the reports as neither were adopted for financial reporting purposes (e.g., see Zeff, 1972).

2

BROAD ACCOUNTING PRINCIPLES☆

ABSTRACT

In five pages, the study summaries the proposed principles; twenty-four pages summarize committee members' comments, some of which are in support and others in dissent.[1] The latter include reservations regarding the lack of convincing logic, adequate reasoning, and limited examination of objectives. In particular, it could have been helpful if specific principles had been coordinated with individual postulates, and the concept of realization seems to have been weakened by focusing on the reporting of holding gains and loss as a matter of principle. Yet, there was a time when "theory" was considered to mean "the impractical." But research activities such as these, and the discussion they generate, carry much promise for refining conceptual bases; thus, strengthening accounting technology and its associated profession by cementing its foundation blocks.

The report appropriately begins by reporting from the prior research publication fourteen postulates expected to serve as the foundation for accounting principles. The next five chapters, forty-three pages of discussion, lead up to Chapter 7 where five pages summarize the resulting principles. The last twenty-four pages, before a four-page bibliography, present comments

☆This chapter has been reproduced courtesy of *The Accounting Review*, the official journal of the American Accounting Association. The original citation for this article is Littleton (1963a).

by nine members of the committees on broad principles and on basic postulates.

The published comments, in some instances, offer support for the report whereas others indicate dissent. Among the latter, these points are made: significant departures from prior practices; proposed changes not supported by convincing logic; insufficient critical exploration of alternatives; inadequate reasons and justifications; limited examination of accounting functions, purposes, and objectives.

To these might be added the reviewer's overall impression. It could be helpful to readers if individual principles were coordinated more often with individual postulates. The concept of realization as the test for recognizing profit calculations seems to have been repudiated by making a matter of principle the calculation and reporting of holding gain or loss. This could be considered as favoring the idea that enterprise profit would be reflected by a calculation of increase in enterprise well-being. Such a preference would seem to indicate belief that accretion from unrealized value changes, and profit emerging from management-originated exchange-price transactions in the market, would together tell of enterprise income.

Section D, the largest of eight parts of the summary of principle, elaborates on the thought that "the problems of measuring (pricing, valuing) an asset is the problem of measuring its future services ..." This might be considered the key section of the summary, and as speaking for a substantial part of the text. It is of course difficult to write about accounting without using the words "value or valuation." But substitute terms are badly needed because of the non-accounting connotations attached to those words by general usage and in economics. Surely, accounting technology will necessarily be more occupied with recorded transaction price than with the interpretation of possible significance of future expectations; that is, with value judgments that have not yet become objective reality for the given enterprise.

The text seems to equate three words: measuring, pricing, valuing. In being skeptical of such a close relationship, something more is involved than semantics. Using the three words interchangeably can add little clarity to technical languages. Valuations either are outright subjective judgments or represent the repricing of an asset. Some changes of acquisition prices recorded in the accounts cannot be ruled out, but the initiative comes from outside the range of accountants' responsibilities. Yet, professional accountants are in a good position to protest an acceleration of the practice of casual repricing.

The term "measuring" is used throughout the report. The associated emphasis thus given to money dollars and quantification suggests that "measuring" expresses a key note. It is not made clear that quantification is basically outside of accounting responsibility, and that the "quantities" come to accounting ready-made. As such, accounting is in fact only equipped to organize the "measurements" given to it and to apportion them reasonably and justifiably *toward* generating, in the user, an understanding of the given business enterprise. Pushing accounting to do more would be attempting to give this technology responsibility for indicating what the facts of enterprise experience mean. Yet, its logical function should be that of making understandable the experience-facts that exist.

In one section (p. 7), the five postulates named in the first report as those speaking of the environment of accounting are indicated as leading to a statement of accounting functions. Two of these functions refer to assigning data to periods of time and to using money as a common denominator. Periods, like accounts and the enterprise itself, are categories for assembling data to make them more comprehensible. This is a compelling concept of an objective and using these "categories" constitutes a means to the end of making an enterprise more readily understood. Assigning data to periods is therefore more a necessary technique than a function; the function is to increase understanding.

As for the use of money, this is indeed a common denominator but it is not accounting that makes it so. Use of money is a necessity of trade, whether accounts are kept or not; accounting looks upon money price as a fact, not as a measurement function. It is confusing to speak of money in account as if account figures tell of measured value. Money price and the dollar sign are used in accounts to indicate a service rendered by a medium of exchange.

The other three items at this point in the text seem to present an overly compact view of function. This too deserves careful attention, for surely principles would be at least as close to functions and objectives as to actions and technique.

Compressed, these three items point toward the function of measuring resources held by a claims against an enterprise entity and of measuring changes in these elements. It is not clear whether the functions there visualized are those of measuring as such or of reporting on measurements. If the latter, financial statements would be a means, not an end. If measuring, as seems logical, comes before reporting, the simplest rudiment of bookkeeping would become acts of measuring, by this reasoning. If we view the rudiments realistically, the picture noted is one of marshaling into various analytical categories data already "measured" by having been stated in terms of the medium of exchange used in actual transactions in the markets. The assembled data therefore tell of enterprise experience, and accounting has been functioning as a type of data processing apparatus working with enterprise experience.

Some fundamental questions emerge. When do account data cease to express enterprise prior experience? When and why does accounting technology (or principles) take over responsibility for modifying consummated prior experience into something else? At what point does a function of analytically marshaling factual data convert into a function of undertaking to inject into accounts interpretative changes, sponsored by conditions and events not yet "measured" by managerial decision-actions in the market? Would it not be useful if these two functions should be carefully differentiated in both theory and practice-that of marshaling data and that of extracting meaning from the data marshaled?

It would seem appropriate for technical means to be designed and used toward fulfilling a deeper function; that is, means which could separate analysis and synthesis on one hand and interpretation of significance on the other. But perhaps thought has been so strongly focused in the literature toward financial statement communications so as to push aside some underlying characteristics which could do much to explain the capabilities and the limitations of accounting. It may be that the interlocking of real and nominal accounts could have more significance for accounting service than money considered as measuring values. Interlocked real and nominal accounts, and the logic inherent in interrelated bilateral accounts, provide technical means for communicating enterprise prior experience beyond the power of purely statistical data averages and indexes to duplicate.

Years ago, William James said theory becomes an instrument helping us to move forward. Since further discussion may be sparked by theory questions, some additional ones are presented toward that end.

Is the economic concept of "improved well-being" appropriate for association in accounting with the significance of nominal accounts? These categories provide means of calculating profit and loss from data out of overt transactions. A calculation of change in enterprise well-being would produce, on the surface, apparently similar figure results. But there would be differences. A comparison of enterprise net worth as of differing dates would not provide analytical data (such as expense and revenue) indicating the factors responsible, under management, for the resulting change in totals.

In the absence of regularly used nominal accounts, a direct determination of increase in well-being would call for frequent asset revaluations. Consequently, increase in net worth would be a mixture of value increases and transactions representing earned income. Perhaps it is the presence of this kind of mixture which prompts search for ways to dissolve it. Advocacy in this publication of reporting on holding gain or loss, of consistent use of replacement prices, and periodic revaluation of assets, seems to imply a need to achieve a breakdown into constituent parts of the change in net worth between balance sheet dates or a need to bypass, or modify, factual nominal accounts accordingly. But is the result superior, informatively and logically, to the usual income statement?

Can accounting technology or accounting principles be expected to reveal economic causation affecting a company? Price level change and change in replacement prices are facts of economic life. Their effects on an enterprise could best be exerted through their influence on management's decisions. Must we assume management will be unaware of these facts? Current economic conditions outside the enterprise should logically be considered as collateral and interpretative information. Supplementary disclosures of information of this type have been proposed. They are mentioned casually in this report. A subsequent research publication will deal with the impact of price level changes.

As indicated in the reviewer's earlier examination of the report on postulates, the raising of questions and alternatives might well be considered more as stimulation toward further discussion than as expressing critical dissatisfaction with research in theory undertaken for the ultimate benefit of practice.[2] Practice (technology) in both administrative and financial accounting has grown so rapidly under pressure and need, while theory (ideology) has not been able to keep pace. As such, a great deal remains to be done in the latter area. There was a time when "theory" as to accounting meant only "the impractical." Someone has said in another context that theory gives significance to practice; practice supplies the test that keeps theory vital. No doubt, theory and principles cannot point the path to follow, but they should light up the terrain ahead so we may better choose the path.

The research activities of professional men and accounting teachers carry the promise of helping to round out the full picture of enterprise capital-income accounting; a technology that has made very important contributions to economic society and, along the way, has given rise to a profession that was initiated in the public interest and is still intent upon serving the public interest. The timing, direction, and plan of this research in and for accounting is an earnest of that intention.

NOTES

1. Littleton is referring to Sprouse and Moonitz' research monograph, *A Tentative Set of Broad Accounting Principles for Business Enterprises*, which was published on behalf of the AICPA in 1962.

2. Littleton (1962a) is referring to his earlier review of Moonitz' *The Basic Postulates of Accounting* (1961). This review is reproduced in the previous chapter, "Basic Postulates of Accounting."

3

PRICE LEVEL CHANGES ☆

ABSTRACT

Price level movements have been under scrutiny for forty years. Yet, a need still exists for further classification of the concept of business income. This is so because accounting has a justifiably duty to report on actual transaction experience. General prices, on the other hand, cannot speak so specifically, but business decisions nonetheless need to consider such data. With this in mind, an alternative emerges: include price level adjustments in accounts or report them separately as supplements. The support is given in this study to the latter, while acknowledging that time is needed for the interpretative benefits of supplementary reports to be more widely recognized. Given enough time, it is reasonable to expect that a favorable consensus will emerge. Financial statement users would no doubt favorably receive supplementary data on the impact of inflation, and companies would not suffer from enlightening the people at interest in this manner.

This report of 278 pages presents a penetrating analysis of the problems involved in making evident to users of financial statements the impact on a business enterprise of changing price levels.[1] The primary parties concerned are those who initiate financial communications (management) and people

☆This chapter has been reproduced courtesy of *INSIGHT Magazine*, the Magazine of the Illinois CPA Society and the successor of *The Illinois Certified Accountant* (for the latest issue, visit www.icpas.org/insight.htm). The original citation for this article is Littleton (1964c).

who need the information as part of the basis for investment decisions. Men in the profession of public accounting are in a good position to sense the data problems of these primary users. In that context, the American Institute of Certified Public Accountants, through this research study, has rendered a constructive service in the public interest.

Price level movements have been under close scrutiny over the past forty years. The results of the wild inflation and financial collapse of Germany in the 1920s and the American depression of the 1930s greatly stimulated a continuing interest in the effects of price change and monetary inflation. The profession has deep concern about adequate and dependable information for the investing public. For this reason, the Institute is a logical agency to study the impact on financial statements of contemporary price level change.

"Full disclosure" is more than a rule and more than an accounting principle. It is a moral responsibility of business life, in an era of wide public investments in business enterprises. Full disclosure is a modern responsibility similar to that so clearly recognized a century ago and made the subject of British legislation in the form of several Companies Acts. That recognition of the public interest strongly influenced the early development of a responsive profession of public accounting.

Against this background, *Accounting Research Study No. 6* clearly deserves wide circulation as well as thorough consideration within the financial community and in the decision sections of enterprise management. The chief decisions toward improving accounting communications in this era of monetary inflation must be taken in these two segments of the economy. On its own motion, the profession of public accounting cannot create general acceptance of specific ideas, principles, or practices relating to financial statements.

In this report, fifty-six pages of text are presented in five compact chapters: the problem in perspective; what is meant by price level adjustment; adjustments and generally accepted accounting principles; objections to adjustments; and methods of disclosure. The remainder of the study consists of a five-part appendix of 190 pages: the index number problem; adjustment techniques; gains and losses on monetary items; disclosing effects of price level changes; and cases from the literature. A bibliography of ten pages is also included.

Interest in improved financial reporting was clearly evident in the 1920s, when rising prices were sponsoring write-up of asset values, and in the 1930s, when falling prices sparked asset write-downs. Certain financial practices during the booming 1920s attracted attention because credits from asset write-up sometimes found their way into surplus available for dividends. Analysis of such practices led the Institute to advocate strongly the separation, in the financial statements, of earned surplus and appreciation surplus. Only a full disclosure such as this could make the needed distinction evident. At about the same time, dividend statutes were changed where the wording of existing laws seemed to avoid the issue by simply limiting cash dividends to "surplus."

These actions, sponsored by two professions, achieved clarification of both the concept of enterprise income and of dividend base. These actions also strengthened the logic inherent in the communication function of financial statements.

As the economy steadily moved up from the depths of the 1930s, the accompanying rise in price levels continued farther than reversing prior price trends. By the early 1950s, price data began to take on the colouration of monetary inflation. The public accounting profession, almost a generation earlier, had been interested in strengthening the accounting concept of enterprise net income by identifying it with *earned* income. In the 1940s, there was growing concern that some of the effects of current inflation might be lost to view if the users of financial statements did not, in some manner, take into consideration the seriousness of a growing price level rise. Price level change tends to reflect monetary inflation, and inflation, like fixed asset write-up, might affect the public's concept of reportable net income.

The concern felt in the profession was indicated by the creation of a research group to explore the matter. The results were published in 1952 under the title *Changing Concepts of Business Income*. As the content of that important report clearly indicates, the study and publication was an action of public service rather than an undertaking of direct benefit to the profession. In essence, the book was an examination of the nature of enterprise income; it explored that concept more deeply than had been appropriate in prior studies of the distinction between earned surplus and appreciation surplus.

Income determination was an important service function of accounting long before there was a literature of economics, including income theory. The aspects of business reflected in the word "income" lie at the heart of enterprise activity and related investment activities. Because of this fact, there is need for considering, on a many-sided front, the trend on monetary inflation. For inflation should have a definite impact on decisions in business operation and in the investment markets.

Accounting technology is closely identified with such decisions, but only in specific ways. This technology makes its contribution primarily through the meaning that can be interpreted out of enterprise prior experience data, which is reported by the technical processes of enterprise accounting. Study of these data can lead thought, and emerging decisions, toward separate and collateral appraisal of the significance for the enterprise of present and probable future economic, financial, and political conditions. Obviously, these will involve non-account data.

Here is ample justification for *Accounting Research Study No. 6*. An important need exists for still further clarification of the concept of business income. Once more, certain aspects are involved of what business is not. Such negatives cannot be included in a definition. Yet, a negative may be as enlightening as a positive characteristic. It is fair to consider *Accounting Research Study No. 6* as an endeavor to foster better understanding of a very complex matter.

The existing literature gives ample evidence of that complexity. That evidence is thoroughly explored; the monograph indicates the variety of possible approaches to understanding the impact of price level change. Many selections from the growing literature present analysis based on data from published company reports. This permits the reader to observe by hypotheses, the apparent impact of price level change on reported account data. It is regrettable than so few company reports undertake, on company initiative, to give readers similar interpretive analyses.

Whenever the nature of enterprise income has been brought under close scrutiny, whether in the 1930s, 1950s, or 1960s, a major problem has arisen as of ways and means for making appropriate disclosures. And always the functional logic and the natural limitations of enterprise accounting have contributed to the selection of the means proposed. This fact suggests that awareness of functions and limitations should be clearly present when clarified concepts point toward improved types of actions.

The separate disclosure of earned surplus and appreciation surplus emerged a generation ago from rational concepts of the relation between enterprise management‘s prior decision actions (enterprise transaction experience) and the creation of enterprise earned income. Management could order write-up of asset values but that decision would be unilateral and hypothetical, lacking confirmation by overt action in the markets by the given enterprise. A rational basis would therefore not exist for reporting the resulting credit as earned income. Unless, of course, accountants' basic concepts changed wherein "accretion-income" could come from a judgment as to the enterprise's improved status of well-being. The issue would rest on the question whether or not "improved status" and "earned income" were so close in meaning that the terms would be synonymous in effect.

Write-up of asset values, in addition to raising the question of economic versus accounting concepts, gave point in the 1920s to a legal question: was "surplus" an appropriate term for use in a dividend statute? The legal question was settled by statute amendments in certain states. Additional accounting questions also appeared, such as depreciation calculated on appraised values, and whether part of that charge should be made against appraisal surplus. By the 1950s, the price level rise had more than offset the price fall of the 1930s. Some of the methods developed earlier to encourage recovery seemed to continue effectively after their asserted function had been fulfilled. This persistent rise in price level generated fresh questions of the adequacy of accounting reports of the day. Again, the nature of enterprise income became a focal issue.

In the *Journal of Accountancy* for May (1950), George O. May expressed the view, as an accounting postulate of the day, that "... fluctuations in the value of the monetary unit which is regarded as the accounting symbol may properly be ignored (p. 387)." In 1952, May's study group stated, in *Changing Concepts of Business Income*, that "... the assumption of reasonable stability (of monetary unit) is regarded as unwarranted (p. 105)." And, later in the same report, that "large corporations should be encouraged to furnish information that will facilitate determination of income measured in terms of approximately equal purchasing power (p. 150)." In 1953, as part of *Accounting Research Bulletin No. 43*, a restatement of *Accounting Research Bulletin No. 33* (1947) said: "should inflation proceed so far that original dollar costs lose their practical significance it may become necessary to restate all assets in terms of the depreciated currency (p. 69)."

As quoted in *Accounting Research Study No. 6*, the Accounting Principles Board "... agreed that the assumption in accounting that fluctuations in the value of the dollar may be ignored is unrealistic ... (p. 1)." Finally, when *Accounting Research Study No. 6* was published, it was indicated that "... special attention should be paid to the use of supplementary statements as a means of disclosure (p. 1)." This leading statement, it would seem, had opened a path around the objections against reporting price level impact through incorporating index adjustments items directly in the financial statements themselves. With the impasse thus removed, the functional logic of accounting would be protected, and the financial statement data would then continue to report on the results of enterprise prior transaction experience.

The study group's report and the associated monographs (1949–1952) had become a broad inquiry into the concept of the nature of enterprise income. In the course of the study, the economic concepts of income and the relation of monetary policy to price level change were carefully explored. One of the conclusions (from p. 105 as indicated above) can therefore be said to have been influenced by economic theory.

The relevant aspects of economic theory, it may be appropriate to note, did not develop in association with the techniques of computing enterprise earnings (net income). Those economic concepts would not have been inspired by the large significance, for the individual business enterprise, of calculating income as being generated by the decision-actions of its own management, thus to reflect the actual experience of that specific enterprise.

It is clear that management decisions would be influenced in part by judgments regarding past, present, and possible future economic conditions. But it would be difficult to avoid the conviction that decisions in and for an enterprise would also be strongly influenced by management's intimate knowledge – through account data – of its own past transaction experience.

A conclusion therefore emerges that two very different kinds of data should be available and used; one concerned with prior transaction experience of the given enterprise; the other with data about contemporary conditions; that is, with data in much greater variety than price level statistics alone. This is so because, from accountants' continuing study of the nature of enterprise income and its disclosure to interested parties, it is clear that accounting has certain necessary functional limitation. These combine to make inadvisable direct modification of its reporting of data from enterprise actual experience. There is no convincing reason, however, why financial statements should not be supported by supplementary and interpretative information framed in any useful degree of detail and arrangement.

The disclosure of supplementary data is receiving more direct consideration now than earlier. Yet, a good deal of the accumulating literature seldom mentions this type of communication as a desirable and useful technique. Readers of the articles are indeed made aware of asserted deficiencies in accounting and of a need for decisions useful statistical data. But they do not also have the benefit of cogent analysis of the limitations which prevent accounting from attempting to be all things to all people through direct modification of its communications. And the point is seldom made that non-experience data, injected into the technical structure of enterprise accounting, could cloud statement users' perception of the individuality of both the given enterprise and its decision-making management.

Instead, improvement in communication become evident when full-scale supplementary analytical disclosures are proposed which can make understandable, side by side with the primary financial statements, the apparent impact of price level change. And the concept of this interpretative technique is not a product of the middle 1960s. Note an example:

> I am questioning efforts to alter the appearance of business affairs (by artificial averaging or smoothing of data) without modification of the objective conditions .... Therefore the solution lie in the supplementary annual reports, not in doctoring them. (Study Group on Business Income, 1950, p. 271)

William A. Paton first gave this admonition in his Dickinson lectures.[2] At the time he spoke in 1940, "stabilized accounting" was a new proposal.[a] A clear preference for supplementary disclosures over index-adjusted primary statements is also indicated in *Accounting Research Study No. 6* (see in particular p. XI, XII, 3, 4, 13, 14, 51, 53, and 250). Persuasive reasons can support this approach.

1. The ratio relationships among elements of supplementary disclosures are not disturbed if all data have been converted by index adjustments. This aspect has special significance for the interpretive analysis of a business enterprise toward an appraisal of the effectiveness of its management.
2. The restatement of non-monetary items, in supplementary reports in terms of price level change will result in a relevant restatement there of ownership equity. This is reminiscent of the emphasis, given in the 1930s, to the use of appreciation surplus in association with asset appraisals. Both then and now the disclosure treatment is significant because, in the certified primary statements, the income tax base is still clearly evident in the income statement and the statutory base for cash dividends in the balance sheet, neither statement being modified by injection of index adjustments.
3. A particularly puzzling problem is avoided. That is the problem of revising, in a period of falling prices, a previous restatement made for data in the primary statements under conditions of rising price levels.

Accounting Research Study No. 6 seems categorically to support the doctrine of separating (1) financial statements based on actual transaction experience of the given enterprise and (2) supplementary interpretive, analytical, and non-accountant reports reflecting a calculated view of the possible impact of price level change on the given enterprise. This constructive approach to a difficult problem of communication deserves commendation.

An apparent attempt to look forward, however, seems to imply a degree of hesitation as to the future. On page 54 "a period of experimentation" is mentioned. This, it seems, would continue in effect until the business community increasingly included supplementary information in the annual reports and until users of company reports had become familiar with the interpretive interrelation of the two presentations.

If the interval proves to be only a time of experimentation, rather than continued advocacy, the constructive work of the present research may ultimately lose its impact. The result could be continued use of the present financial statements alone in the customary form, or in some form directly modified by injected price-index adjustments, or perhaps in the form of the use of asset appraisals. On the other hand, the interval could prove a time of education in the usefulness and use of reporting interpretive details by supplementary disclosures. A growing consensus that this technique was appropriate would make company annual reports much more useful to all interested parties.

But it should be noted, even for the parties most directly at interest, that this degree of improvement in communication cannot alone accomplish all that is needed. Too little explored, thus far, are the problems of penetrating into the significance, for specific types of decision problems, of the data relationships made available in financial statements in association with collateral interpretative information. Indirect, yet forceful support for a careful separate reporting on account data out of enterprise transaction experience, was given nearly thirty years ago by Wesley C. Mitchell in his introduction to *Industrial Profits in the United States* (1934). He states: "... profit statements ... are made primarily as guides to future actions ... Every business man ... must make periodic attempts to ascertain whether his past policies have been successful ... (p. 7)."

Such an "attempt to ascertain" depends directly on use of data reflecting the transactions resulting from the businessmen's own past policies and actions. Enterprise accounting, undiluted, can provide the needed first step toward management's next decisions. A mental image of future potential, particularly when this is attempted in the investment market, can only be conjecture beyond the accomplished facts of prior transactions experience. Any judgment useful information beyond the primary financial statements must be supplementary to them, not within them. For future expectations cannot be overt experience at the same time. If this separation is blurred, experience and expectation will each be denied its right to make its own kind of contribution to decisions in the making.

NOTES

1. Littleton is referring to *Accounting Research Study No. 6, Reporting the Financial Effects of Price-Level Changes*, which was published by the AICPA in 1963.

2. Littleton is referring to Paton's manuscript, *Recent and Prospective Developments in Accounting Theory*, which was presented at the Annual Dickinson Lectures in Accounting, Graduate School of Business Administration, Harvard University.

a. The same author had expressed a similar sentiment for supplementary disclosures in the early 1920s in the proceedings of the Association of University Instructors in Accounting, the predecessor of the American Accounting Association, and in *The Accounting Review*.

4

AN INVENTORY OF PRINCIPLES☆

ABSTRACT

A deductive approach to the principle is demonstrated here. An "inventory" is a presentation of knowns. Knowledge, in turn, offers a basis for critically appraising technical actions. Principles distilled out of experience can provide dependable guidance to subsequent actions. This may sponsor rational innovations, correction, or cancellation of action-types as well as convincing reasons in support of existing action-types.

The American Institute of Certified Public Accountants has recently issued *Accounting Research Study No. 7*. The full title is: *Inventory of Generally Accepted Accounting Principles for Business Enterprises*. Paul Grady may well be considered as director of the research and editor of the report. The volume is a substantial and valuable contribution to the literature of the profession, and this is so for several reasons.

The use in the title of the word "inventory" is itself significant. In early use, this word carried the thought of taking stock to see how things are. In the area of accounting research, the same thought raises a leading question: what is the situation now concerning generally accepted accounting principles?

Knowledge of the present situation can be useful in various ways. The profession can make direct use of this inventory. Various committees of

☆This chapter has been reproduced courtesy of the *Journal of Accountancy* and the American Institute of Certified Public Accountants. The original citation for this article is Littleton (1965c).

practitioners have given long and careful consideration to many separate problems. Their judgments are presented in detail. The volume is a veritable handbook of authoritative opinion about many ideological problems of accounting. The assembled information, therefore, can become a springboard toward refining and expanding this kind of inventory.

The book does not in itself seem suited for a college text and, by design, properly so. Yet, with benefit, much of its material could be selectively incorporated in new works or in later editions of advanced texts. In the offices of professional accountants, the volume will become indispensable, not only for the principles but as educational materials for the staff.

A clear element of strength in the presentation is the adoption of an inductive approach toward principles. Fundamentally, the chosen point of view is that of considering guiding principles as having evolved out of experience. These are tested by use and have survived according to observed results.

The text, in many items, seems to invite penetration beneath conclusions to detect reasons that provide convincing support. It will be clear that compactly stated conclusions will have been strongly influenced by rationally persuasive, perhaps compelling, concepts. This is a significant feature, for beyond principles – these being guidelines for choices – stand known accounting actions for serving as appropriate means for achieving definite ends.

Back of guidelines and actions, there will be definable objectives – the reasons supporting actions. These objectives and reasons could perhaps be formulated as concepts. It is appropriate, therefore, that a chapter on concepts has been included. Concepts are persuasive by their nature, and they can be compelling in effect from their association with definite limitations. And any practical technology will necessarily be subject to specific limitations.

The chapter on "Basic Concepts" marks an area where academicians might conduct exploratory excavations toward uncovering other influential concepts. Possibly, these, too, could presently sponsor acceptable action-types, which, to some degree, could negate less acceptable accounting actions.

At a time, when technical terminology was under early discussion, "generally accepted practices" was rejected as the key phrase. Possibly, this action reflected a feeling that "practices" would too often be identified with custom and thus tend to weaken the force of formulated statements of the generally accepted. Some people now might consider "principle" a weak term, sounding too scientific or philosophic for a context of practical technology like enterprise accounting.

It might be less difficult to overcome the latter deterrent than to strengthen the term "practices." In the context of accounting, the identity of "principle" can be shaped by associating it with rational, realistic, and persuasive reasons why a specific principle is firmly grounded in experience-tested and basic concepts. Concept-based principles would be fundamental; they should speak of ideas appropriate to the resolution of conceptual dilemmas; they would be helpful to professional judgments in choosing among alternatives.

The search for principle-supporting concepts would possibly involve penetrating beneath known accounting actions for concepts, which could justify the better action-type or support rejection of a less desirable type. From this point of view, the present research document is very welcome.

The volume consists of eleven chapters of text, plus bibliography and thirty-four pages of comments by members of the relevant committee. Also included is an excellent index, a feature especially useful for a reference volume. Chapter 3 is also particularly effective, as an aid to reference use. Each of the five topical chapters, following the one on "Basic Concepts," is given a section in Chapter 3. Each section begins with a compact formulation of an objective. Following this are page references to sections later in the book, in which are stated each of the principles relevant to that objective. Again, this proves an extremely useful arrangement.

Also noted in each case are specific references to existing documents offering authoritative support, documents such as accounting research bulletins, opinions of the Accounting Principles Board, *Statements of Audit Procedure*, and statements by the Securities and Exchange Commission. A subsequent chapter deals with price-level changes (12 pages), alternative methods of implementing accounting principles (28 pages), and terminology bulletins (33 pages). Altogether, this research makes for a noteworthy achievement.

5

ACCOUNTING FOR MANAGEMENT☆

ABSTRACT

The book shows that accounting has attained the status of a modest intellectual discipline.[1] This achievement is demonstrated by a skillful weaving of significant accounting terms into a description of the way systematically arranged account data can convey verbal ideas about the situation and the progress achieved by a business enterprise. It is made evident that accounting aims at communication; but "reading" the communication must first be learned.

A hunter was snowbound alone for four days in a mountain cabin. He said later that there had been firewood and canned food so it was not a bad experience. It was pretty lonesome, he remembered, and the only reading material was a dictionary. He recalled enjoying that, under the circumstances, and learned many new things but he also said that the plot was not very exciting.

This author's earlier book, his Dictionary, is similarly lacking in discernible plot.[2] His latest book has now remedied this fact. It skillfully works into a new format a good deal of accounting terminology. The result is a progressive exposition of the significance accounting data can have for

☆This chapter has been reproduced courtesy of the *Journal of Accountancy* and the American Institute of Certified Public Accountants. The original citation for this article is Littleton (1966).

management personnel in general. It is easy to agree with the author's interpretative statement in the preface:

> Accounting today has attained a conceptual level: A modest intellectual discipline that leads ... to understanding financial statements ... [and] also to the addition of scope and depth to the practice of management. (p. iii)

This thought epitomizes the book's contribution. Before accounting, there was enterprise and there was management. Accounting grew from those seeds. After some centuries, investors were offered the benefits of professional audits of the accounting results of management's decision-actions.

In time, management itself grew more professional in character, although not formally so recognized. Inevitably, the technical aspects of accounting and management increased as experience marked out the path. As a result, the investment segment of modern economic society has been faced with increasing needs to understand increasingly complex enterprises and appropriately to evaluate the effectiveness of management. Such understanding requires, on the part of those at interest, an ability to penetrate to the meaning inherent in a mass of data, which speaks directly of management decisions and enterprise results. Any "mass of data" set in columns of digits is more difficult to "read" than are printed pages of words set in sentences. To "read" account data requires a special technique.

This book makes a definite contribution to the art of reading financial statements. It clothes many important accounting and business words with meanings significant for managements and investors by emphasizing words more than digits. Figure size alone is not particularly enlightening; digits need to be tied to verbalized ideas. The account data in financial statements speaks through spatial arrangements and account titles. Because of these characteristics, the verbal language of accounting becomes important.

Part of the first group of six chapters deals with fundamentals of account-keeping in an excellent non-textbook way. *Environment*, by a compact description of economic society, is considered as the atmosphere in which enterprise, management, and accounting will have to function. *Transactions* are described as events significant for the enterprise because they provide the substance of account data. This is equivalent to considering exchange-priced events as transaction experience of the given enterprise emerging from management decisions. That experience needs systematic organization because only by that means can data-mass be made comprehensible.

Accounting Pattern describes the characteristic techniques of debit and credit. Understanding this aspect of accounting is essential to appreciating the unique and logical way events are translated into meaningful categories.

The author quite simply explains "debit" as symbolic term for something owned by the enterprise; and "credit" as a symbolic term for something owed by the enterprise. This is essentially the point of view of the balance sheet reporting of real accounts. It does not apply with equal clarity to expense and revenue. Yet, these groups of nominal accounts provide highly significant data for all parties at interest.

Quite possibly the center of many statement user's interest lies in the data from nominal accounts. It is one of the magnificent accomplishments of enterprise accounting, to have so successfully fitted real and nominal accounts together as to create a very real and significant integration.

The nominal accounts set in contrast efforts to achieve and results achieved. Applicable costs speak directly of quantitative and qualitative efforts; earned revenue speaks of achievements. The calculated relation of the two elements provides a clue to management effectiveness in using the elements of capital indicated by the real accounts. From an approach such as this, it follows that balance sheet assets will speak of achievement potential; items on the other side of the balance sheet will speak of sources of that potential. Thus, enterprise assets flow toward income calculations before they flow toward liquidation of indebtedness.

The rest of the book deals with the extensive scope of accounting service capability. Three chapters explain periodic adjustments of ledger accounts and the preparation of financial statements. Another chapter considers fixed assets and depreciation, a particularly important part of periodic reporting. Details of balance sheet assets, liabilities, and equities; details of income statement arrangement, and of consolidation statements – these matters occupy four chapters.

Subsequent sections of four chapters reach into the use-aspects of account data. "Costs and their Control" and "Accounting & Management" are understandably related to the broad need to recognize the importance for future decisions of adequate, dependable, readable, and organized history of enterprise prior transaction experience. The chapter "Forward Accounting" explains the types of budgets and the significance of careful budget planning. A chapter of "Flow Statements" clearly points toward techniques for study of movement in enterprise experience.

"The Audit Function" outlines this activity as "preventative accounting" and as an instrument for testing and correcting management policies. Sub-topics include *pre-audit* (internal check and controls), *internal audit* (appraisal of organizational behavior), and *external audit* as an "exploratory, critical review" for formulating a professional auditor's judgment of the propriety of the company's financial statements.

The final chapter, "Endproducts," is concerned with the importance of penetrating through account data toward a grasp of the verbal messages that the user might see out by "dissecting the financial statements" and by study of the interrelations among various financial and operating ratios. All this is to help the user to judge the significance of observed change over time.

It is reasonable to believe the book has been written out of two convictions: (1) many words with accounting significance will also have significance in a broader context from being carefully integrated therein and (2) organized accounting figures are themselves a type of language because they tell of enterprise prior transaction experience. If the relations of accounting words and the account digits are recognized as this book shows to be entirely possible, some skill in reading meaning from reported transactions experience could emerge as a result.

NOTES

1. Littleton is referring to Kohler's book, *Accounting for Management*, published in 1965.
2. Littleton is referring to Kohler's book, *A Dictionary for Accountants*, published in 1952.

PART XI

1

BOUNDARIES FOR ACCOUNTING DATA

ABSTRACT

The major service of accounting concepts comes from their association with relevant accounting actions. Decisions by enterprise management generate a continuing flow of transaction experience, which will be systematically organized toward review. Organizing transaction data, in turn, requires recognition and respect for a variety of classification boundaries. Most notably of these boundaries is the enterprise itself, the fiscal period, and the ledger account.

Any pairing of accounting means and related ends could have significance for accounting theory and collaterally for relevant technical actions. Yet, this pairing of specific actions and intentions would not fully indicate the importance of that relationship or clearly convey the deeper connotations implicit in a broad term such as "compelling concept."

Each word in the phrase has meaning sharply relevant for accounting. "Concept" is identified with an idea or explanation capable of being put into words. Being an idea-image in the mind, a concept can only be symbolized by words. A same-word, a phrase, or a sentence definition used alone may not be completely adequate to communicate the underlying concept. Nevertheless, as word-pictures, cumulatively produce a growing pattern of interrelated ideas, the significance of accounting concepts will emerge from their association with relevant accounting actions.

Accounting concepts may well be ingredients for accounting theory, since theory may be considered as being, basically, explanation of actions.

Theory will influence rules and principles so they may serve as guides to actions. Concepts will thus influence actions without serving as guiding directives. As such, concepts tend to lend their influences by contributing ideas about relationships, patterns among actions, and by suggesting underlying reasons that point to the need to choose among alternatives with great care.

"Compelling" is indeed stronger than persuade, motivate, and influence; yet, it is not as forceful as command, order, or restrain. And the compelling aspect of a given "concept" may be strengthened by a lack of appeal on the part of alternative concepts. Uniting both of those words can provide a useful angle of insight into the relation of accounting ideas and actions. Each concept of a basic objective, whether large or small, each idea of accounting action, as a means toward an objective, will need to be to some degree compelling, influential, persuasive, and explanatory. Concepts will need these qualities, because they will condition some action; they will stimulate design in action; and they will connect action with action in discernible patterns.

In a coordinated body of ideas, the several concepts involved will support each other and, by this mutual support, form conceptual beams and girders capable of uniting the purpose that generate and justify a complex of detailed techniques, procedures, and other accounting actions. It will be useful, therefore, to note the compelling qualities of some basic concepts.

One example refers to the substance of accounting – enterprise transaction experience. A business enterprise and its managerial activities generate a continuing flow of enterprise experience. This concept is compelling for several reasons. The enterprise exists as a social entity for the service it is able to render. The service and preparation for serving is expressed in overt transactions originating in the enterprise and executed in the markets. The accumulating effects of that experience reflect management decisions confirmed in the markets. Lacking this transaction substance to work with, enterprise accounting could not function.

Another basic concept refers to the relation accounting bears to the enterprise as the enclosed environment within which this technology originated and wherein it continues to make its social contribution. An understanding of the close relationship of accounting to the management unit can increase the realization that conceptual limitations exist that will affect the service capacity of accounting.

This is so because, before there was accounting, there was enterprise; and because of enterprise, there was management. As such, a business enterprise serves as an operating unit engaged in some particular type of economic activity. Those activities are selected and limited; outside of these boundaries, there is a magnitude of non-accounting actions. None of these can be actual experience of the given enterprise. From this, it is clear that the "enterprise entity" identifies a boundary of accounting action.

Management is the decision center. Its action generates specific and verifiable facts of enterprise experience. Those exchange-priced transactions constitute direct evidence of effects intended and of the associated persuasive considerations necessarily also involved. The resulting accumulation of many transactions creates an intermixture of effects, which, in mass, would be almost unintelligible without being systematically organized. Hence, enterprise transaction experience identifies another aspect of boundaries necessary for accounting.

The nature and service of accounting will be conditioned, to some degree, by the type of enterprise and by the informational needs: first of its management and second by investors' need for enterprise data. This fact binds enterprise accounting, enterprise entity, and enterprise management into a tight triumvirate, surrounded as it were by boundaries common to all three. And perhaps the word "conditioned" should be examined in this context. It is conceivable that it might seem to imply that accounting would be subservient to managerial whim; thus, to be forced, if desired, to report such figures as might be thought most useful.

Yet, it is part of the theory function to point actions strongly toward creation of appropriate and honest records of actual experience. This is a sharp contrast with the thought that accounting might be flexible to wish. And this presents another boundary. Only accounting theory that is logically based can aid the choice of actions, which will be reasonable, appropriate, and factual. It can render this kind of aid, precisely because theory encourages search for convincing reasons supporting technical actions and for ways of appraising the intentions back of the objectives, which, in turn, condition the form taken by those actions.

In other words, a natural and functional logic provides a boundary that encloses various pairs of ends and means to those ends. Enterprise is a means to the end of providing service and management is a means to the end of operating the specific "economic engine." Accounting is a means toward two ends: recording the facts emerging from transactions and organizing those data toward analytical review of the accumulating results of managerial decisions. Accounting thus conceived is not as flexible as is statistical method. Conceptual boundaries separate the two technologies.

Management decisions are efforts to accomplish the service objectives of its enterprise. Accumulation of enterprise assets represent effort potential;

expenses represent effort applied, derived from distinct service acquisitions in the markets or from conversion of assets represented by internal transfers between accounts. It can be said, therefore, that asset potential flows toward the achievement of earned revenue. And that earned revenue is evidenced by new assets; thus, completing the cycle of the functional service characteristic of enterprise operation. And all of these actions are inside the boundaries.

One side of the balance sheet, the reported unapplied effort-potential, acquired at specific invested costs, becomes a direct part of the accounting cycle, representing the sequential flow of productive actions. Study of these relative data, reflecting, as they do, movements of capital from assets to expense, revenue, and back to assets, can be very helpful to many next decisions. This is so because the actions are taken within limiting boundaries. The functional logic of accounting directs data into this circular flow, by constantly and persistently reflecting expense-cost in amounts, which were established by the initiating exchange-price transactions.

It is significant in this connection that subjective valuations lie back of, and not in, an emerging exchange-priced transaction. Hence, price, not value, enters the accounts from transactions. Consistent adherence to this boundary means that data movements between accounts are kept faithful to the acquisition price, which speaks of overt experience of that specific enterprise. Furthermore, by using data from exchange-priced transactions, accounting has rendered very important services to society over the centuries through the impulse given toward well-managed business enterprises. Whereas good businesses have been allowed to thrive, the poorly managed businesses have failed from some inadequacy in the services rendered or from inability of management to keeps costs below revenue. It is, therefore, logical to consider enterprise net income as compensation for effective services produced by good managerial decisions made within the boundaries of specific enterprise.

It is inadequate, however, to consider the chief function of accounting to be the calculation of profit or loss. It is closer to the fact to see its function as pointing account data sharply toward use in interpretative analysis of management effectiveness. The last figure in the income statement, even when viewed for a series of years, cannot alone be very revealing. The details of charges and credits will be more important because they are more enlightening. Those details tell of changes in enterprise efforts (cost and expense) and changes in enterprise accomplishments (customer acceptance).

A corollary, more directly related to accounting than to management, points toward the technical interlocking of real and nominal accounts.

This relation is a highly significant characteristic of accounting, perhaps even so significant that it deserves the status of a deep and purposeful concept. This intertwining of two different classes of accounts makes very effective use of the logic hidden in the dualism that is a characteristic of every exchange-priced transaction, regardless of whether or not accounts are kept.

A significant part of the contribution made by nominal accounts comes from the fact that they report on the results of management decision-actions in the markets. Furthermore, they avoid trespassing the enterprise boundary that excludes effects attributed to value changes in which actions by management of the given enterprise have had no part. This is so because management's effectiveness cannot be clearly demonstrated by price changes in the markets until management enters the market through overt transactions for the given enterprise.

Economics, on the other hand, may consider change in welfare status as significant. But the close interrelation of enterprise entity, enterprise management, and enterprise accounting (within the limiting boundaries) makes it illogical for accounting to attempt to calculate change in enterprise well-being. Data having such an intention should be prepared outside the framework of enterprise accounting. Interpretive adjuncts of these kinds are not subject to logical limitations such as those conditioning accounting.

A business enterprise justifies its existence by rendering effective service for society. The effects on the enterprise of management's decision-actions produce clues to management's attempts to discharge its wider responsibilities. It is a fact of profound significance for accounting that its techniques can systematically organize the data from enterprise transaction experience in ways that make understandable the nature of the relation of enterprise entity and enterprise management.

For management, modern accounting is an avenue toward interpretative self-knowledge, just as its earlier forms were for partners in sea-borne trading ventures centuries ago, and for the same reasons. Enterprise experience, as a mass of separate events, is not readily understood. Transaction events translated into data and then organized into significant categories, each with its own defined boundaries, can make a mass of events intelligible. Future decisions, toward additional enterprise transaction experience, will benefit from management's appraisal of the need for continuing, discontinuing, or changing prior lines of enterprise action.

These concepts help make clear how rational enterprise accounting is tied into enterprise and its management by strong elements of functional logic. In a sense, accounting mediates between entity and management and between these two as a unit and the investing public outside. Because of its mediating aspect, it becomes increasingly important that accounting technology should differentiate enterprise transaction experience as such and information in the form of non-experience data. As such, if logic indicates an active relation between accounting functions and enterprise transaction experience, the injections of non-experienced data in the midst of transaction data within the accounts would be a confusing violation of analytically necessary boundaries.

To undertake to interpret enterprise experience without giving any thought to surrounding conditions and plausible expectations could result in faulty decisions. Such possibilities could be avoided, by communicating non-experience data by means of supplementary non-account disclosures. In this manner, two areas of data would be available as a base toward next decisions. The decision significance of each kind of information could then be separately appraised and the decision problem reviewed from different angles.

Definitely associated with an experience-centered function is the idea that such a function necessitates creation of conceptual boundaries, which should be clearly recognized as such in all accounting actions. The concept of an enterprise entity establishes such data boundaries. Enterprise experience is individual. The effect of exchange-priced transactions, by various enterprises on other enterprises, does not constitute experience for an enterprise that is not a party to the event. A concept of boundary is not a matter of definition; it is an idea essential to the service function of accounting. Trespass of any such boundary would record extraneous and irrelevant elements as if they were experience of that enterprise and its management.

The fiscal period is an example of conceptual boundaries. In a way, these are boundaries of convenience. It is at least conceivable, for short-lived and single ventures, that enterprise and management would be associated but briefly. If this were the case, data showing results of venture experience could be made understandable by direct comparison of enterprise status at the beginning and at the end of enterprise life. Today, ventures are so much the exception that concepts logical for them can scarcely be logical for modern corporations.

Each account, by intention and design, sets conceptual boundaries for the classification of details from enterprise experience. Misclassification of transaction data is a violation of boundary; it may proportionally distort part of the factual picture of enterprise experience. And financial statements are influenced by all these boundaries. Lack of full disclosure or an inappropriate combining of details will be objectionable for the reason that violations of boundaries can distort the meaning interpreted by the user for his study of the data communicated.

Recognition of conceptual boundaries is, for several reasons, a necessary aspect of a technology for marshaling enterprise experience data. Boundaries make data meaningful by including the relevant and excluding the irrelevant for each category, and by providing a basis for recognizing omission or displacement of the relevant and the presence of irrelevant elements. A system of recognized category boundaries is needed, because accounting is a complex of means that reflects the effect of a complex of motivating objectives. The existence of conceptual boundaries provides definite aid to recognizing interrelations connecting these two major complexes. This thought is significant, because appreciation of the appropriateness of technical actions can be enhanced from awareness of the strength of these interrelations.

To the extent that violations of limiting boundaries are not recognized or accepted, there will be risk that basic objectives may be prevented, to some degree, from being fully achieved by the basic actions of accounting. If those actions do not provide insight into enterprise experience and the effectiveness of enterprise management's actions, the achievement of a very basic objective will have failed.

These considerations point toward another compelling concept. The functional logic implicit in the necessary relations among accounting means and ends is the force that gives unity and strength to the various aspects of accounting purpose and limitations. The logic of analytical necessity requires definite recognition of two facts: (1) that each accounting category shall have specific boundaries regulating its content and (2) that disregard of such boundaries can weaken accounting fidelity to the experience-reporting objectives, toward which its actions are focused. It would be highly appropriate for accounting actions to be guided toward being in clear harmony with category objectives.

Some actions affecting accounts have long been rejected, because they were unacceptable violations of some conceptual boundary. Investigation, sometimes leading to legal actions, has revealed the use of specious invoices to help cover embezzlement of funds. This, of course, is a case of outright fraud. But an accidental inclusion of a purchase invoice, not related to any transaction authorized by the management of the given enterprise, would be just as much a trespass of the conceptual boundaries of that enterprise as an entity, of the fiscal period that includes the item, and of one or more specific accounts. Inadvertent errors in posting an item to the wrong account would violate one boundary in a positive way and another in a negative way. Neglect to apportion the cost of prior transactions, which continue to affect the enterprise, would distort the facts in more than one fiscal period. These are examples of actions that are undesirable because of their effect; a clue to their recognition is the concept of boundary significance for accounting.

Recognition, correction, and avoidance are necessary in order to maintain the data integrity of the several categories involved. Yet, some accounting actions that show disregard for conceptual boundaries have not been rejected. Customary usage (such as cost-or-market inventory pricing) may have made it difficult to hold to strict accounting logic. Or, as some desire, some kind of pressure for injecting interpretive elements into the midst of account data, which reflect enterprise actual experience, may sometimes be considered stronger than fidelity to the functional logic of accounting.

Violations of accounting logic produce illogic, even though the action may be taken with the best intentions. Authoritative regulation of the actions of accounting would be no solution. An enforceable rule or law may compel acceptance, and the rule may be supported by a choice among alternatives, but the resulting accounting action could not rest on functional logic. As a result, the objective of the rule would come into question.

Yet, most accounting actions reflect the influence of appropriate and functional logic. And exceptions will need very strong support in order successfully to defy that logic. It is, therefore, necessary that exceptions are examined closely and that the search for compelling concepts continues toward those that can illuminate the functional logic of accounting.

2

NEGLECTED LOGIC

ABSTRACT

The figure pictures in financial statements may seem motionless. Yet, movement is essential to an enterprise. The analytical service of an account is best reflected by the relative rates of inflow and outflow of data. At the same time, the functional logic inherent in capital-income accounting does not support "valuation" as an appropriate part of accounting objectives. This is so because transaction experience is objective in nature whereas valuation is subjective. And the logic relevant to accounting actions would seem to include relevance as a key term because boundaries are functional aspects of accounting.

Accounting logic is unlikely to play its full part in this technology out of decree or urgings. Instead, recognition of the need must grow from understanding. The basis would be realization that some kind of logic had evolved as accounting was evolving; that this logic can be persuasive and enlightening because it is grounded in good sense supported by experience and will, therefore, appeal to reasonable men.

Along the road toward recognition of accounting logic are certain spots revealing examples of actions in which logic would seem to have been ignored. Often, such deviations will be found to mix two techniques that more appropriately might be distinguished: (1) techniques of marshaling enterprise actual transaction experience and (2) techniques for casting interpretive light on accumulated experience data. Dissolving such mixtures should lead to a closer accord between accounting actions and accounting logic.

The figure pictures presented by financial statements may impress the viewer as motionless and static. The balance sheet may seem like a camera snapshot, since it shows enterprise financial status as of a given date. The income statement may seem like a still-life painting, since it shows an arrangement of details about earned income.

The latter statement, however vaguely, does suggest movement and change. In this, it is more like a mosaic picture of birds in flight than like a still-life painting. The effects of many individual transactions have been assembled in this statement. Each one of these effects, like the small pieces set into a mosaic, has contributed a bit of individual "color" out of the intention and content of each transaction. Each account is a sub-area for processing details toward final arrangement into meaningful relation. The "message" finally opened to the financial analyst has been built, tile by tile as it were, into a discernible pattern, which, like a picture, can stimulate imaginative understanding toward an interpretive appreciation of antecedent movement and change behind an apparently static communication picture.

Movement and change are essential to the existence and purpose of a business enterprise. Enterprise management is deeply concerned that its decision actions will generate appropriate changes. Enterprise accounting is therefore strongly committed to showing transaction data as moving in and out of the enterprise, and between accounts, toward arrangement into informative and factual communications. As such, mobility is an essential characteristic for account data. This is not mobility dictated by whim of desire, but mobility always in harmony with systematic progress toward fulfilling the logical function of accounting; that of providing a useful degree of insight into a given business enterprise and the effectiveness of its management.

The frame contributes a boundary to a painting mosaic. In like manner, conceptual boundaries play a part, along with data organization, in framing an intelligible communication. Only data clearly appropriate to a given category should be lodged in that category. If data movements in or out are not logically relevant to the categories' functions, the action constitutes logical trespass and is questionable for that reason.

An important aspect of internal movement of data from account to account often involves apportionment of a prior transaction according to the degree that its effect is logically related in part to the current fiscal period and in part to future periods. This is not merely an innovation related to a modern concept of enterprise continuity as a going concern. Long ago, when membership in a partnership was different, it was customary (logically necessary) to consider, as of the date of change (the boundary line between different enterprises), the rights of partners on each side of the boundary.

For incoming, outgoing, and remaining partners, the situation was in effect similar to the purchase or sale of an enterprise. Frequently, some elements would appear at this time that we would now name as items to be "accrued" or to be "defer." Taxes unpaid could be an example. Among a number of bookkeeping textbooks of the eighteenth and nineteenth centuries, only about ten per cent of those examine mentioned items we came to call periodic adjustments. Unpaid wages were mentioned in 1712, interest payable in 1788, bad debts in 1840, and fuel unconsumed in 1877.[1]

Such examples indicate recognition of a date-line boundary. An apportionment over this boundary is not "trespass" but fulfillment of the inclusion-exclusion function of a category. Both estimates, from then and now, would be made of the continuing effect the original transaction should logically have upon the account data, on both sides of the boundary. The basis of that estimate would be a rational judgment of relevance to the present and the future. This is necessarily largely subjective, but, the decision, nevertheless, stays within the transaction experience.

Neglect to "spread the effect" would overstate one account in one period and understate the showing in the other. Where refinement of disclosure or calculation is considered important, this objective would counter-balance any preference for neglecting an apportionment. Basic to apportionment decisions would be a justifiable concept of a fiscal period as a logical category, capable as such of contributing to the achievement of the experience-data marshaling objectives of accounting technology.

More recently, the use of the type of accounting action called apportionment has been expanded within the boundaries of a fiscal period. In industrial accounting, costs are apportioned among production centers, between production processes, and between production units. These and other actions of apportionment involve rational decisions toward interpretatively useful internal computations, capable of reflecting significant movements of data related to significant physical movements within the productive process. In all such allocation situations, decisions must be made which balance usefulness of refinement in computations against the reliability of subjective judgments as to the basis used to guide the act of quantitative apportionment.

A typical action of accounting apportionment comes into view in connection with inventory. Goods and material are required for their use-potential. As potential use becomes actual use (by manufacture or sale), a decision is necessary in order to associate part of the acquisition with the present use and part as deferred toward future use. Again, an estimate must be made. This may be approached from two different directions. Estimate the goods moving into the sales market (or material moving into production) or estimate the goods retained for future use. If these were true alternatives, there would be little basis for a persuasive choice. But they are not true alternatives. In the light of the functional logic of a category such as an account or a fiscal period, whose integrity should be respected, one type of inventory assignment would seem preferable; that is, more logical.

The word "inventory" is not the only accounting term inviting some measure of confusion from having different meanings. The accounting importance of this aspect of work with transaction data suggests closer examination. Inventory could refer to physical goods as well as materials in bins or on shelves segregating type from type. Confusion would result here, as with accounts, from mixing the contents of different categories. Inventory could also refer to a list of items in possession. Such a listing would serve as a helpful adjunct to merchandise or material management decisions. Finally, inventory could refer to a bilateral account category having the usual in-and-out characteristics. Movement of data would be indicated, as with all accounts, by assignment of items to one side or the other.

There is a clear similarity with many other accounts in the third concept of inventory. The logical functioning of a bilateral account, well typified by a cash account, leads to the calculation of a figure for net change in the category by contrasting data inflow and data outflow. It is clear from the service nature of a cash account, and of an income statement as well, that the informational content of a category's balance is less than that to be gleamed from study of relative rates of inflow and outflow. For the balance may become what it is, at a given time, because of increased inflow or decreased outflow in the past, or vice versa.

The operation of a cash account accords closely with the concept of category function: inflow coming from certain types of management actions; outflow coming from quite different types of management actions. The analytical service capacity of an account is more closely related to rates of flow than to the balance that remains. Moreover, a cash account balance lends itself well to verification; the integrity of reporting on inflow and outflow can be tested by comparing the count of cash with the account balance.

These characteristics are typical of nearly all asset accounts. An inventory account, however, is frequently treated as if it had different characteristics. A materials inventory account will contrast acquisitions and withdrawals; thus, like a cash account, result in a remainder of acquisition not yet withdrawn – a balance which may be verified by count. On the other hand, the merchandise inventory account usually does not conform to this logical pattern. Its balance is often determined by count-and-price; the resulting figure compared with acquisitions is considered to produce a residual figure speaking of withdrawals (i.e., the cost of goods sold). The last phrase seems to reflect a quite different concept, but the calculated facts may not be in accord with the meaning of the words.

The accounting treatment just described, put into words, says in effect "whatever acquired goods are not found to be still on hand must have been sold." To the extent the verbalization is factually true, the phrase and the account will both be logical; that is, faithful to the category's function. It will be observed, however, that some acquired goods may have been lost, stolen, or damaged beyond selling. If these are omitted from the "count," the calculated figure called "cost-of-sales" no longer properly identifies with the clear meaning of the words.

This treatment, if applied to cash account, would scarcely be acceptable. Cash received, less cash on hand, would not produce a reliable figure for cash disbursed. This result is more than a matter of semantics. It presents an issue of illogic; that is, a violation of a conceptual boundary necessary for data integrity. If goods are known to be lost, stolen, or damaged and are removed from the inventory account in the amount of the invested cost of each, the cost-of-sales figure would be properly identified with the words used in this item of profit calculation.

The inflow to the inventory account is objectively determined from cost of purchase transactions or the calculated cost of manufacture. In order for this account to function completely as a category, the outflows would also have to be objectively determined. This can be done systematically in manufacturing accounting, but is more difficult in merchandise accounting. Yet, the same logic would be available to guide actions in both situations.

It may well be impractical and expensive in merchandising to "cost each sale" thus to accumulate a cost-of-sales total directly. In searching for acceptable alternatives, recognition might be given to the significance of different types of "outflow" other than sales. Items can be destroyed or stolen, become obsolescent, or out of fashion. Here, loss recognition is at first a matter of subjective judgment and of writing a new price ticket. Actual loss would be objectively determined only by sale at some price.

A clue to a logical treatment under these conditions could be found in the technique used of providing a reserve for uncollectable accounts. The operation is based on two ideas: that selling on credit involves some risk of losses from bad debts; that experience with credit selling can result in dependable estimates of probable losses and thus lead to the creation of an acceptable reserve for uncollectable accounts. Losses actually demonstrated, in respect to individual cases, will be removed from the asset and charged against the reserve. The essence of this technique is in the action of delaying specific designation of a particular receivable as "loss" until known facts can support this change in the asset.

It would seem quite appropriate to adopt this technique for use with certain kinds of inventory losses. Experience in markdowns from damage, obsolescence, or overstock would guide the creation of a reserve for inventory losses by charging an "allowance" account. When, as and if sale below cost occurred, the loss would be charged against the reserve and the purchase invoice cost credited to sales. The reserve account balance would be reported on the balance sheet as a deduction from receivables, and the "allowance" debit would be reported as a deduction from revenue. The more complex procedure is the more logical; the simpler procedure can only be justified for its simplicity.

Another kind of repricing of an invested cost appears when the traditional rule of the "lower-of-cost-or-market" is applied to individual items in the inventory list. As usually applied, this rule will change the cost-of-sales without clear disclosure of that specific effect.[a] A cost-of-sales figure will scarcely preserve the integrity of that account, if the amount indicated includes a possible loss on goods not yet sold as if they had actually been sold. Whatever justification may be advanced in support of this action (e.g., convenience or conservatism), it cannot negate the injected trespass of a conceptual boundary (that of a category or cost-of-sales) or the effect on account data integrity.

Two other aspects of this kind of accounting action need to be examined. Since it has been customary to recognize falling repurchase prices for items already standing in inventory, it has been suggested, as a matter of consistent reporting, that rising prices for inventory items may also be recognized. Consistency can have a certain logical appeal, yet neither prices that are higher or lower that acquisition cost could speak of enterprise actual experience. More persuasive would be the practice of completely divorcing changes in current market prices from the techniques or reporting actual transaction experience data in financial statements. Such changes in the market would have even more interpretive significance if disclosed outside of accounting technology as such.

A choice of alternative to cost-or-market is available: (1) a reserve for inventory losses could include a factor for probable sale of some items below cost and (2) a supplementary disclosure of the probable impact on inventory "value" of change in general price level. Opposed to these alternatives is the pull of established procedures, which lack a persuasively logical basis under present conditions. Customary procedures are not illogical because they have been long in existence; nor can they become logical because they are time tested. A more significant matter is whether earlier procedures are now as appropriate as they once were.

In a very early text (Pacioli, 1494), an opening entry included some items at current prices and some at customary prices. The author comments: "make the prices higher rather than lower so you can make a larger profit."[2] This is hardly a desirable precedent for today; that is, unless we are ready to reprice inventory so that later sales will produce "normal profit." It is not pricing – especially unilateral pricing – that produces a profit; customer acceptance is vital; and the contrasting of acquisition cost is vital to profit calculation. From the fifteenth century to the twentieth is a long time for a precedent to survive. The seventeenth century is closer; perhaps the precedent comes from that day.

The French Commercial Code of 1673 included certain rules for preparing a balance sheet. Following that statue closely, a text in 1712 made the following points among others: the inventory of goods should be priced at no more than it is worth so that a profit next year would be possible; if goods had deteriorated, reduce the price; if prices at the factory are now lower, use the current price.[3] The Napoleonic Code of 1807 followed the law of 1673, where the context seems pointed toward the use of account data in litigation in connection with fraudulent insolvency, possibly involving falsely high balance sheet assets. Perhaps this situation could be interpreted as pointing toward the desirability of conservative accounts (Littleton, 1961a, pp. 507–521).

It would seem evident from this early background that a concept of "valuation" was associated with the idea of the financial statement function. The persistence of this idea is evident. Yet, the functional logic inherent in enterprise capital-income accounting points most strongly toward financial statements in which assets will speak of invested cost carried forward (risked) into the future, thus leaving for later consideration the timing of recognizing, as definite facts, the service contributions, if any, of those investments.

There seems little clear evidence that pricing rules, which were given a statutory status on the European continent, were transplanted to Great Britain as recognized accounting practice. Yet, it is quite likely that knowledge of the rules existed. The laws of France seemed to have been made against the backdrop of possible accounting insolvency and loss to creditors. British common law would be similarly concerned, and perhaps the courts would expect trustees in bankruptcy to report factually upon the value of assets available to cover the obligations to creditors. Out of the experience of lawyers and accountants before the courts in cases of bankruptcy may have come such a deep concern for honest accounts as to produce a tendency to favor conservative account figures, even in cases were bankruptcy was improbable.

British statutory sections affecting business were quite drastic in the early eighteenth century; formation of stock issuing joint stock companies had been prohibited after a rash of misuse of company promotions. Legislation directly affecting use of accounts and reports to shareholders came in the first half of the nineteenth century. But this did not set up valuation rules for specific balance sheet items. The Company Acts, especially that of 1862, required registration of companies, the keeping of proper accounts, the audit of financial statements, and the circulation of the audited statements to all shareholders.

The legislation is not directly significant for inventory pricing. It was significant, however, in that it laid the foundation for a profession of public accounting and, by specifying the keeping of proper accounts, left those details to be worked out by businessmen and auditors. And it would be difficult to say whether American ideas and practices regarding inventory pricing were more influenced by knowledge of continental statutory laws, by professional views of British accountants, or by conditions characteristic of American business in the latter half of the nineteenth century.

It became customary for the American merchant to borrow from his bank in order to be able to gain a discount from his supplier for cash payment on a bill of goods purchased. In these cases, the inventory item, along with cash and receivables, would be critical items for the lender to know. Conversion of inventory into cash would provide the primary means for later paying the bank loan. Since cash flow budgeting by businessmen were not practiced at that time, the future status of the borrower's cash would not be specifically forecast. The banker, however, could take a close look at balance sheet evidence for the present liquidity position. Significance here would be the ratio of current assets to current liabilities. Although this figure pertained only to the present, it could be a factor to be considered along with the banker's knowledge of the borrower's reputation and business experience.

A banker, considering a short-term loan, would not be as interested as management would be in account data reflecting invested costs. Ideally, he would prefer a financial statement with overtones of values toward the future. To the extent that this kind of presentation would be feasible, it would afford a better basis than cost for mentally projecting the situation toward the time when the loan would be due. Here appears a conflict of concepts not confined to inventory. An interest in actual cost is characteristic of management; an interest in values is characteristic of people who wish to consider reported account data as a springboard for judgment as to enterprise "expectations."

Future conditions must necessarily receive consideration. They will be vital factors for decision toward the future. Yet, the future can, in the present, only be a matter of informed opinion. Financial statements should be, to the maximum degree possible, presentations of facts out of past enterprise transaction experience. This conflict of ideas has been resolved in favor of the modification of inventory pricing in the balance sheet, and toward the acceptance of that presentation by the force of local customs. Expediency also seems to play a part in merchandise accounting. This is so in connection with the count-price approach to calculating cost of goods sold and in modifying that pricing downward (when market conditions change) in order to produce "conservative" figures for current assets in a balance sheet, which, in turn, support applications for a short-term bank loan.

Bank lenders have had experience with overstated current assets and understated current liabilities. It would be natural for a lending banker to scrutinize a borrower's report of current assets and current liabilities. What is important, however, is that any conservatism actuated by this study should be by the banker. The accounting statements need to do no more than to reflect the actual experience of the enterprise. It can hardly be an "accounting principle" that directs use of the lower-of-cost-or-market. A principle should be related to functional logic and not to custom. A banker, considering a loan request, would be no more concerned about deviations from logic (since he is the appraiser) than would a bankruptcy court (also an appraiser) be concerned, as it focuses on the creditor's legal rights against a debtor.

An honest financial statement (actual experience) is as praiseworthy as is a banker's conservatism. Such a statement could disclose supplementary information and still hold close to the primary function of accounting. Direct and unilateral modification of enterprise actual transaction experience would represent an act of will and would not reflect the force of accounting logic. As such, a variation from accounting logic need not be considered as an intentionally misleading act. It is perhaps better considered as an opportunity to take note of the existence of a logic having significance for accounting and, in so doing, to reach a basis for critically examining the logically rational versus the expedient appeal of deviation. Critical examination of the issues would lead to appraisal of the arguments, reasons, and presence of misunderstandings that offer support for and against actions that depart from accounting logic.

An examination of circumstances beneath a fall in repurchase prices might cast doubt on the adequacy of a rule of "lower of cost or market." Prices in the purchase markets may be clearly below the invested cost of items already in an inventory; they may be falling but not yet below our costs; or they may presently go below our cost with prospects of either falling further or of reversing the trend. Such varying factors could undermine confidence in a rule of thumb.

Moreover, experience may indicate that the selling prices, in the merchant's line of business, have not shown a tendency to follow closely general price changes in the purchase markets. Alternatively, product obsolescence may be judged imminent or popular taste may be changing favorably. Such factors can change merchandise policies very quickly. Price tags are easy to change accordingly. But the accounting facts of prior actual transactions are still facts; they still represent effort honestly made to be in a position to serve customers. Furthermore, changing recorded facts, derived from prior experience, cannot help to serve customers and earn revenue. If changing the ledger facts seems to change costs, this is only a delusion.

Recognition of accounting logic would not make accounting actions rigid in pattern. An appropriate degree of flexibility is implicit even in association with a guiding logic. A reserve for uncollectable receivables is not illogic, nor is it an open door for misrepresenting either the asset or the revenue. It is an action, which gains its logical status out of enterprise experience with selling on credit. Experience suggests that the amount to be tentatively reserved; subsequent experience indicates continuing or changing amounts to be reserved. The action is more disclosure than modification. It would be similarly be a logical disclosure to use an allowance and reserve for "inventory losses" based on tested prior experience.

In summary, it will be noted that the various categories characteristic of accounting are essential features of its capacity for making enterprise experience understandable. Logical boundaries are necessarily a part of every category, for they will control the content of each by directing inclusion and exclusion of data. The existence and location of these boundaries are dictated by a functional logic derived from interrelated objectives, which unite to control the pattern of accounting actions. The function (objectives) of these categories can be concisely epitomized as follows:

1. Transactions are categories with the function of factually expressing management's intention to affect its enterprise in certain ways.
2. Accounts are categories with the function of assembling data about like efforts and direct opposites made to further enterprise objectives.
3. A fiscal period is a category with the function of separating into informative time segments the effects on the enterprise of those transactions whose capacity to affect extends beyond one fiscal period.
4. A business enterprise is a category with the function of creating an enclosed sphere of managerial action and of service to society.

These several categories relate to a close alliance consisting of enterprise entity, enterprise management, and enterprise accounting. The same functional logic, which influences the service of the underlying categories, also binds these three elements into a significant three-party unit whose reason for being underlies all the objectives of all the several categories.

Forward budgeting of flow of cash, through current assets and current liabilities, could produce information for supplementary disclosures (or basis for reserves), which would make unnecessary valuations of current assets, especially those of receivables and inventories. The issue raised here is two-fold: how compelling, as to accounting actions, is the functional logic inherent in this technology? How significant for accounting is the fact that the impact of events external to an enterprise falls upon management's later decisions and not on prior actions or on the account data generated by the prior actions?

These issues cannot be resolved by a categorical answer. The consideration here is given to inventory accounting. While this example might not resolve all problems, it may point toward a need to explore, in various ways, the limitations of enterprise accounting technology. It may also point toward a need to perceive and interrelate significant facts of economic life, which influence the forms and capabilities of accounting. Work of this kind could sharpen the image of enterprise accounting, as a technical means capable of becoming, under the influence of functional logic, an even more suitable agent serving convincingly desirable ends that have definite social significance. As such, if there is a *guiding principle of relevance* in accounting, it could epitomize the significance of conceptual boundaries. After all, what can be more compelling in accounting than data integrity and what can better insure data integrity than respect for conceptual boundaries?

NOTES

1. Littleton gives no references for these dates.
2. Littleton provides no page number for this reference.
3. Littleton is referring to Jacques Savary's book *The Complete Tradesman* (*Le Parfait Negociant*).

a. Verbal indication, at the inventory spot on the balance sheet, that lower of cost or market has been used, is a rather superficial disclosure of the effect of cost-of-sales.

3

CONCEPT OF A PRINCIPLE

ABSTRACT

An accounting principle should be supported by clear concepts of the needs to be served by reporting on actual transaction experience. This is so because account data are able to speak authoritatively only of transaction experience of the specific enterprise. In addition, some actions are justified by principles resting on moral grounds. Some of the characteristics of an accounting principle that emerge are that these are persuasive, relevant, and reflective of the truth.

Because a principle should offer guidance to action, principles in general, and accounting principles in particular, should reflect certain characteristics. An accounting principle should express ideas capable of being traced back to supporting concepts of needs to be served and of limitations restricting that service. Elements such as these give a principle its vitality and significant meaning. An accounting principle should also be clearly relevant to the preparation and communication of data that are realistic, honest, informative, and have been derived from actual transaction experience of the given business enterprise.

Close adherence to actual transaction experience will supplement reality. Strict regard to preserving the integrity of all classification categories will mark the data as honest; that is, as undistorted by self-interested desires or dissatisfactions. The quality and information content is strongly influenced by accounts, so interlocked to facilitate the analytical interpretation of significance inherent in data magnitudes and movements over time.

The needed influence of basic concepts can be destroyed by willful distortion of experience reality, or by strongly independent decisions as to the kinds of data accepted by a specific amount. Possibilities such as those suggest that simple account names and simplified definitions for technical terms may not suffice to produce trustworthy account data or dependable and informative communications. With this in mind, there is need for clear understanding of the limited objectives of each account and of significant and meaningful relations among accounts. If the technical processes of accounting have been modified, away from firm contact with the realities of enterprise transaction experience, later analytical interpretation of that experience may be handicapped.

It would seem appropriate in accounting to consider a principle as a relevant persuasive truth. Here, "truth" would mean conformity with reality; thus, to possess power to carry conviction. "Relevant" would mean having particular acceptance of ideas capable of influencing rational actions. This approach to concept of an accounting principle would turn away from dictionary definitions as a base. This should not be a concern; since dictionaries are prepared to serve the widest uses, most of the ideas found there are not sharply appropriate for use as cornerstones for accounting thought.

Under the concept indicated, an accounting principle should point thought toward accounting-type actions. Users of the account data would thus direct these actions at organizing transaction data toward subsequent rational decisions. Such a concept, thus applied, would press account data to be realistic, honest, and informative. That is to say that the concept should be clearly actual and convincingly factual; be without deceit or distortion; and be capable of conveying dependable knowledge useful for decisions. If account data are influenced away from contact with this kind of three-fold concept, the real messages lying within those data may be to some degree obscured.

For example, it is clear that the concept of "dividend" should include (as definitions cannot) certain effective limitations and those limitations should influence accounting communications that include company earnings and surplus. Disregard for such limitations could lead to cash dividends out of appraisal surplus. Actions of this kind, a generation ago, led to subsequent changes in the dividend laws in several states and to new formulations of relevant accounting usage.

In another example, self-interest might sponsor a fast write-off of fixed asset depreciation. Yet, such treatment would misrepresent the still unused investment in the asset involved and the related cost applicable for present and future income calculations. Those actions would constitute disregard for the principles of realistic and objective reporting of enterprise prior experience. It would not void the basic principle to point to statutory limitations on tax-deductible depreciation or to statutory authorities for accelerated write-off.

Legalized fast write-off may have rested on expectation that resulting actions could stimulate socially desirable outcomes, such as increased investments in new assets; thus, improving the business capital segment of the Gross National Product. What the law can authorize, the law can change. On the other hand, pressure from income taxation, which is considered burdensome, could foster efforts on the part of business management to explore ways to lighten that pressure. Some efforts may perhaps go beyond the realistic. Again, governmental action as to depreciation deductions may have produced accounting results somewhat more in line with the businessman's concept of depreciation realism.

In general, when ideas seem lacking in realism, one can recognize some hint of falsity or bias therein. Where ideas seem to reflect reality, of course, exercise of judgment is still necessary as to the nature of reality in the stated context. No rules can take over that responsibility. By experienced exercise in the faculty of judgment, we can learn to identify reality in familiar situations. In accounting, we can at least find bases for preferring one type or degree of significant reality to another

Here, then, is the basis for testing the acceptability of an idea, even an idea that undertakes to express an accounting principle. Quite plausibly, a principle could be usefully judged as persuasive and truth-related to the ultimate usefulness of data derived originally from enterprise transaction experience. Data of this sort will regularly be needed for business decisions. Under these conditions, an asserted principle could be examined as to its truthfulness and its persuasiveness. An assessment, as to the truth of a principle, could very well seek out its relation to relevant reality. An assessment, as to the persuasiveness of a principle, could very well look for convincing reason that would support and justify specific actions toward ends sanctioned by that principle. Several formulations will afford examples for comment along these lines:

1. Decision makers – management and investors – need knowledge of the results of prior transaction experience of the specific enterprise.

The truth herein is persuasive, from its relevance to decisions in the making. That truth is capable of usefully stimulating accounting actions in preparation of relevant and knowledgeable data, which reflect the results of prior judgmental decisions within the specific enterprise. Some decision makers would like information about estimated current values. Yet, it is not part of the technical function of enterprise accounting to supply such information mixed with data from exchange-priced transactions of the specific enterprise.

The last phrase carries an implication that an enterprise entity constitutes an outer shell, which contains the effects of all its prior transaction decisions. The accounting actions here involve the production of realistic and useful records of enterprise experience. Such recorded data, projected against significant non-account data, which is also relevant to impending decisions, can provide a firm platform for well-founded and forward-looking decisions. Consider the following principle:

2. Accounting technology has demonstrated, by use, its capability for making enterprise experience knowable and, thus, to serve some of the needs of interested parties.

As above, this example also expresses a persuasive truth about the use significance of organized account data reflecting enterprise prior experience. The logical and moral aspects of this technology limit its capability from remaking prior results or recording future expectations as facts. This leads us to the third principle:

3. The tight relation between the accounting function and the enterprise function dictates the type of data that can provide realistic evidence of enterprise transaction experience.

These types of experience data justify major groupings of account data: data on capital dedicated to enterprise objectives (i.e., capital sources); data on capital productively employed (i.e., capital kinds); efforts made to use capital (i.e., applicable costs and expenses); and achievements of enterprise service acceptable to customers (i.e., revenue earnings). By the basic tests indicated above, these several items could be considered as principles, as they are persuasive truths that have a guiding capability for accounting sections. This guidance function of basic principles underlies the framework for integrating data classification categories and the informative accumulation of data from the results of management decisions. A fourth principle:

4. Data in accounts and in financial statements are able to speak authoritatively of actual transaction experience of a specific enterprise.

The basis of "authoritatively" is the fact that the events back of those data are solidly identified with a specific business enterprise and with decisions of its management. It is outside of the accounting function and technical capacity to indicate what the enterprise experience might have been. General or specific replacement prices are not experience of any enterprise, although they could have been made experience by overt transactions of the moment. An index of average price moments is even farther away from speaking of the experience of a specific enterprise. Nevertheless, significant price-level changes, studied outside of the accounts, may be quite useful when decisions are being formulated. Consider the following principle:

5. In order for authoritative data to be convincingly communicative, it is necessary that the integrity of the classification categories, the integrity of the data there accumulated, and the integrity of the summary report, shall be assured.

Any type of violation of data integrity can distort the readability of the message about enterprise prior experience. Each distortion could make more difficult the interpretive efforts to penetrate to the significance inherent in the message. This leads us to the final principle:

6. Hidden misinterpretation of actual transaction experience, whether originated by oversight, neglect, or intent, can undermine the authenticity of reported account data.

If not detected and corrected, misrepresentations would debase the technical function of enterprise accounting and restrict is service capacity. Each of these formulations of principles can express a basic and persuasive truth, because of several unmistakable conditions. It might be useful, though not attempted here, to group an array of formulated accounting principles into these categories: (1) persuasive, (2) convincing, and (3) compelling. The existence of differing qualities could materially strengthen the association of the principles with technical actions and limitations. The core facts about transaction experience are solidly identified with a particular enterprise; carefully maintained integrity for the categories and their data is essential in their acceptance and use. These qualities can dependently facilitate rational business judgments, and through those can foster good business decisions by enterprise management and enterprise investors.

The wide range of freedom to make individual decisions is demonstrative of an economy where self-interest is a key concept, but it also makes it possible for bias to influence and for dishonesty to falsify the record. This fact reflects a significant truth – if not an accounting principle – about human nature under conditions of freedom. Furthermore, this truth can usefully sponsor a degree of skepticism as to automatic dependability of unaudited financial reports. From this fact, in association with the functional obligations of enterprise accounting, it seems that the profession of public accounting would be strongly committed toward accepting and attesting financial statements that clearly reflect actual and realistic prior experience of the specific enterprise.

Although not verbally formulated as a principle in the early days, there is good reason to believe that such a concept of the attest function was active in the first half of the nineteenth century. That is, before the English Parliament established statutory audits and, in effect, laid the basis for a recognized profession of public accounting. It seems reasonable to believe that the elements of accounting principles were also active at the time the Securities and Exchange Commission was established. And at the time, in the early 1930s, when the American Institute of Accountants, in cooperation with the officials of the New York Stock Exchange, began to require the certification of financial statements to be tied to generally accepted accounting principles.

In another contemporary action, also in harmony with unformulated accounting principles, the American Institute of Accountants established and justified the practice of sub-classification of corporate surplus in ways which would distinguish between earned surplus – as available for cash dividend – and capital surplus and appreciation surplus-as not being available for cash dividends. More was involved in these situations than clarified account definitions. There were also moral grounds for the actions in England and in the United States. In both instances, there had been a background of disregard for the public interest and evidence of loose financial practices associated with speculative excesses.

The terminology in principle 5 above may seem to supply guidance for corporate and accounting actions rather than guidance to business judgments. Yet, this principle, in association with the principle of data integrity (number 6 above), can, by its influence on accounting actions in the enterprise, offer reassurance to the investor as to data reliability. This assurance can be a factor in a party's judgment to invest or not invest.

An important collateral factor is the investor's ability to read significant meaning, for his purpose, out of the communicated data of enterprise prior experience. Such ability is not a natural talent; it must be learned. And it is doubtful that professional accountants can accept responsibility for interpreting, out of financial statement data, meaning that would be directly relevant to the basic decision problems of specific individuals. There are techniques of analytical interpretation, and the use of these could be taught. But, at best, the ramifications of an individual's investment problems can only be sensed through direct consultation. The professional accountant could no doubt helpfully serve as consultant. Nonetheless, in so doing, he is acting outside of his attest function and, perhaps, without the special knowledge and experience of an investment consultant.

PART XII

1

ALLOCATION PROBLEMS – INVENTORY PRICING

ABSTRACT

Because of pressure from a concept of analytical necessity, account data must be reported for comparable periods of time. This is so because accounting is committed, by its reporting function, to hold its data as closely as is reasonably possible within realistic classification boundaries. The entity is the most prominent of these categories, but the fiscal year is another prominent category. With these two categories in mind, account figures speak with authority of transactions where the output price of the seller and the input price of the buyer are identical. Only by review of his account data can either party review in retrospect his prior valuation judgment.

The present interest in accounting principles reflects concern that the existence, in certain situations, of a variety of acceptable alternatives may impair accounting reporting effectiveness. This may well be the case, as not all alternatives can be equally persuasive. If choice is unrestricted, personal opinion will be free to dictate the choice. Conceivably, personal advantage may not be a satisfactory basis for published financial reports. Personal bias could influence the choice of method for pricing inventory or for calculating periodic depreciation. Nonetheless, the potential effect of such bias would hardly be sufficient to justify enforced limits of choice, whether by statute, tax regulations, or other compelling pronouncement.

The concept of general acceptance has served a useful purpose, because it provided a middle ground between wholly free choice of techniques and forceful limitation of choice. Nevertheless, there were weaknesses: the phrase "generally accepted" was practically undefinable and the available techniques had long been debated in the literature without settling the issues. Discussion seems not to have identified the best among alternatives, nor has discussion clearly identified distinctions that might provide clues for recognizing the least desirable.

As a case in point, perhaps the conceptual problems of periodic reporting, of reapportioning account data between the current fiscal period and future periods, have not been penetrated deeply enough to provide guidance as to the most defensible choice. It is necessary to assign inventory figures between cost of sales and the residual asset; and it is similarly necessary to assign depreciation figures. This necessity stems from facts of business life and its allocation should therefore be strongly influenced by the functional limitations that are characteristic of accounting.

One can argue the same for periodic reporting. Because a business enterprise continues as an operating entity over a succession of years, data allocations by accounting action cannot be avoided. Rational operations could not be expected if only irregular appraisals produce account data; if assets having long service life were immediately charged off; or if these were left intact in the records at full original cost. As such, periodicity for reporting data is a necessity; it should be treated in accounting as rationally as possible.

Accounting neither creates management's need to know nor the transaction experience it records. Accounting, however, does have a clear functional responsibility: that of dependably marshaling the factual data of enterprise transaction experience in ways that will permit data users, management, and investors, to penetrate to the meaning lodged in the events themselves and made interpretatively visible through data relationships. As such, because people will seek to interpret account data, accounting has a functional obligation to keep its data faithful to the actual experience of enterprise.

Management's efforts to achieve acceptable service is represented in the transaction experience that accounting records. Initial acquisition judgments are confirmed and, in a sense validated, through sales revenue later achieved. The action core of accounting has always been centered on the relation of that effort and that achievement. The symbol of effective management is found in the relation of that effort to that achievement. This constitutes the most significant single result of the use of accounting techniques.

These aspects of the technical function have a direct bearing on the accounting actions of rationally apportioning acquired productive-effort potential over a pre-determined series of fiscal periods. This task must be accomplished by methods and directed by ideas. These ideas have to be those that will not result in distorting the reporting of productive and operating costs nor distort the data pictures of the enterprise's financial positions. Such an assignment is not easy to fulfill. "Productive potential" may seem only a fancy name for assets; yet the term is aptly descriptive of the reasons for acquiring resources. "Rationally apportioning" of inventory and depreciation may seem vague, because the first term could mean different things to different people. "Reasonably" might seem more useful, but it could not completely remove all interpretative doubts. Perhaps "realistically" would be acceptable. However, whatever descriptive words are used, apportionment should be given qualifying terms that would exclude whim or wish.

Preferred types of apportionment should be those enjoying support from persuasive reasons. These are the reasons associated with the compelling concepts that shape the accounting function and its limitations. It should be possible to find persuasive concepts that would help to narrow the range of alternatives, such as the choice of pricing inventory into cost of sales and the pricing of equipment depreciation into cost of product. In fact, the existence of alternative ways of reporting on specific items invites attempts to find basic and compelling concepts of accounting functions and limitations, which could point the way to a choice of actions, or at least provide a basis for sequential preference.

One such influential idea is the concept of analytical necessity. This necessity underlies all accounting actions of assigning transaction data among account categories and fiscal period categories. Periodic allocation is a necessity for clear reasons. Between enterprise efforts to serve, and the achievements resulting there from, there is the creation of analytical significance, which makes the study of this significance indispensable. These efforts to achieve sponsor the existence of an enterprise; and these efforts should be open to regular review at short intervals. From inventory, cost of sales data tells of efforts relevant to a specific period of time. Depreciation charges tell of the use of assets to produce salable products; these will then become elements in costs of sales and express effort to achieve revenue.

Inventory items first speak of cost-price or effort-potential. That is the same as the reporting of potential awaiting its destiny of furthering sales-price achievement. Items of inventory, in passing to other owners, transfer their service capacity to the advantage of both parties. The seller achieves, because he has effectively made the necessary effort. From the recorded results, he is then in a position to study, in retrospect, the results of his price-margin policy. The record, therefore, reaches from the past, through arithmetic and the study of account data, and stretches toward present judgment of enterprise policies in general. As such, it is worth keeping in mind that accounting techniques and account data have never been ends in themselves. Instead, they have always been means by which management, and later investors, are put in a position to rest future decisions on knowledge of prior decision results.

The analytical necessity of reassigning data from prior transaction experience poses a problem of conceptual alternatives. Inventory, as an important asset, stands opposite various liabilities and is a part of the statement of financial position. Inventory, as a revenue potential, stands ready to contribute cost-of-sales data to the statement of periodic earnings. The choice of treatment of the relevant asset, however, will affect the allocation to cost of sales. Furthermore, the choice of treatment in the earnings statement of cost of sales will affect residual amounts in the balance sheet. If the residual asset is priced above or below actual cost, the net in the earnings statement will be affected by the difference between value and invested cost. If the cost of sales is entered at transaction cost, the asset's residual value will also be reported as cost in the balance sheet.

Involved here is the concept of the earnings statement. Is there an alternative of using data exclusively from transaction experience of the given enterprise or of introducing data reflecting contemporary prices established by other enterprises? Resolving the alternative could be aided by recognition of a strong compelling concept of functional limitations. A limiting factor is the necessarily tight interrelation of the enterprise as an operating entity, of its management as a decision center, and of enterprise accounting as technical methodology particularly useful for organizing the transaction results of prior decisions, which have been made in the markets by the management of the given enterprise for the benefit of that specific enterprise.

This formulation can be considered a compelling concept, because market decisions and market prices to which this enterprise has not been a party cannot realistically furnish data capable of reflecting this enterprise experience history. It is also not capable of reporting on the effectiveness of its managements' prior decision. In other words, only transactions initiated and affected by its management can rationally be considered as realistic as the overt experience of this enterprise and, thus, as the proper basis for its account data.

There is nothing in the historical development of enterprise accounting that would indicate that this technology has ever been more than a well-designed procedure for realistically organizing the transaction experience of a specific business enterprise. Some of the deviations – such as lower of cost or market – from a strict reporting of actual inventory transaction experience (acquisition price or invested cost) seem to reflect an urge, perhaps not clearly recognized, to make modifications of recorded prior transaction experience. However small these departures may be – even when explained as conservative and forward looking – they nevertheless constitute subjectively determined modifications of objectively determined actual experience. It would not be persuasive to consider opinion as being superior to fact as a guide for next decisions.

All types of inventory actions pose the same conceptual problem. Shall inventory be treated as a valuable current asset or as deferred revenue potential? By one view, inventory is a significant item in an enterprise's financial position; by the other, inventory is an accounting element waiting its destiny of moving, bit-by-bit, into possession of specific buyers. In the case of the latter, it could also be waiting to move along the assigned path into production cost of new items. Since inventory is to serve both the balance sheet and the earnings statement, it is difficult to see how such an asset item can be priced at one level and then reproduced to cost-of-sales at a different dollar level at some later point.

The same kind of service capacity permeates both the items sold and similar items that have been retained in the enterprise. The contribution that inventory makes to revenue comes from the buyer's judgment of that service capability to him and from his acceptance of the offered sales price. He has no knowledge of the seller's acquisition cost. Therefore, the use, by the seller, of any other figure than acquisition cost in his earnings statement will constitute a unilateral and hypothetical modification of overt fact.

These concepts can also be usefully related to the pricing techniques labeled "last in, first out" in order to identify the presumed type of flow movement of inventory items. A flow pattern is characteristic of inventory, if the units are indistinguishable and mixed together, as in crude oil. Yet, this LIFO pricing for the cost of sales has been advocated even for mercantile situations where varied stock is essential. This lends support for the thought that one key to inventory accounting (i.e., contribution to revenue or product cost) has been replaced by another pattern of accounting actions, one which could favor using replacement prices for inventory.

It could be the case that LIFO acquisition prices are higher than those reported from earlier purchases. In that event, cost of sales would be charged with a higher unit price. The remaining low-cost inventory would be reported in the balance sheet. LIFO acquisition cost could also be lower than earlier costs, if replacement prices have moved lower. Consistent use of the LIFO method would then charge cost of sales with lower unit prices with the corresponding change in the balance sheet. Another possible alternative: abandon the LIFO method when prices turned lower, perhaps then substituting LIFO pricing. In that case, earlier and higher acquisition prices would be shunted to cost of sales leaving lower priced inventory for the balance sheet. Such a policy would continue the tendency to favor costs of sales data regardless of the effect of that action on the balance sheet.

In these situations, the factual events have all originated in overt transactions of the given enterprise. But this fact alone is not conclusive. It is still an analytical necessity to apportion inventory between the present (cost of sales) and the future (balance sheet). Even so, indecision exists: some part of the transaction experience should pass to cost of sales. Some should also be put to the balance sheet. Which action shall control both entries? This issue needs to be resolved. If consistency is still a virtue, some version of the LIFO method should be used and the expedient cost-or-market idea should be abandoned.

Perhaps, in some cases, consistency over persistency might be relatively immaterial. If the result were judged material, perhaps the use of computers could reveal the real cost-price characteristics of inventory inflow, thus offering a pattern to guide the charge-off to cost of sales. Guidance for charge-off would be preferable to guidance for determining the balance sheet item. The reason for this would be the fact that the compelling concepts of accounting, as a whole, strongly direct preference for holding account data, as closely as reasonably possible within realistic classification boundaries, and confining that data to sources clearly identified as overt transaction experiences of the specific enterprises.

Data accuracy such as is expected in science is not appropriate for enterprise accounting, but this distinction should not open a door to personal preferences over factual accuracy. The logical tie of accounting to overt transaction experience of the given enterprise is strong enough to make irrational certain types of action. One such action would be that supported by the intention to choose whichever alternative would favorably influence reported net revenue.

It is worth remembering that one characteristic of modern practice – that of pricing inventory items at the lower-of-cost-or-market – was evident long ago. In eighteenth century France, severe penalties were prescribed for bankrupts. Probably, as a result, the recognized practice of the day tended to underprice inventories. Perhaps this kind of reporting would have been considered a convincing indication of the merchants facing certain intentions to overstate them. It would reflect efforts to avoid such overstatements of assets based on action that could be considered false reporting.

It is difficult to escape the conclusion that an eighteenth century concept and practice of inventory pricing was operative much later only as an inherited custom. It could scarcely be considered a principle, even in the eighteenth century. The weakness inherent in this custom, in the context of American business in the twentieth century, could not be erased by taking recourse in a theory of "recoverable cost." A proposed doctrine of "normal profit" would also lack persuasive power. Accounting is not an engine to create profit by figures; it is only a technology for reporting on actual and overt transaction experience of a specific enterprise. It has never been anything else.

The function of accounting falls into question when alternatives exist such as those examined here. It is not a true alternative to contrast the choice of (1) a functional obligation of calculating enterprise profits conservatively and (2) a functional obligation of using data from overt transaction experience, in order to bring into view actual costs of efforts made by the enterprise to achieve its service objectives and corresponding revenue from those efforts.

The reason for this is that the price tags of salable goods do not produce enterprise net profit. Profit is generated by management's achievement of revenue and its success in holding effort-costs below the revenue obtained. By marshaling the data of transactions, accounting makes possible a calculation of periodic profit. Yet, that result is not the reason for this technology, as enterprise accounting evolved to provide clues indicative of management effectiveness. This aspect of management is to be read, not from the final net figure, but from the interpretive analysis, over time, of accounting evidence of management's controls of effort-costs and its ability to influence customer transactions.

In this pattern of relationships, there are clues to concepts that lie beneath the capability of enterprise accounting to render its own type of essential service. If the relevant compelling concepts of limited service function are ignored or weakened, the accounting service is affected accordingly.

The LIFO method and cost-or-market are departures from pricing inventory into cost of sales at acquisition cost. If these departures continue as acceptable alternatives to the cost-pricing method, they probably would continue to provide precedent for further modifying reported account data out of its tie to overt transaction experience. Furthermore, it is likely that the idea of applying price level adjustments to account data and the basic financial statements may have benefited from the precedent.

The LIFO method, cost-or-market, and price level adjustments, if admitted into the accounts and statements, would bring in data reflecting general economic conditions quite outside the pre-transaction experience of the specific enterprise. The issue is not the "usefulness" of information about economic conditions. Movement of prices can be collaterally useful as a separate aid to interpreting the significance of prior transaction experience. Nonetheless, for understanding an enterprise and for appraising management effectiveness, it is indispensable that account data shall speak authoritatively of enterprise overt experience. Statistical information about economic conditions, price change, and other external conditions cannot speak with that authority.

It is unfortunate that the verb "to value" is so often used loosely where "to price" would be more appropriate to describe accounting action. The result of an overt transaction, by independent parties, is a digit expression equally useful to both parties; that is, the price. This price is different from a price tag or price per unit, as its size represents nothing but the agreement between two parties. The valuing, on the other hand, has already taken place subjectively in the minds of these parties, each from his own point of view. Each is satisfied that the transaction is to his advantage. The obvious distinction between the two "valuations" cannot be represented by the same set of digits. The account figures therefore do not concretely speak of value. They do speak only, but with authority, of an equal input price and output price.

For one party, his input is the acquisition price. For the other party, the same digits speak of his output; that is, the action which generated the revenue-price. For both parties, the resulting account data provide concrete and factual motives necessary to accomplishing the function of enterprise accounting – that of organizing transaction data toward review of the results of prior decision-actions of management. Furthermore, only based on such a review is it possible for either party to appraise in retrospect his prior valuation judgment. Stated differently, transaction experience can be convincingly organized for analytical review when it is based on knowledge of existing alternatives and of a persuasive basis for discriminating between them.

2

ALLOCATION PROBLEMS – DEPRECIATION

ABSTRACT

Periodic allocation of asset potential is necessary in order to open enterprise efforts and achievements to analytical study. Productive assets are purchased and used for their inherent power to contribute to the creation of new products and to the achievement of revenue. Management's decisions direct this asset acquisition and use toward the end of achieving earned revenue in excess to applicable cost-expense efforts. Acquisition costs and liability obligations (reported in the balance sheet) are therefore necessary antecedents to enterprise service effectiveness. As such, accounting is failing in its primary function if it deals ineffectively with data expressive of those enterprise efforts and achievements.

As is the case with inventory pricing, depreciation accounting is justified by a compelling concept of analytical necessity. A part of this concept is reflected in the term "periodic apportionment." The allocation of productive potential between the present and the future is an analytical necessity. This kind of action is necessary so that management's effectiveness shall be open to analytical study. As such, fixed asset depreciation reporting is a necessary action because of the antecedent objectives.

Again, as with inventory, a variety of alternative approaches to allocation actions creates complications of choice. Presumably, alternatives came into existence because they seemed to be justified by special circumstances. If strongly differing situations do indeed exist, a presumption would arise that observed differences could not be adequately reported by a single method. For the same reason, situations that differed arbitrarily would not be equally well supported by the special circumstances. Perhaps a desire to influence accounting results, or lack of deterrents to such a desire, could foster a particular alternative over a more logical one.

Few ideas about depreciation penetrate the real essence back of dictionary definitions, but a useful clue to the existence of depreciation can be seen in the purpose of acquiring an asset that has productive potential. Such as an asset is purchased and used because of its inherent power to contribute to the creation of new products and, in its own way, to contribute to the achievement of revenue.

The acquisition price of a productive asset is particularly significant. It tells of the quantity of investment in efforts, which will not be quickly exhausted. That invested effort will need to be apportioned among fiscal periods. The effort thus apportioned over time will then need to be reapportioned among product units that the asset helps to create. This is cost, industrial, and manufacturing accounting. Each term is satisfactory; all refer to accounting actions taken under pressure from the concept of analytical necessity.

If allocation actions such as depreciation entries were not taken, the accumulating data of enterprise operating experience would not be systematically recorded or reported. If this kind of treatment of data were neglected, the needed day-to-day decisions of management would be adversely affected. In order to make appropriate managerial decisions, the collection of data, which can describe prior experience, becomes an analytical necessity.

It would not be realistic to charge off (to surplus) the whole acquisition cost at once, nor would it be rational to hold the whole acquisition cost intact (as an asset) until the equipment had to be discarded as useless. These would be unrealistic accounting actions, because of the existence of an antecedent compelling concept of the nature of enterprise earnings. This is so because management's effectiveness comes clearly into view through account-calculated earnings. As such, it is worth keeping in mind that it is not asset appraisals, or advancing price levels, but management directed enterprise activities that generate earned revenue in excess of applicable cost-expense.

The concept of asset depreciation should be closely related to the concept of enterprise earnings. Because of that relation, the income statement calculations of a period's net income is not a truthful showing until depreciation has been recognized, estimated, and included among the "efforts" to earn revenue. A firm concept of earnings (after depreciation) is therefore helpful in classifying the broad functioning of enterprise accounting. Another and often competitive concept settles on the word "profit." This can be a confusing term. In the context of economics, the meaning is usually associated with an improved state of well-being. This idea, applied to a business firm, would identify "enterprise well-being" as being indicated by the value of resources above the committed responsibility to discharge specific liabilities.

Yet, "profit" is a term poorly oriented to accounting use and to the management function. "Earnings" is much more appropriate. It suggest planning and working for rewarding consequences, particularly those of customer satisfaction. It is the responsibility of management to produce acceptable services. The reward called "earnings" comes from the full achievement of acceptable enterprise service. It is therefore helpful to realize that accounting, especially depreciation accounting, is more strongly influenced by the need to report on effort and achievement (revenue and applicable cost) than by the need to report the assets and equities. The report on management effectiveness is more directly of interest to more data users than the report made by a balance sheet.

This centering of accounting interest is desirable because many people tend to consider that a balance sheet does or should report on asset values, standing in contrast with predetermined legal claims against enterprise assets. It should be realized, however, that accounting technology could not possibly report factually on value possibilities year after year. This fact makes clear the need for a separation, in the data user's mind, between (1) accounting reports on the results of prior overt actions by management and (2) subjective opinions as to present or future values of enterprise assets.

Sometimes it is suggested that depreciating assets represent "the present value of future income." In the context of economic theory, such a concept may often be appropriate. There, it carries a thought that forecasted future income could offer a basis for computing (mathematically) a "value" for a productive asset capable of producing the forecasted result. However, the economics way of thinking does not appropriately carry over into accounting. From the point of view of this technology, an asset is possessed by an enterprise for its capacity to contribute usefully to company production and, through that production, to help create revenue from sales measured by the price customers are willing to pay.

Equipment obsolescence may become known and, if so, it will call for recognition and reporting through accounting actions. The word obsolescence generally refers to a perceived fall in the value of an asset. This judgment is usually based on conviction that equipment that is more modern exists that could perform the same service effectively at lower use-cost.

Known facts of this kind call for management consideration. Their questions may arise about probable operating results and financial policy. Management will evaluate the situation and judge possibilities. But the mere existence of better equipment is not enterprise experience; and the possibility of improved operating efficiency cannot change the existing unused investment in equipment. Until new overt actions follows deliberation, nothing is changed in that experience of that enterprise. Hence, no modification of account data is needed.

Another question is also involved, where obsolescing is recognized. Is the cost allocated to current production to be increased because the asset is thought to be approaching full obsolescence? Is there a persuasive alternative, such as the provision of a specific "valuation reserve" out of earned surplus? Would this action correctly decrease production cost for the use of the asset?

Beneath questions of this kind lies an aspect of the concept of "earnings." Shall that concept be narrowed in this regard? Is it interpretatively advisable to separate the allocation of acquisition cost by sending only a part of that cost into product? Would this be a matter of influencing product cost (and earnings) by "manipulation of obsolescence"?

Depreciation accounting, in the charge to product cost, could include recognition and allocation of both the physical contributions made to production by equipment use and estimates for obsolescence. The latter aspect, being essentially a reflection of the impact of replacement cost, might serve as a precedent capable of giving support to proposals to recognize and introduce, as account data, other types of replacement prices. This action, if accepted, would dilute the reporting of overt transaction experience with an admixture of external prices not yet part of the experience of the specific enterprise.

The statement could be made that it is the function of accounting to report on an enterprise's financial condition. It could also be said that its function is to determine an enterprise's periodic earnings. It is not a compromise to say that accounting should report on both aspects. Yet, the frequent appearance in the literature of terms like value, replacement prices, and obsolescence seems to give special emphasis to financial position. As such, it is clear that accounting faces a problem of alternatives, or a problem of reconciling two types of reporting most concisely identified by the cost versus value debate. Can this technology acceptably report on financial status, essentially in accordance with value, without avoiding responsibility for reporting earnings closely tied to data from the actual transaction experience of the specific enterprise?

It is understandable that value is a concept that has great significance for investors; they are not intimately involved in operations as is management. Many non-accounting matters such as monetary inflation, which would tend to press replacement prices higher, influence their thinking. For a person with this thought in mind, balance sheet items, re-expressed in terms of a price level index, would be considered interpretatively useful. But is this kind of modification of prior experience within the responsibility of enterprise accounting?

The presence of inflation does, and should, influence decisions by management and investors. But decisions should not be rested on accounting reports alone. Furthermore, pressure toward injecting modifications of overt prior experience could prove undesirable in certain respects. Such modification could mask the significance of overt prior experience. Instead of helping interpretation, this could make decisions more difficult. As such, separately weighing management's effectiveness (indicated by reported transaction experience), and the significance to the ending decision of economic conditions (indicated by price level index series), would be a more sound basis for decision-actions.

It is significant for the accounting function that asset and liability accounts shall be recognized as providing a platform from which the efforts to achieve acceptable service-revenues originates. A platform could exist without creating such services, but it would lack a function. The term "service" is the key; the balance sheet (the platform) is the necessary antecedent – a means to an end but not end in itself. As such, the management of operations must successfully create efforts to serve, before it can achieve revenue of significance to investors. For this reason, acquisition cost is more significant, for the balance sheet and investor use, than is current replacement prices reported where acquisition prices would otherwise have been.

The conclusion is that accounting, which deals ineffectively with data from efforts and achievements, is failing in its primary function. Furthermore, the auditor's function of attesting the financial statements to the financial community does not carry with it responsibility for "values." The statements should therefore present only data derived from enterprise overt transaction experience.

In the context of the present, it is increasingly clear that even the best reporting of the results of prior experience cannot alone serve management and investors as their decision problems deserve to be served. It is wholly unrealistic to believe that accounting technology could be so modified as to serve all or even most interpretive needs. The conclusion seems unavoidable: a separate companion technology for account data interpretation is needed. This need seems to be corroborated with by a mild trend that seems to be forming to advocate use of supplementary disclosures to report on the impact on the enterprise of price level change. Regrettably, such reports are not often seen in published company reports, and this evident lack of public acceptance may strengthen desires to use the unfortunate alternative of direct modification of financial statements.

Let us return to depreciation. Calculated depreciation, used in the income statement and for reporting income tax, is an important item in the effort-cost side of computed net earnings. In the event that tax regulations (e.g., investment credits and guidelines to computations) invite or require change in depreciation calculation, governmental fiscal and inventory policy tend to weaken company adherence to depreciation, held closely to the concept of analytical necessity, to some extent. This necessity and the functional limits of enterprise accounting combine to direct depreciation accounting toward the support for the use of depreciation based on acquisition cost. This is so because the procedure is in direct harmony with a compelling concept: the use of an asset's effort-potential makes direct contribution to production in proportion to the acquisition cost of that effort-potential.

Changes in economic conditions can generate ideas about accounting actions in much the same way as taxation or changes in regulations can do. Necessarily, business policy will change because of economic conditions. For example, when monetary inflation is evident, realistic business decisions will be influenced accordingly. But account-recorded results from consummated transaction experience (e.g., acquisition cost allocated by depreciation charges) cannot rationally be considered as inaccurate because of a subsequent condition of monetary inflation.

This leads us to the following proposition: the cumulative effects of the various circumstances, here considered, lend support for the use of interpretive data capable of *supplementing* the usual account data reflecting enterprise prior transaction experience. For example, a report of flow of funds is a well-established separate communication. Reporting the estimated impact of price level change could very well be similarly developed.

The separation between these two types of data is necessary because account data is still required in order to report on the performance of a specific enterprise. This is itself is a major task. Price index series, however, can only provide an indication of a broad range of prices that reflect consumer actions. This is a fact of significance for management's consideration, but present consumer prices are not capable of expressing actual prior experience of a given business enterprise. In fact, long before reported price index data take shape, the specific enterprise has already committed its capital resources (at acquisition prices) into the form of planned efforts to produce revenue from costumers' acceptance of the products or service.

The final thoughts on allocation alternatives may be something less than solid conclusions. Yet, they represent firm conviction supported, it is hoped, by persuasive logic. Accounting technology cannot be a complete and all-purpose information system for management, investors, tax authorities, and other. It must operate under necessary and definite limitations. Its best data will need to be supplemented by useful non-account data beyond the transaction experience of the given enterprise.

Opportunity to choose among inventory pricing alternatives and among depreciation alternatives may invite trespassing on accounting's functional limitation. However, convincingly established preferred practices could foster a growing consensus, and in this way mark enterprise accounting as a rationally based technology for reporting dependability on prior transaction experience. In order to be convincing, the choice of alternatives should be solidly supported by cogent reasons and alternative action types that are not supported should be denied preference.

An opportunity seems present in this context for the profession of public accounting to expand its research activities. It should be for practitioners to convince themselves, and gradually their clients, on such concepts as the following:

1. that it is feasible and appropriate to hold financial statements closely to a function of reporting data from the actual transaction experience of the specific enterprise;
2. that supplementary, analytical, and non-account data can be very useful to all interested parties; and
3. that it would be to the client's advantage for the profession to make available a broad range of advisory services, including that of consulting on the interpretive significance of changes, over time, among the account data of the specific enterprise, and on the collateral significance of those data considered in a context of key economic and statistical data.

This line of actions would seem to fit well with a thought attributed to the philosopher William James: "... interpret the unobserved by study of the observed."[1] Certainly, in business, it would be useful to future decisions to study data reflecting prior transaction experience, and data reflecting economic conditions (the observed), in order to look beneath the experience for clues to the unobserved, such as the relation of enterprise experiences and contemporary economic conditions. This is so because present decisions should be reached from an awareness of the present of both the enterprise and the economy.

Much of the energy of scientists is devoted to intensive study of observed relationships in order to understand aspects not observed. Much of the literature of philosophy is devoted to recognizing, organizing, and justifying elements of knowledge, especially those deserving consideration as dependable truths, convincing reasons, and illuminating relations. Yet, it would be quite pretentious to think of enterprise accounting as having philosophical or scientific overtones. But even with this in mind, it is surely the case that the search of available evidence of the nature and limits of accounting could make more understandable, and for observable reasons, the service capability of a technology that has a long history of effective service and evolutionary growth.[a]

NOTES

1. Littleton provides no reference here, but William James (1842–1910) was an American philosopher, physician, and psychologist. James is considered one of the major contributors to the field of pragmatism, along with John Dewey, the latter of whom Littleton cites throughout this manuscript.

a. Two useful references here would be Goldberg's *Concepts of Depreciation* (1960) and Sprouse's *The Measurement of Property, Plant, and Equipment in Financial Statements* (1963).

3

MANAGEMENT AND THE PUBLIC ACCOUNTANT

ABSTRACT

Account data and computer output can organize facts in aid of decisions, but men must still decide. Education as such is a way of deepening experience, and practical experience is educational from pressing one to think. On one hand, the function of financial statements is to open transaction experience to analytical review. On the other hand, college education should provide some experience in thinking when not all useful facts are available.

It is significant that accountancy was born from the union of enterprise management and enterprise transactions. Before there was a profession of public accounting, there was enterprise and there was management. The profession rests on the historical foundation. Yet, the attest service to investors is only a century old. Action by the profession in the area of management service is even more recent. There is a reason.

Modern business management has become increasingly complex and technical, even to the point where some people use the term "management science." Yet, business decisions cannot be the same as those of a scientist. Far too many imponderables are involved. Business judgments must come from experience; that is, the experience of weighing known facts along relevant imponderables, such as future economic conditions. The latter may be projected from past statistics; but neither past averages nor data projections can do more than encourage thinking toward decisions.

Philosophers give experience the name empiricism; that is, the seeking of knowledge by observation and experiment. Although neither business nor accountancy evolved out of laboratory experimentation, both grew out of experience. The word carries many of the same overtones as the word "education." Education refers to a special way of gaining experience by being pressed to think. Practical experience, in turn, is educational precisely because it too presses one to think.

It is important to note that the word "experience" is a major factor in accounting in more ways than how it is used in CPA statutes. Transactions in the markets, based on management's decision to create such transactions, provide the basic data of enterprise experience. The substance of account data, therefore, is the transaction experience of the specific enterprise. The function of financial statements becomes that of summarizing the experience-results of management decision-actions. As such, the constellation between these entities is as follows: an enterprise is an operating entity; management is a decision center; and accounting is an experience-organizing apparatus.

Although the profession of public accounting is barely a century old, it has experienced a fine growth in service capacity. Its strength is not from its age but from the capabilities of its individual members. The profession's function has been largely that of offering the investing public assurance of the dependability of enterprise financial statements. But dependable financial statements may not be sufficient in themselves. Although they open the enterprise's prior experience to analytical review, both management and investors still have to interpret the data. The problem is also that, while the reporting function and the attest function are clear enough, the art of reading the reported evidence is relatively less developed. Interpreting financial statements is a field waiting for plowing, planting, and harvesting. That field should be particularly attractive to the professional accountant.

The business enterprise and its transaction experience will always be tightly related. Yet, the interpretative significance of that relation has not been fully explored. Complex experience data need to be made increasingly comprehensible. Injecting interpretative elements into the statements is not a good approach. It would be better to improve the techniques of data interpretation. This is a separate art.

Decisions often involve choice among alternatives and consideration of imponderables. These factors cannot be expressed by account data in money digits. In fact, problem answers are seldom directly readable from account data or computer output. These can only provide thought-provoking materials. Nonetheless, professional accountants are thoroughly acquainted with the character and limits of account data. Neither mathematical nor statistical knowledge can substitute for this accounting knowledge. No more can knowledge of economics, finance, taxation, and political science act as substitutes. Studies of such areas contribute to thinking about non-account ideas, but they provide little help when it comes to accounting knowledge.

Professional accountants are strategically situated to take the lead in interpretative analysis. Many useful clues can be accumulated from the techniques of financial statement analysis. The study of interrelations among specific items of enterprise transaction experience can be particularly fruitful. What is more, these changes are already underway. Through the division of management services, professional accountants are moving in the direction of becoming consultants as well as auditors and tax experts.

There is opportunity in this new activity to implement a proactive thought from the philosopher William James, who suggested that one should approach the interpretation of the unobserved by analysis of the observed. For management, the "unobserved" can be the significance buried in changing relations among data. For the professional accountant, as consultant, the "observed" can be data reported by the financial statements. The analytical penetration into the meaning of data interrelations, as viewed by investors, can help management to view its experience data as through the eyes of those investors.

In the *Journal of Accountancy* for December, 1963, the thought was expressed that the common body of knowledge appropriate for the professional accountant should prepare him to serve beyond the attest function and to offer diagnostic service (Roy & MacNeill, 1963). That kind of service would mean exactly what has been described here: interpretatively penetrating to the meaning back of transaction experience data. Out of such diagnosis could come "therapeutic" suggestions; that is, constructive ideas of possible lines of action. Of course, once clients have had the diagnostic, they may prefer to take remedial action on their own motion. As an analogy, a physician may prescribe but this is hardly a part of the accountant's function.

The forthcoming study of the common body of knowledge may be particularly helpful to men in the management services division.[1] The right kind of knowledge can provide a platform for good judgments and rational choice of alternatives, when consulting in an area of widely varying decision problems.

In the matter of educational preparation, it is sometimes clarifying to think of academic education as a type of experience. We might think of field experience as a type of education as well. Indeed, education and experience should be lifelong companions, capable of understanding each other and assisting each other. One kind of education, through the classroom, usually comes first. Classroom studies can be broadly general and often with fine results. At other times, it can be narrowly confined, perhaps emphasizing accounting in all its phases. It can be filled with drills in doing, organizing, and solving data based on earlier examination problems.

Each of these extremes lack something needed. It may prove beneficial, in the end, not to attempt to produce professionals in college. Yet, college should be something more than a screening device to sift out the unpromising. College ought to function toward developing capacity to think, whatever the situation may be. Obviously, not all possibilities can be anticipated. Hence, part of the educator's duty is to provide some experience in thinking in the face of situations where not all useful facts are available. For accounting majors, it is particularly desirable to help students generate the desire and the intention to keep on learning. They must recognize that passing the CPA examination makes them no more a professional than passing grades in college can demonstrate an education. There is no end to learning how to learn to be a professional.

It is doubtful that the time has come for special schools to train professional accountants. If it were educationally questionable to overconcentrate on accounting courses in a university school of business, an even greater concentration in a professional school would involve the same weakness. Moreover, it would probably be necessary there to duplicate much of the non-accounting work now given in the programs of collegiate schools of business. Alternatively, admission to the professional school could prescribe graduation in business as a prerequisite. For instance, if the applicant were a graduate in the liberal arts, a broad acquaintance with important aspects of business would be missing. The graduate from a business school would at least have the initial advantage of having wet his feet in business education, including some accounting.

In further defense of a school-of-business education for prospective professional accountants, the expanding availability of a master's degree is significant. Such graduates will have benefited from programs considerably broader than preparation for the CPA examination. In fact, contact in the program with advanced aspects of management, finance, and economics can ultimately prove as beneficial as accounting courses. This can be especially true in those programs where the teachers all make an effort to tie their courses in with other subjects taken by the students.

Increasingly, educators realize they cannot make students into professionals. This task must rest with the graduates themselves in cooperation with their professional associates. As such, it would seem clear that even the smaller firms have a duty to themselves and to their profession to offer constructive assistance and direction to members of their staff. The larger firms are already geared to offer help in post CPA educational development. It could benefit the profession generally if ways and means could be found to describe some of the educational practices that might be appropriate for smaller firms to use.

It is doubtful that the printed page and text books can of themselves show students how to think. It is the teacher's responsibility, therefore, to create opportunities that can help students to realize that the ultimate use of classroom material is to learn how to think (not to memorize). When one has learned one of the techniques of thinking, from one point toward another, he is ready to learn how to choose, act rationally, and make decisions. But thinking comes before these actions and, in business life as elsewhere, remembering is simply not enough as too many situations will be unfamiliar.

NOTE

1. Littleton is referring to Roy and MacNeill's research report, *Horizons for a Profession: The Common Body of Knowledge for Certified Public Accountants*, which was published in 1967 and would later come to represent a milestone in the development of the educational requirements for CPAs in the United States.

4

A COVEY OF CONCEPTS

ABSTRACT

Accounting concepts undertake to verbalize ideological building blocks. Each represents a unit that may be assembled in varying groups. The resulting organized communication can be represented neither by a list of concepts nor by a collection of definitions. A mere sequence of presentation will not do either. Instead, it is more informative to select several concepts and bring their interrelations under close examination. This is so because concepts associated in groups can illuminate the inner nature of enterprise accounting. Arranging the data from related accounts into groups, such as an earnings statement, will also present a grouping of ideas that give the accounts added meaning. Related to this, it is significant to note that ideas are more basic than words or digits. Learning to write involves more than forming letters and spelling words. A composition or discourse is more an arrangement of ideas than of words. Similarly, in accounting, an exchange-priced transaction expresses an idea made concrete and objective by decisions in the markets. These transaction ideas are distributed among a variety of accounts. Each account expresses an idea; its name, form, and content derived from specific concepts. Awareness of these concepts is a necessary factor for constructing an account category, for arranging a financial statement, and for interpreting meaning from data reported therein.

A distinction is often implied in contrasting "accounting theory" and "accounting practice." Yet, the two ideas are more closely related than the dictionaries indicate. Theory is not purely the hypothetical; practice is not purely the customary. Theory and practice are true companions. As such, their real relationship is complex that warrants examination. Modern accounting, in particular, reflects a complex of technical methodology for dealing usefully with data from enterprise transaction experience. That complex of actions is well-known; the associated complex of basic concepts is less well-known.

It is not enough to say that accounting theory supports accounting action or to say that accounting actions implement accounting theory. Yet, these are meaningful phrases. It may seem an oversimplification to sift a sample of basic concepts out of the body of accounting theory. But this is simplification only in the sense that headlines simplify the news. Headlines, and concepts, serve only as indicators for an essence. As such, a number of compact concepts can offer substantial clues to the capacities of known technical features of enterprise accounting. And, whereas no listing can substitute for an organized presentation of accounting theory, concepts can point thought toward the possibilities of penetrating beneath accounting actions and principles in search of their deep foundations.

It is relatively important whether verbalized concepts are described as persuasive, convincing, basic, or compelling. Some ideas have more strength than others may. If that is the case, the adjective could suggest that fact. "Persuasive" could suggest mild support for action; a "convincing" concept would be somewhat stronger. "Compelling" would mark a concept as necessary. "Basic" implies not so much a degree of force but rather foundations upon which to build upward toward a structure of actions.

Better than definitions, concepts can explain accountancy's reasons for being and its capacity to serve society, its functional directives, and its logical limitations. Awareness of this nature of functions and limits should be evident in any formulation of accounting principles. In the sample below, no importance is implied by the sequence of concepts, and no specific indication is given of the quality of a concept. Conceivably, this could vary with the circumstance under which specific concept is considered relevant to a particular type of accounting action.

It is inherent in the function of accounting to provide a needed insight into a business enterprise, through the reporting of the results of the decision-actions of its management. Financial statements are able to communicate this insight only because of the tight interrelationship of the enterprise entity, management decisions, and the exchange-priced transactions resulting from the relationship between them.

Concepts are the building blocks necessary for fabricating a structure of accounting ideology. Some concepts invite inclusions in the design, whereas some dictate exclusions. Both types of influence combine to strengthen the communication capability of the data from transaction experience.

The structure of accounting actions exists and serves in an atmosphere of men's needs and enterprise objectives. This pragmatic relationship is inevitable, because ideas of desirable ends foster ideas of suitable means. As such, the term "pragmatic" here refers to a program of testing the relation of ends and means to those ends. The suitability of means is judged by the reasonableness of the consequences of their use. This concept can be quite useful in accounting. Recognition of logical relationships can be helpful in formulating concepts; and for that reason those concepts will be more useful and significant than those that exist because they are expedient, convenient, or traditional.

Since accounting actions are technical means employed in the service of specific ends, these adjectives should consciously influence the choice of means. A useful outcome of recognizing this functional logic would be to produce an integrated body of doctrine (as to accounting objectives) associated with a purposeful integration of technical actions (means toward those ends). Such an association could be as logical and convincing as is the relation between real accounts and nominal accounts.

By the force of functional logic, accounting objectives direct preserving, in the accounts, the factual integrity of the items of consummated transaction experience of the specific enterprise. As such, enterprise accounting must function within definable limits. If this was otherwise, the stored digits could not communicate the data essence that users need to study. It is therefore the case that accounting concepts often points to limitations – a type of indicated negative. And definitions cannot cover negative aspects.

A classification category – whether that is the enterprise, a fiscal period, or a single account – should meticulously exclude all that is irrelevant and include all that is relevant. The degree of relevancy of data to category will always be a matter of concern. For example, in the phrase "enterprise accounting," the adjective is useful because it identifies this technology with a specific enterprise entity. By its technical actions, the account data of one enterprise will be isolated from those of all other enterprises. Only in this way can a given enterprise be made understandable as an independent unit.

The communication capability of account data is strongly influenced by limitations inherent in a necessary relation between capital in action and earnings produced by those actions. Value increases (evidences of economic causation) and earned income (management-generated results) cannot escape being misleading, if both are included in the accounts financial statements. Prior economic conditions will have influenced management decisions, which, in turn, generate earned income. But those influences cannot be isolated from management judgment in choosing specific transactions. Moreover, later economic conditions cannot change prior transaction facts.

It is also the case that accretion from unrealized value changes is conceptually very different from earnings emerging directly from enterprise management decision-actions. There is a significant distinction between improved change in enterprise well-being, viewed as change in the status of real accounts, and earned income, computed from nominal accounts designed to report on management's achievement of revenues and control of applicable cost-expense. In fact, invested costs and attributed values speak of two concepts so far apart as to be beyond possible harmonization. The rational structure of each concept needs to be explored in a context of the functional limitations necessary for enterprise accounting.

The necessary concept of the limited function of enterprise accounting will dictate development of special techniques for disclosing non-account data of interpretive significance. Back of the broad concept of the function of accounting stands a concept of business enterprise as a necessary experience-and-reporting unit. Back of this function is a concept of management, much concerned with the functioning of the markets. The functional limitations of accounting make this technology poorly equipped to mix two kinds of data: (1) those limited to the experience of one specific enterprise and (2) those non-transaction data not thus limited, such as replacement prices and price level indices.

It is fallacious to think that accounting technology can satisfactorily undertake to "measure" something that is inherently as subjective as value, while still being faithful to its experience-oriented function. Money, for accounting use, is a medium of exchange, an aspect of transaction bargaining, an aid to the meeting of minds in a specific exchange carrying a two-way benefit. The digits used on such an occasion do not speak of values, for value is a subjective judgment, which must differ between buyer and seller if a transaction is to emerge. What the parties agree upon is a price.

In the investment markets, the mental image of an enterprise's potential can only be a conjecture, projected forward from data derived from the accomplished facts of its transaction experience. Direct modifications of accounting technology could not reach far enough to remove this limitation. The result is that accounting, as such, only has a limited obligation to furnish investors with non-transaction data. Instead, the most significant aspects of enterprise transactions are the intentions, decisions, and actions of management in relation to that consummated event. Accounting data are organized to make these aspects more readily understandable.

For example, raw data suitable for enterprise accounting becomes arithmetically homogenous by being restricted to facts originating in specific exchange-price transactions. By being made homogenous items of experience, account data become well suited to reflect management effectiveness. Although a business might function for a time without a formal accounting system of this kind, management decisions would even then be indispensable. These managerial actions, in turn, become new data for the accounts.

Accounting can make available, to interested parties, dependable figure symbols of enterprise prior experience. But accounting cannot, in the same format, penetrate to the significance, for the user, of the patterns made evident by the figure symbols. Instead, accounting mediates between prior transaction experience and new decision problems faced by managements and investors.

Transaction data come into accounts of the parties concerned as prices agreeable to both parties. Hence, data in accounts will speak of prices but not of value. Yet, each party will have previously reached a considered value-judgment before consummating the transaction. As such, each exchange-priced transaction includes a significant equivalence between a planned intention and a necessary and persuasive consideration. For each party, the transaction will create a favorable and unfavorable effect on his affairs. This characteristic provides the basis for the technical form observed in every ledger account.

This leads to the conclusion that accounting works with the money-priced transaction experience of the relevant enterprise and that it, therefore, does not measure anything. It records quantitative facts provided by the contracting parties. Those parties do not "measure" the transaction; they make separate judgments of the alternatives available. The judgment of the buyer is to accept the offered price by the seller. The seller, in turn, has priced his offer at a point that he thought would be persuasive and yet profitable. The data, resulting from this complex of separate judgments, thus become historical and quantitative facts for both parties. This process would be lost in any proposal to re-imagine these transactions in the future. This is so because history, rewritten, is no longer history.

PART XIII
LATE REFLECTIONS

1

WHY?[☆]

Scientists tell us that the plants in our universe have long been "things in the process of becoming." It is quite believable that our present-day economy is still in the "process of becoming" as well. Similarly and for several centuries, accountancy, as a specific aspect of this economy, has also been on the road of "becoming" what it now is. Because "becoming" signifies evolutionary development, we can note evidence beneath modern accounting of change, growth, and improvement. Furthermore, we have little reason to doubt that change will not continue to be a characteristic. We may well believe that accountancy, through this continuing process, can grow toward new reaches of perfection of its service capacity. In fact, there is little reason to think accounting has reached its peak.

Scientists are interested in finding evidence capable of fostering men's understanding of unchanging forces and the interrelations among the results of those forces – the stability and significance of gravity, for example. Vast structures of wider understanding have been built on such foundations. Understanding can always be strengthened by knowledge of "reasons why." Given this, accountancy may very well be considered as a logically coherent system for consistently organizing enterprise transaction experience. It is logical from being an effective means to desirable ends; it is coherent from consisting of closely interconnected parts; and it is systemic from the use of an orderly plan for classifying data flowing from specific items of enterprise transaction experience.

Accountancy, thus considered, has characteristics and functions which invite inquires of "why" questions. When posing such questions, it seems reasonable to expect that recognizable "forces and interpretations" may be detected beneath accountancy. None of these will be as universal as is the force of gravity. Yet, some may be so basic as to seem primarily responsible (1) for the long continued and usefulness of specific accounting techniques and (2) for promoting modifications appropriate to new needs. Perhaps

[☆]A note accompanying this chapter indicates that Littleton would have finished writing it in December 1966.

some clues to such "basic forces" may be detected when relationships can be observed between specific aspects of accounting techniques and identifiable needs of the times – early and contemporary. It would be helpful if we had a wider understanding of some of the "whys" (evolutionary forces) beneath technical forms and uses antecedent to present-day methodology.

The specific ways and means of the accounting of yesterday and today must have appeared in response to recognizable needs and objectives. So, too, must future technical action. As such, many features of today's accounting will have been foreshadowed in earlier developments. Beneath those earlier techniques, there doubtless was recognition of and reaction to economic conditions, evident opportunities, needs of the times, and contemporary situations. No doubt, future aspects of accounting are being similarly foreshadowed at the present time.

These thoughts raise this question: could accounting have grown to its modern dimensions and usefulness merely from a series of accidents? Surely, the answer must be negative. All use-actions reflect types of empirical knowledge and practical experience. Yet, this knowledge will gain its strongest support from being associated with "... a recognized theoretical structure that is definable, cohesive and susceptible to rational articulations (Welsch, 1966, p. 81)."

In turn, it should be clear that accounting theory would be put to test by the service it renders in making rational and understandable the technical features of accounting actions. This is particularly true for those aspects that contribute strongly to the capability of enterprise accounting actions that open the data, resulting from enterprise transaction experience, to interpretative analysis. The relationship, which presents empirical knowledge (based on practical actions) with early and evolving techniques, is a matter of considerable significance. Modern accounting techniques are strongly indebted to developments taking place during long periods of antecedent growth. For this reason, the "whys" of earlier accounting can have meaning in the present.

It is true that the "whys" of today may derive some of their characteristics from pressures and needs of recent events and contemporary conditions. Yet, it may still be a significant fact that many of the pressing needs of earlier days, having sprouted techniques adequate to those times, may also have produced ways of thinking and acting quite capable of serving present needs.

Even at the conversational level, "why" is associated with reasons, explanations, and justifications. All such elements have significance for understanding. Whether we use the word "accountancy" (an area of knowledge), "accounting" (procedural actions), or "account" (data-classification category), each of the terms is meaningful because the actions involved can be supported by convincing reasons, clear explanations, and persuasive justifications. The strength of those terms and the significance of the related actions will derive from "whys" capable of giving the actions validity and purpose.

Management will have intended the effects transactions have on a given enterprise. Consequently, entries in accounts will reflect results of prior decisions. Thus, account data are able to provide readers with summarized clues to management's effectiveness – a convincing reason for and justification of accounting.

An earlier name for accounting, double-entry bookkeeping, clearly suggests a continuing characteristic: duality. This early terminology and its modern counterpart had and have large significance because it was, and is, a reflection of underlying logic. Fully understood, "duality" can provide a clue to the reason why "accountancy" means more than "accounting."

The logic inherent in enterprise accounting does not reflect a semantic relationship between verbal propositions. It is a logic especially appropriate to a technical instrumentality, which is still faithful to the nature and the limitations of the reasons for its early simple forms.

The same active logic evidenced by the word "duality" continues to be effective today. The persuasive and compelling reasons, the "whys" of this logic, still provide the supporting under-structures for accounting actions appropriate to the needs and pressures of today. It is significant, and illuminating, that the duality in accounts today is a natural reflection of an antecedent duality within items of enterprise transaction experience–a duality evident even before agreement between the parties produces effects on the two enterprises concerned.

This antecedent duality exists in the fact that two parties are necessary to create an exchange transaction. Moreover, each transaction party, before making the transaction decision, will recognize the dual effects he then has in mind: one effect (favorable) that he desires; the other effect (unfavorable), which he would prefer to avoid if that were possible. Thus, each party must first judge whether the transaction on its favorable side will outweigh the unfavorable but necessary aspect. An outright transaction between independent parties emerges only from this reasoned judgment on the part of both parties, each acting in his own self-interest.

The result is that it is evident that the persuasive logic of accounting (its reasons why) begins to exercise an influence before a need for recording has appeared. A transaction, once consummated, creates a dual effect on the affairs of each party. The result is not mechanically produced; each party has clear reasons backing his judgment and decision. Each acts based on his own experience and intentions. Thus, dual effects first become a reality quite outside of accounting as such. The accounts are involved only after these events and, yet, they will have been prepared in advance in a form suitable to their function of preserving a record of the duality of transaction effects.

It is unlikely that men would fail to recognize the effects worked on their enterprise by their transactions. And it is quite likely that such recognition would have influenced the way factual data from the transaction were recorded a long time ago. Both back then and now, awareness of intended effects would stimulate ideas for appropriate organization of those data. For instance, bilateral accounts, as aids to recording transaction effects, would seem almost to have been an inevitable response to the duality so inherent in every consumed exchange-priced transaction. Clearly, each transaction would involve a necessary favorable and unfavorable aspect. These conditions would quite logically lead to use of one side of an account category for entries increasing the balance and use of the other side for decreasing effects. Eventually, the fact would be apparent that, on some accounts, a plus-effect would not necessarily be favorable and that a minus-effect would not necessarily be unfavorable.

Persuasive and forceful elements of accounting logic lie within the interrelations among transactions. Hence, there is logic of arrangement in the design of bilateral accounts, and in the arrangement of account data in financial statements. These technical features were not inventions. Forceful reasons why, needs, and pressures lay back of early technical details and later modifications.

In the early days, and today as well, the influential pressures reflected aspects of men's need to know the cumulative effects of prior transactions, in order to act rationally in the present and toward the future. The result is that the modern characteristics of accounting techniques are no accidents; they strongly reflect men's rational responses to recognized needs. The relation of response to need is a type of logic that is promptly tested by observed results and the suitability of that response.

The technical features of accounts and accounting are capable of rendering useful services because, in use, they systemically reflect two convictions. The first conviction is that significant relations exist among items of enterprise transaction experience. The second conviction is that interrelations among accounts can provide clues to management's ability, within a competitive environment, to generate favorable effects to the advantage of that enterprise by incurring specific unfavorable effects. It is difficult to conceive of a different body of theory and practice equally capable of rendering a comparable service to business enterprises in a dynamic economy.

Periodic reporting of assembled data is made necessary by the fact that most business enterprises must act as a continuum. To be effective, enterprise service must continue to be available; a flow of transaction experiences inward and outward are a necessity. Inflowing events occur in a time sequence; hence should be recorded in sequence. The same is true about outflowing events. Events in each of these categories are related in ways appropriate to the character of the enterprise, decisions of its management, and prior as well as subsequent transaction experience. These inherent characteristics of business transactions can and do provide conditions (needs and pressures) to which accounting techniques are responses. Those characteristics constitute part of the explanations of (reasons for) specific types of accounting actions.

Two flowing streams of events are interrelated. One expresses a variety of efforts to prepare to serve and the actual service. The other expresses the achievement of intended service. Successful efforts, indicated by achievements, make it possible for the enterprise to continue to offer its services. This type of self-renewal also gives effect to recognition of a need for continued growth in the capacity for effective and acceptable service.

Continuity of enterprise existence is strongly influenced by an effective relationship between enterprise efforts and achievements. Accounting serves this function well, by reporting in informative ways on the continuity of that relationship. Evident here are clear reasons why accounting is faced with the need to react suitably to pressures on the enterprise to combine continuity with change. Such pressure produces the necessity to report periodically, in blocks of data, emerging from continuing flow of transaction experience.

The spacing of continuity in efforts and achievements becomes a feasible operation because ways and means have been devised for allocating (apportioning), over successive fiscal periods, the initial costs invested in various assets that have continued usefulness. Among these ways and means are accounting actions (responses to needs) that are named accrue, defer, and depreciate. Use of these techniques helps make continuing efforts and achievements understandable, in sections, as it were. The need for periodic accounting reports lies in the fact that interested parties, both inside the enterprise and outside, cannot withhold necessary decisions until long-lived assets have completed their life of service.

A type of chain reaction is evident here. If accounting techniques were not available for apportioning enterprise transaction experience; if reports from those techniques lacked reliability; if decision makers did not interpretatively study the organized data; then many next decisions would be less soundly based. Such needs exert very strong pressures and accounting technology has responded. As a result, accounting has steadily grown in capacity to serve, as it has grown in ability to respond to recognized needs.

As a result, the user of accounting reports gains knowledge helpful to his decisions. "Knowledge is power." This trite saying can apply to the "knowledge" inherent in account data. In a book dated 1494, the author Pacioli, at one point states in figurative language of his day, "... he who does business without knowing all about it, sees his money turn into flies."[1] Even that long ago, there were pressures capable of influencing men to devise useful responses. The point is that trade is not a modern invention. Through progressive stages, it has evolved into business, as we know it today. Long ago, a great deal of existing wealth was relatively sterile and unproductive in the hands of a few people. When society's need for goods increased enough, and adequate sailing vessels were available, trading ventures abroad put saved wealth to work.

Prospect for profit played a part in inducing capital to take the risks involved. As such, capital was made productive due to its relationship with risks and prospects of profit, and because people at home were willing and able to buy the final product. In other words, adequate economic demand was a basic requirement in this constellation. Capital, thus made actively productive, created a need for records of trading activities. These records, in turn, provided data from which final liquidation of a venture could rationally result. The procedure here was, in effect, a rather simple matter of a "counting" at the venture's start and another "counting" at its completion (liquidation).

In these activities, capital had been productively employed in response to recognized needs. As a result, a social need was met, an investment (venture) had reproduced itself, and an increment (profit) resulted, which would be capable of enlarging later trading voyages. This simple recording and computing procedure set the stage for accounting as a "language of trade." Accounting still is that kind of an instrument of communication, but it has greatly grown in its capability of "composing" understandable reports on prior transaction experience.

Why has a vastly improved power of communication now come into being? We must believe it came because of new pressures and needs. These, plus men's ingenuity, proved capable of generating new responses and capacity for effective communication of the results of prior decisions and actions. As modern pressures grew, accounting responded with useful and dependable additional information, capable of picturing, in data, the effectiveness of enterprise management.

A particular strong characteristic of modern accountancy (periodic apportionment of invested costs) was not foreshadowed by the investment-and-liquidation characteristics of early trading ventures. The response to new needs was completely different and for specific reasons: (1) the later type of enterprise had to have continuity of existence and (2) capital thus employed came from many people distant from the point where operative decisions were made. Such investors were out of direct contact, but had their own decisions to make, hence the need for periodic account information.

The factual reports emerging in response did not speak in words and sentences. Financial statements can only communicate through data totals and sub-totals suitably labeled. In a sense, this is a separate "language." Its data derive from overt transaction experience. Its organization, in bilateral accounts and tabular summaries were communications of ideas about managerial actions (transaction experience), re-expressed in technical forms of data arranged to facilitate study of interrelations and results of prior decisions.

Here were specific responses to conditions not faced earlier, but it is to be noted that periodic financial statements are not completely communicative as they stand. The organized data need to be interpretatively analyzed, in order for the reader to understand the enterprise's prior transaction experience. Here, however, there is some personal responsibility in this matter, for only the user knows what his decision problems are. As such, there is no doubt that interpretative analysis of financial statements is hardly an appropriate responsibility of accounting as such. Yet, all of the technical actions that make up enterprise accounting are clearly focused toward just that; that is, interpretative analysis of meaning that can be significant for the interpreter.

The users of financial statements, especially those concerned with decisions in the investment markets, have a pressing need to read the messages that are inherent within enterprise prior transaction experience. Because so much interest is focused upon understanding the results of management's prior decisions, it is appropriate to consider accounting as a kind of written "language" carrying its message to many "readers" by means of compact and factual financial statement presentations. Furthermore, because some accounting statements are not presented in a spoken language, its written message will need to be "translated." This interpretative action of extracting meaning from reported account data should be a distinctly separate technology. This ought to be the case for the same reason that interpretative analysis of the significance within statistics reflecting price-level change is an activity separate from compiling the data. Drawing conclusions from study of the data is a result of interpretative analysis and not its compilation.

Another significant pressure, which has shaped accounting, can be called the moral aspect of adequate communication. That kind of pressure strongly affects certain aspects of periodically reporting on enterprise transaction experience, and on the auditing of these reports.

On the surface, it would seem that an alternative to the complexities of periodic apportionment of enterprise costs would be revaluations. Yet, this approach could result in a wide departure from verifiable reality of the actual transaction experience of the enterprise. Charging the whole cost of a long-lived asset against surplus, or against the revenue of one period, would misrepresent a rational concept of management's responsibility to absentee investors. A similar misrepresentation of reality would appear if the initial cost of a long-lived asset were left undisturbed in the balance sheet.

It is clear that such an asset is possessed for its power to make continuing contributions to the service needs of the owning enterprise. The asset is held by virtue of its usefulness in creating salable products. Those products "benefit" from the service of that asset. That "benefit" must become a part of the ultimate calculation of the cost of sales of the product produced. If accounting provides no technique for including "machine use" as part of the cost of goods produced, those accounting data will have misrepresented a rational relationship that should be evident in a factual communication to interested parties.

Careful apportionment of asset cost is thus supported by pressure from a moral force. Other examples of such pressures are not difficult to observe beneath accounting techniques. Indeed, moral pressures were a substantial part of the "reasons why" the profession of public accounting began and continued to grow in service capability and acceptance. In other words, the profession of public accounting was not "invented." Like other aspects of accounting, there were "reasons why" which can make its appearance understandable. The related compelling need and pressures were different over the years; yet, they proved capable of producing responses that grew into professional actions and responsibilities.

Highly significant evolutionary developments appeared in Great Britain under pressures from conditions there in the early nineteenth century. Business enterprises were permitted, under the laws of the time, to organize with limited liability being granted to shareholders. By mid-century (1844–1845), statutes required company directors (1) to register their companies with the government, (2) to keep accounts and prepare financial statements, and (3) to appoint one or more auditors – at this time these would have been non-accountants – who might employ an accountant to assist them (Littleton, 1933).

Soon thereafter, the nation experienced a period of wild speculation in company formation and trading in company shares. These activities fostered a variety of deceptions and frauds affecting investors. Moreover, those conditions generated an increasing rate of company bankruptcy. In response, between 1825 and 1883, parliament passed seven statutes concerned with bankruptcy. Necessarily, insolvent enterprises had to face pressures from creditors. From 1870 to 1880, there were 84,778 cases of insolvency. Of these, 10,515 chose full bankruptcy, whereas 64,263 chose liquidation or composition of debts.

Under these circumstances, it would be important that the courts and both interested parties should examine the facts of the company's condition. A "statement of affairs" and a "deficiency account" became useful documents in such hearings. These organized summaries of enterprise accounting data could present factual pictures of the financial conditions of the enterprise at a given date. With these facts at hand, the parties could discuss terms under which agreement might be reached, such as partial cancellation of debt and an opportunity for the company to continue operation in the hope that the residual debt could gradually be paid. And, although preparation of such reports did not require an audit, knowledge of accounting could be a helpful fact. Moreover, this kind of experience could and did prepare men later to offer audit services for solvent enterprises.

Long before these developments appeared in the nineteenth century, the rudiments of audit procedures had evolved under different conditions. Later, those were adapted to the examination of the affairs of solvent business enterprises. Checking the records of local tax collectors offered an early precedent. A more comprehensive framework can be noted in connection with the operation of the landed estates of the time. The records made by various clerks and stewards were carefully examined and summarized by three officers of the nobleman's estate. The resulting statement of data about the activities of the estate would be presented before the members of the nobleman's council. After approval there, the data were used as a basis for planning estate activities for the next year.

Clearly, here was a solid foundation that could be usefully associated with men's accounting experience in connection with insolvent business enterprises in the nineteenth century. The Companies Act of 1865 drew upon this background for precedents. But the Parliament did not outline audit procedures. Yet, companies were required to keep accounts, retain auditors, and send copies of the financial statements and the auditor's reports to the government and to all shareholders. By this time, an increasing number of men had expanded their knowledge of law and accounting. This made them particularly competent to carry out accounting and auditing activities appropriate to the purpose of this legislation. Such carefully drawn legislation would not have been appropriate if men capable of implementing its purposes had not been available.

By this time, "audit" had come to mean more than a search for errors in recording and the organization of account data into informatively arranged reports. Auditing was becoming an activity calling for a technical and critical examination of data from enterprise transaction experience, and for passing judgment on the authenticity of the figure-pictures presented in financial statements.

Here were "reasons why" public accounting, as a profession, began to develop a sense of responsibility for the public interest. The pressures in this direction were these: (1) economic conditions of the times; (2) a wide misunderstanding of the social functions of joint stock companies; and (3) a tendency for speculative fever to distort men's business morality. Recognition of the impact of these conditions led to legislative and technical responses by society that would be in the public interest. The availability of reliable men especially acquainted with business and accounting provided technical personnel capable of supplementing the intentions of the statutes. Over a long period of time, the evidence is clear: under quite different conditions recognized needs continue generate responses in accountancy.

The argument here is that accounting developments have been underway for a long time. Needs, pressures, and conditions existing long before the voyages of Columbus produced very useful responses in the form of early types of accounting actions. As needs have changed, responses have changed accordingly. Economic activities and men's perceptiveness have expanded together. All the while, the logic inherent in a close relationship between recognized needs and responses judged adequate thereto has continued to hold upon a door to wider understanding of business enterprises and business management.

From its simplest beginning, accounting has been an instrument for communications. In simpler times, simple responses were adequate. In the more complex present, new types of needs and conditions influence accounting communication techniques. Yet, the capability for new responses by this particular discipline is necessarily limited by its inherited as well as by its newly acquired characteristics.

Accountancy is not so constituted, or so open to infinite expansion, as to be able to become in itself the factual response to all of man's need for information upon which to base his next decisions, either as management or investor. Enterprise accounting, in all of its forms, has always consisted of efforts (suitable methods) toward effects (desirable consequences). Its efforts have always been solidly committed to reporting dependably on factual data emerging from decisions of enterprise management. The effects toward which efforts have been directed can be compactly expressed in the phrase: "to understand the results of the prior transaction experience of a given business enterprise."

All transaction-generating decisions will be intended to effect desired changes in the financial status and earning capacity of the given enterprise. Such summaries of transaction experience, when compared period by period, can epitomize the effects of management's prior transaction decisions. As such, comparative study of periodic financial statements calls for interpretative analysis, and this provides clues to management effectiveness. Analysis will put under close study (1) the quantitative changes produced in specific accounts and (2) observed differing rates of change among significantly related accounts and related groups of accounts.

Management will know what its policies have been; it will be able to appraise its own policy-based decisions. Non-management analysts, however, are not so well positioned to appraise the results. It is for this reason that independent audits can offer assurance that the summaries are faithfully tied to objective transaction experience. The same reason should influence writers on accounting toward advocating convincingly appropriate data boundaries for specific accounts. The same reason should prompt management to indicate changes in policy relevant to reported account data. Finally, the same reason would also support supplementary use of known interpretative techniques, to the end that the function of enterprise accounting together with supplementary data should make understandable to interested parties.

The argument is that accounting cannot alone generate understanding of enterprise transaction experience. It does not have the flexibility and the interpretative devices of statistical analysis. Nevertheless, data from accounts can be interpretatively analyzed and studied by use of non-accounting techniques. Accounting itself, however, must perform its function strictly within tight boundaries. It must be strictly faithful under the guidance of its own types of moral responsibilities. For example, interpretative observations can be made in enterprise management reports. These can be helpful to outside interests; but this help is collateral to and not an integral part of the enterprise accounting function. This is so because the data from the transaction experience of any given enterprise cannot rationally include data other than those that reflect decisions made in and for the given enterprise.

It is worth noting that the service of accounting is valuable as it stands, and that its service function could be clouded if non-experience data were injected into the accounts. In hidden ways, such an injection could obscure the real effects of the transaction experiences of that enterprise. Instead,

Table 4. Relationship between Conditioning Factors and Accounting.

Conditioning Factor	Accounting Response
Both parties to a consummated exchange transaction will have to incur an unfavorable effect in order to benefit from a planned favorable effect.	Both parties will have prepared account categories in bilateral form, with one side to record favorable effects and the other to record unfavorable effects.
In its search for success, each business enterprise is under pressure to adjust to changing conditions.	In order to prepare data essential to survival, accounting uses the techniques of accrue, defer, and depreciate as means for the periodic and rational association of data on the relation of efforts (costs) and achievements (revenue).
Both enterprise managements and investors in company securities have pressing need for dependable factual data reflecting the results of management's prior decisions.	In order to respond to these needs, for a foundation of reliable and factual information, accounting restricts its data to that originating in the transaction experience of the given enterprise. It excludes from its techniques any attempt to interpret the significance that such data may have for various interested parties.
British experience in the nineteenth century with widespread insolvency of business enterprises, and later with wild speculation in company shares, generated distrust of wholly uncontrolled business actions.	Those conditions sponsored two types of response: (1) accountants were asked to assist the courts by presenting factual presentations of the financial conditions of an insolvent going concern; (2) somewhat later, Parliament, in the public interest, required audits of the company affairs to be made annually by accountants and that the attested reports shall be sent to all shareholders and appropriate governmental officials.

accounting opens to interpretative scrutiny the results of prior transaction experience of the given enterprise. But the accountants of that enterprise cannot know the decision problems facing all users of enterprise account data. They therefore lack the responsibility, even the ability, to offer interpretative insight into the accounts or into financial reports.

In summary, four types of major conditioning factors have existed that slowly pressed accounting toward its destiny: duality of effects; periodic allocation of data; relevant experience; moral dependability (Table 4). Furthermore, many types of responses to conditions are involved in enterprise accounting in specific ways. It is therefore appropriate to consider that accounting has evolved, not on the initiative of accountants, but as a part of men's intellectual and moral reactions to challenging circumstances and significant conditions of their times.

NOTE

1. Littleton provides no page number for this reference.

2

ACCOUNTANCY: A DISCIPLINE

Within the technical term "accounting" is the basic word "count," meaning to determine how many. By prefixing two letters, we get "account." A noncommercial meaning for this word is a statement or report of actual events. The phrase "account for" refers to an explanation (verbal or numerical) of the outcome of antecedent events. Adding three letters produces "accounting"; a term similar in meaning to "account for." "Accounting" therefore refers to a numerical way of reporting on the outcome of antecedent events; specifically, the results of transaction decisions previously made by a given enterprise management.

The great variety of enterprise activities necessitates use of many categories (accounts). By this means, specific types of transaction effects can be clearly identified and grouped together. This segregation of events by kinds and effects proves very helpful in making prior experience understandable. The numerical symbols in the account categories make possible quantitative comparisons and interpretative regrouping of experience data into larger totals and significant remainders.

The basic characteristics of account categories and many of the techniques of dealing with transaction data are very old. It is clear that modern accounting has deep roots in the distant past. And it is noteworthy that those methods, and their successors, were responses to perceived needs for factual information. As such, accounting methods have from the beginning served as means of responding to recognized needs. Such needs to know still press for satisfactory responses and for suitable ways of knowing in order to make judgments. The implication is that accounting is a way of knowing and a path toward decisions.

It is partly for these reasons that enterprise accounting deserves to be considered a discipline – a course of actions disciplined by pressing needs. It is because of these growing needs for knowledge of prior experience that accounting has grown in ability to organize and interpreting the transaction history of specific business enterprises.

Consider the following analogy: a nation's history can provide glimpses into the interdependence of events and into their relation to the actions taken. In much the same way, enterprise accounting can provide illuminating glimpses of the relation of management's recent reactions to contemporary conditions and needs – actions based on new judgments made in the light of results emerging from judgments made under prior conditions. In effect, therefore, accounting data place prior conditions and present conditions face-to-face in and of discriminating judgments regarding actions to be taken toward the future.

Account data speaks directly of prior transaction events of that enterprise; accounting techniques produce a special type of historical record. In providing this "factual history," accounting makes readable the results of previous efforts made in the context of information about even earlier transaction experience.

Factual history of this kind, analytically interpreted in the light of contemporary conditions, can provide an intellectual springboard toward next decisions. Accounting can effectively serve this purpose because its techniques, guided by its ideology, are capable of systematically providing a view of interrelations among prior transactions. Such avenues of insight can lead thought toward the study of observed *effects* in association with the *reasons* behind those effects. It is clear, therefore, that accounting takes in some of the characteristics of history; it opens the doors for critical examination of many factors capable of influencing new decisions.

Professor Henry Rand Hatfield's paper (1924), "An Historical Defense of Bookkeeping," has been justifiably praised as a gem of accounting literature. It deserves recognition for its constructive contribution to accounting education and research. It also deserves recognition for its inspirations drawn from the implicit thought that accounting is a service area that has an intellectual content deeply rooted in a long evolutionary development. Close examination beneath the surface of that long history will reveal other significant aspects.

Accounting began its growth in service capacity under disciplinary pressures of the needs of the times. As pressures continued to multiply, accounting continued to grow toward accountancy. Accounting eventually became an organized technology; in due time a related profession of public accounting appeared because of conditions of that day. The capabilities of accounting are now unquestioned, and it has steadily continued to develop as an effective instrument in aid of disciplined thinking toward decision-actions in business. The result is that the present status of accountancy is secure. But the reasons for the depth and breadth of its inner nature need to be more fully understood.

One path toward penetrating to the inner nature of accounting is the seeking out of the needs, pressures, and conditions that have combined to make modern accountancy something much more significant than a recording and reporting methodology. This discipline now includes a profession and college education in the subject is available up to the doctorate. The techniques of this discipline have been under progressive development for more than five centuries. Those early characteristics were examined some 30 years ago (Littleton, 1933), with the intention of indicating their origins and certain basic characteristics, many of which are still visible within modern techniques.

Obviously, development did not stop at the end of the nineteenth century. When the modern history of accountancy is brought under close examination, a basic fact will at once be clear: accountancy has become more than bookkeeping; it is different in a similar way to how bookkeeping in the days of Christopher Columbus was more complex than the recording methods in early Egypt and Rome.

I hope that a later writing of history will reach deeper than a descriptive chronology of changing methodology. Uncovering reasons, which could have fostered observed developments, could point thought toward attempting consciously to rest further developments on reasons. Perhaps reasons, sponsoring twentieth century developments, may necessarily be somewhat speculative for some time to come. Nevertheless, the results of this kind of penetration beneath the surface would tend to indicate that accounting has become increasingly a discipline shaped by recognizable non-accounting factors. From such an approach, perhaps some aspects of a philosophy of evolutionary development could become apparent.

A philosophy of this kind should be concerned with understanding and explaining. Perhaps the writing of accounting history should be concerned with finding reasons that would seem capable of improving accounting design and organization. Such reasons, being associated with known technical aspects of accounting, could help make modern accounting better understood as an intellectually based discipline. Furthermore, if we have inherited the fundamentals of a discipline of this character of service, and if history shows that men have improved it over the years, then prospects for further constructive developments and uses would seem promising.

It would be helpful to look beneath the events of accounting history for clues to conditions and pressures (acting as causes) which could have fostered the rudiments of accounting technology and ideology. Those rudiments, which were shaped by related needs, set those action patterns that were to be refined by later needs and conditions into accountancy, as we know it today. An inviting area for study emerges. What needs, pressures, and conditions have been modifying and strengthening the early patterns?

What ideas lead to other ideas? What convincing reasons are necessary to support modifications and change?

If a continuity of rational motivation (ends to be achieved) is observable in the past, and if continuation of motivation has then fostered technical improvements (means for achieving ends), it would become reasonable to think of accounting as an intellectual endeavor. Disciplinary pressures from recognizable conditions and needs of the times would have shaped this endeavor. Recognition of these factors, which are considered as motivations for the development of early techniques, should precipitate questions of whether these continued to influence accounting developments into the twentieth century. This would bring further questions as to new types of motivation, which could have influenced those later developments.

Continued early motivation, plus possible new motivation, might provide clues to reasons that might go far toward justifying modern accounting as being an intellectual discipline rather than an improved way of reporting informative data. At the very least, through this approach, it should become clear that changing economic conditions and men's growing ingenuity could unite in influencing accounting and in detecting its limitations.

Accounting reflects many of the characteristics of a discipline. Over a long period of evolution, it has continuously increased in capacity for effectively rendering a particular kind of service. As accounting steadily moved from a routine method to a responsive discipline, this growth in capacity tended to accelerate. Its growth toward responsiveness has been intellectual. That quality was evident quite early. Men long ago responded to a need to review their prior transaction experience. Their ingenuity is evident in their design of a method that continued to respond adequately to newly perceived needs.

Each step was an intellectual response to disciplining influences, the most prominent of which is an ever-expanding need for factual records available for review. Slowly, rudimentary records grew into a disciplined methodology of specific action-types serving specific end-purposes. Clearly, related here were ends to be achieved and actions judged appropriate to such achievement. Here, ends and actions were directly influencing each other: ends inspire actions and use of suitable actions achieve the desired ends. Those convincing elements of logic strengthened enterprise accounting as an intellectual discipline.

Accounting is not only itself a readymade discipline, as it is under continuing disciplinary pressures. It is still being formed, influenced, and directed in various ways toward accomplishing an increasingly important and informative mission. Over time, an increasing variety of accounting actions have brought an increasing amount of transaction experience under disciplined organization. The purpose: to provide more data in aid of the disciplined thinking of businessmen toward effective decisions.

This discipline is discernible in many places. Decisions are disciplined by knowledge of prior experience, and by knowledge of the factors and the judgments that influenced the decisions. Two kinds of experience tend to discipline management: (1) knowledge of conditions and pressures in the general area of economic life and actions and (2) knowledge of the needs and limitations of one's own enterprise. Only the second kind of knowledge comes from enterprise accounting, but the other kind is also indispensable to business decisions.

It is clear that many business decisions will be sponsored by judgmental recognition of the needs of people in that enterprise's market. Successful actions deserve to be repeated, if conditions are still appropriate, and failures deserve to be avoided, but they must first be recognized. Thus, management will be led by increasing experience to choose lines of action for specific reason related to enterprise successful functioning in the past.

The enterprise service function is a contriving objective, continuously sponsoring well-chosen decisions and actions. Thus, a chain-reaction is created of ever-expanding needs, which are pressing the enterprise to expand its action capabilities in effective ways within limits imposed by other conditions. Some of these limits will be evident in the fact that enterprise actions directed toward achievement (favorable results) can only be entered upon by incurring parallel effects that, if considered alone, would be considered as producing unfavorable results. Both sides of the coin need always to be taken into consideration. These various relationships are possible because men have developed certain distinctive capabilities:

1. A capacity for conceptual thought and for using those ideas to lead to other ideas.
2. A capacity for retaining knowledge acquired from experience.
3. A capacity to transmit the results of experience in a readable language. Accounting is part of this language of business.
4. A capacity to interpret significance from accumulative experience.
5. A capacity to accelerate one's intellectual growth by effectively combining his many capabilities, and by conceiving new ways of acquiring new experience for studied review.

Decisions made by businessmen in response to specific needs have, in turn, disciplinary effects on the enterprise, and through those effects, an influence on the economy of the nation. Economic and financial actions of consumers are also responsible to their own needs under contemporary conditions. Therefore, these people are also disciplined by economic circumstances. In addition, their actions, in mass and individually, discipline the enterprise through the effect those actions have on management decisions.

Accounting necessarily became a discipline because it had the function of bringing decisions under the discipline of enterprise prior transaction experience. A result of this service of accounting was that of training (disciplining) management toward experience-based decision-actions. Furthermore, accounting could develop progressively because its earliest techniques had been responsive to men's reactions to their intellectual need to learn from prior experience. As a result, accounting grew up as a responsive discipline, resting on an intellectual basis, which had been shaped and formed by a wide variety of disciplinary factors and pressing needs that demanded effective responses.

The actions of recording transaction data became a sub-discipline of specific ways of recording data under the influence of specific reasons for using those techniques. Transaction recording thus became a discipline because:

1. Its actions rested on underlying – even if unperceived – persuasive logic that could relate ends and means.
2. Its actions could provide planned technical treatment of data judged useful in aid of decisions.
3. Its actions could bring transaction data under controlled organization and in a form that could contribute to management's disciplined thinking.
4. Its actions dealt with data out of prior transaction experience, which, itself, had been influenced (disciplined) by the forces of economic conditions and business competition.

In essence, enterprise accounting became an intellectual discipline because it grew up under the influence of decisions taken by management, in response to recognized conditions in the economy. Because accounting is still growing under similar circumstances, knowledge of its historical development can be particularly useful, and there is no doubt that accounting continues to evolve toward its destiny.

Developments in accounting evidenced before 1900 have persisted; moreover, the rate of growth has accelerated. In the first sixty-five years of the twentieth century, incremental growth has exceeded that of much longer periods of time. A rapid rate of change seems evident in the United States. At the university level, education for business has greatly expanded. Accountancy has been part of that growth. Departments of Accountancy in numerous universities offer courses at the graduate level and some at the doctor's level. This movement has paralleled growth of the profession of public accounting and the widespread acceptance of business management as approaching the scope of a profession.

The general argument here is that a part of accountancy's destiny lies in the future. And, as in the past, that future will be strongly influenced by the present. This influence will be at least as strong as the influence of the past on the present. As such, some acquaintance with accounting history could make the transition more understandable.

Accounting actions have always called for careful consideration of contemporary conditions and conscious reaction to the disciplinary effects. These disciplinary effects come from pressures of the time and impact enterprise activities and management's decision problems. As a result, accountancy has grown as the business economy has grown. As its service capability continues to increase under expanding responsibilities, accountancy will undoubtedly continue to support disciplined thinking toward business judgments and investment decisions. As such, perhaps in its modern functioning, accountancy deserves recognition as an intellectual discipline; being itself disciplined by needs, accountancy has indeed acquired capabilities for disciplining business decisions.

Accounting has long been evolving toward a future destiny. Evolutionary development is a continuing force. The end of the nineteenth century only marks a brief pause in the thought of the viewer of history; time flows smoothly over every date. The same generalization fits the onward development of enterprise management; accounting technology and ideology; and the profession of public accounting. The viewer's task, and the participant's problem, is to sense the emerging present from the recent past.

The value of reading history – whether that is the history of the economy, business, management, or the profession of public accounting, accounting theory, and techniques – lies in this: it can help us become aware of the significance of continuous change and the forces which promote it. History makes us aware that change will come out of the push of discernible reasons; aware that acceleration of accounting development since 1900 has come, in part, from the continuing pressure of early reasons and, in part, from pressures out of contemporary reasons (the two types need to be examined separately); and aware that the accounting of the future will be influenced by similar combinations of response.

History capable of serving these purposes will need to present many persuasive reasons why the orderly growth that is already evident in accountancy will continue. This kind of history could serve two purposes: (1) making the inner nature of enterprise accounting more readily understandable and (2) providing readers with a platform from which to watch and appreciate future growth. As such, thoughtful observation of emerging history can help men pursue opportunities that will help the process.

Many significant antecedents of the known present can be noted in early accounting history. These were themselves evolutionary growths; that is, effective responses to contemporary conditions and needs. The observable persistence of characteristic techniques offers evidence that early effectiveness was so feverishly supported by logical reasons for being; hence, the techniques are still able to contribute today. This indebtedness of today to the past deserves consideration, especially as a part of accounting education.

Many of the characteristics of modern accounting may seem to be mainly responses to modern needs and contemporary conditions. This might well be the case. Recognized needs still press for adequate responses. Yet, part of present pressures will have been influenced by reasons that remain persuasive. In fact, a part of the explanation of the continuity of desirable action types lies in the fact that many of the sponsoring reasons are still driving accounting actions. As such, motivation similar to that effective in earlier years is often present even now. This is why similar responses prove similarly acceptable. In other words, today, as was the case long ago, logical relationships exist with power to influence. The relation of desirable ends (motivation) and means to those ends (responses) would be as persuasive, perhaps even as compelling, now as earlier.

It would seem that understanding the influential logic reflected in accounting actions, then and now, could deepen our appreciation of the rich magnificence of modern accountancy, and add credence to a belief that it deserves to be considered an intellectual discipline. In fact, evidence grows that enterprise accounting is a disciplined discipline and that an effective logic is visible within it – a logic of effective responses to recognized needs. Those needs call out for adequate responses; the needs become ends to be achieved. Without pressure from recognized needs (ends), accounting techniques (means) would not have been designed, tried, or changed as use dictated. Techniques, which repeatedly proved satisfactory in use, would become accepted as appropriate means for achieving desirable ends. Here is an effective and logical relationship; that is, one that is repeatedly tested by use.

Recognized needs are motivating in their effects and they provide reasons for seeking suitable technical responses. Use of those techniques puts their service capability to the test. If their suitability falls into question, other means will be tried until improvement is attained. As new reasons (needs) for actions appear, they provide motivation for modified or new ways of acting.

As an economy grows in complexity and extent, its business enterprises grow in number and in responsiveness. The related responsiveness of enterprise accounting is immediately involved. Thus, economic change disciplines enterprise responses and those responses call up refinements in accounting techniques. As complexity of account data increases, the need increases for more and better techniques for analytical interpretation of account data in search of clues to imbedded meaning.

Conditions such as these will have definite disciplinary effects on the enterprise and its accounting. Meeting those pressures calls for disciplined thinking; disciplined thinking about the significance of choosing or designing suitable means clearly capable of serving persuasive, perhaps compelling, ends towards effective achievements.

Knowledge of accounting history will not provide direct inspiration for new techniques. However, it can point to the compelling concept that accounting actions will always be tested by; that is, their ability to serve adequately as means toward known ends. Knowledge of history can give point to the wisdom of being sharply aware of influential conditions and fertile in conceiving effective responses.

Simple methodology, as is plainly indicated in early accounting history, can adequately serve simple needs. Conditions that are more complex call for increasingly sophisticated responses. When conditions are more demanding, accounting techniques must be more intricate. The problem of technical appropriateness then becomes more acute. This puts new pressure on exploring the reasons for these new needs, and on closely examining the promise of possible responses.

Every type of accounting action, each being intended to have a specific effect, will have a reason for being what it is. All such reasons should be clearly rational and strongly convincing. Thus, the total number of actions will be interrelated because the supporting reasons will have come from a central motivating force. Influential reasons will be united in making the chosen actions understandable. It is the function of accounting theory to foster these relationships. Understood in this way, theory touches all types of actions because theory is essentially explanations consisting of reasons why and reasons why not.

There is an analogy between accounting, as a discipline, and the athlete, who disciplines his body by resolution of his mind. The athlete seeks the disciplining effects of planned training. From persistent training, his physical actions come more under his control. In the same sense, accounting is a series of planned actions designed to bring under discipline the data originating in the transaction experience of a specific business enterprise. These data are "disciplined" into various informative categories (including accounts), which, by prior design, have been so planned as to interrelate informative groups of experience data.

This "disciplining" of transaction data is carefully planned, and the objective of this planning is to make understandable the results of management's prior decisions. Hence, such organized data will be able to discipline (influence) management's future decisions. It is significant of the accounting function that new decisions can be brought under the influence of knowledge of prior experience, through the services rendered by accounting techniques of organizing transaction data. It is therefore evident that accounting can be considered a discipline by a variety of tests:

1. Accounting's technical actions have been planned to conform to specific patterns of factual data; that is, it has been trained to sort out the available data into informative categories.
2. Accounting's technical actions will separate the favorable effects that transactions have on the enterprise from the unfavorable effects.
3. Accounting's technical actions organize transaction data in accounts until summaries are needed; in effect, accounts are trained to remember.
4. Accounting techniques can reveal data movements capable of reflecting the actions of management to induce inflow and outflow of transaction information.
5. Account categories are limited in their scope, in contrast to the greater freedom of statistical methodology.
6. Accounting techniques, by intention, definition, design, and title, have been "trained" to operate within specific boundaries for each type of data category. These boundaries are the enterprise, the fiscal period, and the individual account.

These are examples of the kinds of disciplines that exist in accounting. This is their character and intention. The various disciplines unite in helping to further the main functional objective of accounting; preparing prior experience data to aid in the creation of well-planned new decisions. Some aspects of enterprise accounting suggest that this technology is not only a practical discipline but also an intellectual discipline:

1. The patterns of accounting actions over the years have been conceived and designed by mental effects to respond effectively to recognized needs.
2. The data organized by accounting carry intellectual messages that are very useful to minds engaged in making judgmental decisions in business.
3. Accounting techniques have been developed from specific types of intellectual intentions: to identify distinguishable kinds; to count and remember how many of each; and to speak (report) to interpreting minds.

The evolutionary developments characterizing the long history of accounting indicate that there has been a continuing responsiveness to contemporary conditions and changes. This responsiveness has demonstrated men's ability to react to changing conditions: (1) by steadily improving their ability to use organized knowledge of prior experience and (2) by learning to use the factual results of prior transaction experience as a springboard toward improved enterprise service as new opportunities appear.

The pressures of contemporary needs and conditions are helpfully disciplinary in effect because they work through men's intellectual appraisal of their needs. They are also useful because that kind of recognition can influence the mind toward rational choices and defensible decisions that do not rest upon an emotional outlook. As such, decisions can be stronger from the influence of clearly perceived relations between ends in view (objectives) and appropriate means (actions) to those ends. This is especially true when there are persuasive, perhaps compelling reasons, why a particular end should be sought, and why the corresponding means will likely prove satisfactory.

Accounting can justifiably be considered an intellectual discipline, because its reasons for being – its objectives, theory, and philosophy – can strongly support its chosen array of techniques (i.e., its types of rational actions toward specific ends). As such, even though deep-lying reasons about early developments may not have been more than plausible conjectures, they need not be treated as merely assumptions. Even early methods should have been designed and used because they were judged by their users as adequate to the specific need of that time. For a long time, this kind of disciplinary logic has been providing strong fibers for relating accounting techniques and accounting objectives.

As the service capacity of accounting has grown, the problems of education of this discipline have grown even faster. There is a present need to lever methodology with more ideology, whether that takes the form of accounting theory, philosophy, or history. Much theory, philosophy, and history is available among the subjects in the area of the liberal arts. These are considered capable of contributing to intellectual capacity. It seems reasonable to believe that these subjects, set into an accounting context, could make similar contributions.

The teaching of accounting itself, by appropriately interrelating necessary technology with broadly conceived ideology, could do a great deal to give this subject matter many more intellectual characteristics. Appropriate theory, history, and philosophy, brought into contact with accounting education, would not duplicate broad and specialized courses found in liberal arts programs. Instead, the materials chosen for this use could convincingly indicate that enterprise accounting grew up, and still lives, in contact with developments in economic history and theory; and in contact with philosophical thinking about interrelated actions and objectives appropriate to accounting's special function of making enterprise transaction history reviewable.

In accounting, as elsewhere, there is a need for connecting rational actions with convincing reasons for so acting. This technology would become more understandable, if it was set in the context of men's progressive intellectual growth over time. This is so because accounting has itself been a product of men's increasing power to think rationally, effectively, and practically, while under the pressures of contemporary needs. It has grown as an intellectual discipline out of such a background, and deep understanding of the nature and function accounting can continue to contribute to men's capacity to think from needs to rational responses.

Modern accounting is a late blooming of an early recording methodology. As needs become more complex, better methods became necessary. Yet, men still prove equal to the challenges they find. Conditions still stimulate ideas; ideas still produce improved types of actions. Men still grow from their experience; they accept that kind of discipline; and they thrive on it because experience is educational. They also become more sensitive to the significance of experience, because so many have learned that education is expensive; that experience is educational; and that experience grows from thinking as well as from doing (i.e., from theory as well as practice).

The thought that accountancy deserves to be considered an intellectual discipline can be compactly summarized:

1. Accountancy broadly embraces the areas of accounting theory, technology, education, and the profession. These elements are attractive to a trained mind; they also contribute to the further training of that mind toward orderly thinking, rational discrimination, and questioning that seeks insight and understanding.
2. Accountancy is an area of action and experience, with its own methodology, ideology, and aid to interpretative analysis. Its study and use is therefore capable of further sharpening and disciplining the user's mental processes.
3. Accountancy is a combination of ideas and actions set into convincing relationship. It is a union of motivation and achievement. Its action, techniques, and achievements begin in discernible reasons, which are persuasive and often compelling.
4. Accounting ideas call for implementation by actions; accounting actions find justifying support in recognized purposes and objectives.

Accountancy can become a stronger discipline from enlarging and implementing a framework of basic concepts. Sections of this framework could include such items as the following:

1. Concepts of aims, ends, objectives, purposes, and reasons, each stated in broad terms and for sharply specific situations. These concepts would call for actions capable of implementing those desires, intentions, and limitations. All such concepts need to be appraised according to relative degrees of necessity or desirability.
2. Concepts of ways and means, of techniques, and of methods. These will constitute actions likely to fulfill specific ends and purposes. All such actions need to be examined as to specific appropriateness to certain purposes and as to evident capability for achievement.
3. Concepts of significant relationships. This is needed because understanding does not come directly from masses of data but from interpretation of the meaning inherent within related data.
4. Concepts of categories appropriate to the data. These need to be appropriate to the informative segregation of data by types and appropriate to interrelate with other categories.
5. Concepts of boundary limits for categories and of the undesirable results of trespassing category boundaries.

6. Concepts of interpretative analysis. These are needed to extract meaning out of movements within a category and out of rates of change in the data of related categories.

Previous pages have considered enterprise accounting as a discipline that grew in response to disciplinary pressures of needs and conditions. The primary pressure came from the very basic need management and investors have for factual knowledge of the results of prior decisions and actions. Centuries ago, there were investors in trading ventures abroad and there were managers who were responsible for those voyages. The needs of modern security investors and corporation managements are better known. Accounting techniques, early and simple, as well as modern and complex, were concrete responses to such needs. The patterns of accounting, then, and now, have been influenced (disciplined) by men's needs to know.

The basic step toward effective communication of transaction experience began slowly a long time ago. Written memoranda about transaction events began to prove inadequate for summary analyses. Transaction data needed to be brought under discipline that was more effective. As a result, accumulated transaction data (in memorandum form) came to be disciplined into an increasing number of specific account categories. This "pressing" of transaction data with a few informative kinds could greatly compact transaction experience; thus, making it more readily reviewable. That very basic and logical development still makes its typical contribution to understanding, even after centuries of increased complexity of the data and the many new problems of reaching rational decisions.

Despite this effectiveness, a general problem gradually arose: that of being confident of the dependability of the large amounts of data. Out of such needs came the profession of public accounting. This development deserves more extensive analysis than is possible here, but a few highlights can indicate the type of responses to recognized needs that appeared.

The prototypes were the annual reports of stewardship in England several centuries ago. These were examined and tested in detail. The procedure was essentially a simplified "audit" of the calculations and organized presentation of the year's activities of the community of the estate. Here, the validity of the report was under examination. Later, about a century ago, "audit," in an almost modern sense, grew out of statutes by the English Parliament. These required accounts to be kept by all business enterprises. The resulting financial statement summaries were to be closely examined (audit) by experienced accountants.

The audited statements were then to be sent to officials of the government and to all holders of company securities. Thus, accounting and account reporting were brought under statutory discipline. Moreover, the effect of the audit and specific reporting to stockholders placed enterprise management under the discipline of publicity. As so often in the evolution of accounting, here, again, a recognized need generated an effective response. The need became evident from an increase in security speculation, often accompanied by loose, if not dishonest, actions by some enterprise managements.

Let us now return to the topic of education. Instruction in keeping accounts has been evident in a very long series of bookkeeping textbooks. The most famous early text, the first put into print, was that by an Italian, Pacioli, in 1494. Instruction in keeping accounts continued for centuries to be a matter of teaching the routine actions of recording and marshaling enterprise transaction experience. Now, almost 500 years later, education in the subject matter has greatly expanded and broadened as is fitting for an intellectual discipline. Accounting study, and preparation for the profession of public accounting, is now available in many universities and the coursework often extends to the postgraduate level. This, too, is a disciplined response to recognized needs.

It would be unrealistic for accounting education to fail to make clear to college students of business the interrelated body that is enterprise accounting. This could happen whenever a clearly mechanistic approach would set the pattern of instruction. A better approach would be based on questions and the production of adequate response.

Since accounting has been disciplined over centuries of development toward its present status, it would seem important that every opportunity be used to make clear the way separate aspects of the technology can be articulated within a conceptual whole. It might be quite useful, early in the sequence of courses, to indicate the end and the means involved. The end is to make understandable an accumulating mass of transaction experience and the means to that end is the technical language of accounts, the bilateral categories, and the thought processes of translating those events into data sorted into appropriately named account categories.

Students need to realize early that transactions tell of enterprise history; and that the financial statements, which emerge from the accounts, undertake to make that transaction history meaningful to the reader. Yet, ideas such as these may seem to emphasize theory too early. On one hand, it would not be appropriate to load early courses with theory in the raw, so to speak, and especially theory treated as abstract thought or as product of deductive logic. On the other hand, theory, considered as rational explanations of the reasons for a special situation or action type, could enrich the task of learning to use techniques. This is so because the student would be able to approach those actions from the point of view of the purposes that call those actions into being.

The aim of this approach would be to build firm foundations of actions and reasons; thus, to serve as bases for later courses and advanced preparation. This approach holds promise because all actions rest on their reasons for being. Motivation, therefore, should be a thought that is frequently injected. The instructor should ask questions around fundamental issues, such as the purpose of the bilateral form of accounts and the rationale behind the routine meaning of "debit" and "credit."

Recent growth in the literature on accounting theory and history indicates increasing recognition that (1) accounting actions are aspects of a special technology of marshaling data toward revealing meaning and (2) that actions originate in, and are justified by, an understandable ideology; that is, ideas of needs and of possible alternative actions in response. In other words, needs generate actions and accounting actions are efforts to communicate messages inherent in the transaction experience of a given business enterprise. Recognition of aspects of the functions of accounting such as these, and the ways its techniques serve those functions, can be more educational than the rote learning of making entries and constructing financial statements, in accordance with contemporary custom, but without support of reasons for the peculiar arrangements of data.

With the preceding propositions in mind, the argument is that accountancy is indeed a discipline. It has reached that status over a long period of development, starting with very simply elements. It has grown greatly in ability to respond effectively to the disciplinary pressures of urgent needs. In doing so, accountancy has itself become a disciplined way of thinking and acting. It has grown in capability to respond rationally to new needs. As a result, accountancy has become a sharply disciplined technology dedicated to a particularly useful type of factual communication.

3

ACCOUNTING: A LANGUAGE

It has been said: "Double entry developed early in Italy in response to the needs of nascent capitalism (De Roover, 1956, p. 174)." Both the need and response are supported by convincing reasons. Increasing complexities of business activities were pressing men, even then, to organize the data from their transactions experience. Their response was to devise means likely to aid the understanding of the significance of that experience, ultimately with the goal of aiding future decisions.

It has also been pointed out that "the fourteenth and fifteenth centuries were perhaps the most brilliant and progressive period in the history of accounting (De Roover, 1956, p. 174)." The results were indeed a brilliant product of the times and the men of those days. Evident was a high sense of originality and recognition of pressing need – that of a technical language capable of organizing for review the results of prior transaction experience. As such, from its beginning, enterprise accounting was disciplined by recognized needs. Continued responses to continued needs produced increasingly useful communicative abilities. Language of some sort was an early necessity. This is so because the use of language by men is associated with thinking, and thinking becomes increasingly dependent upon increased language skills.

Consider the following analogy: reading is a way of absorbing the thoughts of another person; that is, to perceive communicated meanings. Similarly, accounting is a form of language. It records the results of prior thinking, which, in turn, leads to further thinking. Furthermore, like any other language, the accounting communications may often need to be translated (interpreted) for better understanding of the messages therein.

With this analogy in mind, those who prepare account data toward interpretation of its messages need to realize that many users will have little knowledge of the procedures that make transaction experience informative. They need also to realize that users of accounting reports could, with benefit, learn to "read" financial statements with understanding, especially if they acquired some knowledge of the accounting language that provides the organized information and influences the arrangement of the data in the reports.

A part of effective communication is the grammar involved. This guides the use of words in structuring sentences in conformity with established usage and clear communication. Syntax undertakes to guide the choice of ideological symbols (including words) in ways that can facilitate communication and stimulate thought. Mathematics, for instance, affords an example of a specific type of non-verbal symbols. Accounting makes effective use of a few very appropriate symbols. In both cases, however, it is necessary to understand the meaning of the symbols and the way they are manipulated under the rules of the related grammar and syntax.

Accounting uses only a moderate amount of grammar found in the normal usage of words. Therefore, the function of conversation must employ non-verbal symbols to create the needed readability. The basic symbols used in this connection are (1) quantitative data – usually expressed in terms of mutually agreeable exchange prices – derived from actual transaction experience of the given enterprise and (2) bilateral account categories for grouping transaction data by kinds.

Just as words and phrases are a form of "thought-shorthand" for ideas, so too are bilateral accounts symbols of relationships between ideas. The digits in an account will usually be thought to be symbols of quantities of dollars. Yet, it would be more logical to consider the digits as quantitative symbols of transaction events; that is, items of the activity history of an enterprise. It is especially confusing, for both students and report readers, to be led to think of account data as expressing past, present, or future purchasing power. Perhaps this is one spot where ideas from economic are less appropriate to the context of accounting.

Transaction data and account categories have combined into very effective mediums of communication. They greatly simplify an otherwise unintelligible mass of accumulated transaction experience. This is a clear contribution to communication, as the reorganization of account data into the form of financial statements further facilitates readability and understanding, which are important factors in aid of business decisions.

The study of the grammar and syntax of accounting usually begin with exercises in translating the facts of specific transactions into uniformly quantitative data, distributed among appropriately named account categories. The routine of translating can be learned, after a fashion, by following examples and a few rules-of-thumb. An example of this would be the rule-of-thumb to debit what comes in and credit what goes out. Yet, although this might help with cash transactions, it can hardly strengthen the thought processes involved in dealing rationally with most other situations. This time-honored approach is a very elementary and mechanical way of beginning to develop analytical ability for making events intelligible.

The general argument here is that rules and illustrations will seldom lay firm foundations for thoughtfully rational organization of data masses. Mental perception is needed. Simple but compelling reasons and practical logic are also readily available. These elements need not be complex; and their use is well adapted to developing the mental processing of making the decisions involved in translating events into data in account categories.

This approach to transaction analysis does not imply that a highly theoretical introduction to elementary accounting is recommended. Whatever the method, it should be influenced by the educational level at which accounting techniques are first presented. It is possible, for example, to underestimate the capacity of college freshmen and sophomores to group clearly presented reasons for the peculiarities they meet in accounting. It will be clear to the thoughtful teacher that convincing reasons exist for the various technical actions and that knowledge of these reasons can be educational in their effect.

Such reasons could be persuasively associated even with the simplest types of accounting thought toward accounting actions. Specific action types are supported by specific reasons why those actions are part of the results of thinking about accounting as a way of making data more understandable. It might even be quite useful to view simple data in the context of its usefulness, in aid of next decisions for the enterprise, at an early stage. This would have the advantage of beginning to present usefulness as the goal of record keeping and data organizing. Therefore, somewhere in a program of business education, preferable earlier rather than later, the student would benefit from realizing the persuasiveness of simple use-logic in a context of enterprise accounting.

Like mathematics, accounting is more a language than a body of knowledge. Both "languages" have a proper and orderly usage, which we refer to with the term "grammar." The orderly uses of this language persist because the resulting data are made more meaningful. They are meaningful precisely because accounting actions are motivated by reasons, conditions, and needs, which unite in pressing for informative organization of data mass. Those needs sponsor the recording actions as means to the end of providing information as useful responses to decisions in the making.

This logical relation between ends and means is part of the "grammar" of accounting. Basic knowledge of this relationship should be part of elementary accounting study, because understanding, as well as doing, has a place there just as well as it does in advanced courses. This is so because, throughout accounting, relationships have major significance. Furthermore, because relationships make up the basic subject matter of both logic and accounting, it is permissible, perhaps necessary, to consider that accounting includes numerous aspects of persuasive logic. For accounting, like language, is a "logically rational system."

Accounting has slowly been fashioned into a medium of communication; it has rapidly increased in degree of perfecting that function. It follows, therefore, that compilers of account data need to know the "language" well in order to facilitate that function. Likewise, users of account data also have a need to know this language well in order to read the messages embodied in the organized data.

This leads to two related observations. First, the modes of expression found in accounting make little use of graphic symbols. Extensive and effective use is made, however, of recognizing and indicating relationships among quantitative data derived from transaction experience, in the markets, of the given enterprise. Second, although accounting actions make extensive use of quantitative data, particularly those expressed in money prices, this use does not directly express value.

The argument is that, although accounting uses some arithmetic, it is not mathematical in function. It uses the quantitative data from transactions as elements to be organized into a variety of informative categories; those being designed to assemble similar and contrasting kinds of experience information. This disciplined (planned) use of account categories increases the analytical potential, by assembling like data in specifically named accounts and by naming accounts so that they can readily be assembled into significantly related groups of accounts (i.e., by related transaction experience types).

These observations are rooted in the use of language. Buried in the word "accounting" is the word "count" (enumeration of how many). Yet, a stress on "how many" is likely to over-emphasize many as "measuring" the quantitative side of transaction experience. It also almost inevitably associates the process with measuring value. Nonetheless, the recorded digits "measure" only in a very limited sense. Both parties to a consummated transaction have agreed upon a mutually acceptable "bargained price," which will move the transaction forward. A term such as this turns thought back, as it should, to the reason behind the transaction rather than toward the local currency involved. The parties have each separately evaluated the transaction. Each has a different value in mind. The same digits cannot represent both.

Use of the term "money figures," on the other hand, almost inevitably opens a door to confused thinking. The reason: money, denominated in a national currency, is widely considered as changing in value as commodity prices change. We refer to this change as a change in the purchasing power of money. This is a rational concept of economic relationship. Yet, its use in connection with accounting theory lays a foundation for distrusting and misinterpreting the messages communicated by accounting data.

This confusion comes from a misunderstanding of the transaction event. It is a fact that all items of account data have derived from transactions expressed in terms of agreed (bargained) price. However, the only "valuing" involved has been in the mental judgments of the two parties regarding the desirability for each of that exchange. Strictly speaking, therefore, money in this situation is not consciously a measure of value. Instead, it is a medium of exchange; a generalized technique of equating the differing value judgments of the two parties.

As an alternative, the term "bargained price" carries a connotation closer to "medium of exchange" than to worth or value. For that reason, it can better describe this aspect of accounting. Furthermore, the titles of the various accounts provide better clues to the messages in the data than do the quantitative digits. In other words, the resting place of the data – that is in the account of each party to the transaction experience – will be more significantly informative than the digits can be.

Enterprise accounting may properly be considered a special kind of history: a factual story of the transaction experience of the given enterprise. That enterprise exists to generate an acceptable service; and enterprises vary in many ways according to their type of service. Yet, all enterprises provide that service to customers bit-by-bit and transaction by transaction. As this is the nature of a business enterprise, its living history consists of day-by-day inflowing and outflowing transactions with other entities. A significant and inherent duality of actions therefore is at once evident in all types of business transactions.

These movements, inward and outward, must be initiated by intention and decision. The eventual results of these controlled movements will have large significance to people who make transaction decisions (management) and for people who supply enterprise capital (investors). Naturally, management wishes to review their transaction experience in order for next decisions to be based on the knowledge of the results of prior decisions. Investors wish to review periodic summaries of enterprise transaction experience as well, in order to form judgments as to management's effective creation of earnings and the continued financial health of the enterprise.

Under these conditions, the need for effective communication of the essence of enterprise transaction history is clearly evident. The needed communication will necessarily be sharply different from most kinds of communication. It cannot be communication by musical sound, color, or painted forms. It cannot be by direct speech as two men on the phone; it cannot be like a letter between two distant parties. A closer analogy would be to compare accounting communication with a letter in English sent to a Paris correspondent and then translated into French. Accounting would be even closer to a communication in the form of a technical paper using previously researched materials. These would have been informatively interrelated and organized for other people to study.

Accounting data, out of transaction experience, have, in a sense, been researched (collected) and organized (translated) into informative group (account categories). The result is that the kind of transaction experience typical of the given enterprise will be compactly summarized for the reader in the form of financial reports.

By the nature of their content, accounts will easily fall into recognizable groups for the reports. A group of asset accounts will have a common focus: they all speak of production potential. These elements of potential derive from a variety of sources: loans by creditors, capital by investors in shares, and earnings retained in the business. Together, these sources constitute equities – claims against company assets. It is inevitable that the two resulting totals will be equal; someone will claim the last asset if the company liquidates. Set together as a report, asset accounts and equity accounts present to readers a statement of logically related elements – a compact communication of enterprise financial position as of a specific date. It is to be noted that the figures involved do not speak of values; they report on summaries of remaining elements of enterprise transaction experience.

The operational function of a business enterprise is that of producing acceptable services. Accounting language, therefore, must include a way of communicating evidence of services accepted by customers. One group of related accounts (revenue) provides this evidence out of actual transaction experience. Before acceptance by customers, the offered services must be made available. The assets used to prepare for that service and to secure customer acceptance (appreciable costs and expenses) will be related to, and opposite to, the revenue from sales. The resulting summary of these elements is particularly informative report on enterprise experience.

The accounting communication of these related elements of prior experience will offer clues as to management effectiveness. This is differently indicated by the two major sections: (1) evidence of achievement in satisfying customers (thus earning revenue) and (2) evidence of achievement in holding total applicable cost and expense below the amount of revenue earned.

This report – earnings statement – and the report of assets and equities – financial position statement – compactly summarize the results of a multitude of managerial decisions. What is more, together they open to study several aspects of managerial activities. These are activities in acquiring capital from indicated sources; activities in converting assets into cost-expense capable of attracting revenue from customers in larger amounts than the cost of applicable factors; and activities in satisfying customers' demands, to ensure the financial health and capability for growth of the enterprise.

These two reports compress a year of transaction experience; they compactly summarize a year of multiple decisions and multiple results of the judgments there involved. In a very definite sense, they reflect, in factual data, a section of enterprise operating history. They can serve this function because they emerge from twelve months of accounting activity in organizing a large volume of transaction experience data. As a result, it is obvious that a vast accumulation of documents will lie back of the accounts and the reports. Without those raw materials of experience, the year's history could not be prepared. Without planned organization, the mass could not be made intelligible.

Enterprise transaction history cannot be completely presented in a verbal text. It can be made usefully informative only to the extent that its data can provide clues to activities and decisions of specific types. This necessitates extensive classification of the emerging transaction data. Each significant type of transaction activity will be segregated into one specifically named account. The name of the category can provide clues to the reasons why capital was assigned to that purpose, which is derived from the source indicated by the account name. The result is that those account names refer to specific segments of enterprise transaction experience. If the content of an account were to include elements not clearly identifiable with the name, this would be an example of misclassification. It could result in a serious distortion of transaction truth.

It will be obvious that all items of transaction experience will have been sponsored by recognizable purposes; that is, by intentions that make necessary specific actions for implementing certain ends. This being the case, an "accounting language" will be needed: the events will need that discipline in order to bring the elements into an informative communication. This "orderly discipline" can help the data user to associate purposes and ends with related actions as ways and means. By knowing something of the functions of accounts and transactions, the user of reported account data will be reminded to always think of the management decisions back of the reported data.

Over a long period of evolutionary development, accounting has gradually become a highly effective technology for organizing complex transaction experience. It is part of the function of accounting history to open this to examination. It is particularly important to trace the early steps by which its use could marshal masses of transaction data into a compact report of enterprise transaction history. That detailed history speaks of many types of actions sponsored by many types of enterprise objectives. This is necessarily so because enterprise experience consists of the union of many ends and intentions, and with many ways for achieving those ends. The user of account data will benefit from thinking through reported data to find glimpses of these influencing ends and purposes. Without this mental penetration back of account figures, these data cannot serve their basic function.

Inherent in the pairing of ends and means, there are strong elements of persuasive logic. If the results of prior decisions seem unsatisfactory, this fact may come from faulty selection of the means or from choosing a specific objective that proved unsuited to the means at hand. The choices actually made (of means and of ends) will come from management decisions. These, in turn, should be based on knowledge, experience, discretion, and judgment. Given this, it would be an important part of the accounting function to provide account data that, when analytically interpreted, could carry thought deep enough to suggest weak spots in the matching of enterprise actions and objectives.

History, even the history of a year's transactions, can open to the mind avenues for seeking light on questions of why or why not. The user of account data must seek clues to reasons why the results are to some degree unsatisfactory. Were the ends suitable? Were the means inadequate? Furthermore, in searching beyond the springboard of such questions, the interrelations among accounts need to be closely studied for clues to ill-advised proportions. Those interrelations among accounts have been designed into the system; and the transaction data have been carefully assigned into categories according to the planned design of interrelations. If decision-makers do not analytically study interrelations, they will pass over much of the service capability of accounting. As a result, significant clues to improved decisions may not be recognized.

The enterprise function is that of providing acceptable services. Accounting must be organized to provide evidence of achievement in that area. A variety of accounts will be needed to permit analytical insight into the results. If those account data are not closely studied, the accounting function has been defeated in at least some measure. To avoid this, transaction data must be organized in ways to make readable the evidence of efforts made in order to achieve certain outcomes. Expense and cost data speak of effects exerted by conversion of the effort-potential residing in assets. Management judgment and actions will have initiated the creation of debts and liabilities as sources of those assets. Management will be judged, according to the effectiveness of this relationship – commonly referred to as the financial position of an enterprise – as well as by the effectiveness of the relation of cost-expense to revenue.

The apparent status of the well-being of an enterprise can be read from the statement of financial position, provided "well-being" is not defined as reflected by the contemporary value of its assets in relation to its obligations to investors and creditors. It is not persuasive to consider that upward changes in the "net value" of the enterprise will reflect the favorable results of management's efforts to earn new assets from revenue by keeping costs and expenses below the aggregate prices customers will pay. In other words, hypothetical appreciation of assets does not generate profit. It may even be questionable whether asset reappraisal creates something that can appropriately be called "capital surplus."

The objectives of reporting on the results of enterprise transaction experience will influence the types of accounts to be used and their significant interrelations. The choice of accounts and the closeness of their relationships are important elements in the "language" in which transaction experience will be expressed. That "language" is quite important to the user of account data as well. This is not to say that users need not be experts in accounting technology, but their own self-preservation should dictate some interest in this "language" and how it to communicates understanding.

Appropriate design of the data marshaling mechanism is of course the first step. This design will be influenced (1) by knowledge of the type of enterprise and of the kinds of transaction experience to be expected and (2) by knowledge of the way enterprise accounting serves as a type of language. This language is a "logically rational system" that is designed for capability in maneuvering masses of data toward interpretative understanding.

Operation of the system requires close knowledge of the broad function of reporting transaction experience as well as the purposes and limitation of each account in the system. It also requires understanding of the intended effect on the enterprise of specific types of transaction experience. It is here that the raw materials of communication are, in effect, "researched" (processed) into a form that is more intelligible. Some of this data, after being initially processed into specific accounts, must later be gradually processed over a period of years into accounts that adhere to the annual interpretative association of periodic expenses and revenue.

After marshaling and reporting of a period's transaction experience, the use made of the data communicated depends on the interpretative skill of the user. He will receive some help from the spatial arrangement of the data in reports and from contrasted data-totals, such as assets and equities as well as revenues and expenses. Yet, the full meaning of reported transaction experience cannot be read directly from data as it is presented. It is therefore necessary to study relationships for clues.

Relations among reported summary data will have interpretative significance because these represent relations among the decisions that created the transactions. It is these deeper relations from which the reader seeks clues. It is the intention of the system, and of the separate accounts, that this should be the case. On the same basis, changes in account data between one period and another can be very informative. This is so because the change has been management's intention in creating the chosen transaction experience.

On the surface, accounting activities may seem clerical; hence, easily learned from rules and examples. But accounting has become much more than bookkeeping. Even the simplest and traditional accounting actions were supported by convincing reasons. It is therefore regrettable that so little effort is made by writers of elementary texts to show students that rational reasons can make routine actions more understandable. In fact, regardless of how elementary the exercises may be, transaction analysis is an intellectual process of thinking transaction events into "logical pockets" whose names provide clues to their contents. The result is that texts need not seem philosophical or theoretical in order to make some of those fundamentals clear to beginners. Account categories are appropriate means to desirable ends. This can be made clear without introducing pragmatic logic as such.

Keeping accounts and translating transaction experience; that is, to sort events in accordance with appropriate pockets, is a complex means to a very understandable end. This end is that of making prior transaction experience understandable, through the review of the effects that the events had on various aspects of enterprise operations. The summary, however simple it may be, of those effects can be very helpful to people (investors) outside the enterprise. Presumably, they would wish to see evidence of changes among the firm's assets; changes in the relation of assets to liabilities; changes in the relation between revenue and applicable expense; and changes in the relation of the period's net profit to total assets and other accounts.

These concepts of objectives are not too complex, in simple form, for beginners. They can be presented as very practical aspects of accounting. These practical aspects reveal various purposes beneath data and the accounting treatment of those data. Some of the revealed events are chosen by management to produce desired results (e.g., service to customers). Other events are chosen to enable the enterprise to offer its service (e.g., applicable expenses that began as enterprise assets). Management's choices of transactions, therefore, are helpful means to very definite ends. The result is that overall costs are lower than total revenue, precisely because management planned it that way in authorizing specific transactions by types and amounts.

Students can appreciate the logic inherent in accounting, without realizing the part that logic, as such, plays in human affairs. Nonetheless, it would seem clear that they could still benefit from knowing that accounting actions are not merely traditional actions supported only by custom. A repeated association of management intentions with its actions could help foster realization that accounting has always been purposeful. Elementary accounting is not too early to introduce students to the thought that other people, besides management, will be interested in examining organized data, which, in turn, can reveal evidence of management's efforts and achievements. For example, to what extent are people who supplied part of the capital that the enterprise uses interested in this organized data?

Regardless of particular timing, somewhere in accounting education the persuasive and responsive logic inherent in enterprise accounting should be made clear. Because accounting is an intellectual discipline, its foundations in simple pragmatic logic, in particular, should be made evident to students. Recognition of the essence of this logic could add vitality to the basic concept that accounting deals with transaction history, and that it deals with this transaction data rationally, understandably, convincingly, and usefully. In other words, it deals with this data *logically*.

One of the very noticeable characteristics of enterprise accounting is the frequent appearance of duality. An early and rather inadequate descriptive term, "bookkeeping by double-entry," reflects this aspect. It does so, however, quite incompletely. This concept was presumed to be highly characteristic, which it was, and thoroughly explanatory, which it never was. Accounting, or bookkeeping by double-entry, was considered as a grouping of certain kinds of actions. Duality of entry was traditional. As such, it had to be accepted and used. This usage could be mechanical, if necessary, and without justification. Surely, accounting technology has progressed far enough now to be approached from a higher level of thinking.

First, duality is one characteristic and bilateral accounts is another one (duality again). After that, transaction analysis becomes necessary, as transaction events must be translated into pre-arranged account categories. Meshing these, as if they were two gears, is the first prerequisite to recording. This is essentially a process of translation or converting. The analogy follows that, as French must be converted into English, events must be converted into data in an assortment of categories. This, in turn, is an intellectual challenge and a learning process that can help develop one's mental powers.

In many respects, transaction analysis is simpler than the translation of language. Yet, accounting, as with language, is a medium of communication but with a simpler grammar. Accounting is largely controlled by penetrating into the logic of interrelations among data. The bilateral aspect of every business transaction and ledger account provides a very useful springboard: a basis for the logic of accounting.

"Logic" may sound like the name of a college course in the department of philosophy. Although it may be doubted that such a department would be the place to start the study of accounting, it is indeed a department well suited to exercises in learning to think clearly. However, it is also reasonable to believe the study of accounting can provide exercises in learning to think logically. Consider transaction analysis, which is a highly significant aspect of accounting language. In what respects is this an exercise in mental discipline?

Exercise of this kind is called up whenever a specific transaction event, already consummated in the markets, needs to be reasoned into appropriate spots within a "logically rational system" of account categories. The need is to translate specific events into specific bilateral categories. This will necessarily be an intellectual process. What bases are available for guiding the decisions along rational lines? How has communicative powers been designed into accounts and communicative needs been designed into transactions?

The communicative powers of accounts are affected by the use of two features: (1) the specific name of each account-category and (2) the bilateral feature of a left column and a right column. The account name separates kinds, and the separate columns closely contrast opposites within a given kind. The feature both double the amount of information and produce a residual remainder, which is reporting on the difference between like kinds with contrasting plus or minus effects on the enterprise.

This bilateral feature is not the "double" feature of "double-entry." That term can only refer to one event having two effects on the enterprise; hence, it will involve an entry in more than one category. Instead, these two differing concepts provide clues to certain plausible and rational relationships among various accounts and between transactions and accounts. As a result, these designed but quite natural relationships, and a certain amount of useful and persuasive logic, help bring about the dual placement in the accounts of transaction data. This logic deserves careful analysis because it contributes strongly to the power of all accounts to join forces in making informative communications; thus, justifying their status as elements of a "language."

Transaction analysis is an intellectual process of deciding the distribution of data among a variety of account categories. The action taken originates in recognizing the two elements involved: (1) the effects on the enterprise of the specific transaction event; and (2) the specific accounts to which the transaction's effects are related as indicated by the nature of the transaction. This analysis and action will produce a clear example of duality of entry, from the duality of the transaction effect on the enterprise.

This treatment may raise questions of theory. Why is duality a necessary aspect of a transaction, an entry, and of an account? Are these aspects of duality matters of rational choice or merely accounting? Is duality indispensable to the analytical function of enterprise accounting? What persuasive reasons can support the most plausible answers here?

First, perhaps duality began as an undesirable aspect inherent in all exchange-priced transactions between two independent parties. Second, perhaps duality proved to be a particularly useful means to the end of enabling men to review all of the effects of their prior decisions. Third, perhaps duality is inescapable because each party must consider how his proposed transaction will have a hoped-for favorable effect for him; and how, in order to produce that desired effect, he must experience an unfavorable effect. Under these unavoidable circumstances, any consummated exchange-priced transaction would call for a dual recording in the accounts of both parties.

Obviously, judgment and decision would have been involved for both parties. The ultimate appropriateness of the transaction would need to be judged by the ultimate effect on the firm's operations. Moreover, it is clear that enterprise managements have made a value judgment. Do the digits entered in the parties' accounts therefore express values?

To answer this, it is necessary to note that "value" is a highly personal concept. Two transaction parties will have in mind differing "values"; otherwise, no exchange would take place. The same digits will be found in the accounts of both parties, although under different account names. Yet, the "values," in the eyes of each party, will be different. This should make it clear that some confusion of terms could be involved.

For both parties, the transaction was desired; for each, the prospective favorable effect out-weighed the necessary unfavorable effect. This recognition lies at the heart of both decisions; it is the essence of valuing. Yet, a fallacy underlies considering the digits as "meaning value." In that connection, it is necessary to note (1) that each party records two elements identical in quantity; (2) that one of these two refers to the aspect unfavorable to the specific party; and (3) that the unfavorable effect is the price that one party sets in order to achieve the favorable aspect. Perhaps there is a clue here, which can put the emphasis on price, not value, as the aspect indicated by the digits in the accounts of both parties.

The same digits are lodged in the purchase account of one party and in the sales account of the other. To one, the figures signify a cost-price; to the other, it signify a selling price. The transaction of giving up goods to the party who receives the goods will confer a potential benefit to each party: one expects to use the purchased goods and the other expects to use the cash from his sale in ways benefiting his enterprise. These are the judgmental values in view, when the parties agree upon the transaction exchange and the price.[a]

The dualities so characteristic of transactions, transacting parties, and account entries, disciplines (impose restrictions) accounting theory and actions. These are convincingly logical restrictions. They are far from being *just* expedient. Only through such restrictions can events, planned to have specific effects on the enterprise concerned, be fully related in the record, which can later be opened to analytical review. Interpretations of the meaning are, in turn, necessary in order to see the results of efforts made effectively to provide an enterprise with experience appropriate to its intent and purpose.

"Dualities" is a term expressive of "pairs:" pairs of effects from one transaction; pairs in the bilateral form of accounts; pairs such as plus and minus; pairs such as assets and equities; pairs such as revenue and applicable expenses; and pairs such as a statement of financial position and a statement of operational earnings. There is an observable sequence here: (1) transaction events; (2) accounts are recorded as pluses and minuses; and (3) items are summarized into groups of related and contrasting accounts. All of these elements join in making enterprise experience reviewable. This sequence makes a definite contribution to accounting as a language and a medium for communicating ideas.

Duality also makes its contribution. Used with understanding, it employs seeming complexity to gain clarity of meaning. The bilateral aspect of accounts also contributes to communicative power. So too do the seemingly clashing terms "favorable" and "unfavorable." The influences of these characteristics can almost be diagrammed in their relation with the bilateral feature of accounts.

Given this constellation of dualities, perhaps ones first thought would then be that communication would be aided by recording favorable transaction effects on one side of all accounts and the corresponding unfavorable effects on the opposite side of the accounts involved. Yet, that is not the case; in some classes of accounts, favorable items (pluses) are placed on the left side of a bilateral account and unfavorable (minuses) on the right side. In other accounts, placement of entries, pluses and minuses, is reversed.

In statistical categories, this would seem quite arbitrary. Yet, are there persuasive reasons for believing that this peculiarity in accounting is not accidental or merely customary? If there is a measure of recognizable logic here, it should have, in some way, a rational effect on recording and interpreting techniques. Because of this, it should be a useful aspect of accounting as a language. Two key questions here are these: why are not all favorable transactions effects entered on one side of the account, perhaps the left one, and the unfavorable effects entered on the other side?

The answer is readily evident when we examine such contrasting categories as property and debt as well as assets and equities. Standing alone, a new equity (debt payable) is unfavorable to the enterprise. Standing alone, a new asset is favorable. Reverse effects can also appear: (1) a debt payable is canceled, which is a favorable event to the owing enterprise and (2) an asset is given up, which is an unfavorable event to the same enterprise. These effects of specific actions are only logically reported, as indicated, if they are entered on the proper plus or minus side of the accounts. Hence, the following significant symbols and placement of increases and decreases in the accounting language (Table 5).

These symbols are quite logical, given the oppositeness of "asset" and "debt." Borrowing from a bank creates a liability (debt); alone, this is an unfavorable effect. The money obtained from such a loan, if alone, would be considered solely favorable. One side of the experience is cause; the other side is an effect. One kind of effect is so much desired that the transacting party accept the other effect as necessary to produce the desired outcome.

Table 5. Balance Sheet Symbols and Placement in the Language of Accounting.

Assets		Equity Debts	
Favorable (Plus)	Unfavorable (Minus)	Favorable (Minus)	Unfavorable (Plus)

When a bank loan is repaid, the same kind of reasoning, in reverse, can quite logically explain the recording necessary to reflect both effects (Table 6).

Revenue from sales is clearly favorable; assets are sold in order to attain revenue (i.e., to increase that category). Assets, which are passed on to others by sale, will sometimes move first in the form of an expense-cost incurred in order to expedite sales transactions. In the form of expenses, these costs speak of efforts to attract customers. For example, they may speak of the cost of advertising or the purchase cost of the items sold (i.e., the revenue is the return expected from the effort.)

Usually, a closer association of expenses and revenue than is apparent in the separate accounts is deferred until summary time at the end of the fiscal period. Then, they join in one account; that is, the profit-and-loss account. The favorable balance of revenue will be moved to that summary account. It will appear there on the same side as in the original account; the latter being "balanced" (emptied) by an equivalent amount entered on the side opposite (unfavorable). Similar treatment empties the expense account (by an equivalent entry on the unfavorable side). This process has the following results (Table 7).

In summary: favorable effects are (1) increases in assets or revenue; and (2) decreases in expenses or liabilities. Unfavorable effects are (1) decreases in assets or revenue; and (2) increases in expenses or liabilities. These movements are technical means for rationally implementing the accounting function – that of informatively marshaling data from transaction experience in ways that will make readable the effects that management's choices of transactions have had upon the enterprise.

Management strives to increase enterprise assets. It can accomplish this by acquiring useful assets directly, through incurring debt or issuing equity.

Table 6. Income Statement Symbols and Placement in the Language of Accounting.

Expenses		Revenues	
Unfavorable (Plus)	Favorable (Minus)	Unfavorable (Minus)	Favorable (Plus)

Table 7. Profit and Loss Summary, Symbols, and Placement in the Language of Accounting.

Expenses	Revenues
Total Unfavorable Effect (Minus)	Total Favorable Effect (Plus)

It can also strive to increase assets by sales (revenue) of its products or services and retain some of those profits within the enterprise. To accomplish this, management must have goods to sell and must attract customer by incurring various expenses. As such, throughout the process of operating a business, management tries to achieve favorable changes, but this can only be accomplished by making efforts and the incurring of corresponding unfavorable changes. This makes it clear that the skillful making of management decisions is more difficult than using a special kind of "language" to make the accumulating results understandable.

No mention has been made here of profit. It is clear from the presence of a profit-and-loss account in the recording language that profits should ideally be greater than losses. This calculated net result is sometimes thought to be the prime objective of management, and the primary duty of accounting to reduce a mass of details to that compact figure. But it deserves further analysis.

In economics, much attention is given to "the profit motive" and to "improved enterprise welfare." It should be noted, however, that "motive" is a term applicable only to people. These people do indeed engage in business, but a better statement of the intention of business people is possible. Consider the following statement: the intention of business people is to make decisions wisely enough so the summarized results (in the accounts) will reveal the extent to which a multitude of individual transactions produce achievements (revenue) in excess of the costs of making the necessary efforts (expenses) to achieve. If this describes the management function well, the function of accounting is to use a special kind of language for making it possible for interested parties to read factual evidence relevant to management effectiveness and the results achieved.

This brings us back to the transaction experience. This experience is created, bit-by-bit, through a multitude of management decisions. Accounting undertakes to organize that experience, in compact and logical ways, toward opening enterprise accomplishments and efforts (under management) to interpretative review by interested parties. The results, emerging from skilled use of this highly technical language, will speak of enterprise transaction history. That is what people are interested in; that is the reason accounting must be strongly, honestly, and demonstrably factual. This factual characteristic prevents any arbitrary manipulation of the data based on wishful thinking and predictions about the future.

The calculated net profit, which becomes known in the accounts, is not the answer or the objective of accounting. It is, in effect, the boiled-down essence of a large volume of transaction effects. Again, this cannot be the answer, as the questions people have are too many. Instead, an approach to understanding must come from intelligent penetration back of this glimpse of essence; in other words, understanding must reach into the groups of events, which, in mass, produce that essence; into the interrelations among data groups; and into relative changes in the quantitative relations among the groups of transaction events.

The ultimate aim of interpretation is the most difficult to accomplish. This is to sense the judgmental capabilities of the men whose decisions set in motion, and keep in motion, the continuing stream of effects that constitute enterprise life. A leading question then – as always present in analytical interpretation–is how successful management has been in pairing desired and favorable effects with necessary but unfavorable effects. Clues to this question do not stand clear in the final net figures. They will be most readable from observed changes evident in the figures over time and between related accounts.

It is the intention of accounting language, and the purpose of a plus-and-minus history of experiences, to organize account data toward reflecting relationships. This is the intention of the logic within accounting and the intention of the almost magical interpretative usefulness of bilateral account categories to produce a readable communication of transaction effects. Related to this, it will be noted that the left side (whether increase or decrease) is named "debit" and the right side "credit." These technical names are derived from early Latin terms, but a direct translation would not be satisfactory. These two words have become symbols for left and right. No brief terms could adequately express the logical significance of the related elements in a given transaction, or clearly indicate the interpretative significance of a pair of columns in each bilateral account; that is, one column for favorable events and the other for unfavorable events affecting the named account.

NOTE

a. It will be evident that, for each party, the recorded effects speak of his own factual experience. That experience remains a fact for better or worse. Theories about the fluctuating value of money (price-level change) can lead people to think an account record is misleading if it rigidly holds to reporting the size of the transaction, as that indicated by the agreed-upon exchange. It should be convincing, however, that accounting's logical function is to record transaction history. A later price cannot be prior history; hence, it has no logical place in the record of an actual event.

4

ACCOUNTING: A CONTINUUM

Several reasons lend support to the thought that accounting is more of a discipline than a methodology. First, it inter-relates data reflecting motivations and achievements. Second, its techniques are responses to the needs and objectives of business enterprises. Third, its ends and purposes can be regularly tested, by reviewing the reports of the effects on an enterprise of its transactions in the markets. Fourth, its planned actions are disciplined by two factors: (1) the factual pattern of the transactions, determined by the management, of the given business enterprise and (2) the pattern of classification categories necessary for organizing informatively the emerging transaction data.

Because enterprise accounting must serve certain definite functions, its techniques should be considered a special type of language. In accordance with this, accounting must translate the data from enterprise transactions into compact factual messages. It does so by responding to recognizable needs for making transaction data intelligible. In the process, it makes effective use of interrelated account categories to compress extensive experience into meaningful segments. It also makes use of carefully formulated methods of logically analyzing transaction data into informative placement among the account categories. Furthermore, because a business enterprise normally continues in operation over a period of years, accounting serving that enterprise can also be considered a parallel *continuum.*

The rudiments of accounting techniques appeared more than five centuries ago and their influence can be observed in later accounting actions that they foreshadowed. The ends and purposes of early accounting are recognizable, although now expanded, as still capable of sponsoring specific techniques. This expansion has come from each successive era of growth in trade and industry, which has contributed to the technical evolution and service capacity of accounting. As a result, accounting became an historical continuum and it is likely to continue as such. Going forward, each stage of economic development will continue to have its own characteristic needs. These will influence the type of accounting response.

Examining accounting history, one such period could be called a time of revolution in commerce. The crusades had opened contact between Europe and the East. Overland trade grew rapidly as a result. Overseas exploration followed. Soon, joint ventures in foreign trade became popular because of their effectiveness in generating wealth. This period and these actions provided occasions for "responsibility accounting:" a reporting to venture investors of the results of trading activities, as these became definitely known when the assets brought back were liquidated and the proceeds distributed. The first printed textbook on account keeping (Pacioli, 1494) came out of this background.

In Great Britain, another type of responsibility accounting developed in the operation of feudal manor estates of the landed gentry of the fifteenth century. For the most part, the operating activities there were directed toward sustaining the manorial estate and its population. The work was largely agriculture; the necessary activities were subdivided into specialized types of work.

Each type of activity had its own limited responsibilities, activity records, supervisors, workers, and clerks. As to records, the steward of the granary, for example, would have his clerks charge him in the records with the quantity of grain coming from the harvest. As some of the grain passed to the brewmaster, the granary steward would discharge himself for that quantity. Thus, a control over inflow, outflow, and remainder was established for that steward's responsibility. These records reflect an informal example of duality in data movement – an important and very useful aspect of modern account keeping.

Each instance kept their own account. The brewmaster kept his type of in-and-out recording: keeping track of grain that went in and beer that went out. The miller recorded the grain that went in and flour that went out. The baker recorded the flour that went in and the bread that went out. The dining hall steward charged himself with bread, beer, and other goods of this kind, and then discharged himself for the number of meals served to the stated number of people. These facts, and other pertinent data, were assembled annually into a summary report. This report was then tested for accuracy and studied by the nobleman and his council. On this basis, the stewards were commended and a general plan was drawn up regarding the activities for the coming years. Modern audits are more elaborate and modern budgeting are more safely done, but the underlying logic remain largely the same.

Another early development, although not an example of dual entries, was a simple antecedent of the factory system. In connection with the household industry of the day, cloth merchants developed a rudimentary type of departmental accounting. The merchant would buy raw wool from farmers, and then pass the raw material through a sequence of cottage workers for specialized treatment by separate families such as wool washing, carding, yarn spinning, and cloth weaving, finishing, and dying. In the merchant's series of notebooks would be recorded the quantities of wool, yarn, and cloth that passed to each household for its type of service. The wages later paid each family would also be noted. These simple records were ample to provide the merchant with a rough equivalent of process costs and a calculated cost of finished product.

The real beginning of the industrial revolution and the factory system are associated with the nineteenth century British development of power machinery and with increasingly specialized labor skills. The modern and worldwide pattern of industrial production was built on that foundation. Out of this pattern – pressed into being by management's need for detailed information – ultimately came modern cost accounting. This was and is a substantial sub-area of accounting, closely related to managerial control over manufacturing processes and costs.[a]

Continuity of needs has sustained to produce continuity of accounting response up to the present time. New needs have fostered rationally based new techniques. The Industrial Revolution has also continued. In the twentieth century, it has been almost as revolutionary as evolutionary. Specialization in machine use and in worker skills has greatly increased production capabilities. In tangent with these developments, there has also been in increase in the earning power of workers and the returns of investors.

Accounting, so simple in capacity a few centuries earlier, has grown mightily in response to new needs and, in turn, has itself helped industry grow and people to prosper. In the process of developing with the times, accounting has become a complex technology, supported by a logically rational ideology, and serviced by a recognized profession, which we today refer to as public accounting. Together, these achievements have fostered the development of accounting education at the university level.

Developments such as these have not been legislated into being. They have come, as did so many early rudiments of account keeping, from recognition of needs and conditions of the times. The evidence of history suggests the continued appearance of new needs, capable of pressing for new responses in the further development of enterprise accounting.

Some of these developments are already underway. Take, for example, the revolution in managerial accounting techniques, which has emerged from a strongly competitive economy and the capacity for high consumption among the people. Other areas of expansion are the increased investment in corporate securities; the high productivity of capital; and increased managerial skills of exercising judgment.

In each of these areas of business growth, management was closely associated with the creation of enterprise transaction experience. Contemporary conditions, needs for increasingly better decision, and other helpful information has pressed for developments in accounting that could help meet those conditions and needs. As such, the long segmental pattern of accounting history has repeatedly indicated men's response to recognized pressures of the times. At each stage, new managerial problems emerged from newly evident complications. The task of enterprise accounting became progressively more complex. But, fortunately, there were firm foundations, influential ideology, and useful accounting techniques in existence for enterprise accounting to build on.

Evident here was a demonstration of continuity plus elements of responsive growth. This was not traditional continuation of the familiar. The situation repeatedly called for progressively building new structures of techniques, toward meeting new needs, on foundations of tested concepts and proven ways of dealing informatively with transaction data. With that being said, accounting history also indicates that this selectivity-plus-continuity has been liberally supplemented by men's inventiveness. Each period of growth shows contemporary improvement over the past.

The characteristic service capacity of enterprise accounting became so extensive that a special kind of communication methodology had to be developed quite early. The "writing" of that method had to be learned. The extraction of meaning from communicated data also had to be learned. Those developments took place slowly, over a period of centuries, but developments did indeed take place.

A century ago, in the middle 1800s, accounting and financial statements had developed far enough, and contemporary conditions had generated enough pressure, to bring into being statutory audits and a profession of public accounting. That marked definite and practical progress. Before another century had passed, accounting came to be recognized as having characteristics of an intellectual discipline. As a result, educational preparation in the subject was increasingly offered in universities, first at the undergraduate level and later at the graduate level.

As significant as this is of response to pressures of need, it must be said that the full intellectual content of enterprise accounting has still to be clearly recognized. The ideological (theory) side is but slowly being systematically organized into close association with the operative (practical) side. Techniques are now slowly emerging for analytically interpreting a full measure of meaning out of enterprise transaction history, which is already summarized in periodic financial statements. As such, this aspect deserves considerable attention and acceleration.

Slow development in interpretive analyses, in particular, is unfortunate, as understanding has always been a direct objective of accounting. It is already the case that transaction experience must be organized toward revealing the meaning inherent in accumulated experience. Most aspects and developments of accounting as a language of communication have steadily pointed in this direction as well. The ultimate purpose of accounting actions has been, and remains, to facilitate understanding of management achievements. Yet, relatively little constructive effort has been made to help users of accounting communications to learn to read (interpret) the messages inherent in the reported data out of transaction experience.

It remains true that, for many people, accounting reports seem almost as a foreign language. In a limited sense, that is true. Its techniques of communication use relations among figures rather than relations among words. Nevertheless, many users and their advisors have taught themselves some of the techniques of interpretative analyses. There is need for more of that capability. Even with the written word, attempts to communicate in writing will be incomplete so long as reading is not taught along with writing.

A factual history of details of an area of knowledge, such as enterprise accounting, would be voluminous, even if it were limited to the concise mention of chronological events. Such a history is not a prerequisite for knowledge of present-day accounting, as a useful technology, or for preparing to enter the profession of public accounting. Nevertheless, a deeper appreciation of accounting as an ideology and technology could emerge from acquaintance with its historical development. Again, the key here is to view accounting as an historical continuum. A growing awareness that accountancy is an intellectual discipline in its own right could appear from mating, through history, seed-ideas that are still recognizable in accounting of much later date.

Such items from history could lend support for the thought that accountancy includes a great deal of persuasive logic, which is far more effective than mere tradition. It could also lend support to the thought that a good deal of justification is evident in accounting history for considering accountancy as an intellectual discipline of considerable significance for the business world. This, in turn, means that it has significance for all of us, as the activities of the business world now affect everyone.

One of the central features of accounting is its use of categories as basic elements in its "language." In terms of communicative power, account categories have always served to identify and separate different kinds. Thus, they serve much the same basic function as sentences. A sentence groups separate words into an expression of thought. A group of related transaction data combines to express a thought. This is expressed as a total of kinds or a contrast of kinds of two sub-types. As a group of related sentences expands their meaning, so too does a group of related accounts. It is the function of the account-language to express meaning beyond that found within individual transactions. In much the same way, it is the function of verbal language to expand meaning through the combination of words that individually have separate meanings.

In addition, a little thought about enterprise transactions and account categories will indicate that certain moral aspects were and still are involved in creating accounts and recording experience. Both an enterprise and an account are categories. Disregard for their boundaries is a type of deficit. It can make an apparently factual message become fallacious.[b]

The use of duality in the language of accounts is such an important factor for communication that it deserves close examination against an historical background. It was not an accidental characteristic; it has long been evident in accounting use and history. It is worth explaining because, in its modern forms, this feature may provide a clue to some of the inner logic of accounting. It may make clear the existence of persuasive reasons why duality for accounting is not a simple matter of recording, as opposites, an enterprise's inflows and outflows. In fact, such a vast over-simplification cannot be enlightening. Moreover, almost inescapably, it would tend to associate one entry with plus-effect and the comparison entry with minus-effect. Yet, at the heart of accounting's technical language, it is necessary that some accounts shall report plus-effects on the left side, while other accounts shall report plus-effects on the right side.

As a technical term, the word "debit" cannot refer exclusively to plus-effects. To use it as meaning "left" might seem helpful to beginners. But the message conveyed by the position of data in an account does not come from left or right placement. Instead, the meaning of transaction placement must come from the kind of effect that the event has upon one particular account within a group of related accounts. For example, it would strongly interfere with the interpretative reading of an account to have in mind that a debit (left side) entry increased a liability account.

Another reason for believing that this duality is not arbitrary or mechanical lies in the fact that this novel device has proved so highly useful and for so long a time. Duality and oppositeness of effect is characteristics of enterprise transactions whatever the technical forms of the recording language might be. The fact that the "language" of accounting today makes effective use of these characteristics provides one of the most convincing reasons for believing that accounting is indeed a continuum. It was with great discipline, centuries ago, that this rational pattern of data communication formed; by what forces of chance or of deep understanding we do not know.

Such an all-persuasive conception will not make accounting a science. But, surely, it supports a conviction that accounting has recognizable elements of an intellectual discipline. It will be appropriate, therefore, to think about some items of accounting history against the background of these generalizations. Let us consider the records of early Roman debt contracts, which reflect features that may have later influenced recording practices, in the thirteenth century, of members of the guild of merchants of exchange. In so doing, it passed on influence capable of blossoming centuries later into features of modern accounting.

By Roman usage, a loan would be recorded in the form of a verbal statement of contract: "Do you agree to give me (the indicated sum)?" Answer: "I do." In repaying a loan: "You have received (the sum) I promised?" Answer: "I have." This usage continued to medieval merchants of exchange, who often acted as bankers. These merchants operated under strict regulations of their guild, with a prescribed way of making transaction records. As such, when acting as a banker receiving a deposit, the individual would indicate in the record his responsibility thus: "individual A shall have at his pleasure (the amount) this day left with me for safe keeping." The same banker, upon lending to a borrower, would record his new asset thus: "individual F shall give me at my pleasure (the stated amount) this day loaned to him."

As an example of using these verbal forms to create cross-entries, consider that individual A (as above) has assumed the debt owed by individual F. The banker, being made aware of these decisions, would make two entries: (1) "Individual A (the depositor) shall give me (the amount of individual F's loan)," thus reducing A's prior deposit balance and (2) "individual F shall have (the amount of the original loan)," thus reducing the amount of the loan of individual F. Although such transactions were not at first set in the form of bilateral accounts, the written memoranda and the thought processes, nevertheless, reflect a clear duality. Restated in modern bilateral form, those transactions would appear as follows (Littleton, 1933, pp. 51, 90) (Table 8).

Clearly, transaction 3 constitutes a dual entry, which transfers a borrower's debt to a depositor's account (with the latter's permission).

Table 8. Roman Transactions Restated in Modern Bilateral Form.

Individual A (the depositor)	
Trans. 3 "Shall have (amount)"	Trans. 1 "Shall have (amount)"
Individual F (the borrower)	
Trans. 2 "Shall give (amount)"	Trans. 3 "Shall have (amount)"

In effect, individual A has paid or reduced the debt of individual F, which was owed to the banker for a prior loan.

These hypothetical illustrations indicate how recorded duality became necessary in certain situations, even before accounts were bilateral. One party's responsibility would be discharged by the other party's acceptance of that responsibility in his place. Surely, this would have been a relatively frequent occurrence, as their foreign trade and banking activities corresponds with much of the activities in present day. This is not to say that the verbs "shall give" and "shall have" directly became "debit entry" and "credit entry" respectively. Nor do these terms indicate initial dual entry; duality appears only when there is a transfer between personal accounts in the records of the same person, in this case, the banker. Nor were account records of this early set in bilateral form.[c]

It is evident, however, that a depositor would have protection from the responsibility (moral and legal) of the banker to return the sum deposited, even at this early age. Furthermore, the banker, in granting a loan, would have protection in the responsibility (moral and legal) of the borrower to return the amount as agreed. As such, there is a clear continuation of moral responsibility within accounting over many centuries. Accounting is disciplined by this fact toward some of its techniques. Stated differently, accounting is a continuum because a variety of forces, such as moral and logical, have continued effectively within this technology over the centuries.

Certain brief and standardized phrases in the early records served as verbal symbols for the moral and logical responsibility. The parties were morally obligated to live up to the agreed details of a two-party transaction. These responsibilities, especially on the part of a banker, were covered by guild regulation, which effectively worked as the law. It is therefore evident that those bankers served the needs of contemporary society. Hence, the accounts of the day were under the disciplinary influence of contemporary needs, and under the influence of the guild's disciplinary power of enforcing its rules. The general conclusion from this is that, by the tests of relation between usefulness (of the means) and of necessity (the ends), early actions of recording debts in a specific manner proved to be logical means of satisfying recognized needs (i.e., the socially desirable function of banking services, and the moral responsibilities of the parties directly concerned).

The hypothetical illustration above undertakes to adapt earlier ideas somewhat to modern accounting usage. Early account entries and the terminology of that day were such that in them we can now observe some root-characteristics of modern accounting. From their use in verbalized records of bank transactions, the term "shall give" seems on the surface to mean the same as the modern word "debit." Yet, the latter is not a direct translation of the former term. Some of the steps of terminology evolution are indicated below. In several languages, the key words for placement of account data are closest to the basic Latin terms than are the modern terms in English (Table 9).

These present-day technical terms are symbolic simplifications of the early Latin verbs. Those in Italian and French seem clearly to stem from part of the Latin terms, especially the second words, *dare* and *havere*. The German term, *soll*, is a direct equivalent of shall in the Latin *debent-dare*; the German, *haben*, is a direct equivalent of the second word, *havere*, in the Latin phrase, *debent-havere*. These technical words of accounting originated in the phraseology of sentences speaking of personal debts. Eventually, they lost their true linguistic meaning and became mere symbols referring to the left and right side of bilateral accounts.

It is noticeable that the English usage did not follow the lead of continental terminology, which was more or less tied to give and have. The English began to use *debiteur* (one who owes) and *crediteur* (one who trusts). Refer again to the previous examples of a banker's record of a deposit. His entry says that individual A shall have. In effect, this says that the banker owes individual A the sum deposited. The banker's record of a

Table 9. The Evolution of Accounting Terminology.

"Shall give" is close to a literal translation of Latin: debent dare		
"Shall have" is close to a literal translation of Latin: debent havere		
Present day technical terms are:		
Italian:	dare	Avere
French:	do it	Avoir
German:	soll	haben
English:	debit	credit

loan to individual F indicates that he shall give. In effect, this says that the banker trusts individual F to repay the loan. In English usage, one who owes is called *debiteur*; one who trusts is called *crediteur*. This brings terminology closer to the debit and credit terminology of today.

Even considering these development, there are records that appear to indicate terms that are still closer to present usage. In particular, certain Latin terminology may provide a more fundamental foundation for the terms debit and credit as they are now used. In an account from 1396, the term "should give" appears on the left side. At that point, there is added a contra reference named *scriptos-in-credit*. This is written in the credit side of the account. In the right column, of the same ledger account, is a similar verbal formulation using, first, the term "should have," then referring to the contra entry of the item in another account as *scriptos-in-debito*. Here, then, the terms are very close to the modern spelling of debit and credit. In other accounts, illustrated from a century later, are the terms *debitere* and *creditere* (Littleton, 1933, pp. 89–90, 103).

At first, a variety of terms appeared and these were used differently in several languages. After the terms were increasingly used in conversations, very early records began to be stated in some form mimicking verbal communication. As such, one of the most significant historical developments has been the gradual conversion of verbal language into a symbol language of placement of data in bilateral categories. The old terms "shall give" and "shall have" now seem quite lacking in power to signal the placement of transaction data. So too, for the uninitiated, are the terms debit and credit. Yet, the actions signaled by both the old and the new are the same: data is placed in informative ways to make readable the transaction's effects on the enterprise. In effect, the word-symbols, both old and new, came to be recognized as clues to specific placement of data in a pre-arranged pattern of data groups.

That pattern of data groups would be so planned as to compress a volume of transaction experience. Accounts gradually became "tools" for conveying meaning, as a typewriter is a tool for conveying meaning by printing words. This is to say that, if one is composing directly by use of a typewriter, one is contributing mentally and manually to the communication of thought. From this, it follows that, to communicate, one must know the language and the operation of the machine. To absorb the meaning of the message, the receiver must be able to read the language.

Dictionary definitions of debit and credit cannot make clear the meaning these terms must carry to one who undertakes to record the effects on the enterprise of its transactions. It may seem significant to beginners that debits always enter the left side of accounts and that credits enter on the right. Yet, even the beginner must soon learn that this characteristic does not cue the mental analysis of transaction effect. The real cue lies (1) in recognizing the kind of effects the event has on the enterprise and (2) knowing the unchanging pattern of accounts. Some accounts report favorable effects on the left, whereas other accounts report this on the right. Some accounts report unfavorable effects on the left, whereas other accounts report this on the right.

Confusing as this may seem when verbally stated, the arrangement of plus and minus sides of accounts has a convincing logic. It is based on a few quite convincing concepts. Assets are properties useful to the enterprise function. As such, an increase of assets is favorable to the enterprise and a decrease of assets is unfavorable. Hence, the transaction placement will be a plus for debit and a minus for credit. Liabilities, on the other hand, are unfavorable if increased and favorable if decreased. Hence, the transaction placement will be minus for debit and plus for credit. Note how the debit (plus) in one account can be a credit (plus) in the other. This is logical: some increases in assets will have to come from increases in liabilities. To benefit from the advantage of holding the asset, one most suffer the contra disadvantage.

It is the function of management to make such effective use of the increased asset that it justifies also holding the disadvantage, in this case a liability. As such, the management function stands behind the accounting function. Account data must speak of management actions, but accounting has no responsibility for good or bad judgment.

From the accounts, management will be able to see the effects of his judgment decision. It is the function of accounting to make this kind of review possible. This is the reason the plus and minus pattern of accounts can serve an important purpose in a persuasively logical way. This is also the reason bilateral accounts have, almost imperceptible, become an effective tool for effective thinking. This thinking is applied to building a readable record of transaction experience, which will be useful to the process of interpreting significant meaning out of the organized record of transaction effect.

Returning to the term "continuum," which was used earlier, the point is that the present rises on foundations that are still visible when looking into the past. The result is that – in order fully to appreciate the present capabilities of enterprise accounting – it will be useful to gain some insight into the reasons, needs, and the kinds of pressures that led men to innovate the basic techniques of enterprise accounting. In this review, it would also be helpful to note the force of new needs and continuing pressures similar to those of long ago.

Roman verbal memoranda of debts came from the need to know who, where, and how much. The medieval merchants of exchange, on the other hand, needed to know which borrowers owed the bank and what amounts. They also needed to know how much that was owed to what depositor. These transaction types foreshadowed modern duality of data and bilateral accounts. The records were made in response to specific needs on the part of bankers, borrowers, and depositors. Back of those records – as are back of account records today – were specific actions and responsibilities. Within those actions and records, there were aspects of moral pressure and methodical logic.

Even in very early accounting, there are two indications of basic duality that remain to this day: two parties to each transaction and two effects of a transaction on each party. Although the records of the bankers reveals only his point of view, the depositor, if he too keeps accounts, will wish to record a transaction favorable to himself (i.e., a resource he can use later). If he were analytically minded, he would realize that the transaction had an unfavorable effect as well in that he now has less money close at hand. Of course, at that time, it is unlikely that dual entries were recorded in the records of the depositor.

One of the signs of evolutionary development can be noted whenever historical evidence shows recognition, by both transaction parties, of the dual effects on their affairs of every transaction. Another sign can be noted whenever – now or long ago – oppositeness of asset accounts and liability accounts was recognized; and whenever oppositeness of expense and revenue accounts was clearly indicated. It was a very considerable step forward, when accounting procedure called for (1) a summary transfer of asset and liability account balances to a balance account and (2) a transfer from a profit-and-loss account to the balance account of the net remainder, derived from off-setting expenses and revenues.

Clearly, duality, persistently used, adds greatly to the readability of prior transaction experience, organized in the form of summary reports faithful to this key concept of logical duality. There is a duality between the parties to the transactions; the transaction effects on an enterprise; and in the entries in two accounts. These dualities lead to the final duality of two major data summaries: the balance sheet and earnings sheet (income statement). Despite of this, it is doubtful that "duality" was deliberately invented. No doubt, its basic significance was only gradually recognized, and yet it remains an enlightening key aspect of enterprise accounting.

An important collateral aspect of duality is that of responsibility. Throughout accounting history, this factor has exercised a guiding influence. Fidelity to trust is a definite force in men's actions. Hence, it is understandable that accounting should be designed and used to promote the moral principle of fidelity to trust. It is also understandable that accounting should help make fidelity readable from organized data from transaction experience.

Responsibility reports by functional stewards, on the British landed estates, foreshadowed the later form of reports for an executor and those for a company in receivership or liquidation. British joint ventures in foreign trade, patterned after much earlier ventures, also needed a type of responsibility accounting. Venture personnel were, in effect, managers of a trading expedition. As such, they had several responsibilities: effective trading; the ultimate liquidation of the venture; and the distribution of the proceeds among the investors concerned. We may consider this as foreshadowing the separation of investors and management, which is so characteristic today.

Responsibility accounting continued to evolve. Conditions in the early 1800s sponsored reactions in England, which strongly influenced the beginnings of the profession of public accounting. The law presently required a bankrupt person to file his accounting data with the court. Included was a "statement of affairs." Its purpose was to distinguish secured and unsecured creditors; to report on receivables as good, doubtful, or bad; and to report on the available properties. This came about because the courts desired to search out "modes of deception" and to "read the real situation of the company."

These developments brought questions of business morals and truthful accounts to the forefront. Yet, British developments went further. In the middle 1800s, statutes required companies to make periodic accounting reports to shareholders. But the strongest emphasis was the responsibility delegated to company directors; that is, the keeping of accounts and the yearly reporting to shareholders on the financial status of the company.

These developments in England indicate progress toward increased responsibility accounting. Statutes were designed to prevent further examples of irresponsibility in the formation of companies and fraudulent speculation in company shares. The actions prohibited were considered as being against the public interest. Contemporary conditions indicated a need for more soundly conceived business enterprises and better publicity of company accounts. Here, again, recognized needs and contemporary conditions fostered improvements in accountings. The emphasis was shifting toward adequate reporting, as the technical language of duality of transaction effects and bilateral accounts had now become firmly established. Its service capacity was now broadened.

Although knowledgeable accountants had been offering their services for some time in connection with technical accounting problems, the company regulatory statutes sharply identified an important public service that only expert accountants could perform. The first formal organization of public accountants appeared in Scotland (1854) before the Companies Acts of the 1860s. The comparable English organization was formed in 1870.[1] These two organizations foreshadowed the later development of professional organizations of accountants in the United States.

From these events, it is evident that the need for responsibility and reduction of irresponsibility was pressing accounting toward continued development. This involved both an improved technology and the rise of the public interest as a concern in society. This kind of recognition plainly reflects the capability for evolutionary growth inherent in soundly based and logically constructed technology.

From its early days, accounting was dedicated to the pragmatic function of making transaction effects on an enterprise reviewable in the interest of better decisions in the future. Now, the moral aspect of honest transactions, accounts, and reports was being strongly emphasized. It is a characteristic of accounting that morality had long been noticeably associated with its technical actions. This reality, however, has not always shown on the surface and dishonest data can still be found in ledger accounts when dishonest men attempt to conceal the truth. There may still be those who today remain skeptical about the propriety of charging ledger accounts or items in the financial statements so they can readjust past transactions into present prices. Either way, the former development sponsored the development of the profession of public accounting.

Returning to the title of this manuscript, accounting is a continuum precisely because it has deep roots in the past. Many of its typical actions and uses have distant ancestors; much of the basic logic of its language still works its interpretative magic. For example, before the industrial revolution, there was the wool merchant who employed his home crafts to produce cloth. The cottage industry then eventually became the factory system. His simple memorandum notebooks, which recorded wages paid to each family and the amount of production of those involved, had eventually grown into cost accounting. This phase of accounting language has now become an indispensable part of the management function in making decisions for the enterprise. These decisions, in turn, continue to be influenced by the needs and conditions of the times.

It is highly significant of the nature of enterprise accounting that the foundations of its technical capacity were strong enough, in its basic logic, to associate useful means and recognized needs. These meant, in turn, that these foundations could sustain the technical growth later necessary to meet new needs and conditions. As such, there was a built-in capability to develop appropriate responses as later needs appeared.

This brings me to the conclusion. Accounting was never completed; and it is not complete now. We cannot pinpoint the spots in its structural service capacity that may prove inadequate at some point in the future. With that being said, and viewed in a historical perspective, we may face the future with confidence. This is so because accounting is not like a tall building, which have been long under construction and now functioning very well. It is more like a giant redwood tree, centuries old and still growing. Like those magnificent trees, accounting is also a *continuum*: rooted deeply in the past; formed by those contacts with that past; and ever growing in capacity to serve its present and future function. Perhaps, someday, it will be considered a man-made marvel.

NOTES

1. Littleton is referring to what is today known as the Institute of Chartered Accountants of Scotland (ICAS) and the Institute of Chartered Accountants in England and Wales (ICAEW).

a. A book published in 1817 included an early example of cost analysis of labor and material costs in carriages. These costs were listed by crafts and were allocated among the several product units. This analysis afforded the basis for several journal entries. These charged the warehouse with total costs. Upon sale of the carriages, the warehouse was discharged for unit cost, and the purchaser was charged for the sale price. Profit and loss was charged for a loss on one sale, and discharged for the profit on other sales (Littleton, 1933, p. 323).

b. Interpretative adjustment of properly established account data already in an account, due to change in the purchasing power of the dollar since that date, would be a type of violation of a category boundary. The reason for this is that an entry expresses an actual transaction experience as of a specific date. The facts, digits, and record are in agreement at the time. Later prices can have no direct effect on previously established facts. At best, an evident later rise in price of similar items can have only interpretative significance as for the present. This represents collateral information; it is not a substitute for earlier facts.

c. An English accounting entry in 1522 used somewhat similar phrases: "Oweth to give" (referring to a person) and "Oweth to have" (referring to cloth sold) (Littleton & Yamey, 1956, p. 191).

5

THOUGHTS ON HISTORY AND THEORY

On the fly leaf of the 1933 edition of *Accounting Evolution to 1990*, there is a brief quotation from an early German author. In translation, it reads: "One who would probe deeply into an area of knowledge, must also become acquainted with its history." Because history serves this purpose of deepening knowledge, it should be considered as more than a chronology of events. In fact, an understanding of the pressures back of historical developments can be more significant than the actual events.

In thinking of history, it can also be helpful to realize that change is a continuing element. There will always be need for re-examination of prior motives, and for renovation of contemporary methods. Because this is true, a knowledge of history can create a perspective that is helpful in facing the present. And knowledge of trends in contemporary developments can similarly provide perspective in aid of decisions toward the future.

A good starting point for the present discussion is that accounting is still developing. In the book referred to above is this statement: "Accounting at this time [1933] may be in the midst of its greatest moment." Even casual observation of later years can produce persuasive confirmation that significant progress is continuing. Accounting still provides glimpses into the intermingling of economic forces and social growth along with businessmen's plans, achievements, and failures to accomplish.

Each stage of accounting history has been prologue to later evolutionary developments. Hence, we can well believe that men who built upward from pre-existing foundations have created the methodology and the ideology of today's accounting. Their efforts have been effective because they continued whatever was judged as still appropriate. Likewise, their efforts were also effective because their actions innovated change in areas where such a change was warranted and supported by convincing reasons. As a result, the service capacity of accountancy has reflected a continuing evolutionary growth.

I hope that historical developments beyond the year 1933 will be found to reflect developments even more significant than those developments of earlier years. Ideally, convincing reasons will be found that can explain why some early techniques have persisted in some areas, whereas new techniques have been required in other areas. Such reasons can be more enlightening than could descriptions of methods. This is so because techniques only exist for specific reasons, whereas only the purposes laying underneath can generate methods judged adequate to service those objectives.

It is evident from history that our technological language represented, as it still represents, an analytical integration of two social factors: (1) a business enterprise operating as an active entity and (2) a management serving as the guiding mind of that organizational entity. From the viewpoint of accountancy, the initial result of this union was, and is, the creation of appropriate enterprise transaction experience. That experience continues to provide the data for enterprise accounts. Furthermore, the continuity of this aspect of accountancy provides evidence of the vitality of that union and of those data. The basic reason back of that continuity can be noted in this fact: business decisions need to be rested, as far as possible, on knowledge of the results of prior decision-actions.

Another example of historical continuity is the persistent use of data categories set in bilateral form. The service capacity of this particular technique is still undiminished, even in this day of the computer. And there are convincing reason why this is true. Bilateral accounts would be inadequately explained if they existed only to tabulate inflow and outflow (input and output). Instead, another and more significant aspect is found in the natural characteristic of every completed transaction. Each item of transaction experience will consist of a favorable effect and an unfavorable effect on the given enterprise.

The importance of the analytical study of such effects will need no explanation. However, one technical aspect should be noted. The favorable effects are not all increases and the unfavorable effects are not all deductions. The significance of the technical terms "debit" and "credit" comes from the indicated natural characteristics of transactions, and not from dictionary definitions of the terms or from their meaning in the original Latin.

The basic function of the rather simple techniques of transaction analysis is that of opening the data flowing from transaction experience to later interpretative analysis. Moreover, that analytical organization of data is designed to help men rest future decisions on knowledge of the results of prior decisions. Visible within this function is another deeply rooted characteristic of accounting. It is the built-in interpretative significance of the inter-relation between real and nominal accounts. The importance of this close tie between groups of accounts was only slowly recognized, although the relationship had existed from early years. In fact, appraising that relationship was a part of the early development of accounting theory.

These are some of the basic characteristics of accounting technology. Perhaps they are sufficiently fundamental to lie close to the heart of accounting as an intellectual discipline. The main reason for this would be that prior transaction experience – the history of important decisions – of a given enterprise is made intelligible by the techniques of accounting action.

It is also necessary to consider this fact: back of the simple elements of methodology, and their motivations, are recognizable objectives. Yet, those objectives are not fully served by the organization of transaction data alone. Even the most satisfactory organization of data still needs to be intelligently interpreted, in order that men may benefit from the message. John Ciardi's comment is quite appropriate in this connection:

> Intelligence cannot consist in masses of factual data. It comes from seeing essential likenesses and essential differences, and from relating them, allowing for differences within likenesses and likenesses within differences.[1]

Decisions by management and by investors are strongly influenced, but not wholly determined, by knowledge of enterprise transaction history, which is organized in the accounts. This data need to be carefully studied and interpretatively analyzed against a background of contemporary economic conditions.

Accountancy is more than a data-marshaling methodology; it is more than the vehicle of an established profession. It is an intellectual discipline. The reason for this is clear. Its methods are what they are because, in that form, they can serve recognized objectives. Some of these methods have survived throughout centuries of use. They have continued to gain strength from a continuing capacity to serve effectively. They have been, and still are, able to provide piers upon which rest technical structures capable of appropriately serving specific intellectual needs, such as providing information as to the results of prior decision-actions.

We shall always need techniques, and these must be carefully designed and intelligently used. Accountancy will also always need theory to provide supporting explanations.[a] This is so because the reasons underlying and justifying action types, or justifying changes therein, are not evident on the surface of the actions themselves. Instead, it is a function of theory to carry thought toward reasons beneath the surface.

Accounting history should be more than a sequential narrative of growth. It should also seek to reach into the relations of that subject matter with the needs of the times. This suggestion is allied with interpretation of meaning by analysis of presented account data. Detecting and explaining relations among historical events is a type of interpretation from analysis.

With this in mind, neither accounting history nor a deductive approach to accounting ideology can demonstrate that accountancy has qualities like those of science. Being a combination of analytical technology and stimulating intellectual discipline, its achievements have come out of experience and processes of induction. This is to say that its achievements have come out of evolutionary developments in the effort effectively to serve certain, but not all, informational needs of businessmen.

The pressures of those needs have generated reliable and relevant technical means for converting transactions, made in the markets, into needed account data. Those means, as they were refined, were able to progressively improve and broaden the usefulness of the data of enterprise transaction history. As a result, various parties, with an interest in that history, are aided in their future decisions. Out of this kind of service comes a growing awareness of the capabilities of enterprise accounting. It seems important, therefore, that accounting theory and history should combine forces to clarify the factors that make account data helpfully informative. But what kinds of factors help make accounting informative? Several types come to mind:

1. The initial reason that prompted the design of suitable techniques for marshaling transaction experience as well as information about the size and characteristics of those originating events;
2. The concept of interrelated account categories, and evidence supporting the dependability of those categories and the data therein; and
3. Techniques appropriate for interpreting decision-useful meaning out of movements among account data over time.

Factors such as these give to account data their capacity for making understandable the achievements of the arrangement of a given enterprise.

It is to be noted that the verbalization of factor two is not complete; the phrasing seems to imply that ledger accounts are the only categories involved. It is necessary also to consider fiscal periods as analytical categories. Just as data move between accounts, some account data move over several fiscal periods: that is, their service capability extends over a series of fiscal periods. Hence, accounting techniques must provide for orderly and rational apportionment of some kinds of transaction data over an extended service life of some assets.

Many, perhaps most, controversial aspects of accounting theory originate in this necessity. By spreading original data systematically over a succession of periods, accounting makes an important contribution to data user's understanding of management's achievements. This kind of technical service is indispensable to that kind of objective. And this will be true regardless of whatever ideological problems or controversies the apportionment efforts may generate.

It has been said of science that its interpretative side seeks to relate available data to a logical framework of concepts. We note that the accounting literature today is often concerned about "principles" instead. Nonetheless, the above phrase, "framework of concepts," does not seem to identify with the nature of "principles," even when that word is modified by the objective "logical." This being the case, I suspect that the quoted thought would do well being accepted for use in the accounting literature, although this technical discipline lacks some of the characteristics of a science.

Their relations with a framework of concepts must discipline account data. Accountancy could therefore benefit from an enlarged framework of basic concepts. For example, the concepts inherent in specific bilateral accounts could be clarified beyond a simple definition of each account. The concepts that underlie inter-account relations should themselves also be integrated. Similarly, inter-account relations dictate the arrangement of data in periodic financial statements. This tends to activate the communication function of accounting.

Together with a framework of interrelated concepts, another framework of interrelated techniques could prove very useful. For example, it should be enlightening to examine, critically, familiar techniques in the light of the neighboring framework of guiding concepts.

This brings the argument back to the periodic allocation of original transaction data as an aspect of marshaling account data. Fragmentation and reassembly is involved, and these actions lack clear-cut concepts comparable to those characteristic of transaction analysis. In fact, periodic apportionment becomes an area of controversy largely because of the inadequate ideology as to the reasons and the limitations that should play a guiding role. As such, the situation may call for examination of differences within likenesses, and likenesses within differences. It could be helpful in such a situation to resort to induction; that is, reasoning from the chief problems of communication (the ends) towards a search for the most appropriate techniques capable of producing the best results.

Several questions now emerge. How far should individual desire or judgment, within a given enterprise, be free to determine the extent and timing of data fragmentation among fiscal periods? For example, what degree of flexibility is given in a decision about the potential life span of a specific long-lived asset? Should guidelines be provided from a party outside of the enterprise? Would it be more beneficial to use a consensus within a specific line of business? Other alternatives would be the use of tax regulation, congressional action, or some standard set by a governmental commission.

If it seems that these accounting actions should, preferably, be determined by people closely identified with a given enterprise, would those actions always be expedient and rationally defensible? Would they be completely determined internally or in consultation with professional accountants of broad experience? Should the chosen time-span be a matter of practical and pragmatic judgment? Could the time-span be determined against a structural pattern of rational ideology and interrelated persuasive concepts? Which of these proposals could be implemented? From these questions, it must be clear that a relevant, rational, and interrelated ideology has not yet been formulated. It must also be clear that we have too few basic concepts, which have been uncovered and coordinated into a coherent body of necessary doctrine, to meet pressing needs.

An examination of the early history of accountancy cannot meet the needs described above, but some useful clues as to fundamentals can be found there. More clues could then become available from ideological research among the materials of the twentieth century, and from imaginative research into the nature and service-function of accounting theory. Perhaps we should therefore aspire to improve accountancy as an intellectual discipline—one deeply committed to making the results of managerial decision-actions increasingly understandable and open to penetration beneath masses of factual data in search of the meaning embodied in prior transaction experience.

It is particularly significant for accountancy that its history and theory are so closely related. History is concerned with needs pressing for responses in the form of accounting actions; theory is concerned with the logical relations between the desirable ends (needs) and the means (responses) that are capable of approximately achieving those objectives.

It is entirely reasonable to view enterprise accounting as a complex means toward achieving rational ends. Indeed, we may confidently believe that the accounting function is that of informatively organizing and faithfully reporting the effects all items of transaction experience have on the given enterprise. Such a function (objective) could be explained, justified, and strengthened by analyzing the reasons for an evident relation between

(1) ideas about needs for reviewable data from transaction history and (2) ideas about satisfactory responses to those needs in the form of accounting technical actions. This is the relation between ends and means. A theory of this kind could be supported by an examination of the rationale behind the desirability of the needs and of the appropriateness of the responding accounting actions.

Categories are part of the framework within which accounting actions take place. This comes from a clear and desirable need for carefully organized data from transaction-experience. Long use has demonstrated that account categories proved to be an appropriate response. Moreover, it is now clear that accounts include characteristics not evident in simpler categories, which has served well in statistical groupings of related items.

In fact, the bilateral form of account categories is a unique feature of accounting. It is now essential to the exercise of the experience reporting function of the system. Accounts seem specially designed for collating, in separate categories, logically related elements of transaction experience. These elements are related to the named account but express opposite effects on the enterprise. The service rendered (the objective), by this technical aspect, is that of making reviewable a remainder, which expresses the net results of contrasting favorable and unfavorable effects in a certain limited area of transaction experience.

It is worth noting that the bilateral form of accounts has proved to be a very appropriate response to recognized needs. Men gradually came to recognize (1) that duality characterized all negotiated transactions and (2) that producing favorable effects on the enterprise necessitated parallel unfavorable effects. The specific terms used to describe these aspects came even later, although the aspects were always inherent in transactions in the markets. If it were otherwise, desired exchanges would not have taken place. Nonetheless, the bilateral characteristic of an account may initially have appeared almost accidentally, as when a borrower from a banker agreed with a depositor that the debt of one should be set off against the recorded deposit balance of the other party. The decisions of these two parties created a need to change the records; the banker's recording action was an effective accounting response. As such, the accounting records were disciplined by recognized and rational needs.

A business enterprise is itself the initial identification category for accounting. Only data clearly relevant to that specific enterprise is admissible to its accounts. Any other data would produce false classification. As such, the concept of enterprise entity is a concept of data boundary. A corollary of this proposition is this: it would be a false classification of the actual transaction experience of the given enterprise if a recorded transaction were later restated at a price different from the original amount.

The fiscal period, usually one year, should be considered another category whose boundaries should be closely respected. Distortion of the recorded message, the actual experience, would result from indefensible assignment of experience data among several fiscal periods. Difficult as it might be to apportion asset investments, which have a long service life, a neglect to do so would produce results that are even more questionable.

In a similar way, each account has definite boundaries. It is a violation of a boundary (a distortion of meaning), if an entry is unfaithful to the name and limitations of the specific account. It is also a violation of a boundary if an item is placed on the wrong side of the proper account. The reason for this is that each side of an account has a specific reporting function. Moreover, each side of an account has its own limitation as to admissible data. Failure to respect that internal boundary can distort the record.

The bilateral account is not so much a result of evolution as it is a product of rational thought, almost unconsciously made effective. It seems to be an excellent example of men's mental reaction to contemporary conditions, and their gradual reactions to recognized needs for renewing and understanding the related results of transaction experience.

Pressures from complex economic activities disciplined men's ingenuity toward information systems capable of making their actions and commitments reviewable after the events. In other words, men are disciplined toward better methods when their intelligence recognizes a need to be met. As a system of recording transaction experience develops, it gradually becomes a disciplined way of dealing informatively with accumulating transaction experience. The result is that men were disciplined by need long ago, and that the story is made readable by accounting history. And, of course, men continue to be disciplined by recognized pressures. In fact, the evidence of history strongly supports the conviction that improved ways of responding to conditions are always the results of disciplining factors.

Modern accounting presents characteristic structural features, having deep roots in the distant past. Those features were, and still are, astonishingly effective means to very desirable ends. The bilateral account is a good example of a logical means to desirable, perhaps necessary, end. Technical features such as those were not invented outright in the form we use today. They slowly grew from a few fertile seeds. Some of these origins can now be identified in modern techniques. It should also be clear that the minds of many men, in many centuries, and in different lands, have nurtured rudimentary elements into a logically structured and widely useful communication technology.

Even though evidence is strong that modern accounting grew out of quite simple recording actions, it is easy to be convinced that accounting today is largely supported by accepted customs that are open to change by consensus. Yet, the customary often has more support than that of age. The rationale of a custom should be that its use provides for convincing results. The point is that a change away from the customary will need support from more than current dissatisfaction. Furthermore, both acceptance and change need to be supported by convincing reasons, compelling concepts, and persuasive logic.

It is an important function of accounting theory and of research in theory to seek out the rationale of customary practices. This entails the weighting of the degree of weakness, if any, and the uncovering reasons supporting change. The desirability of expected results of the change needs also to be considered carefully. In effect, this calls for the use of pragmatic logic in aid of assessing rational progress.

The use of pragmatic logic is justified because accounting actions are means that should be sponsored by convincing and compelling reasons. This kind of relationship suggests that a certain amount of logic always influences accounting actions, and, to that extent, tends to restrain expediency.[b] The result is that it should be a recognized part of the function of accounting theory to clarify logical relations. From this, it follows that, in viewing the historical development of accounting, the results flowing from typical accounting actions should be open to at least two questions: (1) as to the appropriateness of the chosen action in view of the reason for its being and (2) as to the desirability or necessity of achieving the apparent end in view.

Questions such as these ask for close and disciplined thinking. Yet, at times, the real significance of the relation of ends and means seems to have been avoided by accepting the phrase that "the end justifies the means." Too often this thought is treated as if it meant "an urgent need to achieve will excuse any means to that end." Thus, a doctrine of expediency has ensued. The problem is that, if expediency alone determines the type of action pursued, this may distort the proper relation of action and purpose. What is worse, if the results of such distortion are accepted without question, this will deny the significance of convincing logic. Instead, an end must be clearly desirable to be justifiable; and only a justifiable purpose invites honest search for appropriate means. A mean that fits this situation justifies its choice solely by the adequacy of the service rendered.

Much of the force of logic, observable in the early aspects of accounting actions, can still support modern action types. Moreover, recognition of logic's persuasiveness can be helpful to the formation of basic concepts capable of illuminating the service capacity of our technological discipline. It is therefore likely that a wise and defensible choice of basic concepts can accomplish much to raise accounting above resort to the expedient, convenient, and traditional. And, again, it is likely that these basic concepts must rest on convincing logical grounds. Perhaps many of such concepts will be more closely related to objectives and limitations than directly to ways and means. This is a natural expectation; ends and objectives exert strong influence on the choice of appropriate ways and means.

Influence of this kind need to be explored and understood. Basic and compelling concepts are building blocks of ideology. Out of these ideas come techniques. Some concepts will point to inclusions; others will direct exclusions. Both types of concepts, being supported by logic and ethics, can improve the capability of account data to communicate understanding of the achievements of enterprise management.

It has been said that "ethics is a condition of the world, like logic." Perhaps accounting could also be considered a necessary condition of the business world. To achieve this status, accounting already makes effective use of both ethics and logic. Even in accounting's early development, the constellation of ends, which were clearly desirable, and means, which were clearly appropriate, was a logical relationship. For example, in the early records of loans and deposits, the words "shall give" and "shall have" were written. This represented an early form of the recognition of moral responsibility to repay.

There also are effective ideas of right and wrong in modern accounting. There are unethical and false entries as well as adjustments of properly established and factual account data. With that being said, logical rationality is still often evident in the modern relationship between accounting ends and the means employed. This reflects the influence of firm concepts about sound reasoning as to alternative ideas, method, and possibilities.

As the above example illustrates, ancestors of present day accounting ethics and logic can be noted in the history of the discipline. A part of the service of that history is that it can reveal the deep roots of these two aspects of enterprise accounting. The seeds from those roots still influence accounting standard toward faithfully adhering to the transaction experience of the given business enterprise for its communication materials.

Accounting techniques have long been disciplined by the logic of appropriate ends and means. Those techniques have moral connotations: each accounting action, in order to justify its purpose, must be truth-oriented and truth-reflecting. With this in mind, it is still the case that the messages inherent in even the most truthful account data will need to be interpreted. Nonetheless, interpretation is not something entered into an account; it must be an action separate from the communicated transaction-experience.

A distinction needs to be made here. A carefully planned arrangement of account data into financial statements is an aid to interpretation rather than being itself interpretation of meaning. Economic conditions may change after prior transaction facts have been recorded in the accounts. This fact may influence the current significance of the experience, but it could not justify changing the recorded transaction history of an enterprise. The result is that truth, for accounting, is one part *economics* in that it is indicated by real transactions in the markets between the given enterprise and other independent parties. At the same time, truth for accounting is also one part *statistics*; that is, under the control of clear concepts of the functions and limitations of each of its several types of classification categories.

The specific enterprise entity is itself the most basic category. Transactions to which the given enterprise is not a party cannot provide truthful events for its records. It is also essential to standards of morality (truthful reporting) that subsequent transaction experience should not be used to restate prior transaction experience. This is so because false classification will always lack a moral basis. This concept is part of the natural logic and technical discipline that provide foundations for the service capacity of enterprise accounting.

Enterprise accounting deserves to be considered a discipline because, within the area of its reporting function and the boundaries of its logic, this technology can make moral standards directly useful. The dependence of third parties on factual reports is a vital aspect of accounting morality. Those parties need to judge the achievement of management based on account information. This places direct moral responsibility upon the accounting discipline and upon knowledgeable accountants.

The significance accounting standards have for professional accountants are clear. The basic data must be the result of the transaction experience of the given enterprise. Auditing will test this much. Certified financial statements are constructed from tested transaction data. The user of the financial statements can trust certified statements to reflect those standards. With this in mind, even the most truthful reports must be closely studied for meaning. The user alone will supply the interpretation of meaning. He will derive it from his analysis and interpretation of the significance of changes in the amounts recorded in the accounts, from one year to the next and of shifts in proportions between related data. Stated in this way, it can hardly be considered a function of enterprise accounting to interpret meaning from the raw data, which has different significance depending on the reader of the financial information.

Interpretation will call up its own type of techniques for studying data movements, patterns of change, and interrelations among observed movements. Fortunately, many of the characteristics of accounts can be of assistance. For example, the logical plus-and-minus relation among accounts is inherent in the nature of different transactions (favorable and unfavorable effects). In interpretative analysis, the rates of change in the accumulation of data on opposite sides of an account will also have more analytical significance than changes in the account balance. Moreover, the data on one side of some accounts will also appear on the opposite side of other accounts where the rate of change may have a different significance. Furthermore, those differing rates of change may have interpretative significance in comparisons to each other, which might not be noted from the study of each change in isolation.

Certain generalizations may be useful at this point. Throughout the growth of accounting and management, after the start of the industrial revolution, there was one significant feature of accounting that was not evident in the earlier days. This was the effect that periodicity of reporting has had on accounting ideology. It was no longer sufficient to report simply on a person's responsibility, as in the management accounting systems of the English manorial estates. Responsibilities were still involved in modern business, but it was instead concentrated on the responsibility of effective management controls of operations. The result meant that certain recognizable new pressures, not evident in earlier history, generated needs for new responses. Some of these pressures can be listed:

1. Enterprises experienced new continuity of existence and actions.
2. Prior transaction experience needed increasingly prompt review.
3. Many types of assets made their contribution only gradually.
4. Certain new response types emerged from new needs.
5. A fiscal period came to be considered an interpretative category.
6. Long-lived asset-cost needed to be carefully allocated over a number of fiscal periods.

The sum of these pressures meant that asset-cost allocations became a significant element in management control decisions. It called for sharp assignment of costs among product output units. The responses emerging from new needs also indirectly exposed the undesirability of careless apportionments. No apportionment at all would produce distortion of the reported costs of securing enterprise revenue. This was so because inaction would leave intact the initial cost of an asset, although it had given up some of its production capacity. On the other hand, immediate write-off of full cost of equipment would have an irrational effect (1) on the analytical comparison of company assets and liabilities and (2) on the calculation of effort-costs used to produce the revenue reported in other accounts.

No long background of history is yet available to provide clues to the "guidelines" supporting apportionment decisions. Yet, actions of this importance need to be rationally supported. The rationale of periodic apportionment should be convincingly logical; and it should be clearly defensible from resting on persuasive reasons. This kind of firm foundation would serve management decisions well.

There seems to be no precedents in early accounting history for the present variety of methods of apportioning costs among successive fiscal periods. That variety seems mostly to indicate men's increased capacity to conceive a variety of sums for achieving a definable end. Yet, beneath different possibilities, some rational bases must exist in aid of choosing among conceivable alternatives. Fertility of ideas may be outrunning powers of discriminating judgment and search for fundamentals. Inventory cost allocation to periods is one such example.

Inventory is, usually, an investment in the cost of assets expected to be sold to customers. The price of the units offered for sale is determined by management's experienced judgment of what would probably appeal to buyers. Management is free to raise the offered price, if demand justifies it, or to decrease the price, if demand makes this advisable. The calculated profit for the year would be affected accordingly – on the revenue side by price and on the expense side by the known acquisition cost of the goods sold. However, the inventory still available at the year-end would not have been affected by changes in price tags or logically affected by contemporary replacement prices.

Convincing accounting treatment here does not rest on assumptions or on selling price policy. The residual investment in inventory is still what it was; that is, the original exchange-priced transaction experience. The supporting reason should be fidelity to prior and actual transaction-experience in the markets, which is an essential aspect of the accounting language.

"Cost-or-market" and "last in-first out" are terms that symbolize a repricing of previously consummated factual experience. These actions are then directed to depart from the historical truth. These departures cannot be considered to be supported by appropriate logic. This is not to argue that changes in inventory pricing may not have a supporting argument. It is to argue, however, that such an argument will lose some persuasive logic for the gain of some expediency. Faithful reporting of prior transaction experience will suffer as a result, and the only thing that is gained is a thinly supported alternative.

It is worth keeping in mind that, throughout its evolutionary development, accounting has been disciplined by pressures and needs rather than by accepting expediency as a guide to action. In achieving its experience-reporting function, accounting has become a technical language in its own right. The reason is clear. This type of communication became necessary because of the difficulty of reading meaning from raw data, and because of management's need to read clear and frequent evidence of the results of prior decisions. Company directors and investors also had a need for factual evidence of management's achievements in operating results and in financial position.

As a result of long and progressive evolutionary development, accounting has now reached the status of an intellectual discipline. A profession of public accounting serves it and its data provide vital information to an extensive and capitalistic economy. Correspondingly, it has become an area of both undergraduate and postgraduate university education.

As a modern necessity; a profession serving the public interest; and an avenue for the development of men's intellectual powers, accountancy today deserves to be recognized as a discipline resting on solid moral grounds. It is sustained by strong elements of pragmatic logic. This logic firmly unites convincingly desirable, and fully defensible, ends and objectives, with convincingly appropriate ways and means for achieving those kind of objectives. The key words here are desirable, defensible, convincing, and appropriate. If the means chosen satisfy those terms, the effects of their use will provide support for the objectives that called them up.

In all questions of alternative treatments (means to ends), thorough research is needed concerning the specific close-up ends and those overall objectives that call for implementation and research into the reasons why these ends and objectives are desirable. The place to start the search is with the ends, as it is the ends that must influence the choice of means. Furthermore, unless the objectives are rationally attainable, no means could be judged as rationally suitable. This is necessarily so because the purpose of the creation of technical means is that they shall reasonably serve convincingly rational ends. These rational ends, in turn, deserve that status only through the reasons why they are the best available way to attaining the specified end.

It turns out, however, that the choice of clearly rational ends is more difficult than the choice of appropriate means. The former are difficult to define, limit, and to identify piece-by-piece. The recognition of possibly alternate means may also pose some questions of the basis for preference. And the better basis for choice may become visible only from prior experience or from trial in association with a particular end in view. In the latter case, the key to acceptance would be found in the results from a trial in the specific use.

Obviously, human judgment would be involved in this process. This, too, would be influenced by prior experience and by an open mind that was not too much impressed with the conclusive value of customs as such. This mind would realize that the customary way is the easy way, only because no real consideration of alternatives would be involved.

Returning to the idea of a trial, one lesson from accounting history is that every method and each type of technique is constantly being evaluated and tested. There are no alternatives to this. Only usage can demonstrate usefulness. Usefulness, in turn, may itself be a matter of opinion. And this opinion may need to be justified. As such, recourse may ultimately have to turn to a study of comparative reasons for implementing one objective over another, accompanied with comparative responses for the probable success of different ways of achieving that end.

To conclude, it is worth reiterating that enterprise accounting is an intellectual discipline for a specific reason. The decision problems there involved need to be approached along intellectual and rational lines. Convincing, even compelling, reasons should be sought in support of each specific accounting objective. This approach could itself prompt ideas of possible and appropriate means to those ends. These means, in turn, could be supported by persuasive, even compelling, reasons why they merited consideration and trial.

NOTES

1. Littleton does not attribute this quote to anyone, but it appears to be from somewhere in a series of articles, titled *Adventures of the Mind*, which was published in installments in the *Saturday Evening Post* and later as a compiled book in 1962.

a. The present and continuing development of a cogent and analytical theory may well prove to be the outstanding contribution of the present generation to the evolution of accountancy.

b. The early forms of accounting techniques were perhaps in a sense experimental. With time, they gradually changed. This change, however, was not set in motion for the purpose of expediency. Instead, there are historical evidence of clearly desirable ends being served by appropriate means.

6

REMINISCING

By his restful position on the lounge chair, the gray-haired figure in sunglasses seemed likely to be a man enjoying retirement and the pleasant winter sun. The circumstances seemed appropriate for napping. Yet, back of the glasses, the eyes were open; the man was thinking of the long series of events, which had preceded the up-coming birthday. Now, there was time to wonder, "how come." Surely, the sequence of those events could not have been pre-planned. Surely, most of them had involved personal choices. It now seemed apparent that these, gradually and unnoticed, had been building a pattern only recognizable in retrospect. If choices had been made, what had been the alternatives that offered a choice?

In retrospect, high school years seemed to have been quite ordinary. It was clear there had been a definite interest in the courses in English literature and written composition. On the other hand, mathematics and science were remembered as unappealing, although so much is vague at present. Moreover, both reactions persisted even in the face of requirements in the college program that eventually followed.

Would that early interest in some way have marked an unperceived path, which, much later, led to writing for publication? Would it be reasonable to believe that a foundation was being laid down when the father read to the small son so often? Certainly, it was that reading that later became a pleasure, which made study in college an interesting challenge, and that continued long after.

The man on the sunny patio reminded himself that a draft of another article waited on the study table for a third critical revision. The habit of reading had grown into a habit of writing—both still hard to turn aside. Reading brings new ideas to mind; and these then calls for probing and experimental development. But revising that draft could wait; the warm winter sun and the train of thought were too strong.

After high school, there was college. It was not clear now why college was even considered. Perhaps it was no more than a liking for reading and study. Perhaps, it was a chance suggestion by a teacher of high school English. Other questions could be more clearly recalled. How would the family finance such a venture and which college should one attend? Both questions would have to be answered.

A person usually tends to consider his actions as resulting primarily from his own decisions, taken in the light of available choices. Yet, ideas and actions of other people will often have revealed the existence of choices to begin with. They deserve much of the credit for the results.

How to finance it? The father's brother was a railroad telegrapher. His tutoring was put to test. In due time, the same railroad put the novice to work in small towns, usually on the night shift. Sometimes the location would be a switching tower, where two rail lines crossed, and the approaches to the crossing would be controlled by operating several semaphore signals and protective derails.

Which college? There was a small local college nearby; but there was also a university, 125 miles away, which offered courses in English and allied subjects. The latter would have been an interesting possibility indeed. Why did the choice not fall to one of these? Another choice appeared; a friend mentioned that his brother was on the football team at a university 50 miles away. The difference in distance does not now seem significant; surely, there was no thought of playing football. A catalogue was obtained; therein was the answer. A program of study was outlined for "railway administration." The uncle, the father, and the son had worked for the same railroad in differing capacities. Perhaps there would be openings in the administration side for a college graduate. The choice now seemed clear: study railroading; there probably was no future in English literature anyway.

The man on the patio recalled various aspects of the freshman year. Details of the early study programs had grown vague, but the satisfaction of those days came through clearly. English literature, German poetry, and economic history. These were well-liked subjects, but they were not "railroading."

Another interim followed of "working on the railroad," before returning to the university. There another choice was made; it had lasting effects. Two students from Chicago, living in the same rooming house, knew about the relatively new CPA law for the state and about public accounting as a career. They had come to college to study accountancy. This meeting set in motion a change of plans. Railroading was out; public accounting was in. And, it came to mind, there in the sunshine, that a high school course in bookkeeping had been liked almost as much as English literature. Chance and choice had again pointed the direction.

Subsequent college years were focused on preparing for the profession of public accounting. Employment in a small firm of public accountants presently followed the bachelor's degree. Many years later, there on the patio, the thought came to mind that during college and subsequent employment, there has been no conscious intention for further study except personal preparation for the CPA examination. Certainly, there had been no thought of becoming a teacher. Yet, here in the sunshine sat a retired professor, with a CPA and a Ph.D., who had taught accounting in one university for nearly forty years.

Suddenly such a grouping of facts seemed incredible. That high school lad: a university graduate; a university teacher of accountancy; a graduate student on the way to a doctorate; author of an article accepted for publication; and a dissertation in the process of becoming.

The return to the university, after some experience in the office of a public accountant, was closely influenced by related events. An unperceived basis for a choice had been building up, while serving as audit assistant to a senior accountant in that office. If that personal contact had never been made; if that accountant had not himself been an earlier graduate of the same university; if he had not presently accepted the university's invitation to return as a teacher; and if he had not later needed another teacher for the elementary courses, the next choice of alternatives would not have appeared. There would have been no teaching of accounting.

Back on the campus, but now as an instructor rather than audit assistant. Presently, the CPA examination was completed and a master's degree finished. A return to the audit staff of some firm was a clear possibility, but other circumstances had begun to exert influences.

Work towards the master's degree had been interesting, especially the courses in economic history, economic theory, and corporate finance. So too, had been the new experience of teaching. By that time, the university's program in graduate accounting, being faced with increased enrollment, had need for expanded course offerings. The man on the patio recalled that he had been asked to propose a new course for graduate students. His suggestion was for a course combing accounting history and accounting theory. After this had been given several times, it was divided and the material was expanded into two courses.

Graduate enrollment in accountancy continued to grow. Ultimately, this made it clear to that teacher that it would give support to the growing program if he had a doctoral degree. This resulted in further study at the graduate level and later a dissertation. Almost inevitably, the earlier efforts to put together a course on history and theory led to research on the evolutionary development of accounting. Presently, the thesis was completed. It later became a book.

Graduate work in accountancy continued to grow along with an ever-broadening expansion of professional accounting and college education for business careers. In time, that university established a Ph.D. degree with accountancy as the major subject. Today, many universities offer such a program of graduate study. And in the emerging literature, teachers have deepened and broadened the subject matter of each programs. As such, accounting instruction has gone far since the days when bookkeeping were the beginning—and almost the end. Accountancy now is being recognized and taught as an intellectual discipline, broadly useful to enterprise management and essential to preparation for the profession of public accounting.

Moments of retrospect can provide a deep sense of contentment. Perhaps some activities of those years may have proved useful to others. Such moments can also sponsor a feeling of amazement that a certain boy long ago, with no thought, or goal, had arrived at this point in life. He was now privileged not only to philosophize on the strange interrelation of events of the past, but also to do so under conditions as favorable as relaxing in the sunshine. Happy in a life of fascinating activities, grateful for past opportunities to make choices which circumstances presented; all this, plus a home with a patio in the warm winter sun. What does it matter that one more birthday is at hand?

APPENDICES

APPENDIX A

Table A1. Doctoral Dissertations Supervised by A. C. Littleton.

Year	Name	Title
1939	John W. McMahan	*The Relation of the Concept of Accounting Cost to Accounting Knowledge*
1940	Charles J. Gaa	*The Federal Income Tax Concept of Corporation Income*
	George B. McCowen	*Logical Transaction Analysis*
1941	Nobert G. Bausch	*The Relation Between Accounting and Certain Recent Developments in the Statutory Law of Business Corporation*
	Ralph L. Boyd	*A Study of C.P.A. Legislation in the United States, 1896 to 1940*
1942	James M. Carrithers	*The Accounting View of the Nature of Business Transactions*
	Robert I. Dickey	*Accounting Aspects of Federal Incorporation*
	Robert K. Mautz[a,b]	*A Study of the Content and Arrangement of the Income Statement*
	William E. Thomas	*Accounting as an Aid to Compliance with the Robinson-Patman Pact*
1943	Leslie J. Buchan	*A Critical Analysis of Recent Formulations of Accounting Principles*
	Yee C. Chow	*The Accounting Theory of Revenue Charges*
	Raymond W. Esworthy	*A Historical View of the Accounting Aspects of the Securities and Exchange Legislation of 1933 and 1943*
1950	James O. Eaton	*An Appraisal of the Relationship Between Accounting and Federal Income Taxation*
1951	William L. Campfield	*An Inquiry into the Nature of Judgment Formation and Its Implications to the Public Accounting Profession*
	Dorothy L. Litherland	*A Half Century of Accrual Accounting Theory, 1886 to 1936*

Table A1. *(Continued)*

Year	Name	Title
1952	Kenneth B. Berg	*Objectivity and Relevance in Accounting Evidence*
	Ling-Sung Chiao	*The Philosophy and Limitations of Social Accounting*
	Ming P. Hsu	*An Appraisal of Literature Critical of Cost Basis Accounting*
	Walter G. Kell	*The Equities Concept and Its Application to Accounting Theory*
	Charles Lawrence	*The Changing Uses of Financial Statements*
	William A. Terrill	*Factors Which Modify the Area of Service of Accounting-to-the-Public*
	Nelson D. Wakefield	*The Historical Development of the Certification of Accounting Statements in the United States*
	Glen G. Yankee	*The Usefulness of Criticism in Accounting*
	Eugene L. Zieha	*Accounting under Conditions of Changing Prices from the Debtor and Creditor Viewpoint*

Source: Based on material presented in appendix one in Zimmerman (1967).
[a]Inductee into the Accounting Hall of Fame, Fisher College of Business, The Ohio State University.
[b]Recipient of the American Institute of Certified Public Accountant's Gold Medal Award of Distinction.

APPENDIX B

Table B1. Graduate Dissertations Supervised by A. C. Littleton.

Year	Name	Title
1924	Ray R. Dobson	*The Application of Statistical Methods to the Interpretation of Accounting Data*
	Greer G. Fullerton	*The Auditor's Use of Statistical Analysis*
1925	Frank R. Harms	*The Accountant's Use of Ratios*
1926	Harold B. Eversole	*Seventeenth Century Accounting in England*
	Ralph S. Johns	*The Natural Business Year*
1929	Raymond F. Smith	*The Effect of Purpose on the Balance Sheet*
	Clarence B. Cox	*Economic and Accounting Concepts of Cost*
	Jeff A. Anderson	*The Historical Development of Bookkeeping in the First Half of the Nineteenth Century*
1930	Henry M. Spack	*Capital Stock as a Trust Fund*
	Hale L. Newcomer	*Early Development of Financial Statements*
	Walter F. Frese	*German Explanation of the Fundamentals of Double Entry Bookkeeping Theory*
	George E. Baggs	*The Historical Development of American Bookkeeping in the Last Half of the Nineteenth Century*
	Essel R. Dillavou	*Appreciation, Accounting and the Law*
1931	C. Rollin Niswonger	*Responsibility for Valuation*
	William H. Stout	*Development of American Bookkeeping from 1900 to 1930*
1932	Kenyon D. Bowes	*The Theory of Valuation Accounts*
	Walter E. Campbell	*Overhead Costs in Hospital Accounting*
	Ralph O. Linville	*The Purposes and Accomplishments of Professional Accounting Organizations*
	Ralph L. Boyd[a]	*A Critical Study of the Illinois Personal Income Tax Law*

Table B1. *(Continued)*

Year	Name	Title
	C. A. Moyer	*A Plan for Reflecting Current Prices in the Ledger*
	Frank Grove	*Defects in Organization and Accounting Procedure which Permits or Facilitates Fraud*
	William J. Jones	*The Appreciation Dilemma*
	James W. McMahan[a]	*The Accounting Problems of the Investment Trust*
1933	Norbert G. Bausch[a]	*Recent Criticism of Auditor's Certificates*
	Raymond A. Hoffman	*Accounting for the Receipt of Stock Dividends*
	Julius P. Joseph	*A Survey of the Accounting Problems in Corporation Finance*
	Nobel J. Litherland[a]	*A Proposed Modification of the Methods of Determining and Analyzing Distribution Costs*
	Gaze E. Lukas	*The Relation of Accounting to Statistics*
1935	Walter F. Lawless	*The Management's Use of Accounting Data in Promoting Efficiency*
1936	Noah Fetter	*Recent Tendencies in State Accountancy Legislation*
	Donald K. Griffith	*A Critical Examination of Proposed Technique for Making Accounting Records Reflect Changes in Purchasing Power*
	Edward C. Konchal	*Legal, Accounting, and Economic Aspects of Stated Capital*
	Tsing-Hao Kung	*Chinese Railway Accounting Practices and their Underlying Principles*
	Margaret A. Lamberton	*An Appraisal of the Accountant's Service to the Investor in Securities*
1937	H. E. Breen	*The Effect of Federal Securities Legislation upon the Accountant*
	Raymond Einhorn	*The Non-Availability of Appreciation Surplus for Cash Dividends*
	Poo-Ren Liu	*The Preparation of Cost Reports for the Use of Executives*
	Kenneth L. Smith	*Economic, Accounting and Legal Aspects of Capital Gains and Losses*
1938	Russell W. Carr	*The American Institute of Accountants, 1916–1936*

Table B1. *(Continued)*

Year	Name	Title
	George S. Cerny	*The Theory of Paid-in Surplus*
	Robert K. Mautz[a]	*An Asset Approach to the Concept of Income*
1940	George R. Catlett	*Accounting for Obsolescence of Machinery*
1941	Kenneth B. Berg[a]	*Some Theoretical Aspects of Accounting for Bond Issues*
	Willis A. Leonhardi	*The Accounting Treatment of Bad Debts*
	Joseph F. A. Schneider	*The Statement of Financial Changes*
	Nelson D. Wakefield[a]	*Evolution of Accountants' Certificates*
	Glen G. Yankee[a]	*The Problem of Pricing Inventory Items*
1942	Howard F. Stettler	*Trends in Auditing Examinations*
1944	Morris S. Kessler, Jr.	*Contribution of Accounting to the War Effort*
1947	Anthony H. Asay	*The Nature of Accrual Accounting*
	Max A. Binkley	*Controversial Ideas on Inventory Pricing*
	Gerald D. Brighton	*Reliance of the Auditor on Internal Control*
	Chin-Kiang Kuan	*The Cost Basis Theory of Accounting*
	Harry G. Marlow, Jr.	*Significance of Independence on Public Accounting*
	Tom G. Secoy	*The Nature of an Accounting Loss*
	Clem O. Smith, Jr.	*Techniques of Working with Figures in Accounting*
	Bernard D. Tarshis	*Developments Significant to Accounting During the Decade 1913 to 1923*
1948	William D. Barth	*The Service of Accountancy to Labor Unions*
	Ming P. Hsu[a]	*Inflation and Income Determination*
	Robert M. James	*Reserves Created by Charges in the Income Statement*

Table B1. *(Continued)*

Year	Name	Title
	Harry T. Magill	*The Meaning of Accepted Principles to the Accounting Profession*
	Troy L. Mallory	*Classification of Auditing Procedures According to Techniques*
	Gerald K. Nelson	*A Survey History of Standard Costs*
	Louis G. Pierce	*The Problem of Full Disclosure in Financial Statements*
	Arthur G. Schafer	*Financial Statements for Employees*
	James K. Stalker	*Peculiarities of Financial Statement Presentation*
1949	Joseph E. Carrico	*The Development of the Last-in, First-out Controversy*
	Edward E. Judy	*Accountancy Training for Non-technicians*
	Hugh W. Matter	*The Work of the Special Committee on Public Utility Accounting of the American institute of Accountants*
	John D. O'Neill	*Developments in Reserve Classification*
	Ramzy K. Rizk	*Comparison in Accounting Ideas About Fixed Assets Depreciation in the 1920's and 1940's*
	William A. Terrill[a]	*Depreciation Problems Related to the Controversy over Restoration of Fixed Assets*
1950	Wesley W. Brown	*Fifty Years of Cost or Market*
	Harry J. Jacobs	*The Relationship Between Accounting Principles and Rules*
	James C. Miller	*Estimates in Financial Accounting*
	Vernon K. Zimmerman	*A Survey of British Accounting Theory*

Source: Based on material presented in appendix one in Zimmerman (1967).
[a]Individual went on to complete a doctoral dissertation under A. C. Littleton's supervision.

APPENDIX C

Table C1. Publications by A. C. Littleton.

Year	Books
1919	*Introduction to Elementary Accounting. Cincinnati,* OH: South-Western Publishing Co.
1933	*Accounting Evolution to 1900.* New York: American Institute of Accountants.
1940	*An Introduction to Corporate Accounting Standards.* Chicago, IL: American Accounting Association (with W. A Paton).
1953	*Structure of Accounting Theory.* Urbana, IL: American Accounting Association.
1956	*Studies in the History of Accounting.* Homewood, IL: Richard D. Irwin Publishing (with B. S Yamey).
1961	*Essays on Accountancy.* Urbana, IL: University of Illinois Press.
1962	*Accounting Theory: Continuity and Change.* Englewood, Cliffs, NJ: Prentice-Hall (with V. K Zimmerman)
1965	*Significant Accounting Essays.* Englewood Cliffs, NJ: Prentice-Hall (with M. Moonitz).
	Articles
1926	The 2 to 1 Ratio Analyzed. *The Certified Public Accountant,* 6(8), 244–246.
	Evolution of the Ledger Account. *The Accounting Review,* 1(4), 12–23.
	Italian Double Entry in Early England. *The Accounting Review,* 1(2), 60–71.
	Research Work at the University of Illinois. *The Accounting Review,* 1(1), 31–38.
1927	The Antecedents of Double-Entry. *The Accounting Review,* 2(2), 140–149.
	Thomas Jones–Pioneer. *The Certified Public Accountant,* 7(6), 183–186.
	Two Fables of Bookkeeping. *The Accounting Review,* 2(4), 388–396.
	Two Pioneers of Accountancy. *The Certified Public Accountant,* 7(2), 35–37.
	University Education for Accountancy. *The Certified Public Accountant,* 7(12), 361–365, 369.
1928	The Evolution of the Journal Entry. *The Accounting Review,* 3(4), 383–396.
	Paciolo and Modern Accounting. *The Accounting Review,* 3(2), 131–140.
	Pioneers of Accountancy. *The Certified Public Accountant,* 8(7), 201–202, 217.
	What is Profit? *The Accounting Review,* 3(3), 278–288.
1929	Value and Price in Accounting. *The Accounting Review,* 4(3), 147–154.
1930	Accounting for Appreciation in Two Typical Cases Described. *The American Accountant,* 15(7), 302–303.

Table C1. *(Continued)*

Year	Books
	The International Congress on Accounting. *The Accounting Review*, 5(1), 70–74.
1931	A Cost Approach to Elementary Bookkeeping. *The Accounting Review*, 6(1), 33–37.
	Early Transaction Analysis. *The Accounting Review*, 6(3), 179–183.
1932	A Check-List of Early Bookkeeping Texts. *The Accounting Review*, 7(3), 194–206 (with H. R. Hatfield).
	Capital and Surplus. *The Accounting Review*, 7(4), 290–293.
1933	Capital Flexibility. *Journal of Accountancy*, 56(2), 102–108.
	Creditors' Interest in Surplus. *The Certified Public Accountant*, 13(4), 199–202.
	Independent Study. *The Accounting Review*, 8(2), 160–161.
	Social Origins of Modern Accountancy. *Journal of Accountancy*, 56(4), 261–270.
	Socialized Accounts. *The Accounting Review*, 8(4), 267–271.
1934	The Dividend Base. *The Accounting Review*, 9(2), 140–148.
	Dividends Presuppose Profits. *The Accounting Review*, 9(4), 304–311.
	The Income Approach. *The Accounting Review*, 9(4), 342–346.
	Socialized Accounts (II). *The Accounting Review*, 9(1), 69–74.
1935	Auditor Independence. *Journal of Accountancy*, 59(4), 283–291.
	Educational Browsing. *Journal of Accountancy*, 59(5), 330–338.
	An Inevitably Mediocre Bureaucracy. *Journal of Accountancy*, 60(4), 264–269.
	Value or Cost. *The Accounting Review*, 10(3), 269–273.
1936	The Professional College. *The Accounting Review*, 11(2), 109–116.
	Contrasting Theories of Profit. *The Accounting Review*, 11(1), 10–18 (W. Staub).
1937	Business Profits as a Legal Basis for Dividends. *Harvard Business Review*, 16(1), 51–61.
	Concepts of Income Underlying Accounting. *The Accounting Review*, 12(1), 13–22.
1938	High Standards of Accounting. *Journal of Accountancy*, 66(2), 99–104.
	The Relation of Function to Principles. *The Accounting Review*, 13(3), 233–241.
	A Substitute for Stated Capital. *Harvard Business Review*, 17(1), 75–84.
	Tests for Principles. *The Accounting Review*, 13(1), 16–24.
1939	Suggestions for the Revision of the Tentative Statement of Accounting Principles. *The Accounting Review*, 14(1), 57–64.
	The Uses of Theory. *Journal of Accountancy*, 67(4), 227–233.
1940	The Integration of Income and Surplus Statements. *The Accounting Review*, 69(1), 30–40.
1941	A Genealogy for "Cost or Market". *The Accounting Review*, 16(2), 161–167.
	Inventory Variations. *Journal of Accountancy*, 72(1), 7–16.

Table C1. *(Continued)*

Year	Books
	Questions on Accounting Standards. *The Accounting Review*, 16(4), 330–340.
1942	Auditing techniques. *Journal of Accountancy*, 74(2), 106–110.
	The Meaning of Accounting Education. *The Accounting Review*, 17(3), 215–221.
1943	Examinations in Auditing. *The Accounting Review*, 18(4), 307–316.
1944	Occupational Levels in Public Accounting. *Journal of Accountancy*, 78(6), 470.
1946	Guidance Tests for Accounting Students. *The Accounting Review*, 21(4), 404–409.
	Inventory Pricing. *Journal of Accountancy*, 81(4), 333–334.
1947	Three Audit Principles. *Journal of Accountancy*, 83(4), 280–282.
	Vocabulary of Auditing Technique. *New York Certified Public Accountant*, 17(10), 639–644.
1948	Extension of Accrual Principles would Help Depreciation Accounting. *Journal of Accountancy*, 86(1), 21–22.
	Inventory Disclosures. *New York Certified Public Accountant*, 18(11), 807.
1949	Classified Objectives. *The Accounting Review*, 24(3), 281–284.
1950	Inductive Reasoning in Accounting. *New York Certified Public Accountant*, 20(8), 449–460.
	Inductive Reasoning in Accounting–II. *New York Certified Public Accountant*, 20(11), 641–651.
	The Social Service of Accounting. *The Accounting Review*, 25(3), 320–321.
	A Third Use Value of Accounting. *The Accounting Review*, 25(2), 192–193.
1951	Preparation for the CPA, Technical or Liberal Education. *The Illinois Certified Public Accountant*, 14(2), 50–53.
	Removing the Mysteries from Accounting. *The Accounting Review*, 26(3), 418–420.
1952	Characteristics of a Profession. *New York Certified Public Accountant*, 22(4), 207–211.
	Significance of Invested Cost. *The Accounting Review*, 27(2), 167–173.
1953	Formal Education for Accountants. *The Certified Public Accountant*, 15(4), 43–47.
	[Limitations on the Significance of Invested Cost]: A Reply. *The Accounting Review*, 28(1), 8–11.
	Variety in the Concept of Income. *New York Certified Public Accountant*, 23(7), 419–424.
1954	But is it Accounting? *New York Certified Public Accountant*, 24(11), 688–692.
	Old and New in Management and Accounting. *The Accounting Review*, 29(2), 196–200.
	The Principles or Irrelevant Effects. *Journal of Accountancy*, 16(3), 21–24.
	Principles under Challenge. *New York Certified Public Accountant*, 24(1), 24–28.

Table C1. (*Continued*)

Year	Books
1955	The Logic of Accounts. *The Accounting Review*, 30(1), 45–47.
	Littleton, A. C. (1955c). Prestige for Historical Cost. *The Illinois Certified Public Accountant*, 17(3), 23–27.
1956	Choice among Alternatives. *The Accounting Review*, 31(3), 363–370.
	Economists and Accountants. *The Certified Public Accountant*, 18(4), 18–24.
	Learning to Write. *New York Certified Public Accountant*, 26(10), 608–612.
	Towards Understanding Accountancy. *The Australian Accountant*, 26(2), 81–84.
1957	Do-it-Yourself Writing. *The Certified Public Accountant*, 19(4), 46–48.
1958	Accounting Rediscovered. *The Accounting Review*, 33(2), 246–253.
	The Search for Accounting Principles. *New York Certified Public Accountant*, 28(4), 247–256.
1960	The Interpretative Function. *The Illinois Certified Public Accountant*, 22(2), 3–7.
1961	History of Public Accounting in the United States. *Journal of Accountancy*, 111(5), 93–94.
	Mission and Method. *The Illinois Certified Public Accountant*, 23(4), 1–5.
1963	The Heart of the Matter. *The Illinois Certified Public Accountant*, 24(4), 1–9.
	What is Accounting Theory? *Journal of Accountancy*, 116(3), 37–38.
1964	Appraising the Knowns. *The Illinois Certified Public Accountant*, 27(2), 7–11.
	Integrity. *The Illinois Certified Public Accountant*, 26(3), 6–9.
	Measuring Values is not a Function of Accounting. *New York Certified Public Accountant*, 34(7), 486.
	Reporting the Financial Effects of Price-Level Changes - A Commentary. *The Illinois Certified Public Accountant*, 26(4), 1–7.
1965	The Continuing Importance of Basic Concepts. *The International Journal of Accounting Education and Research*, 1(1), 55–65.
	An Inventory of Principles. *Journal of Accountancy*, 27(4), 14–16.
	Revolutionary Accounting Proposals may be Deceptive. *New York Certified Public Accountant*, 35(9), 644.
	Valuation is not the CPA's function. *New York Certified Public Accountant*, 35(8), 602.
1966	Accounting for Management. *Journal of Accountancy*, 121(1), 93–94.
	The Significance of Interrelated Concepts in Accounting. *The International Journal of Accounting Education and Research*, 2(1), 25–34.
1970	Factors Limiting Accounting. *The Accounting Review*, 45(3), 476–480.

Table C1. *(Continued)*

Year	Books
	Book Reviews
1929	Der Betriebswirtschaftliche Gewinnbegriff in Seiner Historischen Entwicklung. *The Accounting Review*, 4(3), 207.
1930	Volkswirtschafliches Wörterbuch. *The Accounting Review*, 5(1), 79–81.
1931	Tendenzen zur Aussonderung von Vermögenswertänderungen in Betriebswirtschaftslehre, Wirtschaftspraxis und Steuerrecht/Die nennwetlose Aktie/ Erfassung und Verrechnung der Gemeinskosten in der Unternehmung. *The Accounting Review*, 6(4), 324–325.
1933	Die Betriebswirtschaft/Bilans der Aktiengellschaft/Wirtschaftscpüfung und Revisionwesen. *The Accounting Review*, 8(1), 88–89.
	Abhandlung Über die Buchhaltung. *The Accounting Review*, 8(4), 359–360.
1934	Delaware Laws Affecting Business Corporations Annotated. *The Accounting Review*, 9(1), 101–102.
	Depreciation/Public Utility Valuation. *The Accounting Review*, 9(2), 186–188.
	Proceedings of the Fourth International Congress on Accounting. *The Accounting Review*, 9(1), 102–103.
1935	Glossary of Mediaeval Terms of Business. *The Accounting Review*, 10(1), 119–121.
	The Nature of Dividends. *The Accounting Review*, 10(4), 412–414.
1936	Stabilized Accounting. *The Accounting Review*, 11(3), 296–299.
1937	La Formation et 'Expansion de la Comptabilité à Partie Double. *The Accounting Review*, 12(4), 440–441.
1938	Problems in Accounting. *The Accounting Review*, 13(4), 432–433.
1943	Accounting Developments during the Present Century. *The Accounting Review*, 18(2), 178–180.
1944	Square Pegs in Square Holes. *The Accounting Review*, 19(3), 340–341.
1946	Financial Accounting. *The Accounting Review*, 21(3), 352–356.
1949	Fiftieth Anniversary. *The Accounting Review*, 24(3), 330–331.
	The Medici Bank. *The Accounting Review*, 24(2), 229–230.
1952	Dicksee's Auditing. *The Accounting Review*, 27(3), 405–406.
1955	The American Association of Public Accountants, Its First Twenty Years/English Accountancy, 1800–1954. *The Accounting Review*, 30(1), 160–163.
1958	The Interpretation of Accounts. *The Accounting Review*, 33(1), 157–159.
	Outline of Accounting. *The Accounting Review*, 33(2), 347–348.
1962	The Basic Postulates of Accounting. *The Accounting Review*, 37(3), 602–605.
1963	A Tentative Set of Broad Accounting Principles for Business Enterprises. *The Accounting Review*, 38(1), 220–222.
1967	The Accounting Frontier. *The Accounting Review*, 42(2), 421.

Table C1. (*Continued*)

Year	Books
	Miscellaneous
1920	*Lectures in Retail Merchandising: A Short Course in Business for Retail Merchants.* Champaign, IL: The Chamber of Commerce.
	Adjusting Inventories. *System*, 1153–1155.[a]
	Graduate and Research Work in Accounting (Discussant). *Papers and Proceedings of the American Association of University Instructors in Accounting*, 4(1), 83–86.
1922	Outside Employment (Discussant). *Papers and Proceedings of the American Association of University Instructors in Accounting*, 6(1), 55–57.
1923	An Appraisal of the Balance Sheet Approach. *Papers and Proceedings of the American Association of University Instructors in Accounting*, 7(1), 85–92.
1924	The Principles of Valuation as Related to the Function of the Balance Sheet (Discussant). *Papers and Proceedings of the American Association of University Instructors in Accounting*, 8(1), 14–15.
1925	The Development of Accounting Literature. *Papers and Proceedings of the American Association of University Instructors in Accounting*, 9(2), 7–17.[a]
	The Relation of Accounting to the Business Cycle. *Papers and Proceedings of the American Association of University Instructors in Accounting*, 9(1), 108–116.
1929	The International Congress on Accounting. *The Accounting Review*, 4(4), 234–246 (with L. Morey, D. Himmelblau, & F. E. Ross).
1930	The Definition of Earned Surplus (Comments). *The Accounting Review*, 5(2), 170–171.
	The Accounting Exchange: Foreign Accounting Terms. *The Accounting Review*, 5(3), 262–263.
	The Accounting Exchange: Foreign Accounting Terms. *The Accounting Review*, 5(4), 320–322.
	Fifth Year in Accounting. *Enterpriser*, 11, 20.[a]
	A Symposium on Appreciation (Comments). *The Accounting Review*, 5(1), 57–59.
1931	The Accounting Exchange: Foreign Accounting Terms. *The Accounting Review*, 6(1), 64–65.
	The Accounting Exchange: Foreign Accounting Terms. *The Accounting Review*, 6(2), 147–149.
1937	Accounting Theses: A List Compiled. *The Accounting Review*, 12(3), 313–315.
1939	Accounting Research. *The Accounting Forum*, 21–22.[a]
	Thesis Research. *The Accounting Forum*.[a]
1942	*Directory of Early American Public Accountants (Bulletin No. 62)*. Urbana, IL: Bureau of Economic and Business Research, University of Illinois.
1943	The Accounting Exchange. *The Accounting Review*, 18(3), 269–273.

Table C1. *(Continued)*

Year	Books
	The Accounting Exchange. *The Accounting Review*, 18(2), 156–159.
	The Accounting Exchange. *The Accounting Review*, 18(4), 368–373.
	A Message from the Incoming President. *The Accounting Review*, 18(2), 185–187.
1944	The Accounting Exchange. *The Accounting Review*, 19(3), 315–323.
	The Accounting Exchange. *The Accounting Review*, 19(1), 81–86.
	The Accounting Exchange. *The Accounting Review*, 19(2), 193–198.
	The Accounting Exchange. *The Accounting Review*, 19(4), 451–459.
1945	The Accounting Exchange. *The Accounting Review*, 20(2), 231–240.
	The Accounting Exchange. *The Accounting Review*, 20(1), 104–112.
	The Accounting Exchange. *The Accounting Review*, 20(3), 348–359.
	The Accounting Exchange. *The Accounting Review*, 20(4), 465–471.
1946	The Accounting Exchange. *The Accounting Review*, 21(4), 451–463.
	The Accounting Exchange. *The Accounting Review*, 21(2), 212–219.
	The Accounting Exchange. *The Accounting Review*, 21(3), 337–344.
1947	The Accounting Exchange. *The Accounting Review*, 22(1), 80–88.
	Fixed Assets and Accounting Theory. Paper presented at the Accounting Conference, Urbana, IL.[a]
1951	Educational Theory in Accountancy. *College News and Views*, 4(4), 5–9.[a]
1953	Accounting Theory: 1933–1953. *The Accounting Forum*, 24(1), 11–15, 21.[a]
	Conflicting Ideas. *Hermes*(Spring).[a]
	The Trust and Fund Doctrine. *Hermes*(Spring).[a]
1956	Two Professions in Contact. *American Business Law Association Bulletin*, 6, 21–26.[a]
1958	Education for Professional Accounting. *Western Business Review*.[a]
1962	The Purpose of Accounting Education. Paper presented at the International Conference on Accounting Education, Urbana, IL.[a]
1968	Ancient and Modern Bookkeeping Compared. In M. Chatfield (Ed.), *Contemporary Studies in the Evolution of Accounting Thought* (pp. 48–56). Belmont, CA: Dickenson Publishing Company.

Source: The entries in this list are sourced from appendix two in Zimmerman (1967). Each entry was then verified using Google Scholar and, when possible, the retrieval of the original article. Several entries that did not appear in Zimmerman's original publication has also been added.

[a]These entries appear in Zimmerman's (1967) article but could not be located and verified.

REFERENCES

Accounting Research Division. (1963). *Reporting the financial effects of price-level changes*. Accounting Research Study No. 6. New York, NY: American Institute of Certified Public Accountants.

Adams, H. C. (1918). *American railway accounting: A commentary*. New York, NY: Henry Holt & Co.

Aho, J. A. (2006). *Confession and bookkeeping: The religious, moral, and rhetorical roots of modern accounting*. Albany, NY: State University of New York Press.

Alexander, S. S. (1950). *Income measurement in a dynamic economy five monographs on business income* (pp. 1–96). Sarasota, FL: American Accounting Association.

American Institute of Accountants. (1952). *Changing concepts of business income: Report of study group on business income*. New York, NY: Macmillan.

American Institute of Certified Public Accountants. (1953). *Accounting terminology bulletin no. 1*. New York, NY: American Institute of Certified Public Accountants.

Ashraf, N., Camerer, C. F., & Loewenstein, G. (2005). Adam Smith, behavioral economist. *The Journal of Economic Perspectives*, *19*(3), 131–145.

Bach, G. L., Davidson, H. J., & Trueblood, R. M. (1961). *The future of accounting education – A collection of papers resulting from a conference on accounting education*. Graduate School of Industrial Administration, Carnegie Institute of Technology, Pittsburgh, PA.

Backer, M. (1963). Accounting theory, objectives and measurements. *Journal of Accountancy*, *116*(4), 57–63.

Bailey, G. D. (1948). Relationship of accounting to other factors in accurate reporting of inflationary income. *Journal of Accountancy*, *86*(5), 361–369.

Barnett, L. K. (1957). *The universe and Dr. Einstein*. New York, NY: W. Sloane Associates.

Baxter, W. T. (1971). Depreciation, replacement price, and cost of capital. *Journal of Accounting Research*, *9*(2), 189–214.

Beamer, E. G. (1962). Book review: The future of accounting education – A collection of papers resulting from a conference on accounting education. *Journal of Accountancy*, *114*(2), 92–93.

Bedford, N. M., & Ziegler, R. E. (1975). The contributions of A. C. Littleton to accounting thought and practice. *The Accounting Review*, *50*(3), 434–443.

Benjamin, A. C. (1937). *Introduction to the philosophy of science*. New York, NY: The Macmillan Company.

Bergson, H. (1946). *The creative mind: An introduction to metaphysics*. New York, NY: Wisdom Library.

Brinton, C. (1963). *The shaping of modern thought*. Englewood Cliffs, NJ: Prentice-Hall.

Canning, J. B. (1929). *The economics of accountancy: A critical analysis of accounting theory*. New York, NY: Ronald Press Company.

Chambers, R. J. (1957). Detail for a blueprint. *The Accounting Review*, *32*(2), 206–215.

Chambers, R. J. (1963). Why bother with postulates? *Journal of Accounting Research, 1*(1), 3–15.

Chambers, R. J. (1966). *Accounting, evaluation and economic behavior*. Englewood Cliffs, NJ: Prentice-Hall.

Commission on Standards of Education and Experience for Certified Public Accountants. (1956). *Standards of education and experience for certified public accountants*. Ann Arbor, MI: University of Michigan.

Committee on Accounting Procedure. (1947). Depreciation and high costs *(*Accounting research bulletin no. 33*)*. New York, NY: American Institute of Accountants.

Committee on Accounting Procedure. (1953). Restatement and revision of accounting research bulletins (*Accounting research bulletin no. 43*). New York, NY: American Institute of Accountants.

Cronhelm, F. W. (1818). *Double entry by single: A new method of book-keeping, applicable to all kinds of business*. London: Longman, Hurst, Rees, Orme, and Brown.

Cunningham, G. W. (1924). *Problems of philosophy: An introductory survey*. New York, NY: Henry Holt and Company.

Cushing, B. E. (1989). A Kuhnian interpretation of the historical evolution of accounting. *Accounting Historians Journal, 16*(2), 1–41.

De Roover, R. (1956). The development of accounting prior to luca pacioli according to the account-books of medieval merchants. In A. C. Littleton & B. S. Yamey (Eds.), *Studies in the history of accounting*. Homewood, IL: Richard D. Irwin Publishing.

Dewey, J. (1953). *Reconstruction in philosophy*. New York, NY: New American Library.

Dicksee, L. R. (1900). *Auditing: A practical manual for auditors* (4th ed.). London: Gee & Company.

Dicksee, L. R. (1909). In R. H. Montgomery (Ed.), *Auditing: A practical manual for auditors*. New York, NY: Ronald Press Company.

Dimand, R. W., & Geanakoplos, J. (2005). Celebrating Irving Fisher: The legacy of a great economist. *American Journal of Economics and Sociology, 64*(1), 3–18.

Durant, W. (1926). *Story of philosophy*. New York, NY: Garden City Publishing Company.

Fisher, I. (1922). *The purchasing power of money: Its determination and relation to credit interest and crises*. New York, NY: The MacMillan Company.

Gaffikin, M. J. R., & Aitken, M. J. (2014). *The development of accounting theory: Significant contributors to accounting thought in the 20th century*. London: Routledge.

Goetz, B. E., & Klein, F. R. (1960). *Accounting in action: Its meaning for management*. Boston, MA: Riverside Press.

Goldberg, L. (1960). *Concepts of depreciation*. Sydney: Law Book Co. of Australasia.

Grady, P. (1965). Inventory of generally accepted accounting principles for business enterprises (*Accounting research study no. 7*). New York, NY: American Institute of Certified Public Accountants.

Harman, G. (2011). *The quadruple object*. Alresford: John Hunt Publishing.

Hatfield, H. R. (1909). *Modern accounting*. New York, NY: Appleton and Company.

Hatfield, H. R. (1924). An historical defense of bookkeeping. *Journal of Accountancy, 37*(4), 241–253.

Jones, T. (1841). *The principles and practice of book-keeping*. New York, NY: Wiley & Putnam.

Kaplan, A. (1961). *The new world of philosophy*. New York, NY: Random House.

Knauth, O. (1957). Realism and historic convention. *Journal of Accountancy, 103*(5), 62.

Kohler, E. L. (1952). *A dictionary for accountants*. Englewood Cliffs, NJ: Prentice-Hall.

Kohler, E. L. (1963). Why not retain historical cost? *Journal of Accountancy*, *116*(4), 35–41.

Kohler, E. L. (1965). *Accounting for management*. Englewood Cliffs, NJ: Prentice-Hall.

Kuhn, T. S. (1962). *The structure of scientific revolutions*. Chicago, IL: University of Chicago Press.

Letter to the Editor. (1959). Price-level depreciation in annual statements. *Journal of Accountancy*, *108*(3), 16–18.

Littleton, A. C. (1919). *Introduction to elementary accounting*. Cincinnati, OH: South-Western Publishing Co.

Littleton, A. C. (1926). Italian double entry in early England. *The Accounting Review*, *1*(2), 60–71.

Littleton, A. C. (1927a). The antecedents of double-entry. *The Accounting Review*, *2*(2), 140–149.

Littleton, A. C. (1927b). Thomas Jones – Pioneer. *The Certified Public Accountant*, *7*(6), 183–186.

Littleton, A. C. (1927c). Two pioneers of accountancy. *The Certified Public Accountant*, *7*(2), 35–37.

Littleton, A. C. (1928a). The evolution of the journal entry. *The Accounting Review*, *3*(4), 383–396.

Littleton, A. C. (1928b). Pioneers of accountancy. *The Certified Public Accountant*, *8*(7), 201–202, 217.

Littleton, A. C. (1928c). What is profit? *The Accounting Review*, *3*(3), 278–288.

Littleton, A. C. (1931). Tendenzen zur Aussonderung von Vermögenswertänderungen in Betriebswirtschaftslehre, Wirtschaftspraxis und Steuerrecht/Die nennwetlose Aktie/ Erfassung und Verrechnung der Gemeinskosten in der Unternehmung (Book Review). *The Accounting Review*, *6*(4), 324–325.

Littleton, A. C. (1932). Capital and surplus. *The Accounting Review*, *7*(4), 290–293.

Littleton, A. C. (1933). *Accounting evolution to 1900*. New York, NY: American Institute of Accountants.

Littleton, A. C. (1934). Dividends presuppose profits. *The Accounting Review*, *9*(4), 304–311.

Littleton, A. C. (1935). Value or cost. *The Accounting Review*, *10*(3), 269–273.

Littleton, A. C. (1936a). The professional college. *The Accounting Review*, *11*(2), 109–116.

Littleton, A. C. (1936b). Stabilized accounting (book review). *The Accounting Review*, *11*(3), 296–299.

Littleton, A. C. (1937). Concepts of income underlying accounting. *The Accounting Review*, *12*(1), 13–22.

Littleton, A. C. (1938a). High standards of accounting. *Journal of Accountancy*, *66*(2), 99–104.

Littleton, A. C. (1938b). The relation of function to principles. *The Accounting Review*, *13*(3), 233–241.

Littleton, A. C. (1938c). Tests for principles. *The Accounting Review*, *13*(1), 16–24.

Littleton, A. C. (1939a). Suggestions for the revision of the tentative statement of accounting principles. *The Accounting Review*, *14*(1), 57–64.

Littleton, A. C. (1939b). The uses of theory. *Journal of Accountancy*, *67*(4), 227–233.

Littleton, A. C. (1941). A genealogy for "cost or market." *The Accounting Review*, *16*(2), 161–167.

Littleton, A. C. (1942). The meaning of accounting education. *The Accounting Review*, *17*(3), 215–221.

Littleton, A. C. (1943a). The accounting exchange. *The Accounting Review*, *18*(3), 269–273.

Littleton, A. C. (1943b). Examinations in auditing. *The Accounting Review*, *18*(4), 307–316.

Littleton, A. C. (1944a). The accounting exchange. *The Accounting Review*, *19*(3), 315–323.

Littleton, A. C. (1944b). The accounting exchange. *The Accounting Review*, *19*(1), 81–86.

Littleton, A. C. (1945a). The accounting exchange. *The Accounting Review*, *20*(1), 104–112.

Littleton, A. C. (1945b). The accounting exchange. *The Accounting Review*, *20*(2), 231–240.

Littleton, A. C. (1946a). Financial accounting (book review). *The Accounting Review*, *21*(3), 352–356.

Littleton, A. C. (1946b). Guidance tests for accounting students. *The Accounting Review*, *21*(4), 404–409.

Littleton, A. C. (1947a). The accounting exchange. *The Accounting Review*, *22*(1), 80–88.

Littleton, A. C. (1947b). Three audit principles. *Journal of Accountancy*, *83*(4), 280–282.

Littleton, A. C. (1949). Fiftieth anniversary (book review). *The Accounting Review*, *24*(3), 330–331.

Littleton, A. C. (1950a). The Social service of accounting. *The Accounting Review*, *25*(3), 320–321.

Littleton, A. C. (1950b). A third use value of accounting. *The Accounting Review*, *25*(2), 192–193.

Littleton, A. C. (1952a). Dicksee's auditing (book review). *The Accounting Review*, *27*(3), 405–406.

Littleton, A. C. (1952b). Significance of Invested Cost. *The Accounting Review*, *27*(2), 167–173.

Littleton, A. C. (1953a). [Limitations on the significance of invested cost]: A reply. *The Accounting Review*, *28*(1), 8–11.

Littleton, A. C. (1953b). *Structure of accounting theory*. Urbana, IL: American Accounting Association.

Littleton, A. C. (1955). The logic of accounts. *The Accounting Review*, *30*(1), 45–47.

Littleton, A. C. (1956a). Choice among alternatives. *The Accounting Review*, *31*(3), 363–370.

Littleton, A. C. (1956b). Towards understanding accountancy. *The Australian Accountant*, *26*(2), 81–84.

Littleton, A. C. (1958). The interpretation of accounts (book review). *The Accounting Review*, *33*(1), 157–159.

Littleton, A. C. (1960). The interpretative function. *The Illinois Certified Public Accountant*, *22*(2), 3–7.

Littleton, A. C. (1961a). *Essays on accountancy*. Urbana, IL: University of Illinois Press.

Littleton, A. C. (1961b). Mission and method. *The Illinois Certified Public Accountant*, *23*(4), 1–5.

Littleton, A. C. (1962a). The basic postulates of accounting (book review). *The Accounting Review*, *37*(3), 602–605.

Littleton, A. C. (1962b). The purpose of accounting education. Paper presented at the International Conference on Accounting Research and Education, Urbana, IL.

Littleton, A. C. (1963a). A tentative set of broad accounting principles for business enterprises (book review). *The Accounting Review*, *38*(1), 220–222.

Littleton, A. C. (1963b). What is accounting theory? *Journal of Accountancy*, *116*(3), 37–38.

Littleton, A. C. (1963c). The heart of the matter. *The Illinois Certified Public Accountant*, *24*(4), 1–9.

Littleton, A. C. (1964a). Appraising the knowns. *The Illinois Certified Public Accountant, 27*(2), 7–11.

Littleton, A. C. (1964b). Integrity. *The Illinois Certified Public Accountant, 26*(3), 6–9.

Littleton, A. C. (1964c). Reporting the financial effects of price-level changes – A commentary. *The Illinois Certified Public Accountant, 26*(4), 1–7.

Littleton, A. C. (1965a). "Revolutionary" accounting proposals may be deceptive. *New York Certified Public Accountant, 35*(9), 644.

Littleton, A. C. (1965b). The continuing importance of basic concepts. *The International Journal of Accounting Education and Research, 1*(1), 55–65.

Littleton, A. C. (1965c). An inventory of principles. *Journal of Accountancy, 27*(4), 14–16.

Littleton, A. C. (1966). Accounting for management. *Journal of Accountancy, 121*(1), 93–94.

Littleton, A. C., & Staub, W. (1936). Contrasting theories of profit. *The Accounting Review, 11*(1), 10–18.

Littleton, A. C., & Yamey, B. S. (Eds.) (1956). *Studies in the history of accounting.* Homewood, IL: Richard D. Irwin Publishing.

Littleton, A. C., & Zimmerman, V. K. (1962). *Accounting theory: Continuity and change.* Englewood, Cliffs, NJ: Prentice-Hall.

Mattessich, R. V. (1964). *Accounting and analytical methods: Measurement and projection of income and wealth in the micro- and macro-economy.* Homewood, IL: Richard D. Irwin Publishing.

Mautz, R. K. (1965). The place of postulates in accounting. *Journal of Accountancy, 119*(1), 46–49.

Mautz, R. K., & Sharaf, H. A. (1961). *The philosophy of auditing.* Sarasota, FL: American Accounting Association.

May, G. O. (1950). Truth and usefulness in accounting. *Journal of Accountancy, 89*(5), 387.

Mitchell, W. C. (1934). The problem of measuring profits. In R. C. Epstein & F. M. Clark (Eds.), *Industrial profits in the United States.* Cambridge, MA: National Bureau of Economic Research.

Montgomery, R. H. (1912). *Auditing theory and practice.* New York, NY: Ronald Press Company.

Moonitz, M. (1961). *The basic postulates of accounting.* New York, NY: The American Institute of Certified Public Accountants.

Moonitz, M., & Littleton, A. C. (Eds.) (1965). *Significant accounting essays.* Englewood Cliffs, NJ: Prentice-Hall.

Mouck, T. (1993). The "revolution" in financial reporting theory: A Kuhnian Interpretation. *Accounting Historians Journal, 20*(1), 33–57.

Murphy, A. E. (1943). *The uses of reason.* New York, NY: The MacMillan Company.

Pacioli, L. (1494). *An original translation of the treatise on double-entry book-keeping* (In P. Crivelli, Trans.). London: The Institute of Book-Keepers.

Parker, R. H. (1980). *British accountants: A biographical sourcebook.* New York, NY: Arno Press.

Paton, W. A. (1920). Depreciation, appreciation and productive capacity. *Journal of Accountancy, 30*(1), 1–11.

Paton, W. A. (1940). Recent and prospective developments in accounting theory. Paper presented at the Dickinson Lectures in Accounting, Graduate School of Business Administration, Harvard University.

Paton, W. A. (1959). Depreciation – Concept and measurement. *Journal of Accountancy, 108*(4), 38–43.

Paton, W. A., & Littleton, A. C. (1940). *An introduction to corporate accounting standards*. Chicago, IL: American Accounting Association.

Persson, M. E. (2013). *The rise and fall of comprehensive accounting theories: R. J. Chambers and continuously contemporary accounting*. (PhD in Accounting), London: Royal Holloway University of London.

Persson, M. E., & Napier, C. J. (2015a). Accounting is the message: An undermining, overmining, and duomining critique. Paper presented at the American Accounting Association Annual Meeting, Chicago, IL.

Persson, M. E., & Napier, C. J. (2015b). R. J. Chambers and the AICPA's postulates and principles controversy: A case of vicarious action. *Accounting Historians Journal, 42*(2), 101–132.

Persson, M. E., Radcliffe, V. S., & Stein, M. (2015). Alvin R. Jennings: Managing partner, policy-maker, and institute president. *Accounting Historians Journal, 42*(1), 85–104.

Persson, M. E., Radcliffe, V. S., & Stein, M. (2016). Elmer G. Beamer and the American Institute of certified public accountants: The pursuit of a cognitive standard for the accounting profession. Paper presented at the American Accounting Association Annual Meeting, New York.

Powell, W. (1961). Report on the accounting research activities of the American institute of certified public accountants. *The Accounting Review, 36*(1), 26–31.

Randall, J. H., & Buchler, J. (1942). *Philosophy: An introduction*. New York, NY: Barnes & Noble.

Ratner, J. (Ed.) (1939). *Intelligence in the modern world: John Dewey's philosophy*. New York, NY: Modern Library.

Roy, R. H., & MacNeill, J. H. (1963). A report of plans and progress study of the common body of knowledge for CPAs. *Journal of Accountancy, 116*(6), 55–58.

Roy, R. H., & MacNeill, J. H. (1967). *Horizons for a profession: The common body of knowledge for certified public accountants*. New York, NY: American Institute of Certified Public Accountants.

Rutherford, B. A. (2013). A pragmatist of classical financial accounting research. *Abacus, 49*(2), 197–219.

Savary, J. (1712). *The complete tradesman*. Paris: Guignard et Robuste.

Skidelsky, R. (2010). *Keynes: The return of the master*. New York, NY: PublicAffairs.

Smith, A. (1776). *An inquiry into the nature and causes of the wealth of nations*. London: Methuen & Co.

Smith, J. E. (1963). *The spirit of American philosophy*. Oxford: Oxford University Press.

Solomons, D. (1961). Economic and accounting concepts of income. *The Accounting Review, 36*(3), 374–383.

Sprouse, R. T. (1963). *The measurement of property, plant, and equipment in financial statements*. Cambridge, MA: Harvard University Press.

Sprouse, R. T., & Moonitz, M. (1962). *A tentative set of broad accounting principles for business enterprises*. New York, NY: American Institute of Certified Public Accountants.

Staubus, G. J. (1954). *An accounting concept of revenue*. (Doctor of Philosophy), Chicago, IL: University of Chicago.

Sterling, R. R. (1970a). On theory construction and verification. *The Accounting Review, 45*(3), 444–457.

Sterling, R. R. (1970b). *Theory of the measurement of enterprise income*. Lawrence, KS: University Press of Kansas.

Sterling, R. R. (1979). *Toward a science of accounting*. Houston, TX: Scholars Book Co.

Study Group on Business Income (1950). *Five monographs on business income*. New York, NY: American Institute of Accountants.

Sweeney, H. W. (1936). *Stabilized accounting*. New York, NY: Harper & Brothers.

Tobin, J. (2008). Fisher, Irving (1867–1947). In S. N. Durlauf & L. E. Blume (Eds.), *The new Palgrave dictionary of economics* (2nd ed. pp. 369–376). London: Palgrave Macmillan.

von Mises, L. (1962). *The ultimate foundation of economic science: An essay on method*. Princeton, NJ: D. van Nostrand Company.

Webster (1951). *Webster's dictionary of synonyms*. Springfield, MA: G & C Merriam Co.

Wells, M. C. (1976). A revolution in accounting thought? *The Accounting Review*, *51*(3), 471–482.

Welsch, G. A. (1966). Is accountancy an academic discipline? *Journal of Accountancy*, *121*(5), 81–82.

Whitehead, A. N. (1960). *Adventures of the mind first series: From the Saturday evening post* (Vol. 2), New York, NY: Vintage Books.

Whitley, R. D. (1986). The transformation of business finance into financial economics: The role of academic expansion and changes in the U.S. capital markets. *Accounting, Organizations and Society*, *11*(2), 171–192.

Zeff, S. A. (1972). Chronology of significant developments in the establishment of accounting principles in the United States 1926–1972. *Journal of Accounting Research*, *10*(1), 217–227.

Zeff, S. A. (Ed.) (1982). *The accounting postulates and principles controversy of the 1960s*. London: Garland Publishing.

Zeff, S. A. (2007). The membership of the accounting principles board. *Research in Accounting Regulation*, *19*, 207–214.

Zimmerman, V. K. (1967). The long shadow of a scholar. *The International Journal of Accounting Education and Research*, *2*(2), 1–20.

INDEX

Printed and bound by CPI Group (UK) Ltd, Croydon, CR0 4YY

13/09/2026

14961031-0003